걸프 사태

미국 동향 1

걸프 사태

미국 동향 1

한국학술정보

| 머리말

　걸프 전쟁은 미국의 주도하에 34개국 연합군 병력이 수행한 전쟁으로, 1990년 8월 이라크의 쿠웨이트 침공 및 합병에 반대하며 발발했다. 미국은 초기부터 파병 외교에 나섰고, 1990년 9월 서울 등에 고위 관리를 파견하며 한국의 동참을 요청했다. 88올림픽 이후 동구권 국교 수립과 유엔 가입 추진 등 적극적인 외교 활동을 펼치는 당시 한국에 있어 이는 미국과 국제 사회의 지지를 얻기 위해서라도 피할 수 없는 일이었다. 결국 정부는 91년 1월부터 약 3개월에 걸쳐 국군의료지원단과 공군수송단을 사우디아라비아 및 아랍 에미리트 연합 등에 파병하였고, 군 · 민간 의료 활동, 병력 수송 임무를 수행했다. 동시에 당시 걸프 지역 8개국에 살던 5천여 명의 교민에게 방독면 등 물자를 제공하고, 특별기 파견 등으로 비상시 대피할 수 있도록 지원했다. 비록 전쟁 부담금과 유가 상승 등 어려움도 있었지만, 걸프전 파병과 군사 외교를 통해 한국은 유엔 가입에 박차를 가할 수 있었고 미국 등 선진 우방국, 아랍권 국가 등과 밀접한 외교 관계를 유지하며 여러 국익을 창출할 수 있었다.

　본 총서는 외교부에서 작성하여 30여 년간 유지한 걸프 사태 관련 자료를 담고 있다. 미국을 비롯한 여러 국가와의 군사 외교 과정, 일일 보고 자료와 기타 정부의 대응 및 조치, 재외동포 철수와 보호, 의료지원단과 수송단 파견 및 지원 과정, 유엔을 포함해 세계 각국에서 수집한 관련 동향 자료, 주변국 지원과 전후복구사업 참여 등 총 48권으로 구성되었다. 전체 분량은 약 2만 4천여 쪽에 이른다.

2024년 3월
한국학술정보(주)

| 일러두기

· 본 총서에 실린 자료는 2022년 4월과 2023년 4월에 각각 공개한 외교문서 4,827권, 76만여 쪽 가운데 일부를 발췌한 것이다.

· 각 권의 제목과 순서는 공개된 원본을 최대한 반영하였으나, 주제에 따라 일부는 적절히 변경하였다.

· 원본 자료는 A4 판형에 맞게 축소하거나 원본 비율을 유지한 채 A4 페이지 안에 삽입하였다. 또한 현재 시점에선 공개되지 않아 '공란'이란 표기만 있는 페이지 역시 그대로 실었다.

· 외교부가 공개한 문서 각 권의 첫 페이지에는 '정리 보존 문서 목록'이란 이름으로 기록물 종류, 일자, 명칭, 간단한 내용 등의 정보가 수록되어 있으며, 이를 기준으로 0001번부터 번호가 매겨져 있다. 이는 삭제하지 않고 총서에 그대로 수록하였다.

· 보고서 내용에 관한 더 자세한 정보가 필요하다면, 외교부가 온라인상에 제공하는 『대한민국 외교사료요약집』 1991년과 1992년 자료를 참조할 수 있다.

| 차례

정 리 보 존 문 서 목 록

기록물종류	일반공문서철	등록번호	2012090520	등록일자	2012-09-17
분류번호	772	국가코드	US/XF	보존기간	영구
명 칭	걸프사태 : 미국의 대응, 1990-91. 전6권				
생 산 과	북미과/안보과	생산년도	1990~1991	담당그룹	
권 차 명	V.1 1990.8.2-20				
내용목차	* 1990.8.3 미국.소련, 이라크군의 쿠웨이트로부터의 무조건 철수 측구 공동성명 발표 8.7 미국, 지상군 사우디아라비아 파견 8.10 백악관, 미국의 대이라크군 교역 전면 금지 시행령 발표				

0001

	분류번호	보존기간

발 신 전 보

번 호 : WUS-2550　900802 1742 DY　　**종별 :** 긴급

수 신 : 주　수신처 참조 ~~대사//총영사//~~

WUK -1277	WFR -1472
WJA -3270	WCN -0782
WAU -0529	WCA -0258
WSB -0277	WIR -0250

발 신 : 장 관 (중근동)

제 목 : 이라크, 쿠웨이트 침공

　　　　표제 사태 관련, 주재국 반응(영문) 및 사태 평가 내용 긴급 파악

보고 바람. 끝.

　　　　　　　　　　　　　　　　(중동아프리카국장　이 두 복)

　　수신처 : 주미, 영, 불, 일, 카나다, 호주, 이집트, 사우디, 이란

1990. 12. 31. 애 억고문에
의거 일반문서로 재 분류됨.

보 안 통 제	
	外信과통제

앙고재	90년8월2일 근동과	기안자 성명		과 장		국 장		차 관	장 관

0002

외 무 부

관리번호 90/2046

종 별 : 긴 급

번 호 : USW-3544   일 시 : 90 0802 1644

수 신 : 장관(중근동,미북)

발 신 : 주 미 대사

제 목 : 이락-쿠웨이트 침공

대:WUS-2550

대호, 국무부 및 현지 언론을 종합한 전황 및 주재국 반응하기 보고함.

1. 전황

O 금일 새벽 1 시 시작된 이락의 쿠웨이트 전면 침공으로 현재 부분적인 쿠웨이트군의 저항이 있지만 사실상 주요 산업시설 및 관공서등이 이락의 군사점령상태에 있음.

O 쿠웨이트 수상 및 왕자등 주요간부는 현재 사우디에 피신중이며 이락에 대한 저항을 계속 다짐하고 있음.

O 전쟁 피해는 현재까지 알려져 있지 않으나 상당한 쿠웨트군 희생자가 발생한 것으로 추측됨.

2. 미국반응

O 부쉬 대통령은 8.2(목)오전 기자회견을 통해 이락의 군사행동을 강력히 비난하며 이락군의 즉각적, 무조건 철수를 요구하는 한편, 미국내 이락및 쿠웨이트 자산 동결조치를 취함(TEXT 별첨 송부)(USW(F)-1681)

O 미국은 쿠웨이트와 함께 금일새벽 안전보장 이사회를 소집, 이락의 대 쿠웨이트 침공을 비난하고 이락의 즉각 철수를 촉구하는 결의안을 14 대 0 으로 통과시켰음.

O 현재 미국은 이라크군의 철수를 위한 외교적 노력을 기울이는 한편, 인도양상의 항공모함 인디펜더스호를 페르시아만으로 급파하고 페르시아만 배치 미해군의 비상 경계를 강화하는등의 조치를 취하고 있으나 상금 군사적 개입에 대한입장 표명을 유보하고 있음.

3. 표제 관련 진전사항 추보위게임.

(대사 박동진-국장)

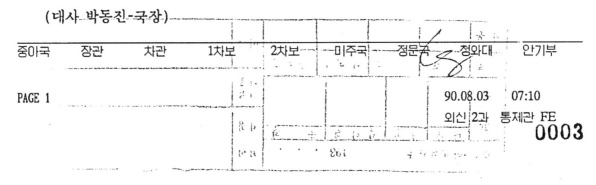

중아국	장관	차관	1차보	2차보	미주국	정문국	청와대	안기부

PAGE 1

90.08.03 07:10
외신 2과 통제관 FE
0003

예고:90.12.31 까지

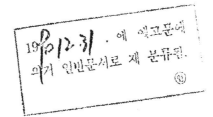

외 무 부

종 별 :

번 호 : USW-3558   일 시 : 90 0802 1959

수 신 : 장관(중근동,미북,기정)

발 신 : 주 미 대사

제 목 : 이락의 쿠웨이트 침공

대 WUS-2550

연 USW-3544

본직은 금 8.2(목) 오후 국무부 KIMMIT 차관원 초치로, NATO 및 일본, 호주등 주요
우방국 대사와 함께 이락의 쿠웨이트 침공에 대한 국무부 브리핑에 참석한바 동 요지
다음 보고함(유명환 참사관 배석)

1. 미국의 입장

-금번 이락의 쿠웨이트 침공을 미국의 주요 이익을 위협한 심각한 문제로 간주하고
있으며 미국은 앞으로 이에 대하여 SERIOUS 하게 대처할것임.

-미국은 정치, 경제, 군사적인 모든 가능한 조치를 검토하고 있으며 어떠한방안도
배제하고 있지않음.

-미국은 집단적인 대 이락 제재 조치가 가장 효과적이라는 판단하에 모든 유에
회원국의 협조를 요청함.

2. 미국이 취한 조치

- 유엔 안보리에서 만장 일치로 이락의 쿠웨이트 침공을 규탄하고 즉각 90.8.1
국경선으로 철수토록 촉구함.

-미국은 지난밤 미국내의 이락 및 쿠웨이트와 관련된 모든 재산을 동결한바특히
쿠웨이트 재산 동결은 점령군이 불법으로 쿠웨이트의 주요 재산을 반출할가능성에
대비하여 취한 조치임.

-미국은 항공 모함을 걸프만으로 이동시켜 미국 시민 보호등 만일의
사태에대비토록함.

-각 우방국에 대하여 집단적인 대이락 경제 제재 조치를 요청함.

3. 금후 조치

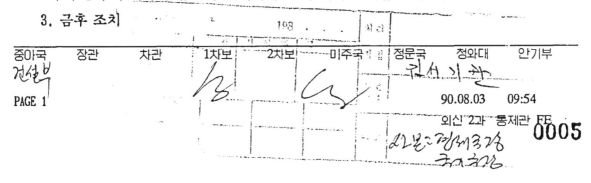

중아국	장관	차관	1차보	2차보	미주국	정문국	정와대	안기부

PAGE 1

90.08.03   09:54

외신 2과 통제관 FE

0005

-유엔을 통해 헌장 제 7 장에 명시된 제재조치(MANDATORY SANCTION 포함)를 취하기 위해 계속 협의 중에 정임.

-이락의 경제적 약점을 이용, 이락 정부 재정을 교란시킬수 있는 방안을 강구하기 위해 사우디, 이집트, 요르단, 예멘등 역내 국가와 긴밀한 협의 실시 중임.

-아랍 형제국들이 중심이 되어 해결 방안을 모색하도록 하는것이 아주 중요한바 미국은 이를 위해 계속 노력 경주예정임.(현재 아랍제국의 반응이 미온적임을 지적하고 있는것이 주목됨)

4. 소련과의 협조

-이루크츠크 미.소 외상회담에서 이문제가 즉가 거론된바 소련은 미국과 협력하는데 적극적으로 나오고 있으며 대 이락 무기 판매를 즉각 중지할것에 동의하여옴.

5. 우방국에 대한 당부

-어떠한 조치든 COLLECTIVE ACTION 이어야만 효과가 있다는 판단인바, 모든우방국및 국제기구가 이락을 규탄하고 경제 제재 조치에 공동 보조를 취하여 주기 바람(이미 조치를 취한 국가에 대해서는 사의를 표명함)

-이락에게 무기를 판매할수 있는 위치에 있는 국가는 즉각 부품및 모든 군사 장비 공급을 중단하도록 촉구함.

6. 기타 질의 응답시 KIMMIT 차관 언급 내용

-사우디 정부의 반응은 경제 제재 조치 관련 만족 스러운것으로 생각함.

-미국은 대이락 경제 제재 에도 불구하고 현재로서는 외교 관계는 계속 유지하여, 대화가 가능하도록 할 생각임.

-쿠웨이트내의 소위 괴뢰 정권에 관해서는 아직 충분한 정보는 없으나 이락이 철군하면 자생력이 없을것으로 봄.

-이스라엘은 이락에 대해 군사적 조치를 취하지 않겠다고 말하고 있음.

-이락이 철군한다고 해도 90.8.1 현재 국경선이 아니라 일부 쿠웨이트 지역을 계속 점령하고 있을 경우도 가정할수 있는바, 그 경우 문제가 더욱 복잡하게 전개될 가능성이 있음.

7. 한편 금일 의회에서도 대이락 제재 결의안이 만장 일치로 채택되어 미국의 대이락 수출.입 및 원조를 금지할것을 행정부에 촉구함으로서 행정부의 대이락 제재 조치를 뒷받침하고 있음.

(대사 박동진-국장)
90.12.31 일반

쿠웨이트 사태에 대한 미국반응

90. 8. 3.

미 주 국

┌─────── 〈현재까지의 주요조치〉 ───────┐

ㅇ Bush 대통령의 비난 성명

ㅇ 미국내 이라크.쿠웨이트 자산 동결

ㅇ 대 이라크 통상관계 단절(원유 포함)

ㅇ 미국 인도양 함대 일부 걸프로 향진

ㅇ 각국 정부에 대이라크 제재 요청

ㅇ 외교단에 대한 국무부 브리핑

ㅇ 유엔 긴급 안보리 이라크 규탄 성명

└──────────────────────────────┘

┌─────────┐
│ 행정부 조치 │
└─────────┘

1. Bush 대통령의 규탄 성명 발표(8.2. 오전)

ㅇ 이라크의 무력침공을 비난하고, 이라크군의 즉각.무조건 철수 요구

　　- 주 유엔 대사에 안보리 긴급 개최 지시

ㅇ 미국내 이라크, 쿠웨이트 자산을 동결하고 이라크와의 통상금지

　　- International Emergency Economic Power's Act에 근거한 행정명령

　　- 여타국 정부도 유사한 조치를 취할 것을 촉구

0008

o 국무부가 각국 정부와 접촉, 이라크를 비난하고 이라크의 불법행위를 중지
   시킬 방안을 협의할 것을 촉구중

o 걸프내 미국 국익보호를 위해 필요하면 어떠한 조치라도 취할 것임.
   - 금일(8.2.)오전 백악관 안보회의 소집

2. Bush 대통령 기자회견(8.2. 오후)

   o 쿠웨이트 지도부의 복귀를 위한 평화적 해결 방안 희망

   o 쏘련의 대 이라크 무기지원 중단조치 환영

3. Baker 국무장관 기자회견(8.2.)

   o 이라크의 쿠웨이트 침공 비난

   o 셰바르드나제 쏘 외무장관에게 이라크에 대한 군수지원 중단 요청
      * Baker장관은 몽고 방문일정을 단축하고 귀국예정(귀로에 방쏘, 사태협의)

4. 주요 우방국 대사에 대한 국무부 브리핑(8.2. 오후)
      * Kimmit 국무부 차관이 NATO, 일본, 호주, 한국대사등 초치, 실시

   o 미국은 정치, 경제, 군사적인 모든 가능한 조치를 검토하고 있으며, 어떠한
      방안도 배제하고 있지 않음을 설명

   o 집단적인 대 이라크 제재가 효과적이라는 판단하에, 모든 우방국 및 국제
      기구의 협조 요청

   o 이라크와의 대화를 위하여 외교관계는 유지 예정

0009

의회 조치

o 미국 의회 대 이라크 제재 결의안 채택(8.2.)
  - 대 이라크 수출입 및 원조 금지를 행정부에 촉구

미국의 무력 개입 문제

o 인도양 배치 항모 Independence호와 전함 6척이 걸프로 항진

o Al Sabah 주미 쿠웨이트 대사가 Bush 대통령에게 미국의 무력개입을 요청

o Bush 대통령은 8.2. 오전 기자회견에서 무력 개입을 고려하고 있지
  않다고 밝히는 한편, 어떠한 대응방안도 배제하지는 않고 있다고 언급
  * Kimmit 국무부 차관도 외교단 브리핑시 군사적 조치가 배제 되지는
    않았다고 언급

※ 카나다의 반응

o Clark 외무장관 성명 발표(8.2.)
  - 이라크의 침략행위 규탄
  - 전투의 즉각중지, 이라크군의 즉각.전면 철수 촉구

o 유연 안보리에서 이라크 규탄 결의안 공동 제안(8.2.)

o 외무부 실무선에서는 대이라크 경제제재 건의중

외 무 부

종 별 :

번 호 : USW-3566 　　　　　　　　　　　　　일 시 : 90 0803 1623

수 신 : 장 관(봉일,항만청)

발 신 : 주 미 대사

제 목 : 이락/쿠웨이트 사태 관련 해상 안전 대책

1. 이락의 쿠웨이트 침공 관련, 미 해사청은 8.2모든 상선들로 하여금 이락. 쿠에이트 연안에서 12마일 이상 떨어져 있을것을 당부하는 특별주의를 발표하였음.

2. 당관 김해무관이 금일 미 해사청 CHRISTENSEN비상 계획 담당관과 국무성 WAJDA 해운육운 담당관실 과장에서 현지 해운 관련상황 및 향후 미측 추가적인 선박 항행 안전 조치등을 문의한바에 의하면 미 정부는 미선사 소유 편의치적 유조선의 페르시아만 항행 안전 문제에 대처, 국무부를 중심으로 해사청과 해군성간 긴밀한 협조하에 사태 진전 파악등 현지 상황 파악에 주력하고 있으며, 아직 상기 특별 주의외에추가적 조치는 고려되지 않고 있다함.

3. 한편 쿠웨이트 원유 수송 서느사및 동지역 써비스 정기선사들은 동지역 배선을 일시 중단하거나 타지역에서의 양하 조건으로 화물을 BOOKING 하는등 현지 사태를 주시, 신중히 대응하고 있는 것으로 알려지고 있음.

(공사 손명현-국장)

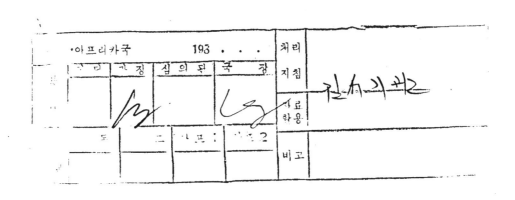

외 무 부

종 별 :

번 호 : USW-3583
일 시 : 90 0803 1922

수 신 : 장 관(중동,미북,동구일)

발 신 : 주 미 대사

제 목 : 미소 공동 성명

연: USW-3571

1. BAKER 장관은 8.3(금) 모스크바에서 쉐바르드나제 소련 외무장관과 이락군의 쿠웨이트로부터의 무조건 철수를 촉구하는 공동 성명을 발표하였음.

2. 동 성명에서는 소련이 이미 대 이락 무기 수출금지 조치를 취하고 미국이 이락의 자산 동결조치를 취한점을 거론하면서 국제 사회가 이락에 대한 무기 공급을 중단 할것을 촉구하고 특히 ARAB LEAGUE 등 인근국들이 유엔 안보리결의가 효과적으로 수행되도록 가능한 모든 조치를취할것으로 촉구하였음.

3. 동 성명 내용 별첨 FAX 송부함.

첨부: USW(F)-1699

(대사 박 동진--국장)

추 ·아프리카국				198 . . .	처리지침	
공 람	담 당	과 장	심 의 관	국 장		
					자료이용	관리기관
배 부	수 동	고	아 프		비고	

중아국   1차보   미주국   구주국   정문국   안기부

PAGE 1
90.08.04   10:37 WG

외신 1과 통제관

0012

EXCERPT OF JOINT US-USSR STATEMENT
DEMANDING IRAQI WITHDRAWAL FROM KUWAIT
AS READ BY
SECRETARY OF STATE JAMES BAKER, III

FRIDAY, AUGUST 3, 1990

.STX

SEC. BAKER: In response to this blatant transgression of the
basic norms of civilized conduct, the United States and the Soviet
Union have each taken a number of actions, including the Soviet
suspension of arms deliveries and the American freezing of assets.
The Soviet Union and the United States reiterate our call for
unconditional Iraqi withdrawal from Kuwait. The sovereignty,
national independence, legitimate authorities, and territorial
integrity of the state of Kuwait must be completely restored and
safeguarded.

The United States and the Soviet Union believe the
international community must not only condemn this action, but also
take practical steps in response to it. Today, we take the unusual
step of jointly calling upon the rest of the international community
to join with us in an international cutoff of all arms supplies to
Iraq. In addition, the Soviet Union and the United States call on
regional organizations, especially the League of Arab States, all
Arab governments, as well as the nonaligned movement and the Islamic
Conference, to take all possible steps to ensure that the United
Nations Security Council resolution is carried out.

Governments that engage in blatant aggression must know that
the international community cannot and will not acquiesce in -- Bend
of available feed) --

.ETX

END

0013

쿠웨이트 사태에 대한 미국반응(2)

90. 8. 4.

미 주 국

┌─────────────〈주요 반응〉─────────────┐
│   │
│ ० 이라크의 사우디 침공시 무력개입 의사 천명   │
│   │
│ ० 이라크의 철군 발표 내용에 대해 불만 표시   │
│   │
└──────────────────────────────────────┘

┌─────────┐
│ 행정부 반응 │
└─────────┘

1. Bush 대통령 기자회견(8.3.)

   ० 이라크가 사우디를 침공할 경우 어떠한 원조라도 사우디에 제공할 것임.

   ० 현재 사우디.영국.터키 등의 지도자와 협의중
     - Ozal 터키 대통령과는 터키 통과 이라크 송유관 폐쇄 가능성 합의

2. 미.쏘 외무장관 공동성명 및 기자회견(8.3. 모스크바)

   ० 모든 국가에 대 이라크 무기 금수 요청

   ० 이라크군 철수 요청

   ० 유엔 안보리에서의 지속적 협조 다짐

   ० 쿠웨이트와 이라크내 미.쏘인의 신변안전 침해시 심각한 결과가 초래될
     것임을 경고

   ० 세바르드나제 외무장관은 이라크군이 곧 철수할 것이라는 통보를
     받았다고 언급

0014

3. 백악관 대변인 기자회견(8.3.)

   o 이라크의 철군계획에 관해서는 언론보도 이외에는 접한 바 없음

   o 현 쿠웨이트 정부는 이라크의 괴뢰정부이므로 합법적 정부가 아님

4. 국무부 대변인 기자회견(8.3.)

   o 미국은 이라크군의 즉각적. 무조건적 철수를 희망

| 의회 반응 |

   o Thomas Foley 하원의장, Les Aspin 하원 군사위원장 등, 이라크가 사우디를
     침공할 경우 무력 개입하여야 함을 주장

| 미 해군 이동 상황 |

   o 인도양 함대 이동에 이어서, 8.6-7경 항모 Saratoga호와 전함 15척이 미국
     동해안에서 지중해로 이동 예정
     - 국방부는 동 이동이 쿠웨이트 사태와 무관하다고 발표
   o 군사 전문가들은 걸프지역내 미 지상기지 및 공격력 부족으로 인해 미국의
     무력개입에 한계가 있을 것이라고 분석

0015

Iraqi Threatens U.S. Interests, CIA Says

By David Hoffman and Dan Balz
Washington Post Staff Writers

President Bush, who vowed yesterday that Iraq's invasion of Kuwait "will not stand," has ordered U.S. government agencies to begin a secret planning effort aimed at destabilizing and eventually toppling President Saddam Hussein from power, according to informed sources.

Bush initiated the effort over the last several days after a series of meetings at which Director William H. Webster outlined the Central Intelligence Agency's evaluation that Saddam, a ruthless leader bent on making Iraq the "Arab superpower," has already put himself in position to manipulate world oil prices.

In angry public remarks yesterday, Bush refused to discuss specific options, but advised reporters: "Just wait. Watch and learn."

In private, the president and his senior advisers have been told by Webster that Saddam poses a threat that goes beyond the immediate Kuwait crisis and extends to the critical long-term economic interests of the United States, the sources said. The CIA evaluation is that Saddam, flush with newly seized Kuwaiti oil reserves, will become a powerful, intimidating force inside the Organization of Petroleum Exporting Countries, driving up oil prices, fueling inflation and possibly throwing the United States into recession and unmanageable fiscal difficulty.

CRISIS IN THE GULF

Pages A13 - A17

The CIA declined to comment.

After deciding it is now in the U.S. "national interest" to stop Saddam, Bush authorized planning for what sources said will likely be a multifaceted effort to strangle Iraq's economy, foment discontent in the military and support resistance groups inside and outside the country. Sources said this effort will include covert activity, which could be difficult if not impossible given that Iraq is organized as a police state and Saddam has brutally repressed any internal opposition.

It could not be learned what timetable Bush has set for making decisions about how to actually implement the campaign against Saddam. The president has asked for the broadest possible set of options and plans for dealing with what is being treated as a major challenge to his presidency and his political standing at home, the sources said.

Tense and angry, Bush arrived back in Washington from Camp David just after 3 p.m. yesterday and spoke briefly with reporters before convening a meeting of his national security advisers to review the situation in the Persian Gulf.

Although his rhetoric was not substantially different from the warnings he has issued since Iraq overran Kuwait on Thursday morning, his demeanor was. He appeared tired, ill-tempered and firm, cutting off one reporter with a testy comment: "What's the question? I can read."

Bush was sharply critical of the failure of other Arab leaders to force Iraq to withdraw its troops from Kuwait, especially Jordan's King Hussein, who defended the Iraqi invasion and called President Saddam "a patriot."

"I want to see the Arab states join the rest of the world in condemning this outrage, and doing what they can to get Saddam Hussein out," Bush said. On Jordan's

POLICY, From A1

Hussein, he added, "I am disappointed to find any comment by anyone that apologizes or appears to condone what's taking place."

Three days ago, Bush said Arab leaders had requested time to handle the invasion on their own, and at the time he appeared to put some hope in that regional effort. By yesterday, however, his patience appeared to have worn thin.

"I was told by one [Arab] leader that I respect enormously . . . that they needed 48 hours to find what was called an Arab solution," Bush said. "That obviously has failed."

Bush said he was continuing his talks with other world leaders in an effort to bring about a "united front" to "isolate Iraq economically," adding, "There is no intention on the part of any of these countries to accept a puppet government [in Kuwait], and that signal is going out loud and clear to Iraq."

Asked how the United States and other countries could prevent Saddam from installing a puppet government in Kuwait, Bush replied curtly, "Just wait. Watch and learn."

The president said he wants the United Nations "to move soon" with economic sanctions against Iraq to reverse what he termed "vicious aggression" against Kuwait. "This will not stand," he said. "This will not stand, this aggression against Kuwait."

Bush refused to discuss military options, especially if the Iraqis move against neighboring Saudi Arabia. But he said "you can assume" he is working to persuade

Saudi Arabia and Turkey to shut off Iraqi oil pipelines that run through their countries. He said he was expecting a telephone call from Turkish President Turgut Ozal and that he planned to talk again later in the day with Saudi King Fahd.

"All options are open," Bush said.

Bush was unyielding in his condemnation of Iraq. Asked whether Iraqi troops appeared to be dug in in Kuwait, he replied, "Iraqi lied once again. They said they were going to start moving out today and we have no evidence that they're moving out."

Bush said the NATO countries were in agreement about how to move against Iraq. He said he had talked with Canadian Prime Minister Brian Mulroney and French President Francois Mitterrand and that British Prime Minister Margaret Thatcher would meet with him here today for further discussions.

He also praised Japanese Prime Minister Toshiki Kaifu for his country's decision to "crack down on imports from Iraq."

Bush said he did not believe American lives were in danger in Kuwait but added that "you know how I feel about the protection of American life and the willingness to do whatever is necessary to protect it."

A decision to look for ways to topple Saddam represents a marked turnabout from the administration's previous attitude toward the Iraqi leader. Saddam received explicit U.S. backing during the Iran-Iraq war, including intelligence sharing, increased non-military trade and food shipments and Bell executive helicopters which he converted to mil-

1016-1   August 6, 1990

0016

itary use. This was largely an effort to use Iraq as a strategic counterbalance to Iran and keep the oil flowing.

After the 1988 Iran-Iraq ceasefire, Baghdad's relations with Washington deteriorated dramatically with Saddam's campaign to crush the Kurdish rebellion, whose leaders had sided with Iran. His increasingly bellicose statements, his stockpiling of the Third World's largest chemical weapons arsenal, and his quest for strategic weapons also strained relations with the United States.

But as recently as last week, the administration was still trying to work with Iraq, in part because Saddam had served as what officials thought was a moderating influence in negotiations over a Palestinian role in peace talks with Israel. Assistant Secretary of State John H. Kelly, in testimony to the House Foreign Affairs Committee last Tuesday, said the administration remained opposed to broad economic sanctions on Iraq.

But by taking Kuwait, the Iraqi president now controls nearly a quarter of OPEC's total oil production, second only to Saudi Arabia. U.S. officials fear this and his military might will give Saddam enough sway in the cartel's quota and pricing deliberations to intimidate Saudi Arabia. "If he installs a puppet regime in Kuwait, he will get enormous leverage over the Saudis," said a senior official. "If you allow him to do that, he's achieved his objectives." The Saudis would be "paralyzed," the official added.

Saddam needs higher oil prices to meet his problems at home, including a massive foreign debt, an expansive weapons program and unmet consumer needs. Analysts said they fear that other OPEC members, including ravaged Iran, would be only too happy to see world oil prices rise.

Yet Bush's efforts to oust Saddam could be extraordinarily difficult, as were earlier attempts to overthrow Libya's Moammar Gadhafi. The sources said the most promising immediate avenues appear to be strangling Saddam financially, hoping that without oil exports, additional money

and new arms supplies, he would face discontent at home and in the military.

The sources said Bush and his advisers had ruled out any attempt at assassination, which is against the law.

A member of an Iraqi opposition group in London, who asked not to be identified, said that while talks have been held with American officials in the past, none has occurred since the invasion of Kuwait.

The opposition is badly splintered and largely in exile. Tiny exile dissident groups exist in European and U.S. cities, but are reluctant to operate publicly.

The opposition coalesces around two poles: Kurdish nationalism and Islamic fundamentalism.

There are a few groups of fundamentalist Shiite Moslems, the most prominent of which is Dawaa Islamiya (the Islamic Call). During the war with Iran, Dawaa Islamiya received support or shelter from Iran and Syria and claimed responsibility for bombings and assassination attempts against Saddam. Iranian exiles say the group maintains an underground presence of some sort within Iraq, including the military.

Iraq's Kurds, who form an estimated 15 to 20 percent of the population, have long resisted rule from Baghdad. The main Kurdish opposition to Saddam, the Democratic Party of Kurdistan (DPK), was helped by Iran during the war and fought Iraqi troops in the northern Kurdish homeland. But the cease-fire allowed Saddam to crush military opposition by the Kurds and to pursue a campaign to relocate them to other parts of Iraq.

There is also a small Communist Party, which broke with Saddam after he purged its leaders in 1978-79. Since then, the communists have been allied with the DPK and another Kurdish group, but appear to have posed no real threat.

Staff writer James Rupert contributed to this report.

1716-2

August 6, 1990
WP

0017

STATE DEPARTMENT

REGULAR BRIEFING

BRIEFER: MARGARET TUTWILER

1:40 P.M., EDT

MONDAY, AUGUST 6, 1990

Number one, an overall update. We continue to view the situation as extremely serious. Iraqi forces, notwithstanding Saddam's pledge to withdraw, seem to be increasing rather than decreasing their presence close to the border with Saudi Arabia. This morning our charge Mr. Wilson met with President Saddam Husayn. President Husayn asked to see our charge. Our charge raised the safety of Americans and the need for Iraq to withdraw immediately and unconditionally. They met for a couple of hours. We view this as a very serious meeting.

Our embassy in Kuwait confirmed that westerners, including Americans, were taken from three hotels in Kuwait and have been placed on buses by the Iraqis. Preliminary hotel lists indicate that about 28 Americans are in these groups of westerners. We do not know their destination and I am not going to speculate about where they have been taken. The President has made clear to the Iraqi government its responsibility to safeguard the lives of those who wish to leave. We hold Iraq responsible for the safety of Americans and of all foreign nationals. Many governments as you know are communicating this same message to the Iraqi government.

We and other governments are working for the safe and orderly departure of all those who wish to leave, regardless of nationality. There are reports that some civilians, including Americans, have been able to leave or have left.

We view this particular matter, obviously, very seriously. Assistant Secretary Kelly has called in the Iraqi ambassador. Our charge in Baghdad is making inquiries with the foreign ministry, and we are trying to find out the facts on the whereabouts of these individuals.

On Secretary Baker's activies since we returned here on Saturday morning approximately at 9:00 a.m. at Andrews Air Force Base, as you all know he left the next morning at approximately 7:00 a.m. for the meeting up at Camp David. This Saturday and Sunday he has been on the phone with Ambassador Pickering; with our Ambassador in Kuwait; with our charge in Iraq; various departmental officials; the President throughout the weekend, any number of phone calls, including a number of times this morning.

1727-1

Number two, he has talked to Foreign Minister Shevardnadze this morning. He called the Foreign Minister approximately at 8:45 a.m. They had a 30-minute phone conversation. When they were in Moscow, they had agreed to stay in touch. Foreign Minister Shevardnadze sent the Secretary a written message this weekend; and the Secretary, as I said, called him this morning. They discussed the overall situation in Kuwait. They discussed the UN vote, and agreed that they should seek to have it voted upon quickly, to move quickly. And they agreed that they both are very much in agreement on the need to continue to work closely together.

Secretary Baker today has also talked to his counterparts in Egypt, France, Japan, and Oman. As you know, he will be attending the President's meeting this afternoon with Secretary Woerner and with Prime Minister Thatcher. He may be talking to additional foreign ministers throughout the day, but I don't have a list for you right now, or any that are in the works.

As you know, the White House announced that the Secretary will be going to Turkey. Turkey, as you know, is a long-time important ally of the United States that occupies a strategic position, both with regard to Europe and the Middle East.

As you know, the President has spoken with the President of Turkey several times in the last week. And it was decided that the best way to continue this series of important consultations was for the Secretary to travel to Turkey.

He will be discussing with the Turkish leadership the crisis in the Persian Gulf and the importance of our coordination in response to it. We will -- tentatively, our plans are, as you know, the Secretary of State is hosting the US-Mexican Bi-national Commission all day Wednesday ending with a dinner here in town.

We will probably be leaving immediately after that dinner from Andrews, flying all night, which puts us into Turkey approximately early afternoon on Thursday.

Secretary Baker, unfortunately, had to postpone his meeting with Foreign Minister Levy. It has been rescheduled at a mutually agreed upon date of September 6 and 7. He would like to stress, even though he had to postpone this, that our commitment to a workable peace process remains strong.

Iraq's aggression doesn't alter that fact at all. It underscores the need to deal peacefully with other conflicts in the region. An Israeli-Palestinian dialogue is an important first step in dealing with the Arab-Israeli conflict. Obviously, there cannot be peace in the Middle East, without peace between Israel and her Arab neighbors. We want to make clear that there is a pathway of reconciliation and peace. That's another way to counter Saddam Husayn's objectives in the area.

1776-2

On the UN, the Council met informally this morning to consult further on a draft resolution which would impose comprehensive sanctions on Iraq under Chapter 7 of the UN Charter. I was just told that they are expected to go into formal session in the next few minutes. We hope the Council will be ready to vote formally on this resolution very shortly. And we are actively working and have been all morning towards that end.

Iraq's dangerous act of naked aggression must be met with swift, decisive action by the Security Council and the international community.

Swift passage of the resolution will demonstrate to Iraq the Council's resolve to enforce UNSC Resolution 660, which demands complete and unconditional withdrawal of Iraqi forces from Kuwait.

The draft resolution would impose a comprehensive trade embargo, economic and military, against Iraq and Kuwait until Iraq withdraws and the sovereignty and independence of Kuwait is restored. The decision to impose these measures would be binding on all UN member states, and we want a total trade embargo, both economic and military.

And that is basically what I had for you all.

Q   Margaret, going back to the 28 Americans --

MS. TUTWILER: Mmm-hmm. (In acknowledgement.)

Q   -- do you now consider them to be hostages?

MS. TUTWILER: We believe that it's premature to call them hostages. Our consultations are going on; our conversations are going on. As I said, we are not going to speculate about where they have been taken, and we have just learned this basically, or been able to confirm it for you, in the last 60 minutes. And so we think it's premature to call them hostages.

Q   The figure we were given the other day was several thousand -- I think 6,000 Americans in Kuwait.

Q   Three thousand.

Q   Three thousand, so we're told.

MS. TUTWILER: Correct. That's the same number.

Q   So what are -- are the rest of them out now and safe or what?

MS. TUTWILER: No. I didn't say that.

Q   Well, I'm just asking.

MS. TUTWILER: No. They are not.

Q   What did Saddam Husayn have to say about the safety of Americans in Kuwait?

MS. TUTWILER: Un——tunately, other than to s—— what our charge said to President Saddam Husayn, I do not have a characterization for you of what was said coming back at us.

Q   Well, when you characterize it as a very serious meeting, what do you mean to convey?

MS. TUTWILER: That we viewed it as a very serious meeting, but ——

Q   Why?

MS. TUTWILER: Because the State Department and the embassy views it as a serious meeting, Bill, but they do not want -- or I'm not at liberty to go into any other detail than the details that I told you of what our charge, Mr. Wilson, raised on behalf of the United States in this meeting --

Q   Well, did President --

MS. TUTWILER: -- and the length of the meeting.

Q   Did President Husayn threaten to hold Americans hostage or --

MS. TUTWILER: I don't have any characterization for you, unfortunately, of what President Saddam Husayn said to our charge.

Q   Margaret, was the US government more or less concerned about these people in the wake of this meeting with Saddam Husayn?

MS. TUTWILER: I've said that we viewed these 28 Americans as a very serious matter and that's what we do. I also said that we have just learned of this, that we are not calling this -- it's premature to call it hostage taking at this moment in time, and that we are ascertaining the facts there on the ground. But we were in a position as of this briefing to come out and confirm for you that 28 Americans were put on buses by Iraqis. Other than that, I'd be totally speculating for you.

Q   At the time Charge Wilson -- I think you said his name was -- met with Saddam Husayn, was he in a -- was he able to discuss these facts or did he not know them at that time, these 28 people on the buses?

MS. TUTWILER: Because of the delay, I don't want to -- I don't want to say which came first to you because we're getting our information, as you know, by cables and phones, et cetera, so I don't want to put it in a time context.

Q   And the rest of the Americans, Margaret, the 2,972?

MS. TUTWILER: I don't have anything specific other than you know they're there. You know that we now, I believe the official number of embassy personnel is 130 and dependents, and approximately 3,000 Americans in Kuwait.

Q   Do you know how many have been able to leave?

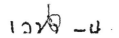

MS. TUTWILER: I don't have a number for you, but we do know that some have -- have left.

Q   What is the Department of State, through the embassy or the consular office, doing for those 3,000-some-odd Americans in Kuwait and the 500 or so Americans in Iraq?

Their families are quite concerned. Some say that they know that the person who is in one of those countries is put up in a hotel. Some are saying that they can't leave and are equating it with a hostage situation. What level of detail can you provide, and what is the US government doing about it?

MS. TUTWILER: As we have been all weekend, which I believe either you or your colleagues have been told, we are in contact with American citizens in Kuwait and in Iraq to the extent that we can. Embassy officials in both capitals have spoken to literally hundreds of Americans, despite the fact that telephones have been unreliable and movement very difficult. We are also in touch with families of American citizens located in those countries and have a large number of officials answering inquiries from Americans regarding families and friends in Iraq and Kuwait.

As you may or may not know, Bill, the State Department put in a hotline phone number which has been published in any number of publications here in the United States just for the very fact of what you're raising, for the information to get out to Americans and their families. But there is a number here at the State Department that was installed for them to call, and my understanding is that it has been heavily used.

Q   Can they get out, as far as you know? Can they get out if they want to?

MS. TUTWILER: We have described it as very difficult, and we have said that the phones are sometimes working, some not; basically just described it as unreliable. And I have said that some Americans have gotten out and have left.

Q   To your knowledge, has anyone been prevented from leaving who wanted to do so?

MS. TUTWILER: Not that I personally am aware of.

Q   Margaret, you said that the Iraqi force

seems to be increasing rather than decreasing near the Saudi Arabian border.

MS. TUTWILER: Mm-hmm. (In agreement.)

Q   Does that mean that there have been no withdrawals? Or overall are there more Iraqi troops in Kuwait now than there were? Or they're just -- just in that one area, have they increased?

MS. TUTWILER: I'm not going to be at liberty to get into troop levels. I would leave the characterization as the President stated it for you yesterday of what he believes as far as withdrawals. And we have said for you today that we believe that -- or there seems to be an increase on the border with Saudi Arabia. But actual levels and types and specific equipment, we're just not getting into.

0022

Q   But you have seen no evidence of withdrawals of troops
back into Iraq?

MS. TUTWILER: I have no new characterization from the
President's last night when he arrived back from Camp David.

Q   How about the story about the pipeline through Turkey?
Has Iraq unilaterally shut that down?

MS. TUTWILER: We can't confirm that, and if we have -- if they
have, if it's true, it's just evidence, in our opinion, that the
economic sanctions are working.

Q   Was the meeting between Kelly and the Iraqi ambassador
laid on in response to something that Saddam Husayn had told the US
charge this morning?

MS. TUTWILER: No.   The meeting with Ambassador Kelly and the
Iraqi ambassador was laid on once our embassy sent us in a cable or
a communique, that what this then confirmed, that these 28 Americans
had been put on buses.

Q   Margaret, what's the status of the Dawaa prisoners,
please?

MS. TUTWILER: We have no information on the status of the
Dawaa prisoners being held in Kuwait.   We've seen the reports that
they have been taken from prison in Kuwait but we cannot confirm
that.   Our policy all along regarding these prisoners has been that
we do not make deals.

MS. TUTWILER: All we know is that 28 Americans, along with
other Westerners, were put on three buses outside of three hotels --
or I don't know how many buses -- three hotels -- and bused.   We
don't know where or what's going on.

Q   How do you know that's a fact?   Is this ---

MS. TUTWILER: Because our embassy sent us a cable.

Q   Were they informed officially ---

MS. TUTWILER: Confirming it.

Q   -- I mean by the Brits, or --

MS. TUTWILER: I don't know how the embassy found out, but they
definitely sent it in confirming it.

Q   The United States positioned off the coast of Liberia
several ships with an effort to be prepared for evacuation of
American citizens there several weeks before that became necessary.

MS. TUTWILER: Mmm-hmm (agreeing).

Q   Have similar arrangements been made in the case of
several thousand Americans in Kuwait?

MS. TUTWILER: That's all under something that I'm not allowed
to discuss.

Q   Can you dra___he distinction for me, e___ain why you could discuss it in one case but not in another?

MS. TUTWILER: I can only say that the President has articulated over and over again throughout the last 72 hours that he is not discussing any possible options that he may or may not take. And so it will be highly irresponsible or inappropriate for me to speculate about what the President may or may not decide.

Q   In the case of Kuwait you mean?

MS. TUTWILER: Mmm-hmm (agreeing).   He sets the policy.

Q   Margaret, Fitzwater said today that one of the goals of the United States was to, quote, "stop Saddam Husayn," unquote. Is the US goal to prevent --- to stop Saddam Husayn from moving further into other countries?   Is it to stop him from continuing to maintain his troops in another country?   Can you --- or is it withdrawal, is it stopping in place?

MS. TUTWILER: Without reinterpreting or interpreting what Marlin said, I will state for you quite clearly what our policy is and there are three parts to it.   One, the immediate and unconditional withdrawal of all Iraqi forces from Kuwait.   Two, the restoration to power of a legitimate Kuwaiti government. Three, ensuring the safety of all Americans in the area.   Four -- I'm sorry, there are four parts -- ensuring the freedom of navigation in the Persian Gulf and the free flow of oil from the region, which has been policy in the United States since 1949.

Q   Margaret, number two of those, "restoration of a legitimate Kuwaiti government," would that be restoration of the former Kuwaiti government or "a" -- because you seemed to say "a" rather than "the" legitimate Kuwaiti government.

MS. TUTWILER: The Emir and his leadership, as you know, remain safe in Saudi Arabia, and they remain the legal government of Kuwait.

Q   Are they the legitimate government of Kuwait?

MS. TUTWILER: Yes.

Q   Can you -- still a couple of more.   Can you tell us anything further about the conversation with Foreign Minister Shevardnadze this morning on this subject?   And also, did they discuss any other subjects other than the Gulf?

MS. TUTWILER: They did not discuss any other subjects, and I don't think, Ralph, that I can go into a more detailed description than of what I did.   They discussed the UN vote and how important it was for it to move quickly.   They discussed the overall situation in Kuwait.   And they discussed, and both agreed upon, staying in contact and the importance of moving quickly in the UN.   I mean ---

Q   Did they discuss the safety of Soviet and American citizens in Iraq and Kuwait?

MS. TUTWILER: Yes.

12/9-7

0024

Q   Margaret, have there been any contacts with -- have there been any contacts with China? On Friday, we were told that such contacts would be instituted.

MS. TUTWILER: Assistant Secretary Solomon, as you know, left our trip in Moscow and went to Beijing. He had two meetings with two different -- I believe they were vice foreign ministers. He has picked back up on his regularly scheduled trip which was to be in Tokyo on August 5, and then on into Korea.

1\}1%\}-8

0025

THE WHITE HOUSE

WASHINGTON, DC

REGULAR BRIEFING

BRIEFER: MARLIN FITZWATER

MONDAY, AUGUST 6, 1990

Okay, again, let me -- please bear with me for this somewhat lengthy summation of events at this point in the -- in Kuwait.

The situation in the Gulf remains extremely serious. There is no information suggesting that Iraqi military units are departing Kuwait. To the contrary, the Iraqi military presence throughout Kuwait, including along the Saudi border, remains extremely large and threatening.

We normally do not comment on stories involving intelligence matter or covert activities; however, because of the sensitivity of the current situation and the blaring headlines in this morning's papers, we must say that there are significant inaccuracies in the stories this morning concerning covert activities. We will not go into details or be any more specific than this. (Light laughter.)

However, it is true that Iraq's invasion of Kuwait threatens regional and world stability, threatens OPEC, and could force severe economic consequences in the United States. From the moment the first Iraqi soldier entered Kuwait, it has been clearly in the national interest to stop Saddam Husayn.

This is an overt situation. His tanks are real and moving. Our response is real and moving on all fronts; diplomatic, economic, political and military.

MR. FITZWATER: Yes, I'm sorry. The United Nations Security Council will resume informal consultations today, possibly to be followed by a formal vote this afternoon --- don't have a specific time, but they are expected to vote this afternoon. They will be considering sanctions that they can take under Chapter 7 of the United Nations charter. Last week, the Security Council passed Resolution 660 calling for immediate and unconditional Iraqi withdrawal from Kuwait. Because Iraq has not complied with this resolution, the US and other Security Council members have been consulting on steps that may be taken.

Just to summarize briefly, that resolution will call for a ban on all trade with Iraq, a ban on weapon sales, a ban on economic assistance and financial transactions. In effect, it will isolate Iraq and seek to force compliance with Resolution 660.

0026

The State Department has ordered all non-essential official embassy personnel and dependents to depart Iraq and Kuwait as soon as the situation permits. We urge all American citizens present to depart as soon as possible. All American citizens are asked to stay in close contact with our US embassies in those countries.

There have been a number of American citizens who have left the countries. You've seen television

reports and interviews with people who have been leaving by bus or automobile in the last several hours.

There are reports, within the last few minutes, on the wire services of people being rounded up or otherwise detained in hotels, and so forth. We do not have any information confirming those reports at this time. We obviously are looking into them and I will let you know as soon as we get any update on that information.

I don't believe I need to go into the military situation. It's essentially the American ships in the Gulf are the same in terms of their configuration, the movement, as we laid out on Friday. So I won't go into that.

Q   Marlin, can you describe what Secretary Cheney is seeking today in his talks in Saudi Arabia and what Secretary Baker will be asking for when he sees Prime Minister Ozal?

MR. FITZWATER: We can't be too specific. In Saudi Arabia, quite obviously, we are discussing the possible threat by Iraqi forces directly to that country. The Iraq forces are consolidating their strongholds in Kuwait. They are close to the Saudi Arabian border and as the President said yesterday, we are very concerned about that and believe that there is a threat there that we need to discuss directly with the Saudis.

Again, I do not want to

confirm details, but it's quite clear that that would involve appropriate ways to defend their country.

Q   Marlin, there's been some obvious unhappiness with Hussein. What was the gist of the telephone conversation this morning with him?

MR. FITZWATER: That was last evening after the NSC meeting. The gist of the conversation was simply to discuss the viewpoint of King Hussein. King Hussein had two television interviews yesterday. He's been quite public about his feelings. President Bush simply reiterated once again that the United States does have an interest in the Gulf. We have significant interest in terms of the oil supply, in terms of our friendship with Saudi Arabia and other countries, in terms of keeping the sea lanes open, and in terms of regional and international stability and the threat to it that's posed by Saddam Husayn's takeover of Kuwait. We wanted to make certain that King Hussein is aware of that situation.

Q   Hussein said yesterday that the Arab summit idea is apparently dead. The President said yesterday that giving the Arabs time has apparently failed. And you're saying that this is clearly a matter in our national interest. Are we now taking the lead in

12M-2

0027

determining what will happen, what the United St__ s response will be, no longer waiting on Arab -- the Arabs to be up-front?

MR. FITZWATER: Well, I hope there has never been any question about that. The United States has been considering its own interests and has taken the lead internationally in this matter from the -- as I said, the day the first soldier crossed the border. We do have very strong interests here. The President has been working tirelessly personally and through international organizations and diplomatic channels to organize international opposition, a United Nations opposition, Arab interests in the region to consolidate their feelings. So the short answer is affirmatively yes.

Tom?

Q   Marlin, have we been in contact, anyone in the administration, in the last 72 hours with the Iranians, either to seek their help in counterbalancing the Iraqis, to maybe open -- use this opportunity to open relations? And for a quick follow-up, do we have any idea about the hostages that -- not the hostages, the Iranian prisoners that were in Kuwait's jails that are reportedly -- have been taken away by the Iraqis?

MR. FITZWATER: The last time I asked, which was yesterday, we did not have any information to suggest a change in the status of the prisoners in Kuwait. We have not had any direct contact with Iran -- again, that I'm aware of. We have had reports -- through third parties, again -- of Iranian interests and Iranian moves in one way or another in the region, but nothing direct.

Q   What's your response to the provisional Kuwaiti leader's threat to Americans in that country?

MR. FITZWATER: The President has expressed his deep concern for the safety and well-being of Americans in Iraq and Kuwait. And we -- our position is quite clear that we consider that a prime responsibility and will not shirk from it.

Q   -- this, if I can. Are we going to be able to provide some means of evacuation for people from Kuwait, private citizens, not just non-essential embassy personnel?

MR. FITZWATER: Well, again, we have not reached that point, and we have advised people to leave. We are in constant contact with our embassies in both countries, and we're in telephone communication. We are -- we know what their situation there is. And we will be prepared to act appropriately, but there's no signals at this time.

Q   Marlin, has the United States considered severing relations with Iraq?

MR. FITZWATER: I don't believe so. Our feeling is at this point that the embassy there is important in terms of maintaining an influence in the area and a source of communication on events there. These things are always subject to change at any time in a fluid situation like we're in. But at this point that action has not been taken.

Q   How about with the government? I mean, are we withdrawing our diplomatic staff from Kuwait?

MR. FITZWATER: Well, as I said in this -- in this statement, we are

urging some people to leave. So there will be s = reductions in
terms of --

     Q   He's not going to close it?

     MR. FITZWATER: As of -- there are no plans at this time.

     Charles?

     Q   Marlin, is there any evidence of Americans being
prohibited from leaving either Kuwait or Iraq?

     MR. FITZWATER: Well, it's somewhat difficult to define. In
the terms of a direct prohibition, probably not. On the other hand,
the situation in Kuwait City and in Baghdad is chaotic. And there
are constraints, just given the normal situation on people's
movements and their abilities to communicate and move around. So we
are hopeful that people there would be allowed to leave or can leave
as they want to. But, clearly, it is not total freedom-of-movement
situation.

     Q   A second point, if I may. When you say it's in the
national interest to stop Saddam Husayn, what exactly does that
mean, "stop him"? Does that mean the withdrawal of Iraqi troops?
Does that "remove" mean remove Saddam from power?

     MR. FITZWATER: Let me reiterate once again -- (pauses to
look through guidance) -- our policy. And I want to read it,
because -- (pauses to look through guidance) -- because every word
is important. And this has been our policy ever since the beginning
of this matter. (Pauses to look through guidance.) Of course the
words I have are not the ones I wanted to give you. (Laughter.)

     MR. FITZWATER: We want the unconditional and complete
withdrawal of Iraqi forces and the restoration of the legitimate
government.

     Q   -- to clarify on the NATO question, the Middle East has
always been outside the realm of NATO; it's not part of their
assignment, their responsibility. Traditionally they have resisted
getting involved in the Middle East. Is this is a change? Is NATO
-- (clears throat) -- excuse me -- going to now actively take a
Middle East role? Is that what President Bush wants?

     MR. FITZWATER: Well the President, of course, has been leading
efforts to internationalize this situation as much as possible.
When you talk about the actions of the Gulf Cooperation Council, the
Arab League, the United Nations, the EC and NATO, I would put these
consultations in the category of being a part of all that
international focus. And in this case, the NATO countries, of
course, are part of the EC, part of the UN Security Council; so
they're all tied together.

     Q   I understand the overlap, but it is not part of NATO's
mandate to deal with the Middle East. Are you seeking to extend
it?

     MR. FITZWATER: No, NATO's mandate concerns its members, and of
course there are at least one fairly direct -- one member fairly
directly involved, and all of the members are directly involved in
the sense of getting oil from that part of the world and having
interests in the Middle East.

                         기차 -4

                                                      0029

Q   But not as a military alliance.

MR. FITZWATER: Well the alliance in general has vast responsibilities, political and military.

Q   Marlin, is the United States interested in seeing the destabilization and eventual toppling of Saddam Husayn?

MR. FITZWATER: We're interested in seeing Iraq completely pull out of Kuwait, and the restoration of that government.

Q   Marlin?

Q   But is the United States interested in seeing the destabilization and toppling of that leader?

MR. FITZWATER: We aren't -- we aren't commenting on internal affairs of -- in terms of any direct threats. The problem here is we have a country whose leader has very personally attacked Kuwait with enormous force, who threatens another country, and as a belligerent in that sense, we have very deep concerns, possibly military concerns, and -- but it serves no purpose to be making any personal accusations one way or another.

Q   But -- Marlin, could I just follow up? Did the President order any actions that would lead to the destabilization and eventual toppling of Saddam Husayn?

MR. FITZWATER: We've only -- would comment on discussions that have been had concerning his attack and invasion of Iraq. We would not offer any comment on that story this morning beyond what I just told you.

Q   Is the reason that you're saying there are major inaccuracies in the report about destabilization of Iraq, is it -- are you saying, in effect, that the United States is not -- does not want to mess -- interfere in the internal affairs of Iraq?

MR. FITZWATER: I'm saying that we don't comment on covert activities and intelligence matters. And in this case, it's virtually irrelevant anyway, because this -- we have a war situation. The man has attacked another country and invaded it. Certainly it threatens Saudi Arabia. Any response by the United States would be very overt and known to all.

Q   Why are you making at least a partial denial of the story? What are the reasons for it?

MR. FITZWATER: We just think it's important not to let a story like that stand without some kind of challenge, even though we are very reluctant to get into denying these kind of things, because then you get into having to deal with every rumor, every story, that comes out on covert activities.

Q   In any way, does the United States feel that Turkey might be threatened by Iraq?

0030

MR. FITZWATER: W▩ ▩elieve every country in ▩▩ region has a degree of threat by vi▩▩e of this action, that there is a threat both directly in terms of the -- of Iraq possibly attacking any country. We don't know what Saddam Husayn's intentions are. And certainly every country suffers the more indirect threat of OPEC takeover and oil supply controls and the expansion of Iraqi control, of Iraq as a country.

Susan?

Q   Have we offered Saudi Arabia and Turkey specific assurances on what the US military response would be if they cut off the Iraqi pipeline and as a result were attacked by _____ Saddam Husayn's forces?

MR. FITZWATER: We have discussed military possibilities and our abilities with all the countries in the Gulf.

Q   But have we assured them that if they take this action we want them to take that we'll be there for them if they get attacked as a result?

MR. FITZWATER: Well, I can't comment on that question.

Q   We're committed to the defense of Turkey in any way in case of that through NATO.

MR. FITZWATER: That's correct, yes. Frank?

Q   Marlin, in your statement at the top you talked about extremely large and threatening developments, including along the Saudi border. Are there recent indications overnight or over the past 24 hours that, in fact, Iraqis are fortifying their deployments along the Saudi border? Is there additional troop movement toward that region?

MR. FITZWATER: Well, I can't put too fine a point on it, but there clearly are massive forces in the southern part of the country. They are close to the border and I don't want to try to characterize their strategic posture or their tactical posture, but clearly it is such that we believe a threat exists and such that we believe that it's important to be discussing the defense of Saudi Arabia.

Q   Is there actual movement over this period of time or are these forces that have been there since ---

MR. FITZWATER: There has been movement.

Q   A follow-up the question about conciliatory gestures from Iraq. Other than public pronouncements, has there been any effort to establish some kind of diplomatic repertory -- repertoire (sic) with Iraq?

MR. FITZWATER: We have diplomatic contacts with Iraq. Our embassy there is functioning, and we have people who have been in touch with Iraq officials continuously, yes.

17▩ -6

Q   Marlin, ▪▪ have mentioned in your ▦▦ing statement that the situation in the Middle East poses an economic threat to the US. Could you detail a little bit what that threat is and how it would come about?

MR. FITZWATER: I wouldn't go beyond, of course, the -- the explanations that I'm sure you have heard before about the impact of disruptions in the oil supply, the possibilities of Saddam Husayn taking over OPEC and having a controlling authority on OPEC pricing and production or certainly a huge influence on that, general instability that his ruthlessness in the region offers to continued oil flow.

A HOSTAGE THREAT

Provisional Government Also Hints of Taking Assets in Kuwait

By JOHN KIFNER
Special to The New York Times

CAIRO, Aug. 5 — Iraq's new proxy government in Kuwait threatened to take hostages or nationalize foreign property today in the face of international calls for sanctions in response to President Saddam Hussein's takeover of his oil-rich neighbor.

"Countries that resort to punitive measures against the provisional free Kuwait government and fraternal Iraq should remember that they have interests and nationals in Kuwait," the proxy government's Foreign Minister, Walid Saud Abdullah, said in an Iraqi radio broadcast.

"These countries should also not expect us to act honorably at a time when they are conspiring against us and other brothers in Iraq in an aggressive way," Mr. Abdullah said. "If these countries insist on aggression against Kuwait and Iraq, the Kuwaiti government will then reconsider the method of dealing with these countries."

Iraq Strengthens Army

In the Iraqi capital, President Hussein ordered the formation of 11 new Iraqi Army divisions to bolster what is already the most formidable military force in the Arab world, totaling more than a million men in uniform.

Rather than easing his posture of belligerence, Mr. Hussein appeared to be increasing his efforts to intimidate other Arab nations, particularly Saudi Arabia, into accepting his seizure of Kuwait and its oil fields and his ouster of the long-ruling Al-Sabah family. The invasion has given Iraq control of 20 percent of the world's oil resources.

Iraq asserted today that the 100,000 troops that poured over the border early Thursday began to pull back around 8 A.M. today in the first stage of a phased withdrawal from Kuwait.

But there was no independent confirmation that any Iraqi troops had left.

In Washington, the chairman of the Senate Intelligence Committee, David L. Boren, said American intelligence reports showed no sign of a withdrawal, and he warned that Iraqi troops were in position to invade Saudi Arabia.

"Intelligence reports this morning do not indicate that the Iraqis are really moving out, especially along the southern border where they are pretty well dug in," Mr. Boren, an Oklahoma Democrat, said in an interview broadcast on the ABC television network.

Iraqi radio asserted that the first units to depart were seen off by representatives of the new Kuwaiti government and "a huge number of reporters." Only a few foreign journalists were in Kuwait when the invasion began, however, and none are known to have successfully entered the country since.

A 'Popular Army'

An announcer on Kuwaiti radio, speaking Arabic with an Iraqi accent, said the Iraqi troops would be replaced by a new Kuwaiti "popular army" open to all nationalities. His announcement seemed to indicate that Iraqis and perhaps Palestinians, who make up a sizeable proportion of Kuwait's

Don't 'expect us to act honorably,' Baghdad's proxy in Kuwait warns.

population, would be recruited for the new force.

The Iraqi radio said on Saturday that about 140,000 members of Iraq's own reserve force, also called the popular army, had been mobilized near the border and were volunteering to "aid brethren in Kuwait." The new provisional government of nine military officers, also announced Saturday on the Iraqi radio, is described by Kuwaiti diplomats and other officials abroad as totally made up of Iraqis.

The Saudi Government held an emergency cabinet meeting today on what its official news agency described as "the regrettable events" that "are a cause of concern and dissatisfaction to the Arabs as well as the entire world."

Without further elaboration, the official statement said the Saudi ministers "expressed deep satisfaction with the efforts undertaken by the King to deal with the current crisis." However oblique, the reports by the news agency's represented the first official Saudi mention of the invasion.

Jordan Warns Against Pressure

King Hussein of Jordan asserted tonight in an American television interview that the Iraqi President had told him he would not invade Saudi Arabia, and he warned against Western pressure.

"I do not believe he intends to go into Saudi Arabia, he has told me that," said the King, who like President Hosni Mubarak of Egypt reportedly received assurances last week that Iraq would not invade Kuwait.

"During the last few days there were pressures applied to bring not only the majority of the world in line but to also influence Arab logic," the Jordanian monarch said.

"Please believe me that intimidation does not work, that it could be counterproductive," King Hussein said. "We could be in a far worse situation that we are facing at the moment." -

But the Jordanian leader appears to be caught in the middle of the standoff. Officials of his Government said today that Amman would not recognize the Iraqi-installed government while Arab efforts to mediate the crisis continue.

Amman Defends Abstention

Prime Minister Mudar Badran defended Jordan's abstention on Friday from an Arab League vote condemning the invasion, saying, "Our abstention is only for the time being, in order to keep our door to Baghdad open and be able to settle the crisis."

A Kuwaiti diplomat said that 15 convicted Shiite terrorists linked to the seizure of the American hostages in Lebanon had been taken from a Kuwaiti prison and moved to the Iraqi capital. The Shiites, supporters of Iran's Islamic revolution and opponents of Iraq, were convicted in 1983 car-bomb attacks against the American and French embassies and other targets in Kuwait.

Kuwait's chargé d'affaires in Amman, Faisal al-Mukhaizem, said the Shi'ite prisoners were taken to Baghdad on Friday and that the Iraqis planned "to use them as bargaining counters."

In Washington, the White House said that the 11 American oil workers rounded up after the invasion of Kuwait had been brought to Baghdad and had talked with American Embassy officials there. With their arrival, the White House said, all missing Americans have been accounted for.

August 6, 1990
NYT

0033

외 무 부

종 별 : 긴급

번 호 : USW-3620 일 시 : 90 0807 1923

수 신 : 장관(중근동,미북)

발 신 : 주 미 대사

제 목 : 중동 사태 관련 해상 봉쇄 가능성

금 8.7 오후 현재 당지 방송등 언론에서는 중동지역 미 함정 배치 현황등을 중점보도하면서, 소련, 영국, 불란서등과의 공동 해상 봉쇄 작전 실시 가능성을 예측하고있는바 요지 다음 보고함.

1. 현재 항공 모함 INDEPENDENCE 호를 주축으로한 1개 항모 전단이 호르무즈 해협에서 페르시아만으로 항진중에 있으며, 또한 항공모함 EISENHOWER 호를 주축으로 한 1개 항모 전단이 동부 지중해에 배치되어 있음.(특히 EISENHOWER 호를 주축으로하는 항모 전단은 이집트 정부의 수에즈 운하 통과 허용에 따라 동 운하를 경유,사우디 서부,홍해 지역으로 이동 예정임)

2. 그밖에 COMMANDSHIP 인 LASALLE 호를 주축으로한 함정 전단이 페르시아만내를 항진중이며, 항공모함 SARATOGA 호도 금일 오전 플로리다의 MAYPORT 기지를 출발, 동부 지중해로 향발함.

3. 레이건 행정부 시절 리비아 공습에 사용된 전폭기종인 F-111 전단도 현재 터키내에 배치되어있으며, B-52 전단도 인도양의 디에고 가르시아기지에 배치되어 있음. (B-52 기종은공중 재급유시 중동 지역 출격이 가능함.)

4. 한편 소련의 유도탄 탑재 함정및 영국, 불란서의 군함등도 페르시아만내에서 항진중이며, 사우디측의 기지 사용 허가에 따라 미 본토 주둔 미군 병력이 금명간 사우 디 영토내로 이동할 예정임.

(대사 박동진-국장)

중아국	1차보	2차보	미주국	정문국	안기부	차관	장관

90.08.08 08:59 FB

외신 1과 통제관 0034

외 무 부

종 별 : 긴급

번 호 : USW-3621   일 시 : 90 0807 1923

수 신 : 장 관(중근동,미북)

발 신 : 주 미대사

제 목 : 국무부 브리핑중 중동 사태 관련 부문

연: USW(F)-1740

금 8.7 국무부 정례 브리핑시 TUTWILER 대변인의 중동 사태 관련 언급 내용중주요 부분 1하기 요지 보고함(동 대변인 언급 내용 전문 연호FAX 송부)

1.중동 사태 관련 협의를 위해, BAKER 국무장관은 명 8.7 오전 터키 향발 예정이며, 이어서 8.10(금)에는 브랏셀에서 NATO 회원국 외상들과 동 사태 관련 대책을 협의 예정임.

2.이라크군은 현재 쿠웨이트로 부터 전혀 병력을 철수 시키지 않은 상태인바, 현 쿠웨이트 주둔병력을 사우디 국경 부근으로 이동 배치시키면서 동시에 전부 태세 강화를 도모하고 있음.

3.현재 39명의 미국인이 바그다드 소재 RASHID호텔내에 일종의 연금 상태(호텔내에서는 자유로이 행동할수 있으나, 호텔을 떠날수는 없음)하에 있는바, 이중 11명은원유 채취 관련기술자들이며, 25명은 작일 쿠웨이트 시내 호텔에서 버스로 이송되어온 미국인들임.

(대사 박동진-국장)

중아국   1차보   미주국   정문국   안기부   차관   장관   2차보

90.08.08   08:59 WH

외신 1과 통제관

0035

	분류번호	보존기간

발 신 전 보

번 호 : WUS-2630   900808 1947 FC   종별 : _____

수 신 : 주   미   대사 . 총영사

발 신 : 장 관 (미북)

제 목 : 부쉬 대통령 연설

1. 외신보도에 의하면 현지시간 8.8(수) 09:00에 중동 사태 관련 부쉬 대통령의 연설이 있을 예정이라는 바, 동 연설 주요내용을 긴급 보고 바람.

2. 동 보고시 청와대에 사본이 배부되도록 조치바람.   끝.

(미주국장 반 기 문)

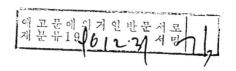

앙 고 재	90년 8월 8일 북미과 박천어	기안자		과 장 신의완	국 장 권병		차 관	장 관		보안통제	외신과통제

0036

NNNN
!
ZB ZM YK0362

ZS YK0363

800932 :BC-GULF-ANNOUNCEMENT URGENT´´´
  IRAQ SCHEDULES MAJOR ANNOUNCEMENT
    NICOSIA, AUG 8, REUTER - IRAQ SAID ON WEDNESDAY THAT IT WAS
ABOUT TO MAKE A MAJOR ANNOUNCEMENT, FUELLING SPECULATION THAT IT
MAY ANNEX KUWAIT.
    BAGHDAD RADIO AND TELEVISION REPEATEDLY TOLD IRAQIS TO
PREPARE FOR THE ANNOUNCMENT AT 1830 (1430 GMT), 90 MINUTES AFTER
U.S. PRESIDENT GEORGE BUSH WAS TO SPEAK TO THE NATION ON THE
GULF CRISIS.
MORE MNK DLR YA

NNNN

쿠웨이트 사태 관련 미국의 조치

1990. 8. 8.

미주국 북미과

1. 군사 조치

가. 군사조치 관련 행정부 입장

° Bush 대통령

- 걸프내 미국의 국익보호를 위해서 필요한 어떠한 조치라도 취할
  것임(8.2.성명)

- 이라크가 사우디를 침공할 경우, 사우디가 원하는 어떠한 원조라도
  제공할 것임(8.3. 기자회견)

- 이라크 경제를 질식시키기 위해 군사적 봉쇄를 포함, 모든 방안을
  검토중(8.6. 기자회견)

° Fitzwater 백악관 대변인 발표(8.6.)

- 이라크군 배치가 사우디에 급박한 위협을 가하고 있으며, 미국은
  모든 가능성에 대비하고 있음

° Kimmit 국무차관 우방국 외교사절에 대한 브리핑(8.2.)

- 미국은 정치.경제.군사적인 모든 가능한 조치를 검토하고 있으며,
  어떠한 방안도 배제하고 있지 않음

° Cheney 국방장관, 사우디방문(8.6.)

- 사우디, 미 전폭기 및 지상군에 대한 기지 제공에 합의

0038

나. 군사 이동 상황

(1) 현재 상황

○ 항모 3척(탑재기 250대), 라살 전함, 구축함 등 총 49척 투입

- 인도양 배치 항모 Independence호 및 전함 6척 페르샤만에 정박

· 걸프로 전투기 발진 가능

- 항모 Saratoga호와 전함 15척 미국 동해안에서 지중해로 발진(8.6.)

· 미 해병대 2,100명 탑승

· 전함 Wisconsin 호, Saratoga와 합류 위해 버지니아 출항

- 항모 Eisenhower호 지중해로 발진

· 이집트, Eisenhower호의 수에즈운하 통과 허가

○ 미국의 F-111, 전폭기 영국에서 터키의 인시르리크 (이라크 국경에서 680Km)로 이동

- 86년 리비아 공습시 사용한 전폭기임

○ B-52 중폭격기 편대, 인도양의 디에고 가르시아 기지에 배치

- 사우디로 출동

○ Bush 대통령, 지상군 및 전투기 사우디 파견 명령(8.7.)

- 이라크의 사우디 침공에 대비한 다국적군의 일부 (이집트, 모로코 등 참여설)

- F15, F16 전투기 파견

- 18공정대, 24 기계화 사단, 101 공정사단 소속 지상군 파견

· 초기파견 병력 2,000-4,000명 추정

- 한국시간 8.8. 22:00 공식발표 예정

(2) 추가 투입 가능 병력 : 신속배치군(RDF) 약 3만명

○ 82 공정대(노스캐롤라이나 주둔) : 24시간내 투입 가능

- 89년 파나마 침공시 투입.

0039

o 7경보병사단(캘리포니아 주둔) : 2-3일내 투입 가능

　- 89년 파나마 침공시 투입

o 24기계화 사단(조지아 주둔) : 페르샤만 배치에 28일 소요

(3) 평 가

o 현재까지의 군사 이동은 직접적 군사 행동을 위한 것이라기 보다는
외교적, 경제적 제재의 효과를 높이기 위한 수단인 것으로 분석

　- 이라크에 효율적으로 대항하려면 최소 5만-30만의 병력이 필요
하며, 이러한 병력의 동원.배치에는 45일-3개월 소요 추정
(미 국방부 관계자 분석)

　- 이라크의 막강한 군사력에 대한 경계심(87년 이.이전 당시
유조선을 호위중이던 미국 프리깃 "스타크"호가 이라크의 엑소세
미사일 공격을 받은 경험)

o 그러나 이라크의 행동 여하에 따라서는 실제 무력행사로 발전 예상

* 기타 국가의 군사 조치
　- 영 국 : 햄스요크 구축함, 프리깃 2척 페르샤만 파견
　- 프랑스 : 함정 3척 지중해로 파견
　　　　　　(엑소세 함대함 미사일, 크로탈 대공미사일 탑재)
　- 쏘 련 : 키닌급 구축함 1척, 보급선 2척 페르샤만 파견(유도 미사일 탑재)
　- 사우디 : 쿠웨이트 국경 지대로 병력 이동(미사일 부대 및 탱크 200-
　　　　　　-300대 증강 배치)
　- 이집트 : 사우디에 2개사단 파병 예정(미 국무부 관계자 언급)
　- 모로코 : 사우디 파병에 합의(미 의회 소식통)
　- 이스라엘 : 모세 아랜스 국방장관, 이라크군 요르단 진입시 이라크를
　　　　　　　공격할 것임을 발표(8.7.)

0040

2. 기타 조치

가. 경제 제재

  ○ 미국내 이라크.쿠웨이트 자산 동결

  ○ 대이라크 통상관계 단절(원유 포함)

나. 외교적 조치

  ○ 여타 국가에 대한 대이라크 공동 제재 요청
    - Bush 대통령 성명, 기자회견
    - Kimmit 국무차관, 우방국 외교사절에 대한 브리핑

  ○ 유엔을 통한 제재 교섭
    - 8.2. 유엔 안보리 이라크 규탄 결의안 채택
    - 8.6. 유엔 안보리 대이라크 제재 조치 결의
      • 쿠웨이트 및 이라크와의 통상 금지(원유를 명시하지는 않음)
      • 대이라크 무기 수출 금지
      • 쿠웨이트 정부 자산 보호를 위한 적절한 조치
      • 의학적.인도적 목적이외의 재정적.경제적 지원 및 상업적.공업적.
        공공의 이익 제공 금지
      • 이라크가 수립한 쿠웨이트 정권 불인정
      • 비회원국에도 결의사항 준수 촉구

  ○ Baker 국무장관, 터키 방문(8.8.)후 NATO와의 협의를 위해 브럿셀
    방문 예정(8.10.)
    - 8.6. 쏘련.이집트.프랑스.일본.오만 외무장관 접촉

다. 미국내 반응

  ○ 의회 반응
    - 8.2. 행정부에 대이라크 수출입 및 원조 금지 촉구 결의안 채택

0041

- Foley 하원의장, Aspin 하원 군사위원장 등, 이라크가 사우디 침공시 미국의 무력 개입 주장

○ 언론 반응
- 이라크의 침략행위 비난
- 걸프지역내 미국의 국익 보호를 위한 효과적 수단 부재 지적
- Washington Post 지는 경제제재가 미국 경제, 미국 국내정치, 우방국과의 관계에 부작용을 초래할 수도 있음을 지적

3. 아국에 대한 대이라크 제재 요청

가. 요청 사항

○ 이라크의 쿠웨이트 침공 공개 강력 규탄
○ 이라크군의 즉각.무조건 철수 요구
○ 아국내 쿠웨이트 자산 동결
○ 아국내 이라크 자산 동결
○ 이라크 및 점령 쿠웨이트와의 통상관계 단절
○ 대이라크 무기 공급 중단
○ 이라크가 수립한 쿠웨이트 정권 불인정

나. 요청 경로

○ Bush 대통령의 성명 및 기자회견

○ Kimmit 국무차관의 브리핑(8.2.)

○ Gregg 주한대사, 장관대리 방문(8.2.)

○ Paal 백악관 아시아 담당 보좌관, 주미 참사관에 전달(8.3.)
- 대이라크 제재가 미온적이어서 실효를 못거둘 경우, 세계 석유 공급에 중대한 차질이 올 우려가 있음과 김일성의 남침 도발을 유혹할 우려가 있음을 언급

0042

- 쿠웨이트 거주 미국 시민이 4,000명이나 되는데도 불구하고
  대이라크 제재를 가하고 있는 점을 강조

o 미 국무부 한국과장, 주미 참사관에 전달(8.7.)
  - 8.6. 유엔 안보리의 대이라크 제재 결의에 호응 요청
  - 미국이 이번 사태를 매우 심각하게 생각하고 있으므로 우방국의
    협조가 매우 긴요하다고 부언

o Solomon 차관보 장관대리 면담(8.8.)

0043

미국의 대이라크 및 쿠웨이트 자산 동결 조치

ㅇ 근   거 ：International Emergency Economic Powers Act(1977년)

ㅇ 내용(요지) :

- To deal with any unusual and extraordinary threat, which has its source in whole or substantial part outside the United States, to the national security, foreign policy, or economy of the United States, if the President declares a national emergency with respect to such threat.

- the President may
  (A) investigate, regulate, or prohibit
      (i) any transactions in foreign exchange,
      (ii) transfers of credit or payments between, by, through, or to any banking institution, to the extent that such transfers or payments involve any interest of any foreign country or a national thereof,
      (iii) the importing or exporting of currency or securities ; and,
  (B) investigate, regulate, direct and compel, nullify, void, prevent or prohibit, any acquisition, holding, withholding, use, transfer, withdrawal, transportation, importation or exportation of, or dealing in, or exercising any right, power, or privilege with respect to, or transactions involving any property in which any foreign country or a national thereof has any interest ; by any person, or with respect to any property, subject to the jurisdiction of the United States.

0044

- The President, in every possible instance, shall consult with the Congress before exercising any of the authorities granted by this Act and shall consult regularly with the Congress so long as such authorities are exercised.

쿠웨이트사태 관련 미국의 군사조치

90. 8. 9

미주국 북미과

1. Bush 대통령 특별담화(8.8)

ㅇ 사우디의 요청에 따라 다국적군의 일부로 미 공군 및 육군을 사우디로
   파병 명령(8.6)

ㅇ 파병 목적은 방어적임.

ㅇ 이번 사태관련 미국의 입장 천명(4가지 원칙)

   - 이라크군의 즉각, 무조건, 완전 철수 요청

   - 합법 쿠웨이트 정부의 복귀

   - 페르샤만의 안전 확보

   - 재외 미국인의 생명보호

ㅇ 이번 사태는 전 세계의 문제임.

   - 영국, 카나다 등 정상, NATO 사무총장 등 접촉

* 이와 관련하여 Kimmit 국무차관이 외교단 브리핑 (별첨 참조)

2. 군사 이동 현황

가. 사우디 파병 내역(미 국방부 소식통)

ㅇ 1단계 파병 내역

   - 82 공정대(노스캐롤라이나) 소속 2,300명

   - F-15 전투기 48대

0046

o 추가 파병 예정

  - 101 공정사단(켄터키)

  - 24기계화 사단(죠지아) : 배치에 약 28일 소요

  - F-16 지상 공격기

  - B-52 폭격기(현대 인도양의 디에고 가르시아에 배치)

o 파병 병력수는 상황에 따라 40,000명선까지 증가 가능

나. 기타 병력 이동 현황

o 항모 3척(탑재기 245대), 라살 전함, 구축함 등 총 49척 투입

  - 항모 Independence : 호르무즈 외해에 정박

  - 항모 Eisenhower : 수에즈운하 통과, 홍해 진입

  - 항모 Saratoga : 8.7 플로리다에서 지중해로 발진

                    (다음 주말까지 작전가능 지역 도착 예정)

o F-111 전폭기 14대, 터키의 인시르리크에 배치(이라크 국경에서
  680Km)

o AWACS 5대 추가 파견

o 사우디에 F-15 전투기 12대 인도예정

  - 현재까지는 사우디의 F-15 보유 한도를 60대로 제한하는 Metzenbaum
    Amendment 때문에 인도 불가 상태였음(현재 사우디는 F-15기 58대 보유)

3. 기타 국가의 반응

o 이집트

  - 긴급 아랍정상회담 소집(한국시간 8.10. 01:00 개최 예정)

  - 이라크와 사우디 사이에 주둔하는 아랍 평화 유지군이 파견될 경우
    참여할 용의 있음을 표명

  - 사우디 파견 다국적군 참여 약속 사실은 부인

0047

o 모로코 : 다국적군 참여설 부인

o 영 국
   - 햄스요크 구축함, 프리깃 2척 파견
   - Hurd 외무장관, 다국적군 참가 발표(해군·공군력 추가 파견 시사)

o 프랑스 : 다국적군 불참 의사 표명(현재 함정 2척 파견)

o 이태리, 스페인 : 다국적군에 대한 군수지원 기지 제공 계획 발표

o 쏘 련 : 다국적군에 불참 선언하고 정치적 해결 촉구(현재 키닌콥
            구축함 및 보급선 2척 파견)

o 이스라엘
   - 모세 아렌스 국방장관, 이라크군 요르단 진입시 이라크를 공격할
     것임을 발표(8.7)
   - 미 하원 군사위 소속 존·매케인 의원은 다국적군에 이스라엘의
     참여를 요청할 수도 있다고 언급.

o 카나다 : 다국적군 참여에 관해 요청 받은 바는 없으며, NATO 외상회의
            (8.10. 브릿셀) 결과를 보아 필요성 여부 검토 예정(8.8. Mulroney
            수상 기자 회견)

o 케야르 UN 사무총장의 반응
   - 미국 등의 군사행동은 사우디와 공동 결정한 사항임.
   - 동 결정이 긴장을 완화하는 데 도움이 되기를 바랄 뿐임.

첨부 : Kimmit 국무차관 브리핑 요지

0048

첨부

Kimmit 국무차관 외교단 브리핑(8.8.)

1. 사우디 파병 취지 설명

   o 사우디 파병은 사우디.쿠웨이트의 요청에 따른 것이며, 이라크의 침략
     확산 방지에 목적이 있음.

2. 미국의 외교적 노력 설명

   o 현재 미 행정부는 유엔안보리의 대이라크 금수 결의의 효과적 시행과
     사우디 파병의 다국적화에 외교 노력을 집중하고 있음.

3. 지상군 대치 동향 설명

   o 현재 쿠웨이트내에 이라크군 부대가 증강 투입되고 있음.

     - 국방부는 이라크군의 지대지 미사일, 화학 무기 반입 가능성 우려

   o 이라크군은 현재 사우디에 대한 공격이 가능한 포진

   o 현재 사우디내 미군은 취약한 방어 태세에 있으나, 참호 구축 및 병참
     장비 투입중

4. 다국적군 구성을 위한 노력 설명

   o 미 행정부는 다국적군 구성을 낙관함.

   o 다국적군의 지휘계통은 사우디와 각 외국군을 유엔 산하에 두고, 서방
     동맹국군 및 범 아랍군의 2원적 작전 통제 체제를 구상중

   o 이집트와 모로코는 참여 가능성을 배제하고 있지 않음.

     - 궁극적으로는 양국 모두 참여할 것으로 기대

     - Mubarak 이집트 대통령이 긴급 아랍 정상 회담을 소집한 것은 범아랍군
       구성을 제안하려는 것으로 이해함.

   o 영국은 사우디의 요청에 따라 해.공군 지원 발표(8.8)

   o 쏘련은 다국적군 참여에 동의하지는 않았으나 서방과의 채널은 열어 놓고
     있는 상태이며, 참여도 불가능하지는 않을 것으로 봄.

5. 기타 이라크의 쿠웨이트 합병 가능성, 외국인 소개 문제등 언급

0049

발 신 전 보

<table>
<tr><td></td><td>분류번호</td><td>보존기간</td></tr>
<tr><td></td><td></td><td></td></tr>
</table>

번 호 : WUK-1318   900809 0100 DN   종별 : 긴급

WFR -1517   WGE -1136
WIT -0721   WUS -2634
WJA -3358

수 신 : 주 수신처참조   대사. 총영사

발 신 : 장 관 (중근동)

제 목 : 이락크의 쿠웨이트 합병

사담 후세인대통령은 8. 8 쿠웨이트를 합병한다고 발표하였는바 이에 대한 주재국의
공식반응과 언론 반응을 지급 보고바람.

수신처 : 주 영국, 불란서, 서독, 이태리, 미국 및 일본대사

(중동 아국장 — 이두복)

<table>
<tr><td rowspan="3">앙 고 재</td><td rowspan="3">90년 8월 8일 과</td><td>기안자
성 명</td><td></td><td>과 장</td><td></td><td>국 장</td><td></td><td>차 관</td><td>장 관</td></tr>
<tr><td></td><td></td><td></td><td></td><td></td><td></td><td></td><td></td></tr>
<tr><td></td><td></td><td></td><td></td><td></td><td></td><td></td><td></td></tr>
</table>

보 안
통 제

외신과통제

0050

외 무 부

종 별 : 긴 급

번 호 : USW-3632   일 시 : 90 0808 1115

수 신 : 장관(미북, 중근동, 청와대 ,기정)

발 신 : 주미대사

제 목 : 쿠웨이트 침공(미군 사우디 파견)

중동 사태관련 8.8 (수) 오전 당지 언론 보도 내용 요지 다음 보고함.

1.미국은 8.7. 약 4,000 여명의 지상군을 미 본토로부터 사우디에 파견함.

(파견 부대는 제18 공수단 소속 제82 공수부대, 제 24기계화 보병사단, 제 101 공정 사단등임)미국은 또한 미 동부지역으로부터 F 15기 48대(제1 전술 비행단과 제 354 비행단) 를 파견하고, 영국에서 터키로 F-111 전폭기를 이동 시킴과 동시에 미본토에서 B-52 폭격기 (6-8 대)도 중동 인접 지역으로 이동 시킴.

2. 이집트 는 PAN-ARAB FORCE 의 일원으로 참여하는 것을 검토중이라 하며, 무바락 대통령은 24시간내 긴급 아랍 정상회담 소집을 제의함.

또한 모로코도 숫자 미상의 병력을 파견할것으로 보여 다국적 파견군의 성격이 될것임.

(현재로서 이집트의 병력 파견 여부는 불확실하다고 보도)

3.베이커 국무장관은 8.8. 터키 방문에 이어 8.9 에는 브라셀에서 나토 사무총장 및 동 회원국 외상들과 회의를 갖고 ,금번 사우디에 대한 병력 파견은 쿠웨이트를 탈환하기 위한것이 아니라 이락의 대사우디 공격에 대비하기 위한 방어적 성격임을 설명 할 것이라 함.

또한 미국은 경제 제재조치의 실효성을 높이기 위해 나토 회원국들에게 페르시아만에서 군사적 지원태세를 갖추도록 요청할것이라함.

(대사 박동진- 국장)

미주국   1차보   중아국   정문국   청와대   안기부   차관   장관

외 무 부

종 별 : 긴 급

번 호 : USW-3634   일 시 : 90 0808 1115

수 신 : 장관 (미북,중근동,기협, 청와대)

발 신 : 주 미 대사

제 목 : 부쉬 대통령 연설

대:WUS-2630

연:USW(F)-1743

대호, 금 8.8. 09:00 실시한 BUSH 대통령 연설 주요 내용 요지를 하기 보고함 (연설문 전문은 연호 팩스 송부)

1. 연설 주요 내용

가. 금번 미군 병력의 사우디 파견은 CAUSE OF PEACE 를 위한 결정인바, 이에 대한 지지를 호소함 (체니 국방장관의 사우디, 이집트, 모로코 측과의 성공적 협의 강조)

나. 동 미군 병력은 사우디 내에서 방어적 태세를 견지할것이라는 점을강조함.

(쿠웨이트를 탈환하기 위한 것이 아님을 분명히 천명)

다. 여사한 파병결정 이전, 미국으로서는 전례없이 긴밀하게 관련국간 협의 과정을 거쳤으며, 군사력 동원이외의 가능한 모든 수단을 동원하여 사태를 해결코자 노력하였음.

라. 이락은 쿠웨이트 공격개시 직전까지도 여사한 공격은 없을 것이라고 장담하고서도 아무런 이유 없이 미사일등을 동원 쿠웨이트를 전격 침공하바 이락에 의한 쿠웨이트 괴뢰정권 수립 및 영토적 획득은 미국으로서는 결코 용납할수 없음. 어떠한 침략도 격퇴하려는 미국의 결심을 과소 평가해서는 안될것임.마. 미국은 금번 사태 해결을 위한 다음의 4 대원칙을 천명함.

-쿠웨이트로 부터 이라크 군의 즉가적이고 , 무조건적인 전면 철수

-쿠웨이트 합법 정부 (왕정) 의 복구

-중동지역의 안정과 안전 유지

-동지역내 미국민의 안전확보

바. 이락 후세인 대통령의 쿠웨이트 불침공 약속 및 쿠웨이트로 부터의 조속 철군

미주국 안기부	장관	차관	1차보	2차보	중아국	경제국	정문국	청와대

약속등은 식언으로 끝났는바, 1939 년 히틀러에 대해 취했던 유화 정책과 같은 방식으로는 금번사태를 해결할수 없을것임.

즉, 이락이 사우디를 침공하지 않을 것이라고 가정하는 것은 현명치도 않고 비현실적인 가정임.

이락은 현재 추가적 증원없이도 사우디를 공격할수 있을 만한 병력을 사우디 국경에 배치하고 있음.

사. 금번 쿠웨이트 침공사태로 야기된 위기는 미국만의 문제가 아니라 세계전체의 문제임. 따라서 유엔 안보리의 규탄 및 의무적 제재조치 결정을 환영하며, 일본, 영국도 적극 참여하고있음. 쏘련, 중공도 대 이락 무기 공급을 중단하기로 결정하였음. 미국은 유엔 안보리의 제재조치가 실효를 거둘수 있도록 계속 자신의 역할을 수행할것임.

아. 사우디의 주권과 독립은 미국의 VITAL INTEREST 인바, 미국은 방어적인 자세를 견지하면서 우방국인 사우디를 지켜 나갈것임. 미국도 많은 원유를 중동에 의존하지만 여타 우방국은 더욱 취약한 상황임. 미국은 이지역에서 의 평화 유지 의무가 있음.

자. 또한 금번 사태관련, 산유국의 원유 생산량 증가, 미국등 서방동맹국들의 전략비축 원유 사용, 석유소비 절약 운동 전개 및 정유회사의 가격조작. 부당이윤 행위등의 자제등을 촉구함.

2. 당관 평가

가. 금일 연설을 통해, BUSH 대통령은 미국의 파병 결정이 국제적인 협조하에 이루어 졌다는 점을 강조하고, 또 이락의 후세인 대통령을 히틀러에 비유함으로써 , 이락의 호전성을 중점 부각하고 미국의 단호한 입장을 천명 하였는바, 사우디 파병 결정에 대한 국내외의 지지를 확보키 위한것임.

(특히 , NUNN , DODD 상원의원등 및 ASPIN 하원의원 등 민주당계 중진의원들이 부쉬 대통령의 파병 결정에 전폭적인 지지를 표한점등을 감안할때, 금일 연설은 국가위기 사태시 애국심의 고취를 통해 국민적 단결력을 고양시키는 " RALLY- AROUND- THE- FLAG" 의 효과를 거두는데 도움이 될것으로 보이며 , 실제로 국민 여론도 부쉬 대통령을 크게 지지하고 있음)

나. 또한 , BUSH 대통령은 금일 연설시 미측의 파병 성격이 "방어적" 임을 두 차례에 걸쳐 강조하고 사우디의 안전이 미국의 사활적 이익 이라는점을 지적하였는바, 이는 현단계에서 미국의 목적인 대이라크 전면전을 통한 전쟁 발발 이전 상태로의

회복에 있다기 보다는 , 이락의 사우디 침공은 곧 대미 선전포고에해당한다는 점을 이락으로 하여금 인식 시킴으로써, 현상태에서 이락의 군사행 동 확대를 우선 중지시키고 이락이 국제원유가를 좌지우지 하게되는 결과를 방지코자 하려는 것으로 분석됨. 또한 미국은 계속 아랍제국의 지지 확보를 통해 주 사우디 병력을 다국군화 하도록 시도할것으로 보임.

　　　(당지 전문가에 따르면, 미측이 이락과의 전면전 수행을 위해서는 2 개 중무장 보병 사단과 약 700-800 대의 전폭기 동원이 필요 하다함)

　　　한편, 당지 일부 언론은 HUSSEIN 의 실각을 위한 대안도 검토하고 있다고 보도한바 있음.

　　　(대사 박동진- 국장)

　　　예고:90.12.31. 까지

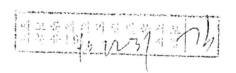

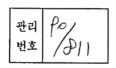

외 무 부

종   별 :

번   호 : USW-3636   일   시 : 90 0808 1413

수   신 : 장관(중근동,미북)

발   신 : 주 미 대사

제   목 : 대 이락.쿠웨이트 경제 현황

대:WUS-2606

대호, 주재국의 대 이락 및 쿠웨이트 경제 현황은 하기와 같음.

1. 대이락 관계

가. 체류 미국인 :500 명

나. 수출(89 년) :12 억불 (농산품)

수입: 24 억불 (원유)

2. 대이쿠웨이트 관계

가. 체류 미국인 :3,000 명(일부 언론등은 4,000 명으로 보도)

나. 수출 (89 년) :10 억불 (자동차 , 담배)

수입:9 억불 (원유)

(대사 박동진- 국장)

예고:90.12.31. 일반

중아국   미주국

PAGE 1   90.08.09   07:19

외 무 부

종 별 :

번 호 : USW-3637

일 시 : 90 0808 1213

수 신 : 장관(중근동, 미북, 기협, 청와대)

발 신 : 주 미대사

제 목 : 이락측 언론 발표문

연: USW(F)- 1744

1, 금 8.8. 당지 언론은, 역사적으로 쿠웨이트는 이락 영토의 일부 였음을 주장하고, 후세인 대통령을 아랍권의 지도자로 영웅시하는 요지의 이락 정부 언론발표문을 중개 방송 하였는바, 동 발표문 (발췌) 연호 팩스 송부함

2.또한 이락측은 금일 발표문에서 이락 -쿠웨이트 간의 단결을 강조 하였는바, 당지 언론에서는 이를 이락의 쿠웨이트 합병 조짐으로 간주하고 있음

(대사 박동진- 국장)

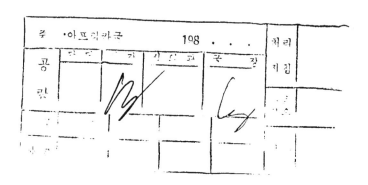

중아국	1차보	2차보	미주국	경제국	정문국	안기부	

PAGE 1

90.08.09   05:29 DA

외신 1과 통제관 0056

외 무 부

종 별 :

번 호 : USW-3638   일   시 : 90 0808 1400

수 신 : 장 관(미북, 중근동, 기정)사본- 대통령 비서실장

발 신 : 주미대사

제 목 : BUSH 대통령 기자회견(이락-쿠웨이트 침공)

　1.주재국 BUSH 대통령은 금 8.8 (수) 정오 백악관 출입 기자들과 기자회견을
가진바 요지 다음과같음. (금일 오전 9:00 발표에 따른 질의 응답 형식으로진행
하였기 때문에 회견 모두 의 별도 발언은 없었음)

　가. 당국적 파견군 관련

　-미국은 사우디 방어 목적으로 군대를 파견한 것이며 아직 전쟁 상태에 돌입한것은
아님

　-영국도 사우디 국왕의 요청으로 군대를 파견할 것으로 알고 있는 바 다른 나라의
참여 문제는 기본적으로 사우디가 결정할 문제임.

　나.이집트 및 모로코의 입장 관련

　-이집트 와는 많은 의견의 일치 (CLOSE AGREEMENT) 를 보았으며 모로코도
매우협조적임. 체니 국방장관의 순방 결과는 무척 만족 스러움

　다.이락의 화학무기 사용 가능성이락이 화학무기를 사용하지 않기를 바라는 바,

　ㅇ 만약사용할 경우 세계가 이를 용인하지 않을것임.

　라.소련의 반응

　-상금 소련의 반응은 매우 건설적임 .작일에도 미.소 외무장관간 접촉이 있었는바,
미국은 좀더 소련의 적극적인 대응을 요청한바 있음. 소련은 유엔 안보리에서 결정한
대 이락 제재 조치에 참가 하고 있으며 무기 금수 조치를 취하고 있음.

　마. 쿠웨이트 무력 탈환 가능성-사우디에 대한 병력 파견은 사우디 방위를
위한조치 임.

　-이락으로 하여금 쿠웨이트에서 철수토록 하기 위해서는 경제 제재 조치가
매우효과적일것으로 생각함.이락은 이미 경제적으로 큰 어려움이 있기 때문에 오래
지탱하지 못할 것임.

미주국　　1차보　　중아국　　정문국　　안기부　　청와대　　그처실　　차관　　장관

　　　　　　　　　　　　　　　　　　　　90.08.09　　07:14 WH
　　　　　　　　　　　　　　　　　　　　외신 1과 통제관

0057

바.정보 부재에 대한 비판-관계 정보 기관은 훌륭한 역할을 수행 하였으며 금번사태관련 비난을 받을 이유가 없음.

-이락의 전격적 작전을 사실상 중단 시킬수는 없었음.

사.식량 금수 조치-대이략 무역 제재 조치에도 불구하고 인도적 견지에서 식량거래는 별도 고려할 필요가 있음.

2.상세는 별첨 기자회견 TEXT(FAX 송부)참고바람(USW(F)- 1745)

(대사 박동진)

PAGE 2

0058

발신 : USW(F) - 1745

수신 : 경   군(미북, 중근동, 기타)   발신 : 주미대사 | 보안 | 품절 |

제목 : Bush 대통령 기자회견 (사본:대통령비서실장) (9 매)
(USW-3638 의 관련)

PRESS CONFERENCE WITH PRESIDENT BUSH

WEDNESDAY, AUGUST 8, 1990

.STX

PRESIDENT BUSH: Terry?

Q   Mr. President, how many American troops have you sent to Saudi Arabia? How long are you committed to keeping them there? And why not use them to drive Iraqi forces out of Kuwait?

PRESIDENT BUSH: There will be a military briefing at the Pentagon, I think it's within an hour, and so I will leave the numbers to them. I would expect there would be some reluctance to give out specific numbers at this point for very obvious reasons.

What was the last part of your --

Q   The other parts, sir, were how long will you keep American forces in Saudi Arabia, and why not use them to drive the Iraqi troops out of Kuwait?

PRESIDENT BUSH: Well, as you know from what I said, they're there in a defensive mode right now. And therefore, that is not the mission, to drive the Iraqis out of Kuwait. We have economic sanctions that I hope will be effective to that end, and I don't know how long they'll be there. They just got there -- are just getting there.

Q   Is this an open-ended commitment? I mean, could this drag on for years?

PRESIDENT BUSH: Nothing is open-ended, but I'm not worrying about that there at all; I'm worrying about getting them there and doing what I indicated in our speech in there is necessary: the defense of the Saudis and the trying, through concerted international means, to reverse out this aggression.

Q   Mr. President, are we in a war? And what other nations have agreed to join our forces in defending Saudi Arabia? And I take it you also have included other Gulf nations in that umbrella.

PRESIDENT BUSH: We're not in a war. We have sent forces to defend Saudi Arabia. Other nations -- I will leave announcements about what other

1745-1

0059

nations will be participating to the Saudis. But I believe Margaret Thatcher, after talking to King Fahd, has announced that forces will be going in, and then I think you'll see other such actions, but I'd much prefer to leave that to Saudi Arabia, who -- indeed, it's their country.

Q But was Cheney's mission successful in rallying support with Egypt and Morocco?

PRESIDENT BUSH: Well, I -- I, having talked to Mubarak a couple of times myself, feel that we are in very close agreement with him. Who was your other country you asked about?

Q Morocco, Yemen.

PRESIDENT BUSH: Morocco -- very, very supportive of the Saudis and of our overall position on the Mideast. So, they're -- I was very pleased with the Cheney mission in that regard.

Brit?

Q Mr. President, there are several dozen Americans in Baghdad apparently not able to leave (at this point ?) and perhaps hundreds more in Kuwait, and perhaps elsewhere in Iraq as well. In view of the extreme political sensitivity of Americans toward this whole question of hostages, why should not Saddam Husayn feel that he holds very high cards now in dealing with the United States?

PRESIDENT BUSH: Well, I've been encouraged that there had been -- have been actually announcements, I believe, saying people were free to leave. So I'm not going to speculate or hypothecate beyond that. I want to see them out of there obviously. But what he does, that's a bit unpredictable. But I'm not going to heighten tensions in this regard by responding to hypothetical questions that might go beyond your question.

Q Well, what -- I just wonder what assurances you might be able to provide so that our policy in this instance will not become, as it has in the past, hostage-driven.

PRESIDENT BUSH: I can provide only the assurance that I consider the protection of American life fundamental to my job and responsibilities as president.

Yes?

Q Mr. President, the question of chemical weapons. There are reports that the Iraqis were seen loading airplanes with chemical weapons. How concerned are you that he would use these over our troops that are there?

PRESIDENT BUSH: Well, I think any time you deal with somebody who has used chemical weapons on the battlefield, you are concerned about it, and I would think that he'd know that, given the way the world views the use of chemical weapons, that it would be intolerable and that it would be dealt with very, very severely. So I would hope that there would be no use of chemical weapons.

0060

Q   Mr. President, I am being told in my ear that there is a report or a rumor out of Jeddah that Saddam Husayn is dead. Have you heard anything of this?

PRESIDENT BUSH: I've not heard anything of that.

Q   Do you know if the Saudis will -- do you know if the Saudis will follow -- do you know if the Saudis are going to follow the Turks' lead in shutting off an Iraqi pipeline, the one --   (inaudible)? Have you had any promises from the Saudis or any other oil-producing countries that they will increase production to make up for this shortfall?

PRESIDENT BUSH: Well, I'm convinced -- I believe that the Venezuelans have announced a significant increase, and I expect you'd find others to follow. And what was the first part, John?

Q   Are the Saudis cutting off the pipeline to -- (inaudible)?

PRESIDENT BUSH: That matter will be discussed, I'm sure, and I know that the Saudis are fully in accord with the action taken by the United Nations in terms of Chapter 7 sanctions.

And so I -- but we have no deal with them in that regard.

Q   Sir, it's difficult for us to get information from Saudi Arabia, one reason being the American news media were not permitted to accompany American troops into Saudi Arabia. Was that your decision or King Fahd's?

PRESIDENT BUSH: That decision didn't come to me. But there's plenty of reporters in Saudi Arabia right now.

Q   Well, do you think there should be a Pentagon pool, as there was for example in Panama?

PRESIDENT BUSH: Well, I'd have to discuss that with the Secretary of Defense. I'm glad that the matter --- that that many forces could be moved with not too much advance warning, and with not too much, therefore, risk to Saudi Arabia or to these troops.

Yeah?

Q   Mr. President, was there any one single thing that tipped your hand into deciding to send US troops and aircraft into Saudi Arabia? And secondly, how supportive have the Soviets been about your decision?

PRESIDENT BUSH: There was no one single thing that I can think of, but when King Fahd requested such support we were prompt to respond. But I can't think of an individual specific thing. If there was one, it would perhaps be the Saudis (sic) moving south when they -- til they were withdrawing.

1945-3

0061

Q   You mean the Iraqis, sir?

PRESIDENT BUSH: I mean, the Iraqis -- thank you very much, it's been a long night -- moving -- the Iraqis moving down to the Kuwait-Saudi border when indeed they had given their word that they were withdrawing. That heightened our concern.

Q   How supportive have the Soviets been to your decision, sir?

PRESIDENT BUSH: The Soviets have been very responsible, in my view. They have joined the United Nations on that resolution, and Jim Baker, as recently as yesterday afternoon or evening, was in touch with Shevardnadze again, and you know, I can't ask for a more favorable response than he received.

Yes, Jerry.

Q   Mr. President, is it your intention to let economic pressure alone provide the force that drives Iraq out of Kuwait? Are you prepared to wait several months, which is how long it might take for the economic sanctions to really bite?

PRESIDENT BUSH: Well, we've taken this first significant step to defend Saudi Arabia. The economic sanctions should begin to bite pretty soon. There will be further steps taken to ensure that they are fully effective, and then we'll wait and see where we go from there. But I have no -- we're not -- we're not -- I'm not beyond that in my thinking. There, obviously, is a lot of contingency planning that always goes on and prudently should go on.

Charles, then Ann.

Q   Mr. President, I can understand the need for individual countries to announce their own attentions with regards to the multinational force, but it's our understanding that the Saudis wanted an Arab component in that force. Is that in fact the case, and will there be one?

PRESIDENT BUSH: They didn't tell us that, but it would not be at all surprising if there was an Arab component in that force, not at all.

Q   But you do not have one at this point?

PRESIDENT BUSH: Well, I'm not going to comment on -- on -- because I think announcement of all components really should come from the participating countries.

Yeah, Ann?

Q   Not even broader, to define it as Arab, if not by nation?

PRESIDENT BUSH: No, I told you I wouldn't be surprised if that happened, but I think that I'd much prefer to have that -- the announcements of that come from others. This -- I think it is important that the focus be on Saudi requests and on [the] defensive nature of the move we've made with these forces.

1945-4

0062

Yes, Ann?

Q   Mr. President, you've told us several times of Saddam Husayn's lies in his dealings with other leaders and with the United States on his intentions. Why do you now believe the Iraqi government's statements that they will let Americans go if there are no -- if there is no evidence of an American being let go?

PRESIDENT BUSH: I'm not sure I totally

believe them.   I hope they're telling the truth.

Q   Do you have assurances from any intelligence source, any other source, that indicates movement by those Americans, or any --

PRESIDENT BUSH: Well, I've had a source of movement by some foreigners, so I would hope that this would then apply to Americans.

Yes?

Q   Mr. President, you said in your speech this morning that the puppet regime in Kuwait was unacceptable, and so was the acquisition of territory.   At the same time, though, you said that the -- that the deployments are wholly defensive.   The question is, how do you actually expect to force Husayn to withdraw from Kuwait?

PRESIDENT BUSH: Economic sanctions in this instance, if fully enforced, can be very, very effective.   It is a rich country in terms of oil resources.   They're a poor country, in a sense, because he squandered much of the resource on military might, and there are some indications that he's already beginning to feel the pinch.   And nobody can stand up forever to total economic deprivation.

Yes?

Q   If I could follow that up -- if I can just follow real quickly.   Could you -- will you rule out preemptive strikes against Iraq --

PRESIDENT BUSH: I am not going to go into hypothetical situations.   We've been very careful not to do that, and I'm simply not going to respond.

Maureen; and then we'll go to the aisle.

Q   Mr. President, could you share with us the precise military objective of this mission?   Will the American troops remain there only until Saddam Husayn removes his troops from the Saudi border?

PRESIDENT BUSH: I can't -- I can't answer that because we have -- we have a major objective with those troops, which is the defense of the Soviet Union.   So I think it's beyond --

(Cross talk.)

PRESIDENT BUSH: (Laughing) -- a defense of Saudi Arabia -- so I think it's beyond the -- I think it's beyond just the question of the tanks along the border.

0063

Q   Sir, are you preparing for a prolonged ground ---

PRESIDENT BUSH: A lot of air power, for example.

Q   Are you preparing for a prolonged ground war in the
Persian Gulf?

PRESIDENT BUSH: I'm not preparing for a long ground war in the
Persian Gulf. There's not a war going on there right now.

Q   But, I'm just saying, could you just tell the American
people what your specific military objective is?

PRESIDENT BUSH: My military objective is to see Saudi Arabia
defended -- that's the military objective. Our overall objective is
to see -- see Saddam Husayn get out and go back and to have the
rightful regime of Kuwait back in place.

     Yes?

Q   Mr. President, can you tell us what US and Saudi forces
will be up against? You mentioned surface-to-surface missiles,
you've spoken previously of the chemical warfare capability of the
Saudis (sic: may mean Iraqis). What are they up against? And the
second question is -- the second part of the question is, did we
misread Saddam Husayn? A couple of months ago, your people were up
on the -- the administration was up on the Hill deflecting a move to
put sanctions on -- on -- on --

PRESIDENT BUSH: Let me -- let me ask you -- I'm not going to
take the question on the exact military problem there because we're
going to have a thorough briefing at the Pentagon -- I think they're
much better equipped to handle that kind of detail.

     On Saddam Husayn, look, we have tried very hard to see if there
wasn't a way to have somewhat improved relations -- there's no
question about that. But -- and I have no regret about having tried
to have discussions that might have led to a better relationship.
But that had to stop the minute you have this -- this kind of
aggression. But I don't think having -- having tried tentatively to
have a little better relationship with a person over the last couple
of years -- we've still been very, very wary all along of his -- of
his intentions.

Q   But did our intelligence let us down or -- or

did you know that what has happened -- when did you get an
indication of -- (inaudible) -- as far as moving into Kuwait and
that sort of thing?

1945 — 6

0064

PRESIDENT BUSH: III, I don't — I don't feel let down by the intelligence at all. When you plan a blitzkrieg-like attack that's launched at 2:00 in the morning, it's pretty hard to stop, particularly when you have just been given the word of the people involved that there wouldn't be any such attack. And I think the intelligence community deserves certain credit for — for — for picking up what was a substantial boycott — (correcting himself) a substantial buildup and then reporting it to us. So — and this information was relayed properly to interested parties, but the move was so swift that it was pretty hard for them to stop it.

I really can't blame our intelligence in any way — fault them in this particular — in this particular go-round.

Yeah, Ellen?

Q   Mr. President, you said this morning that our troops will also defend our other friends in the Gulf. Do we view the American troops there as peacekeepers throughout the Gulf?

PRESIDENT BUSH: We view them there to defend Saudi Arabia, and hopefully their presence there will deter adventurism against any of the other Gulf countries.

Yes?

Q   What other countries, sir, are we prepared to defend in the Gulf region?

PRESIDENT BUSH: Well, I'm not going to give you a list, but — but we're certainly interested in the freedom and the independence of all those countries in the GCC, just for openers.

Yeah?

Q   Mr. President, do you see any domestic impact on the budget talks or deficit from this situation in the Middle East, impact on the gasoline tax possibility or in any other way?

PRESIDENT BUSH: Well, an operation of this nature has considerable expense associated with it. But I've asked for some estimates now as to what that —

what that price may be, but whatever it is, we're going to have to pay it. But I don't have the exact figures yet.

John?

Q   Mr. President, the national security analysts say that this crisis demonstrates once again the vulnerability — constant vulnerability of the oil fields in the Middle East. Doesn't this suggest that this force that you've sent over there may be there for some time, or at least fragments of it will be there to make sure that there is a steady flow?

PRESIDENT BUSH: Well, you might interpret it that way. I'm not prepared to say that I think that's what the outcome will be, because I think if there is this pull-back that the world is calling for, and if the sanctions are effective, I think you would reduce the risk of future adventurism.

0065

Q   In your c__ to the producing countri███ to pick up the slack, do you expect that to begin immediately?

PRESIDENT BUSH: Well, I think it will start very, very soon. I don't know about today, by any ---

Q   Mr. President, with the economy tipping close to the edge of a recession, do you think we still can afford to raise taxes or cut spending, or won't that increase the risk of a (deep ?) recession?

PRESIDENT BUSH: I still think it's absolutely essential to get a budget agreement, and that's going to require a lot of compromise and it's going to require a lot of principle. But you know, what I want to do is separate out my feelings about the budget now that I feel uninhibited by an agreement not to say anything, because I want to tell you exactly how strongly I feel about it. But I don't want to do it here today. I don't want to mix it into this briefing that is largely, you know, dominated by the world concern about the Middle East. But I feel like a liberated human being now. I don't feel bound by --

Q   Why not?

PRESIDENT BUSH -- by -- may I finish what I'm saying here? (Laughs.) I don't feel bound by an agreement that I've told the congressional leaders is no longer in effect. And we've been getting one side of that,   ,

r*v

mainly from the Democrats in the Congress. And now you're fixing to get the other, but not this minute; you have to stay tuned.

Q   Mr. President, to follow up, do you think the spike in oil prices which has occurred significantly at home as a result of the Persian Gulf problem could edge the economy into a recession?

PRESIDENT BUSH: I have not been advised of that. I hope that is not the case, and what I hope to do is see a reduction in oil prices once a -- once it becomes clear that there will not be shortage. There's an overhang now of oil in the marketplace, thank God. We have a Strategic Petroleum Reserve that we can draw from. Other countries have the same -- a couple of other countries have SPRs themselves. And I hope that this rapid spike on oil prices will not be permanent, and I think if we -- if the world begins to see assurances, that there will not be a dramatic cutoff -- or cutdown on oil, that then things will return much more to normal in the market.

Yeah?

Q   Mr. President?

Q   Mr. President, assuming that --

PRESIDENT BUSH: One more after this.

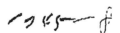

0066

Q   -- assume that we achieve the goal of Iraqi forces
out of Kuwait, Saddam Husayn is still going to sitting there on
top of a million-man army -- (inaudible). What happens in the long
run after that, and can you contain that with -- short of removing
Saddam Husayn from power?

PRESIDENT BUSH: I would think that if this international
lesson is taught well, that Saddam Husayn would behave differently
in the future. And that's what has been so very important about
this concerted United Nations effort, unprecedented you might say or
certainly not enacted since 19 -- what was it? 23 years ago? --
19-- 23 years ago.

So, I -- I -- I don't think we can see that clearly down the
road, but a line has been drawn in the sand. The United States has
taken a firm position, and I might say we're getting strong support
from around the world for what we've done. I've been very, very
pleased about that. Large

countries and small countries. The world reaction has been
excellent. And I would hope that all of this would result in Saddam
Husayn or some calmer heads in Iraq understanding that this kind of
international behavior is simply unacceptable, and we see where we
go.

Q   Mr. President?

PRESIDENT BUSH: Yes, Sarah?

Q   Sir, would you please --

PRESIDENT BUSH: This is the last question.

Q   I understand that we provide most of the food for Iraq
and have done so on the long term and short term and subsidy
payments, credit (assistance ?) for some time. That means that
we've been letting them have a lot of food and a lot of other
products from our farmers at probably low rates, arranged by the
Department of Agriculture. Now, do you -- would you please discuss
the effect of your embargo; and how much do you think that the
Iraqis already owe us for food?

PRESIDENT BUSH: Well, I don't know what they owe us for food,
but I know that this embargo, to be successful, has got to encompass
everything. And if there are -- you know, if there's a humanitarian
concern, pockets of starving children or something of this nature,
why, I would take a look. But other than that, this embargo is
going to be all encompassing, and it will include food. And I don't
know what Iraq owes us now for food. Generally speaking, in normal
times we have felt that food might be separated out from -- you
know, grain, wheat, might be separated out from other economic
sanctions. But this one is all encompassing and the language is
pretty clear in the United Nations resolution.

Thank you all very much. And let me just say this, on a
personal basis. I've screwed up a couple of times here and I'm very
grateful for your assistance in straightening it out. God, I'd hate
to have had some of those answers stand.

Thank you.

1765-9

END

0067

관리
번호 PO/810

외 무 부

종 별 : 긴 급

번 호 : USW-3649   일 시 : 90 0808 1841

수 신 : 장관(중동,미북,국연,봉이,경이,기정) 사본:주사우디대사-중계필

발 신 : 주 미 대사

제 목 : 미국의 대이락-사우디 조치(국무부 동맹국 브리핑)

연 USW-3627,3634,3638

대 WUS-2634

1. 국무부는 8.8 오전 지난 8.1-2 이르쿠츠크에서 있었던 미소 외무장관 회담
결과를 NATO, 일본, 아국, 호주등 동맹국측에 브리핑하는 기회에 미 행정부의대이락
조치의 배경과 현황을 설명하고, 동맹국들의 이해와 지지를 요청하였음(중동 문제에
대한 브리핑시에는 사우디, 쿠웨이트 대사관측도 참석하였음)

2. 금일 브리핑시 KIMMIT 정무차관과 JACK COLBY 중근동 서남아 담당 부차관보가
실시하였으며, 당관에서도 이승곤공사(김영목서기관 배석)가 참석하였는바 미측
브리핑 요지 다음임.

가. 금번 사우디 파병 조치의 취지

-금번 사우디 파병 조치는 이락의 침략 확산을 방지하는데 목적이 있으며, 동
조치는 사우디, 쿠웨이트 정부의 요청에 따른 것임.

-현재 베이커 장관등 미 행정부측의 주요 외교 노력은 유엔 안보리의 대이락 금수
결의를 효과적으로 시행하는것과 사우디 파병을 다국군화 하는데에 집중되고 있음.

나. 이락의 원유 수출 봉쇄

-현재 이락의 터키 관통 송유관은 이미 효과적으로 차단되었으며, 사우디를봉한
송유도 중단되고 있음.

다. 지상군 대치 동향

-현재 쿠웨이트내의 이락군은 증강되고 있으며 , 이락으로부터 신규
부대가투입되고 있음(국방부측은 이락군의 지대지 미사일 반입, 화학무기 반입 가능성
우려)

-이락군은 현재 사우디에 대한 공격이 가능한 포진을 하고 있음.

중아국	장관	차관	1차보	2차보	미주국	국기국	경제국	통상국
정문국	정와대	안기부						

-사우디내 도착한 미군은 현재로서는 취약한 방어 태세에 있는바, 참호 구축및 병참 장비 부입등을 통해 방어 태세를 취하고 있음.

라. 다국적군 구성을 위한 미국의 노력

-미행정부는 이락의 사우디 침공을 저지하기 위한 다국적군 구성을 낙관하는바, 이미 사우디-이락 국경 인전지역에 GCC 연합군(5개 연대)이 배치되어 있고, 이집트와 모로코도 다국적 참여 가능성을 배제하고 있지 않고 있음(미국은 이집트, 모로코가 궁극적으로 다국군에 참여할것으로 기대)

-금일 영국 정부는 사우디 정부의 요청에 따라 영국 해.공군 지원을 발표하였음.

-MUBARAK 이집트 대통령은 범 아랍군이 구성되지 않는 경우, 사우디 방어 다국군에 참여치 않을것이라고 언명하였으나, 동 대통령이 긴급 아랍 정상회의를소집한것은 범 아랍군 구성을 제안하려는것으로 미측은 이해하고 있음.

- 미국이 구상하고 있는 다국적군의 지휘 계통은 사우디 및 각 외국군의 지휘를 유엔의 우산아래 두고, 서방 동맹국군과 범 아랍군이 2 원적으로 작전 봉제체제를 갖는것임.

-소련은 상금 다국군 참여에 동의하지는 않았으나, 최소한 서방측과 협의 채널은 OPEN 하고 있는 상태이며, 참여도 불가능하지 않을것으로봄.

마. 외국인 소개 문제

-현재 미국은 연호 보고(USW-3627)와 적십자를 통한 서방국 공동 소개를 추진하고 있음. 이락 및 쿠웨이트내 외국인의 현황과 동신변에 대한 이락측의 보장문제는 각 채널별로 일치하지 않는바, 미측으로서는 외국인 문제 대한 정보 교환을 환영할것임(미국은 주 이락 공관원의 감축을 추진하고 있으나 상금 이락측은 공관원의 출국을 금지)

-미측이 어제(8.6) 발표한 걸프만 지역에 대한 여행 지침은 신규 여행의 금지와 동 지역 체류자의 자발적인 철수를 권고하고 있는바, 동 지침 작성에는 사우디 원유 증산 필요성을 고려, 미국 기업의 급격한 철수를 방지해야한다는데 주안점이 주어졌음.

-한편, 소련측도 이락내 소련인 신변 문제에 지대한 관심을 보이고 있음(약8,000 정도 체제 추산)

바. 이락의 쿠웨이트 합병 가능성

-현재 이락측은 이락-쿠웨이트 연맹(UNION)을 거론하고 있는바, 동 UNION 이 구체적으로 어떠한 형태가 될지는 현재로서는 알수 없음.

-다만, 이락측은 쿠웨이트가 식민세력에 의해 이락으로부터 불법적으로 분리되었으므로 이락과 쿠웨이트는 통합되어야한다는 주장을 해온점에 유의하고 있음.

3. 관찰

-미 행정부는 현재로서는 미군 파병및 다국군 구성을 통한 이락의 사우디 침공 방지와 국제적 금수 조치를 통한 이락군의 쿠웨이트 철수라는 이원적 전략을 추진하고 있는것으로 보이며, 특히 이락과의 교역 금지를 위한 유엔 안보리 결의가 구속적(MANDATORY)이라는점을 강조, 실질적인 대이락 경제 봉쇄가 가능토록 하는데 주력해 나갈것으로 보임(다만 인도적 차원에서의 식량 교역 문제는 터키등 관련국의 입장과 유엔 결의 내용을 고려, 다소 신축적 입장을 보이고 있으나, 미국으로서는 모든 물자, 용역의 교역 일체를 금지하였음)

-미측의 다국군 구성(이집트, 모르코 동참등)에 대한 기대는 매우 낙관적이나 일부 관측통들은 요르단의 이락 동조등으로 범 아랍군 구성등은 상당히 어려울것으로 보고 있음. 현재 베이커 장관이 명 8.9 터키측과 협의를 마치고 8.10 NATO 외상들과 협의를 갖을 예정인바, 다국군 구성을 위한 동맹국들의 참여 방식은 동 일련의 협의가 종료된후 보다 분명해질것으로 예상됨.

-원유의 전략 비축분 사용 문제와 관련, 미 행정부는 상금 주요 선진국들에대해 구체적 제안을 하고 있지는 않은것으로 관찰되는바, 동 비축분의 구체적 사용 방법과 관련, 일본등 일부 국가들은 국제 에너지 기구 또는 OECD 에서의 토의를 선호할 가능성도 있음.

-현재 미 행정부 인사들은 아국의 대이락 경제제재 조치 참여 여부를 문의해오고 있는바, 이에 대한 아국 정부의 입장 지급 회시 바람.

(대사 박동진-장관)

예고:90.12.31 일반

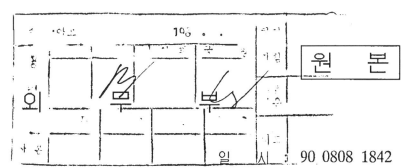

종   별 : 긴 급

번   호 : USW-3650   일   시 : 90 0808 1842

수   신 : 장 관 (중근동,미북,미안,기정) 사본: 대통령비서실장

발   신 : 주 미 대사

제   목 : 중동사태 관련 미 국방장관 및 합참의장 기자회견

　　　연: USW (F)-1752

　　　금 8.8 중동사태 관련 실시된 CHENEY 국방장관 및 POWELL 합참의장의 기자회견 내용중 특기사항등을 요지 아래 보고함.

　　　(기자회견 전문은 연호 FAX 편 송부)

　　　1. 금번 미군 병력의 사우디 파견은 사우디측의 요청에 따라 이루어진 것인바, 파병의 주목적은 사우디군의 방위능력 증강을 통해 이락의 추가적 침략행위를 억지하는데에 있음.

　　　2. 현재 중동지역 배치 미 해군전력의 주종은 군함 LA SALLE 호를 기함으로 하는 JOINT TASK FORCEMIDDLE EAST 및 항공모함 INDEPENDENCE 호, EISENHOWER 호, SARATOGA 호를 각각 주축으로하는 3개 항모전단, 그리고 전함 WISCONSIN 호임. 사우디 영토내에 기도착한 미 공군기는 F-15 (C및 D형모델)및 5대의 AWACS 기가 주종이며, 보병전력의 주축은 제 82 공수부대 소속 DIVISION READY BRIGADE 임. (파병병력의 규모,구체적 이동계획등에 대해서는 사우디 파병이 현재 진행중인 작전임을 이유로, 작전참가 병력의 안전을 고려, 상세 답변을 회피함)

　　　3. 이라크군의 화학무기 사용 가능성을 미측도 예측하고 있으며, 방독면 및 특수복장 지급등을 통해 미군병력은 적절한 화학전 대책을 강구한 상태임.

　　　4. 기존 미 국내법상 미측이 사우디에 판매할수 있는 F-15 는 60대를 초과할수 없도록 되어 있었으나, 부쉬 대통령은 동 상한선을 관련 규정에 따라 직권으로 철폐하였으며, 또한 미측은 사우디측과 사우디 전력증강 방안을 협의해 나갈것임.

　　　5. 미측으로서는 금번 사태해결을 위해 가능한한 많은 수의 국가가 참여하는 다국적 군대가 바람직할 것으로 봄.

　　　그러나 작전지역이 사우디 영토인 만큼 여사한 다국적 군대에의 참여를 희망하는

중아국   미주국   미주국   안기부

PAGE 1

국가는 우선 사우디정부와 접촉해야 할것임.

　(대사 박동진-국장)

발 : USW(F)- 1752
신 : 장 관 (국방동, 이병, 미안또) 사본: 대월경 빅터스(참) 사
주 : 국동사예난연 미 국방장관 및 남참의남 기자회견 (11 매)
(USW- 3650 의 속부)

보안
급

PRESS CONFERENCE WITH
SECRETARY OF DEFENSE RICHARD CHENEY
AND
CHAIRMAN, JOINT CHIEFS OF STAFF GENERAL COLIN POWELL

THE PENTAGON

WEDNESDAY, AUGUST 8, 1990

.STX

MR. WILLIAMS: In just a moment, the Secretary and the Chairman will answer a few questions. They'll both make short statements. The Secretary will go first and then the Chairman and then after that we'll entertain your questions for about 15 minutes or so.

So with that, Secretary Cheney, Mr. Chairman.

SEC. CHENEY: Well good afternoon. There obviously have already been a number of comments, discussions of the operation in the Middle East. I think everybody has had the opportunity to see the President's speech and his press conference over at the White House. And General Powell and I have been asked to do a briefing, to respond to questions. We both have brief opening statements and then we'll be happy to take your questions.

I would, at the outset, though, emphasize for all of you, especially those of you who remember the Panama operation in December, that this situation is different. There are obvious limitations on our ability to speak with respect to what is an ongoing operation. The normal kinds of questions that I'm confident everybody wants answers to are, in many cases, unanswerable with respect to what particular units might be doing or where they might be going or when they might be arriving. So we obviously will, of necessity, be cautious in terms of what we're prepared to talk about.

I thought I would open with a brief statement about my trip this past weekend. The decision was made on Saturday for me to travel to Saudi Arabia. The actual decision to go — that is the planning began on Saturday. The actual decision to go wasn't finalized until Sunday, and I left Sunday afternoon about 2:30 accompanied by Bob Gates, General Scowcroft's deputy; by General Schwarzkopf, who is our CINC in charge of that part of the world; Paul Wolfowitz, the Undersecretary for Policy; and our Ambassador to Saudi Arabia, Mr. Freeman, who was in the country at the time.

We arrived in Saudi Arabia on Monday; met with King Fahd Monday evening, as well as the Crown Prince and other officials. At that time, we discussed in general the intelligence that was

1752 — 1

0073

available to us on the situation in the Gulf, reviewed with them the diplomatic developments and all of the work that had been underway by the President with respect to efforts to impose economic and political sanctions on Iraq in regard to its invasion of Kuwait. We then discussed with them in some detail the military situation on the ground in the Persian Gulf region, and we also presented to the King a rundown on our military capabilities.

Subsequent to those discussions, the King made the request for the deployment of US forces to the Kingdom of Saudi Arabia. I conveyed that request by telephone to the President. The President authorized me to deploy those forces, and I subsequently then gave instructions for those deployments to the Chairman by telephone back here in Washington, and of course, to General Schwarzkopf who was with me in Jedda, Saudi Arabia.

Subsequent to that, I had a meeting the next morning with Prince Sultan, who is the Saudi Defense Minister. We discussed in greater detail the deployments that are now underway. When I left Saudi Arabia at the direction of the President I stopped and visited, as I think's been announced, President Mubarak in Alexandria, Egypt. And then last evening, King Hassan in Rabat, Morocco.

The basic purpose of the deployments the President's already covered. Specifically, our purpose in sending forces at this time to the Gulf region and to Saudi Arabia in particular is to deter any further Iraqi aggression, also, to work with Saudi forces to improve their military and defensive capabilities, and should it become necessary, should deterrence fail, to defend Saudi Arabia against attack.

At this point I'd like to call on General Powell, the Chairman of the Joint Chiefs for discussion on the force deployments involved and then we both will be happy to answer your questions.

GEN. POWELL: Thank you, Mr. Secretary.

Ladies and gentlemen, let me reinforce a couple of points the Secretary made with respect to the amount of information we'll be able to provide you. As the Secretary mentioned, this is an ongoing operation, and because we want to ensure the safety of our troops and because we want to ensure operational security for missions we may be called upon to perform, I will necessarily be limited

in what I can tell you about forces in country, who else might be coming, schemes of maneuver, and matters of that kind. I also would ask for some restraint on your part as you find out information if you would always measure it against the need for operational security to protect our troops. That should be uppermost I think in all of our minds.

Within those limitations though, I will try to share with you today, and in subsequent days through normal briefings, as much information as we can about where our troops are, what they are doing, so that the American people can be informed and so those families will have some understanding of where their young soldiers, sailors, airmen and Marines are.

Let me begin by first saying that, after the Secretary called back, orders were issued for the deployment on Monday evening, and the first element lifted off the ground — early advance party elements lifted off the ground at 7:35 yesterday morning, and the flow has continued with the major part of the flow beginning last night with the departure of the F-15s from Langley Air Force Base.

At the moment, the following forces are in the area of operations or are soon to arrive within the area of operations. Let me begin with the Persian Gulf. As you know, for a long time we have had a presence in the Persian Gulf, and that's the Joint Task Force Middle East currently consisting of seven ships -- Antietam, England, Vandegrift, Ray, Rentz, Barbey, and then the flagship, La Salle, and the Bradley is also part of the force right now. They have been there for some time and were prepositioned and are not part of the new deployments.

Coming to the southeast, we had the arrival of the aircraft carrier Independence and its group on Monday, and it was prepared for operations on Tuesday. And you see additional forces with the Independence group -- some of those are combatants and some of those are resupply ships. With respect to additional naval forces moved into the region as part of the direction given to us by the President and the Secretary, the Eisenhower battle group has now passed through the Suez Canal and has taken up a position generally where you see it in the Red Sea along with the Scott and the Ticonderoga.

As you also know and have seen on television, the Saratoga battle group as well as the battleship Wisconsin, departed east coast ports for a normal deployment -- not part of this operation, just a normal deployment. But obviously, as these ships arrive in the Mediterranean and operate in the Mediterranean, they will increase our overall naval presence in the region.

With respect to the deployment of air forces, as I mentioned F-15 model Cs and Ds left Langley Air Force Base last evening -- during the course of the evening. They are continuing today. And the first planes have
landed in Saudi Arabia and are taking up positions at various locations within Saudi Arabia.

And finally, with respect to ground force deployments so far, the Division Ready Brigade, DRB -- that brigade that is always kept in the highest state of readiness in the 82nd Airborne Division --- left beginning at 3:00 this morning for duty in Saudi Arabia and will be arriving in Saudi Arabia in the course of the afternoon and evening.

That is all I'm going to say now with respect to those deployments that are underway or units that have already arrived in country. Thank you.

Q   General, could you at least say how many men are in the Division Ready Brigade?

GEN. POWELL: No. I'm not going to give specific numbers with respect to the size of our forces in country or in the Division Ready Brigade at this time.

Q   The President said that this was mainly a defensive force, suggesting that they were there to protect points where these aircraft are. Could you say that there's at least a chance that this force might swell greatly if the situation changes or if it will not swell greatly if the situation doesn't change?

0075

GEN. POWELL: ■ iously, the President gav——he correct answer. . That's the initial mission of these forces. We're prepared for other missions that may be assigned to us, but I don't want to get into speculating about what those possible missions might be or the size of forces needed to accomplish them.

Q   General Powell --

Q   Just one more follow-up. Under the current mission, would you need additional troops from what are being deployed now? _

GEN. POWELL: You can be sure that, for the mission we have been given, we will put in adequate forces for that mission. But I'm not prepared to say whether this is the adequate force level for that mission.

Q   General Powell, how vulnerable are these troops during this transition period when you're putting troops and equipment into place?

GEN. POWELL: We thought of that, and I think they are pretty secure. Even though these aircraft and ground troops are just arriving, the Independence is in a position to provide support now, as is the Eisenhower battle group. So we have the ability to cover these movements. And, of course, the Saudi armed forces are quite capable. They have AWACS aircraft. They also have top-of-the-line fighters. So I'm reasonably sure that we can get in in good order without presenting any vulnerabilities. I think I also failed to mention the five AWACS that are also arriving just about now in Saudi Arabia.

Q   General Powell, what is the --

Q   General, we have reports---

Q   -- chemical threat --

GEN. POWELL: Excuse me. Dave?

Q   What is the threat of chemical warfare on behalf of the Iraqis? Have they moved any chemical weapons down to within range of Saudi Arabia?

GEN. POWELL: The Iraqi armed forces do have chemical weapons, artillery-delivered as well as delivered by other means. They have used them in the past. It's a threat that we're concerned with. And I treat it as a capability that is there and could be used. I am not -- I don't want to heighten any concern with respect to that because the intelligence
is somewhat ambiguous. But it is a capability that they have demonstrated in the past that they will use, and we understand that and we have --- are preparing our forces accordingly. But I don't want to heighten tension any more over that issue.

Q   General ---

Q   General, can you give us an esitmate of how trained and ready your troops are to fight a force of a million men that's already been through an eight-year war with Iran?

1952-4

0076

GEN. POWELL: My mission right now and the mission of the armed forces of the United States is to take up defensive positions, to work with the government of Saudi Arabia and other governments who may wish to contribute forces to this mission on a defensive mission. And even though there may be one million people in the Iraqi army, it is not an army that is currently postured to come storming across any border with one million people. I am confident of our ability, when we have finished our deployments, to be able to accomplish the mission the President gave us.

Q   What about training? It's a big turn for the Saudis to allow foreign forces on their soil.

GEN. POWELL: We have trained with the Saudis in the past. It is a change for the Saudis to do this. I think it's a recognition of the seriousness of the situation. And I am absolutely confident in the ability of the armed forces of the United States to operate in this kind of environment. We've trained for it, we've exercised in it, and you've got the finest peacetime armed forces this nation has ever enjoyed.

Q   General Powell?

Q   General?

GEN. POWELL: Over here.

Q   Could you tell us if these troops that have already been deployed to Saudi Arabia -- are they equipped with specialized gear to deal with gas warfare?

GEN. POWELL: Yes.

Q   They are?

GEN. POWELL: Yes.

Q   Could you get into some detail of exactly what kind of equipment that entails?

GEN. POWELL: We have protective masks, we have overgarments that will protect the body from chemical contamination, and we have necessary medicines that will serve as antidotes to chemical agents.

Q   Well, sir, are the ---

Q   General ---

Q   General ---

Q   --- typical warfare --- (inaudible)?

Q   General, can you tell us -- can you give us some idea of the airlift requirements; specifically, what airfields were used for the tanker refilling operation for the F-15s? Did you, Mr. Secretary, get permission to use airfields in Morocco, for example?

SEC. CHENEY: Let me -- the arrangements that we worked out with other nations in terms of the course of my travels and discussions, I think, are obviously of some delicacy in some cases.

1952-5

We have already existing arrangements that will be of benefit in some circumstances. One of the things I asked President Mubarak for when I was in Alexandria yesterday was for permission for the Eisenhower, for example, to pass through the Suez Canal, which was granted.

At this point I don't believe we anticipate using any bases in Morocco. We have not made any such request.

Q   Mr. Secretary ---

Q   As a follow-up, where did the tankers come from that refueled the F-15?

SEC. CHENEY: Well, they're stationed along -- go ahead, Colin. You want to --

GEN. POWELL: A variety of locations. I can't tell you exactly which Air Force base, but the military airlift command, and Strategic Air Command, which has control over the tankers, has the ability, in practice all the time, to refuel airplanes wherever they may need refueling. So, some of the tankers may have come from CONUS bases, others may have come from European bases. I can't give you a specific location. There was a massive tanking operation, obviously.

Q   Can you tell us if the Saudi government has requested any emergency arms sales? And can you -- if they did, could you describe the equipment they have requested and whether it would come from active US stocks, how soon it could get there, et cetera?

SEC. CHENEY: Well, the discussion with King Fahd on Monday night focused on those subjects I've mentioned already, specifically on the general military situation, on how we perceive the threat, and what our capabilities were and what their capabilities were. But this was a broad-gauged discussion; it did not deal with specific arms sales in any respect.

When I met with Prince Sultan (sp) on Tuesday morning, also present were the Saudi chiefs and other military officials. And at that point, I informed the Saudi defense minister that we were, in fact, waiving the provisions --- the so-called Metzenbaum amendment that had limited our ability to ship to Saudi Arabia the 12 F-15s that they'd purchased. They used to be limited by law to having no more than 60 in country at any one time, but the President is permitted to waive that provision when he believes it's in the national interest to do so, and he has executed that waiver.

Beyond that, we didn't discuss any specific arms sales other than that part of my responsibility as the Secretary of Defense, when I returned to the States, would be to review their requirements that we will, as part of this overall effort, want to make certain that they've got the most capable forces possible. And one of the things, as Colin mentioned in his brief and that I think was also in the presidential statement, is that we hope that will emerge from this, by working together with the Saudis there, that their forces will be stronger, their capabilities will be greater after this exercise is over with than they were before. And part of that is

1752-6

0078

also providing them wi|| the equipment they requi■■. So we will be reviewing any requests they may have and making j■■ments and decisions with them about how we can best strengthen their own forces.

Q   And have they made any requests --

Q   Could you comment on reports

SEC. CHENEY: Pardon?

Q   Did they make any requests as a result of your visit?

SEC. CHENEY: The only specific item that has changed has been the execution of the presidential waiver on the number of F-15s they're allowed in-country. Beyond that, I don't think it would be accurate to say they've made additional requests.

Q   Mr. Secretary?

Q   General, would you give us your assessment, please, of the quality of the Iraqi forces that invaded Kuwait and their readiness, based upon their current positions, to go further into Saudi Arabia should that be the military decision?

GEN. POWELL: Well, they conducted the Kuwaiti operation in a very professional manner. It's an army that is capable. They have had eight years of experience in war. They have the capability to invade Saudi Arabia with forces in contact and they have the ability to reinforce those forces. That's what's caused this problem that we now have. So, we treat them and view them as a capable military force. But they are not invincible and they're not 10 feet tall and we have capabilities that we are now bringing to bear to ensure that we, in concert with the armed forces of the Kingdom of Saudi Arabia, can deal with that threat.

Q   General?

Q   General, US policy for a long time has reserved the right to respond in kind if American forces come under attack by chemical weapons. Do US naval forces and land forces in the Persian Gulf region have the capability to respond in kind if they do come under attack with chemical weapons?

GEN. POWELL: I wouldn't comment on what our capabilities are there. As the President said, we are prepared to defend ourselves.

Q   General Powell, could you give us a fuller picture of how the Iraqi military threat may have changed over the last couple of days? The President mentioned surface-to-surface missiles. Could you expand on that, please, and address what (area/air ?) assets may have been moved close to Kuwait. And I'd like you to address directly, if you could, reports that they have loaded planes with chemical munitions. Is that true or not?

GEN. POWELL: I don't really want to comment on specific intelligence reports. Maybe what we have to do over time is to get an intelligence briefing ready, but I really don't want to get into all the details of our intelligence holdings. But on that one, it is an ambiguous situation in my judgment, but we attribute them with that capability. Whether we actually saw them moving something or not,

1952-9

0079

I know they have that c▓▓bility and I attribute th▓▓ capability to
them and I take it into account in my planning and thinking.

    Q   General --

    Q   On the points the President raised in his speech about
the surface-to-surface missiles, could you explain the concern --

    GEN. POWELL: They have that capability.

    Q   that the President had in mind, particular -- in terms
of particular weapons systems and what those are?

    GEN. POWELL: Well, those weapons systems, as we have seen
demonstrated, have quite a range. And the Iraqis have shown a great
deal of creativity in taking Soviet equipment they had been provided
and modifying that equipment to give it even greater range. And if
you look at the range arcs, that is one of the principal threats
directed against Saudi Arabia. And that's why, I'm sure, the
President highlighted it.

    Q   General, will you tell us --

    Q   Mr. Secretary, are you treating --

    Q   -- if you have updated the overall garment that they wear
in chemical warfare? That was terribly hot, as I recall, and very
heavy. Has there been any update of that in recent years?

    GEN. POWELL: It is a hot garment. We have a variety of models
of it, but it is a hot garment. Once you put an overgarment on that
has the purpose of keeping a chemical agent from penetrating it,
there is weight associated with it. But I would also say that our
forces train with these garments regularly out in the Mojave Desert
at the National Training Center, at temperatures very similar to the
temperatures they will be experiencing in Saudi Arabia. So, I'm
confident that we can operate in it for the period of time that
would be necessary should we be struck by chemical weapons, and I
really hope it never comes to that.

    (Cross talk.)

    Q   Mr. Secretary, were you -- thank you very much. Were you
-- how is the Pentagon treating this overall, as something that
you're locked in for a long-time operation, or something that you
view as short term? And if you view it as long term, what would you
say to the people out there who are worried about their relatives in
the armed forces?

    SEC. CHENEY: Well, it obviously is a major commitment of US
forces to a part of the world where we've operated previously, but I
don't believe on this scale. We had the recent experience, of
course, in 1984 in clearing mines in the Red Sea, 1987 with the
Earnest Will operation in terms of escorting tankers through the
Gulf. But to put forces of significant size, air and ground
forces, into Saudi Arabia is a new departure for us. The
situation's uncertain. We don't know how long it will last. We
don't know when it will end. The mission the President's given us
is to be prepared to deter an attack against Saudi Arabia and, if
deter fails, ▓▓▓▓ There is no way for me to put sort of an end point on
that. We do not

                        1952 -- ▓

know exactly how events 11 unfold over the next ⌐months, but obviously the President's made it very clear that he feels very strongly that this is a part of the world that's of absolute strategic significance to the United States and that we are prepared to use US military forces, if necessary, to protect our interests and those of our friends in the area.

(Mixed voices.)

Q   Secretary Cheney, why aren't reporters ---

MR. WILLIAMS: We have time for just a few more questions.

Q   Secretary Cheney, why aren't US reporters being allowed to accompany US troops? Why hasn't a pool been activated and will it be activated?

SEC. CHENEY: It's Pete's fault.

THE PRESS: Ahhhh! (Laughter.)

SEC. CHENEY: No, let me -- let me respond seriously about it. We -- obviously we will -- we think it's important that you have the opportunity to cover the actions of US forces in the area and Pete will be working on finding ways to make that possible.

You also have to keep in mind, though, that inside Saudi Arabia itself -- that Saudi Arabia's a sovereign nation. They have their own rules and regulations and requirements and they establish the ground rules under which people have access to cover activities inside the kingdom. That's not something that we have control over, but we will do our best to see to it that people have an opportunity to cover the activities of US military forces in connection with this operation.

(Mixed voices.)

Q   Secretary, would you address the multinational aspect of this operation and what other forces you might be getting?

SEC. CHENEY: Sure. The -- as a general proposition, the President has made it clear that he supports the notion of the forces of other nations being involved in a multinational effort. But it is not for us to invite other nations into Saudi Arabia for military purposes. Those are arrangements that have to be worked out between those other countries and the Saudi government.

When I have been asked in recent days about that possibility, we've made it clear that the appropriate way for governments to proceed is to contact King Fahd and the Saudi government. And obviously, whatever they can work out we would generally support and be supportive of. I would expect that in addition to the British who've already announced this morning, with the approval of King Fahd, that they will be sending forces, that there will be other announcements in the not too distant future of the forces of other nations participating in this effort.

Q   Secretary Cheney ---

Q   General Powell, you have ---

(Cross talk.)

1052—8

Q   What was the breakthrough that King Fahd saw in your argument? And, General, those 15 Cs and Ds don't have -- do they have air-to-ground capability -- or F-15s?

(Cross talk.)

Q   King Fahd -- what was the breakthrough?

SEC. CHENEY: Well, the discussion with King Fahd obviously was -- I -- a significant moment. He -- the conversation went on for about two hours roughly, and it was, as I say -- consisted initially of my presentation and that of General Schwarzkopf as we briefed on the situation in Saudi Arabia and Kuwait and Iraq and also briefed on our military capabilities. My impression is -- although obviously the King would want to speak for himself -- but that it had become abundantly clear that the Iraqis had, in fact, committed an act of infamy, if you will, in their aggression against Kuwait; that, having told the Saudis and others in the region that they had no intention to invade, they did in fact invade; that the conduct of Saddam Husayn represented a qualitative shift, if you will, in sort of the rules of behavior in that part of the world.

The King indicated to me that he felt his first priority had to be the safety and security of the people of Saudi Arabia, and that based upon that, based upon the historic relationship of the United States and the government of Saudi Arabia -- specifically, he cited the meeting between his father, King Abdul Aziz, and President Roosevelt on the USS Quincy in 1945, and based upon their fundamental trust of the United States, they were prepared to ask for our assistance. And I think it was that culmination of events of the last few days -- the naked aggression by Iraq as well as the historic relationship of the United States and President Bush's extensive consultations with him and commitment to provide significant forces for the defense of the kingdom, that combination of things -- that led to King Fahd's decision to ask for our help.

Q   Mr. Cheney ---

(Cross talk.)

SEC. CHENEY: -- concentrating on air defense and air superiority in the first aircraft that went in.

Q   General Powell ---

(Cross talk.)

Q   The tanks ---

Q   General ---

Q   The Iraqis have some of the most modern Soviet tanks. We've sent the very lightly armed 82nd Airborne. Are you confident that those troops can adequately defend themselves against the Iraqi tanks, or do you anticipate it will be necessary to send armor?

1952-10

0082

GEN. POWELL: I assure you I am totally familiar with the armored capabilities of the Iraqi army, and we will deal with them in due course should it be necessary.

Q General ---

(Cross talk.)

SEC. CHENEY: Thank you all.

GEN. POWELL: Thank you all very much.

Q General, do you intend to send ---

Q Do you plan to send in F-16s?

Q --- any forces from Korea or Europe?

END

1152 - 11

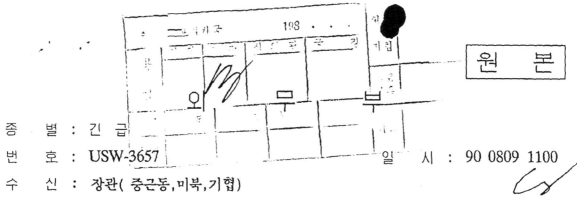

종   별 : 긴 급

번   호 : USW-3657

수   신 : 장관(중근동,미북,기협)

발   신 : 주 미 대사

제   목 : 중동 사태 관련 언론 보도

일   시 : 90 0809 1100

금 8.9.오전 09:00 현재 중동사태 관련 당지 언론보도 내용중 주요 사항 요지를 하기 보고함.

1. 요르단 입장 변화

-요르단도 이락의 쿠웨이트 합병에는 반대한다는 입장을 분명히 함.

-특히, 요르단의 유엔 안보리 경제 제재 결의 동조결정으로 인해, 이락이 사실상완전히 봉쇄되는 결과를 초래함.

(이란-이락전 당시, 이락은 요르단 경유 육로를 통해 무기를 수입한바 있음)

2. 유엔 안보리 동향

-금일중 유엔 안보리는 이락의 쿠에이트 합병을 규탄할것으로 예상됨.

-유엔 안보리의 경제 제재 결의시 기권했던 예멘도 쿠웨이트 합병 규탄에는 동참할것으로 예상됨.

3.아랍 긴급 정상회담

-이집트 무바락 대통령의 제의로 개최되는 아랍정상회담에 사우디, 시리아, 알제리아, 예멘, 리비아는 즉각 참석 의사를 표명한 반면, 후쎄인 이락대통령의 참석 여부는 상금 미정임.

4.미국의 주사우디 주둔 병력

- 최대 5만명까지 증원될 것으로 예상되며, 이미 사실상의 해상 봉쇄 효과를 거두고 있음

5. 미국의 대시리아 및 이란 접촉

-국무부 KELLY 중근동 담당 차관보를 시리아에 파견, 대 이락 제재 동참 교섭예정이며(그간 미- 시리아 관계는 공식적으로는 소원한 상태 였으나, 대화 체널은 상존해 왔음) 이란과도 접촉을 시도할 예정임.

중아국 안기부	장관	차관	1차보	2차보	미주국	경제국	정문국	정와대

PAGE 1

90.08.10   07:26 CG

외신 1과 통제관

0084

6. 다국적 군 문제

　-이집트와　모로코　양국은　즉각적인　병력　파견에대해서는　유보적　입장을
견지하고있으나, 범 아랍군이 결성되는 경우에는 동참이 예상됨.

　(대사 박동진- 국장)

외 무 부

종 별 : 지급

번 호 : USW-3666   일 시 : 90 0809 1610

수 신 : 장관(봉일)

발 신 : 주 미 대사

제 목 : 대 이라크 교역 금지 조치

대 WUS-2622

대호 미국의 대 이라크 교역 금지 조치에 대해 아래 보고함.

1. 법령 제정여부

0 미 대통령은 INTERNATIONAL EMERGENCY ECONOMIC POWERS ACT(77.9.28. 50 U.S.C. 1701)에 의해 외국에서 발생한 사태로 인해 미국의 국가 안보, 외교 정책 및 경제가 심각한 위협을 받게 되고, 동 위협에 따라 국가 비상 사태를 선포했을경우, 해당 외국과의 금융및 상업적 거래를 광범위하게 규율할수 있는 권한을 갖고 있음.

0 따라서 미국의 경우 외국과의 교역 금지를 위한 별도의 법률 제정 절차는필요없으며, 대통령의 행정 명령(EXECUTIVE ORDER)공포로 가능함.

0 8.2 부쉬 미 대통령은 상기 IEEPA 법에 따라 미국내 이락 자산 동결 및 이락과의 교역 금지를 위한 EXECUTIVE ORDER 12722 및 미국내 쿠에이트 자산 동결을 위한 EXECUTIVE ORDER 12723 을 공포하였음(별첨 1,2 참조)

2. 일반 상품 교역 금지의 시행 방법 및 내용

가. 시행 시기 8.2 EXECUTIVE ORDER 공포와 동시에 발효

나. 금지 내용

0 이락산 상품 및 서비스의 미국 수입(출판물등 정보 자료 제외)

0 미국산 상품, 기술 및 서비스의 대이락 수출(출판물등 정보 자료 및 인도적 구호 목적의 기증품 제외)

0 미국인에 의한 대이락 수송관련 거래 이락인이나 이락에 등록된 선박및 항공기에 의한 대미국 수송

0 미국인의 이락 수출품(목적지 불문)구입

0 미국인의 이락내 공업, 상업 및 정부 프로젝트 관련 계약 이행

통상국	차관	1차보	2차보	미주국	중아국	정문국	청와대	안기부

90.08.10   09:21

외신 2과 통제관 CW

0086

0 미국인의 이락 정부 및 기관에 대한 차관및 대출 제공

0 미국인에 의한 미국인의 이락 여행관련 거래 및 이락내 미국인과의 거래(이락내 체류자의 이락 출발 및 언론 활동을 위한 여행 제외)

0 상기 금지 내용을 위반하거나 위반할 목적을 가진 미국인의 거래

0 상기 미국인에는 미국 국적인, 미국 영주권 소유자, 미국 법인 및 미국내체류자 포함.

다. 시행 방법

0 행정 명령 공포와 도시에 각 행정기관은 교역 금지를 위한 기관별 구체적 조치를 강구, 시행함(예를 들어 재무부 소속 OFFICE OF FOREIGN ASSETS CONTROL 은 즉시 연방 준비 은행과 민간 부자 회사에 미국내 이락 자산을 동결을 지시하며, 세관은 대이락 수출품 및 수입품의 봉관 보류 및 압류등의 조치를 취함)

0 금번 교역 금지 조치와 관련 미 재무부가 8.9 현재까지 취한 추가 조치는아래와갈음(별첨 3,4,5 참조)

- 8.2 이전 계약이 체결되어 이미 미국을 수송중인 원유와 관련, 동 원유가8.2 0501 시 이전에 적재되었고 10.1 1159 까지 미국에 도착되며, B/L 이 8.2 이전에 발급되었을 경우 수입은 허가되나 해당 원유 대금은 미국내의 동결 구좌(BLOCKED ACCOUNT)에 예치됨(8.3 자)

-기타 쿠웨이트 관련 기업의 미국내 영업 계속 및 쿠웨이트 관련 증권의 미국내 거래 규제등 자산 동결 관련 조치

0 미 재무부는 과거 이란, 리비아, 니카라구아, 남아공, 파나마에 대한 자산 동결 또는 교역 금지 행정 명령 공포후 2-3 주내에 동 행정명령 실시를 위한 자산 동결 또는 교역 금지의 구체적인 내용, 잠정 조치, 용어정의, 벌칙등을 포함한 시행령을 제정, 공포하였는바, 금번에도 향후 2-3 주내에 이와 유사한 시행령을 제정할 예정임(과거 시행령중 리비아 관련 시행 별첨 6 참조)

0 한편 미국은 자산 동결 또는 교역 금지 조치로 인한 민간 업체의 피해 발생에 대해서는 <u>보상 조치를 해주지 않는다함.</u>

첨부: 관련 자료 USW(F)-1759

(대사 박동진-국장)

예고:90.12.31 일반

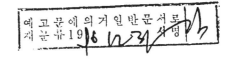

PAGE 2

0087

외 무 부

종 별 : 간급

번 호 : USW-3680

일 시 : 90 0809 1859

수 신 : 장 관(중근동,미북,국연)

발 신 : 주 미대사

제 목 : 미국의 대이락 규탄

　　금 8.9 개최된 유엔 안보리에서 THOMAS PICKERING 주유엔 미대사는 다음 요지 발언을 행한바, 동 발언내용 전문 별첨 FAX 송부함.

　　1. 이락의 쿠웨이트 합병은 무효임.

　　2. 미군 병력은 방어적 목적을 위해 사우디에 파견된 것임.

　　3. 이락군은 쿠웨이트로부터 즉각,무조건적으로 전면 철수하여야 하며, 쿠웨이트합법 정권이 복구되어야 함.

　　첨부: USW(F)-1770

　　'(대사 박동진-국장)

주 　•아프리카국			198 . . .		처리 지침
곡 란					
사 보					

중아국　1차보　미주국　국기국　정문국　안기부

PAGE 1

90.08.10　08:02　WH

외신 1과　통제관

0088

94　걸프 사태 미국 동향 1

보안
동재

(2 매)

REMARKS BY THOMAS PICKERING
US AMBASSADOR TO THE UNITED NATIONS

TO THE UNITED NATIONS SECURITY COUNCIL
REGARDING IRAQI INVASION OF KUWAIT

UNITED NATIONS
NEW YORK, NEW YORK

THURSDAY, AUGUST, 9, 1990

.STX

AMB. PICKERING: Mr. President, we are pleased and gratified by the unanimous approval of the Council of Resolution 662.

The United States does not recognize Iraq's outrageous and unlawful declaration that Kuwait is a part of Iraq. My government therefore is eager to support the legitimate government of Kuwait through the consensus resolution which we have adopted, which declares that any such charade is null and void and without legal effect.

Iraq repeatedly over the last several days has shown its scorn for the international community and for the resolutions of this body. Iraq's declaration is further proof of its continuing threat to the world community, and its disdain for international law.

For our part, at the request of governments in the region, the United States has increased its presence in the area. Mr. President, we are in the course of informing this council officialy, by appropriate letter, of our action taken under Article 51 of the Charter. As President Bush said yesterday, this is entirely defensive in purpose, to help protect Saudi Arabia and is taken under article 51 of the UN Charter and indeed, in consistency with Article 41 and Resolution 661. As Resolution 661 affirms, Article 51 applies in this case.

The Iraqi invasion of Kuwait and the large military presence on the Saudi frontier creates grave risks of further aggression in the area. This being the case, my government and others are, at the request of Saudi Arabia, sending forces with which to deter further Iraqi aggression.

Why is this resolution necessary? It is necessary

1990 -1

0089

because Iraq is attempting to extinguish the sovereighty of a member state of the United Nations.

There is something repugnant, chilling, and vaguely familiar about the statement issued yesterday by the Iraqi Revolutionary Command Council. We have heard that rhetoric before. It was used about the Rhineland, the Sudetenland, about the Polish Corridor, about Mussolini's invasion of Ethiopia, and about the Marco Polo Bridge incident in China. It was used to divide and to swallow up sovereign states, contrary to international law. The world community did not react. The result was global conflagration.

We believe the international community has learned this lesson well. We here will not and cannot let this happen again. We have finally learned the grim lesson of the 1930s, which was succinctly articulated by a Soviet foreign minister of that era, Maksim Litvinov. He said peace is indivisible. We agree.

My government is heartened by the response from the world community to Resolution 661, and we are confident that the procedures to implement it are well underway by the member states and in the United Nations. Resolution 660 and 661 should be used not only to contain this cancerous act of aggression but also to require Iraq to withdraw its forces immediately, unconditionally and totally.

The Council also again today calls for the restoration of the legitimate authority, sovereignty and territorial integrity of Kuwait. By this resolution, the international community again reaffirms that this crisis is not a regional matter alone, that it threatens us all, and that we have learned the lessons of history. We cannot allow sovereign state members of the United Nations to be swallowed up.

The United States stands ready to return to the Council as circumstances warrant to seek further Council action to implement Resolution 660. We are gratified that the Council continues to work expeditiously and effectively in its efforts to deal with this crisis.

Thank you, Mr. President.

.ETX

END

1990-2

0090

관리
번호 PO-1511

외 무 부

종 별 : 지 급

번 호 : USW-3691   일 시 : 90 0810 1630

수 신 : 장관(미북,미안,중근동,서구일)

발 신 : 주 미 대사

제 목 : 미-NATO 협의(이락 사태)

1. BAKER 국무장관은 8.10 NATO 협의를 마치고 가진 기자 회견을 통해 미-NATO 협의 개요와 미국의 기본 입장을 다음 요지 밝힘.

(기자회견 전문 별첨 FAX 송부)

가.NATO 외상 회의 결과

- 미국의 사우디 파병을 지지하고, 각국 나름대로의 방법으로 이락의 침략 확대를 봉쇄하는데 기여키로함(GULF 만 파병은 집단적이 아닌 개별적 차원에서 결정)

-TURKEY 에 대한 공동 방위 의무를 확인함.

-UR 의 제재 조치와 의도를 시행하는데 필요한 조치를 취하기로함.

-금번 회의를 통해 NATO 가 공동의 도전에 대한 중요한 정치적 협의체임을 확인함.

나. 금번 사태와 NATO 의 기능

-NATO 의 집단 군사 행동은 회원국인 TURKEY 에 대한 침공시 TURKEY 를 방어하기 위한 맥락에서 취해질것임.

-IRAQ 에 대한 제재와 이락군의 쿠웨이트 철수를 촉진하는 방법을 모색하는것은 NATO 의 정치적 협의 기능에 속함.

다. 사우디로부터 미군 철수의 조건

-이락군의 쿠웨이트로부터의 즉각 철수

-쿠웨이트 합법 정부의 복구

-미국및 여타 외국국민의 안전보장

-GULF 만에서의 항행 자유에 대한 위협제거 및 GULF 만의 안정과 안보 확보

(BAKER 장관은 상기 항목 전부를 미군 철수의 조건으로 직접 연계하여 언급치는 않았으나, 이락군의 즉각 철수, 합법정부의 복구 필요성과 함께 미군의 파병은 사우디 정부의 요청에 따른것임을 강조)

미주국	장관	차관	1차보	2차보	미주국	구주국	중아국	정와대

2. 금번 NATO 외상 회담을 통해 베이커 장관은 미국의 기본 전략(경제 제재조치의 실효화, 사우디 파병의 다국군화, 터키의 보호 달성을 위한 NATO 각국의 협조를 요청한바, NATO 각국은 터키 피침의 경우를 제외한 군사 행동은 개별적 차원에서 추진키로 합의한것으로 보임.다만 미국은 영국의 해.공군력 파견외에, 불란서, 카나다, 호주, 독일(독일의 경우는 헌법상 동부 지중해 까지만 해군력 배치)등 국가가 걸프만 파병에 동참하는 성과를 얻은것으로 평가됨.

3. 이와 관련, 당관 김영목 서기관은 국무부 유럽 정치 군사과 KDASKY NATO담당관과 접촉, 동 각국의 파병이 다국군 구성을 의미하는지와 지휘 체계의 구성 문제에 대한 협의 결과등을 문의한바, 여사한 법적 형태 문제가 금번 협의시 가장 어려웠던 문제였다고 하고, 지휘 체계의 구성문제 는 NATO 각국 정부와 계속 협의될 예정이라고 답변하면서, 유엔 안보리로부터의 법적 권한 부여를 모색하고 있음을 시사함.

(대사 박동진-국장)

90.12.31 까지

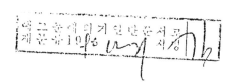

PAGE 2

0092

외 무 부

종 별 : 지 급

번 호 : USW-3692   일 시 : 90 0810 1730

수 신 : 장관(통일,중근동,미북)

발 신 : 주미대사

제 목 : 미국의 대이락 경제 제재 조치

1.금 8.10 미 백악관은 미국의 대이락 교역을 전면 금지하는 시행령(EXECUTIVEORDER) 을 발표하였음.

2.동 시행령에 따르면 미 행정부는 미국 시민뿐 아니라 영주권자, 미국법에 의해동록된 법인(외국 지사)과 기관, 미국적선등 모든 미국인(US PERSON) 이 이락과의 상품,용역, 재정 거래에 개입하는것을 금지하고 있음(수수한 인도적 물품의 기증은 별도 고려).동 시행령 발표문 전문별전 FAX 송부함.

첨부: USW(F)-1772

(대사 박동진-국장)

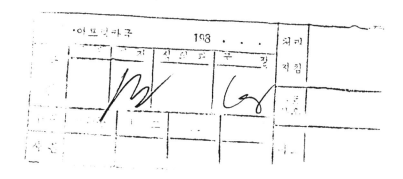

통상국   1차보   미주국   중아국   안기부   2차임

THE WHITE HOUSE
OFFICE OF THE PRESS SECRETARY

EXECUTIVE ORDER

BLOCKING IRAQI GOVERNMENT PROPERTY
AND
PROHIBITING TRANSACTIONS WITH IRAQ

FRIDAY, AUGUST 10, 1990

By the authority vested in me as President by the Constitution and laws of the United States of America, including the International Emergency Economic Powers Act (50 U.S.C. 1701 et seq.), the National Emergencies Act (50 U.S.C. 1601 et seq.), section 301 of title 3 of the United States Code, and the United Nations Participation Act (22 U.S.C. 287c), in view of United Nations Security Council Resolution No. 661 of August 6, 1990, and in order to take additional steps with respect to Iraq's invasion of Kuwait and the national emergency declared in Executive Order No. 12722,

I, GEORGE BUSH, President of the United States of America, hereby order:

Section 1.   Except to the extent provided in regulations that may hereafter be issued pursuant to this order, all property and interests in property of the Government of Iraq that are in the United States, that hereafter come within the United States, or that are or hereafter come within the possession or control of United States persons, including their overseas branches, are hereby blocked.

Sec. 2.   The following are prohibited, except to the extent provided in regulations that may hereafter be issued pursuant to this order:

(a)   The importation into the United States of any goods or services of Iraqi origin, or any activity that promotes or is intended to promote such importation;

(b)   The exportation to Iraq, or to any entity operated from Iraq, or owned or controlled by the Government of Iraq, directly or directly, of any goods, technology (including technical data or other information), or services either (i) from the United States, or (ii) requiring the issuance of a license by a Federal agency, or activity that promotes or is intended to promote such exportation, except donations of articles intended to relieve human suffering, such as food and supplies intended strictly for medical purposes;

1772

-1-

0094

(c) Any dealing by a United States person related to property of Iraqi origin exported from Iraq after August 6, 1990, or property intended for exportation from Iraq to any country, or exportation to Iraq from any country, or any activity of any kind that promotes or is intended to promote such dealing;

(d) Any transaction by a United States person relating to travel by any United States citizen or permanent resident alien to Iraq, or to activities by any such person within Iraq, after the date of this order, other than transactions necessary to

effect (i) such person's departure from Iraq, (ii) travel and activities for the conduct of the official business of the Federal Government of the United Nations, or (iii) travel for journalistic activity by persons regularly employed in such capacity by a news-gathering organization;

(e) Any transaction by a United States person relating to transportation to or from Iraq; the provision of transportation to or from the United States by any Iraqi person or any vessel or aircraft of Iraqi registration; or the sale in the United States by any person holding authority under the federal Aviation Act of 1958, as amended (49 USC 1301 et seq.), of any transportation by air that includes any stop in Iraq;

(f) The performance by any United States person of any contract, including a financing contract, in support of an industrial, commercial, public utility, or governmental project in Iraq;

(g) Except as otherwise authorized herein, any commitment or transfer, direct or indirect, of funds, or other financial or economic resources by any United States person to the Government of Iraq or any other person in Iraq;

(h) Any transaction by any United States person that evades or avoids, or has the purpose of evading or avoiding, any of the prohibitions set forth in this order.

Sec. 3. For purposes of this order;

(a) the term "United States person" means any United States citizen, permanent resident alien, juridicial person organized under the laws of the United States (including foreign branches), or any person in the United States, and vessels of US registration.

(b) the term "Government of Iraq" includes the Government of Iraq, its agencies, instrumentalities and controlled entitites, and the Central Bank of Iraq.

Sec. 4. This order is effective immediately.

1772
-2-

Sec. 5. The Secretary of the Treasury, in consultation with the Secretary of State, is hereby authorized to take such actions, including the promulgation of rules and regulations, as may be necessary to carry out the purposes of this order. Such actions may include prohibiting or regulating payments or transfers of any property or any transactions involving the transfer of anything of economic value by any United States person to the government of Iraq, or to any Iraqi national or entity owned or controlled, directly or indirectly, by the Government of Iraq or Iraqi nationals. The Secretary of the Treasury may redelegate any of those functions to other officers and agencies of the Federal Government. All agencies of the Federal Government are directed to take all appropriate measures within their authority to carry out the provisions of this order, including the suspension or termination of licenses or other authorizations in effect as of the date of this order.

Sec. 6. Executive Order No. 12722 of August 2, 1990, is hereby revoked to the extent inconsistent with this order. All delegations, rules, regulations, orders, licenses, and other forms of administrative action made, issued, or otherwise taken under Executive Order No. 12722 and not revoked administratively shall remain in full force and effect under this order until amended, modified, or terminated by proper authority. The revocation of any provision of Executive Order No. 12722 pursuant to this section shall not affect any violation of any rules, regulations, orders, licenses, or other forms of administrative action under that order during the period that such provision of that order was in effect.

This order shall be transmitted to the Congress and published in the Federal Register.

George Bush

END

1772
-3-

0096

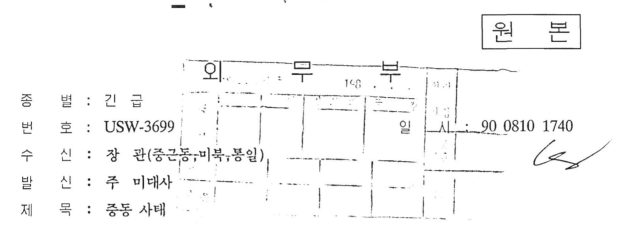

외 무 부

```
종    별 : 긴급
번    호 : USW-3699                     일    시 : 90 0810 1740
수    신 : 장 관(중근동,미북,봉일)
발    신 : 주 미대사
제    목 : 중동 사태
```

1.금 8.10 당지 언론은 하기 요지의 이락 정부 대변인 발표를 중계 방송함.(동 발표 내용 별첨 FAX송부)

가. 서방 제국주의의 침투로 인해 아랍권이 분열되었는바, 이들 제국주의 침투 이후 일부 아랍국가에서는 원유 생산으로 인해 축적된 경제적 부가 사회일부 계층 또는 특권층에 집중되는 부패 현상이 발생하였음.

나.쿠에이트내의 여사한 부패 현상을 일소하고 쿠웨이트에 대한 외국 세력의 지배를 축출하기 위해 이락은 8.2 군사 행동을 취했던 것임.

다.쿠웨이트 해방 이후 제국 주의자들과 시온주의자들이 이락에 대항하고 있는바, 이락은 아랍국가로서 아랍권의 단결을 성취하기 위해 노력할 것이며 이러한 이락의 성전(HOLY WAR)에 다른 아랍국가들도 동참할것을 촉구함.

2.이락측은 특히 전기 정부 발표를 통해 ARABNATIONALISM 과 아랍권 단결의 필요성을 강조하고 금번 미국의 사우디 파병으로 인해 야기된 군사적 긴장 상태를 ''성전''으로 표현함으로서 금번사태를 아랍권 대 서방권의 대립으로 부각시킴.또한 (사우디 왕정에 반대하는 세력들이 봉기할것을 호소함으로서 현 사우디 정권에 대한적대감을 공개적으로 표현함.

3.한편, 부쉬 대통령은 금일 3주간의 하계 휴가를위해 KENNEBUNKPORT 로 향하는 대통령 전용기내에서의 기자들과의 질의, 응답을 통해 여사한 이락측의 발표를 DESPERATE RHETORIC 에 불과하다고 일축하면서 현재의 미-아랍권간 대화와 협조,유엔의 경제 제재 결의에 대한 범세계적지지와 사우디의 이락 침공 저지 결의등을 감안할때 여타 아랍국가들이 이락의 소위 성전에 참여하는 것은 생각키 어렵다는 요지로 답변함.

4.또한 당지 방송에 따르면 카이로에서 개최된 아랍 정상 회담은 이락의 쿠에이트

중아국   1차보   2차보   미주국   통상국   정문국   안기부   차관 장관 결의대

PAGE 1   90.08.11   07:15 WH
                                             외신 1과 통제관
                                                          0097

침공을 강력히 규탄하고 범아랍군을 사우디에 파견키로 결정하였다 함.(동 파병
결정에 대해 이락,리비아,PLO 등은 반대, 알제리아,예멘은 기권 하는등 20개국
회원국중 12개국이 찬성하였다고 함)

    첨부: USW(F)-1782

    (대사 박동진-국장)

ADDRESS BY IRAQI SPOKESPERSON
ON IRAQI TELEVISION
BAGHDAD, IRAQ

FRIDAY, AUGUST 10, 1990

.STX

     IRAQI SPOKESPERSON (THROUGH INTERPRETER):   (In progress) --
wherever you are, your nation is a great nation chosen by God to be
the nation of the Koran.   It was always honored by that choice.   It
always carried the principles of holy religion.   It spreads its
principles, the principles of religion, all over the world, with all
the precepts of [the] prophet, each according to his own
capacities.

     Your nation has always called for humanitarian principles.   It
has thus become a flying banner to be seen in the East and the West
of the world.   Such was your nation -- such is its role, the role
which men who believe in God carried out, men who put wealth at the
service of peoples and populations.   They were responsible men.
They respected their message and their responsibilities.   Their
people thus respected them and their leadership.   They

used all their sources to serve people and populations.

     That's why foreign people respected Arabs and their principles.
Their territory -- the Arab territory -- and Arab shrines should not
be disrepected.   Arabs, by deed as well as by words, were united in
one nation.   Arabs from the eastern places, from Iraq, to the
western places, till Morocco, were proud of their principles and of
the messages they had to carry through in life.

     The leaders -- the Arab leaders -- used to be the most
knowledgeable and the most courageous who would stand on the front
lines whenever wars occurred.   He -- they alway had -- the leaders
always had the front place in the line.   They were always the most
honorable people.   They used to be honest, not lie to their own
people -- honest and respectable, God-fearing and respectful of his
nation.   And Arab leaders knew about religion and daily life, and
used to be an effective leader of the nation.

     The wealth of the nation was distributed on all populations,
even to the poor sectors.   However, newer leaders -- excuse me --
the self-leaders were always working to achieve the goodwill of the
whole nation.   The leaders at that time used to be convincing and
worked according to the will of God, and not following foreign
instructions.   A leader used to be very close to God and far from
everything that is prohibited by religion.

     What has an Arab leader become today?   He has changed, both at
the level of leadership and population level.   After the
introduction -- after the entry -- of foreign forces and the
division

0099

of the Arab nation, weak leaders, weak family leaders, were
installed, providing many facilities to foreigners, helping them to
divide the homeland. Imperialism always cared to divide the nation
so that their interests come foremost. Small oil states were thus
installed, states which were very detached from their people through
their plan. And the new wealth, oil wealth, which was given to a
minority, started to be used for the interest of foreigners and the
new leaders. Corruption, social and financial corruption, spread
all throughout these states. Their leaders used sly methods to help
occupation in their mission.

    The masses that -- in the Arab region were also spoiled.
Corruption spread all throughout the countries. Due to this state
of affairs, the worst image possible of Arabs spread in foreign
countries, due to the bad behavior of such minorities. The first
responsible party

for such a state of affairs is the leaders -- a need that arose to
rectify the shameful image which corrupted the maturity of these
minorities in these mentioned states. Disease spread between --
among these leaders, and poverty was known in these countries.

    That's why the events of the 2nd of August occurred. That day
was a response to bring out Kuwait from corruption and isolation,
where Kuwait was detached from Iraq -- from the original Iraq.
That's why the "day of call" was declared the "day of appeals." So
that we will get rid of all foreign domination, domination which was
mainly concentrated on these minorities. This led to the crazy
reactions on the part of occupiers and occupying foreign countries.

    The problem could not have been solved without this step. But
the liberation of Kuwait and its unity with Iraq became an Arab
battle, a battle to be liberated from poverty and to achieve a good
life far from humiliation and close to God. The new state falls
within the principles of religion. Foreigners should (not ?) accept
Arab -- the Arab way of life. This step was a result of the
intifada as well and of all the objectives which the intifada tried
to achieve.

    Now, coordination on the part of enemies has risen in order
--...

to prevent the liberation of Palestine. We see imperialistic powers
gathering around with their political agents, their Zionist agents,
standing all confronting Iraq. Confronting Iraq because they --
Iraq wants to achieve a unity of Arab wealth and to raise the
banner of Arab honor far from discrimination (?).

    Iraq is an Arab country, it is a torchlight against darkness.
Now that all disbelievers stood in one line, all believers should
stand with Iraq in one line -- a line which is wanted and wished by
God. They should stand against the disbelievers in Saudi Arabia
with Saddam Husayn.

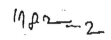

God will make ⊞ victorious. The enemies -- the evil enemies will be defeated no matter how mighty they are, no matter how sly conspirators are -- no matter how -- conspirators -- the Kuwaiti conspirators are powerful.

For all these reasons and under these circumstances, we see Arab -- excuse me -- American troops coming into the region under a false pretext. We tell them that the Iraqi troops will continue their fight, no matter how denials are presented on any part.

We have seen that all conspiracies and schemes with foreigners have failed

to deter Iraq. So the leaders will -- the leaders did not pay any attention to their peoples, who always were against their actions -- shameful actions. The former leaders were not against the Arab and Moslem populations only, they were against the will of God that occurred when Holy Mecca was, together with the tomb of Mohammed, put under foreign protection.

Fellow Arabs and Moslems, all believers in God, wherever you are, this is your day to rise up, to protect Mecca, which is imprisoned by Americans and Zionists. This is your day to stand up and protect the Prophet Mohammed, who carried the honorable and holy message in our holy land so that his message will stay holy and protected.

Fight off corruption and conspiration -- conspiracy. Stand up again for an occupation. Lead occupiers away from our holy land. Raise your voices and try to obtain as many honorable leaders to your part as possible so that we stand in one line and find -- fight against darkness.

Rebel against any person who accepts the situation where Arab women become disrespectable through -- excuse me. Rebel

against anybody who is an agent to the foreigners. Tell all conspirators that they have no more a place on Arab land. They have desecrated Arab honor, burned land under the feet of invaders, invaders who only want the -- who do not want the interests of the Iraqis or the Arabs.

Rise up so that the voice of right in the Arab nation will raise up, especially after all efforts to put your voice down, through rebelling against all efforts to stop you, against all efforts to humiliate Mecca.

Our brethren in Egypt, the grandchildren of believers, the sons of the Ghurabi (sp) Revolution of 1919 and the revolution of 1923, the sons of the revolution of Sa'ad Zaglul, the sons of Gamal Abdel Nasser. This is your day, this is your role. You should stop the foreign fleets from passing through Canal Suez so that your skies and waters will not be desecrated and history will not -- something -- write something which is unsuitable to Egypt.

Egyptians, stop their passage, and put your efforts with the efforts of believers in the Gulf and in Iraq. We call you for the holy war. Do not

1782-3

0101

hesitate to do so. You should stand up against foreign troops. You will thus achieve victory and rights and God's acceptance of you. You will become leaders, honorable leaders of this nation. We will be victorious by the help of God, and invaders will be defeated and will be dishonored. A new sun will rise over the Arab and Muslim world. God will be very satisfied with such a faith, so that all corruption will vanish.

Brethren, you should condemn invaders and conspirators. You should back up Iraq. God will be with you. Victory is always on the part of believers and will be at the side of nationalists.

A quotation from the Koran which says that God has always helped believers in their battle. God is great. Down with the despicable.

Signed by Saddam Husayn on the 10th of August, 1990.

Thank you.

.ETX

END

0102

외 무 부

종 별 : 긴 급

번 호 : USW-3711 　　　　　　　　 일 시 : 90 0811 1400

수 신 : 장관(중근동,미북,통일)

발 신 : 주미대사

제 목 : 중동 사태

　　금 8.11 오전 현재 당지 언론의 중동 사태 관련보도 내용중 주요 사항 요지 하기 보고함.

　　1.쿠웨이트 체류 미국인중 11명의 버스편 육로로 요르단에 도착함(이락 정부로부터 출국 허가를 받은 동 11명 가운데에는 이락의 쿠웨이트 침공 당시 단신으로 동지역을 여행중이던 10세 아동도 포함되어있음)

　　2.미 제 24 보병사단등 미군 증원 부대는 계속 사우디로 향발하고 있으며, 아랍 정상 회담의 파병결정에 따라 이집트군은 이미 사우디에 도착했다함. 또한 시리아 및 모르코군도 금명간 사우디 향발 예정이라함.

　　3.요르단,예멘등 친 이락 성향의 아랍국에서는 반미, 반 사우디 시위가 대규모로 전개되고 있음.

　　4.이락측이 금번 사태를 ''성전''으로 규정짓고 있는 현 상황하에서 미국으로서는 이락및 쿠웨이트 거주 미국인의 안전을 가장 우려함(작 8.10베이커 국무장관이 브랏셀에서 밝힌바와 같이 미측으로서는 상금 이들을 이락측에 의해 억류된 ''볼모''로는 보고 있지 않음)

　　5.이락측이 군사적 행동을 우선 취하지 않는한,당분간 중동 사태는 계속 교착 상태를 유지할것으로 보임.

　　(대사 박동진-국장)

중아국　　1차보　　미주국　　통상국　　정문국　　안기부　　상황실

PAGE 1　　　　　　　　　　　　　　　　　　　　90.08.12　　 07:30 DP
외신 1과 통제관

0103

걸프사태 : 미국의 대응, 1990-91. 전6권 (V.1 1990.8.2-20) 109

보존 : USW (F) -1388
수신 : 정보화 (중동리 사람 1
발신 : 주미대사
제목 : 중동 정세에 관한 논설

Escape Route for Saddam Hussein: Jordan

By Robert Satloff

OXFORD, England

Jordan's King Hussein alienated patrons, friends and allies alike when he initially cast his lot with Iraq and its conquest of Kuwait. For his troubles, he may very well find himself next on the hit list of Iraq's President, Saddam Hussein.

The deployment of U.S. troops in Saudi Arabia, coupled with decisions by Saudi leaders and Turkey to join in the blockade of Iraq, have set the clock ticking for President Hussein. Both he and President Bush are constrained by their posturing over the issue of the restoration of the Kuwaiti emirate, and it is the Iraqi leader's to find a way out of his predicament — restore his economy and popular support — are aggravated.

At the moment, with the world pitted against Iraq, the battle is too one-sided. Baghdad needs to raise the stakes in order to save what it has and complicate Western and Arab countermeasures. To do so, it must create an environment that will permit a resolution without concession.

Robert Satloff is a fellow of the Washington Institute for Near East Policy.

The most logical escape route is through Jordan.

This can be achieved by declaring that Iraq must move its forces into eastern Jordan to defend against either the hostile American presence in Saudi Arabia or the specter of an Israeli attack. Iraq need not actually move troops into Jordan — simply deploying them along the border should be enough to set President Hussein's plan in motion.

The Iraqis' strategy would be to manipulate the divergence in American and Israeli strategic interests that would be highlighted by the threatened entry of Iraqi troops into Jordanian territory. The key factor is the possible split between Washington and Jerusalem on their "red lines" in the Middle East: imaginary markers in the sand that, if crossed, would trigger a military response.

As President Bush first declared and then amply demonstrated, U.S. troops would fight for the Saudi oil fields, though not necessarily for the Saudi regime. America has made no similar commitment to the defense of Jordan. Our red line, for now, is the Saudi border.

In contrast, Israel's "red line" runs along the Jordanian, not the Saudi, border. Any change — or, in this case, the highly credible threat of a change

— in the disposition of forces inside Jordan would almost certainly send Israeli troops into Jordan to seize strategic territory. With their vital interests at stake, the Israelis are not likely to wait for the West's reaction to the Iraqi gambit.

Israel would fight not for the Hashemite regime but for the strategic buffer that Jordan has provided

---

The U.S. must head him off.

---

since the 1967 war. If the Hashemites can no longer maintain that buffer, then the Israelis will do it themselves.

Without firing a shot — without even physically crossing the border — Saddam could transform his lone wolf conflict with the entire civilized world into an Arab-Israeli problem. He will have succeeded in engaging two vital American interests in the Middle East — the security of Israel and the defense of oil resources — moved the focus of conflict away

from the conquest of Kuwait itself and sorely complicated the conflict for all parties concerned.

The threatened deployment of Iraqi troops in Jordan would bring to the fore a number of awkward questions:

Would the U.S. extend its security umbrella to Jordan, and thereby confront the possibility of fighting alongside Israel against an Arab state for the first time?

Would Israel battle Iraq directly or, fearing Saddam Hussein's threat of chemical and biological weapons, limit its actions to Jordan?

Would the Saudis risk perpetual Arab approbrium by offering themselves as the Arab linchpin for a joint U.S.-Israeli campaign against the most popular Arab leader today?

Would Syria stand idly by if it saw Israel and Iraq carving up territory it views as its historic patrimony?

Would America's Western allies keep the faith if the crisis were transformed into an Arab-Israeli contest?

In this scenario, Jordan would become either a battleground or a bargaining chip. In a gesture of good will, the Iraqi President could guarantee Jordan's independence and integrity while demanding the right to intervene there militarily. Its conditions would be the status quo post the conquest of Kuwait — namely the depar-

ture of Western forces and the lifting of the blockade.

In Iraqi thinking, this would provide a neat conclusion to the current crisis. The world has no stomach for war over Jordan. King Hussein would probably plead for the Americans accede to Iraq's demands so as avoid the dismemberment of realm. Only Israel would howl at terrible precedent that had been set. Diplomats on all sides, of course would make it appear as though le peace and honor had been achieved.

America should shut off this escape now, before Saddam Hussein has the opportunity of using it. The Administration must convince Hussein to back up his condemnation of the Iraqi annexation of Kuwait with a public declaration of support for the U.S. deployment in Saudi Arabia. Washington must also seek strategic understandings with Israel regarding the threat of an Iraqi deployment. Finally, with all that is at stake, the U.S. should state clearly that its "red line" extends to Jordan and…

Preventing Iraq's President from playing this "Jordan card" will go far toward maintaining the intensity of the global quarantine against Iraq and help hasten the resolution of the current crisis.

90.8.11. NYT

외 무 부

관리
번호 PO-1526

종 별 : 지 급

번 호 : USW-3713

일 시 : 90 0812 2330

수 신 : 장관(미북,중근동)

발 신 : 주 미 대사

제 목 : 이락사태(미 행정부 조치)

연:USW(F)-1791

1. 금 8.12(일) 미 백악관은 KENNENBUNPORT 에서 대변인 명의 성명을 통해, 쿠웨이트의 AL-SABAH 왕이 BUSH 대통령앞 친서를 발송, UN 알보리 제재결의의 시행을 위해 미국 정부가 필요한 조치를 취해줄것을 요청해 왔다고 발표 하였음.

2. 미측은 여사한 쿠웨이트의 요청은 회원국가의 집단적 또는 자율적 자위권을 규정한 헌장 51 조에 따른 것이라고 설명 하였는바, 미측은 미국등 다국적함대가 해상에서 이락의 교역에 대한 봉쇄조치를 실시하기 위해서는 헌장 51 조에 따른 쿠웨이트의 공식 요청이 필요 하다는 점을 수차 강조 한바 있음.

3. 이와 관련 금 8.12. BAKER 미 국무장관은 미 언론과의 대담을 통해 미국은 향후 이락측의 원유 수출을 위한 선박 이동을 차단 하겠다는 미 행정부의 의지를 명시적으로 밝힘.

4. 한편, 백악관은 상기 성명을 통해 금일 SADDAM HUSSEIN 이락 대통령이 쿠웨이트에서의 병력철수의 조건으로 이스라엘의 아랍점령지로 부터의 완전철수를 요구한데에 대해, 이는 쿠웨이트 점령을 기정사실화 하려는 시도일 뿐으로 동 요구를 단호히 거부 (CATEGORICALLY REJECT) 한다는 입장을 밝혔음.

(대사 박동진- 국장)

예고:90.12.31. 까지

미주국	장관	차관	1차보	2차보	중아국	통상국	정문국	영고국
청와대	안기부	건설부	노동부					

PAGE 1

90.08.13   13:38

외신 2과 통제관 DH

0105

외 무 부

종 별 : 지 급

번 호 : USW-3714   일 시 : 90 0812 2330

수 신 : 장관(미북, 중근동)

발 신 : 주 미 대사

제 목 : 이락사태(미군 파병에 대한 미국내 시각)

　　1. 금 8.12. 미 주요언론들은 이락-쿠웨이트 정세와 미 행정부의 외교, 군사조치를 상세히 보도 하는 가운데 , 미국민의 대다수가 BUSH 대통령의 사우디 파병은 압도적으로 지지하고 (NYT 여론조사: 남자 78 퍼센트, 여자 56 퍼센트) 있으나, 미국이 직접 군사적으로 개입할 만큼 GULF 지역이 미국의 이익에 긴요(VITAL) 하다는 설명과 군사행동 이전의 외교 노력이 다소 불충분하다는 일부 유보적 시각을 소개하고 있음.

　　2. 또한 금 8.12. W.P 지는 금번 미행정부 조치에 대한 종합 분석을 통해 과거 월남개입, 이란 인질사건등에 관련된 미 역대 대통령들이 정치적으로 실패를 경험한 사실을 상기 하면서, BUSH 대통령이 자칫하면 정치적으로 매우 부담스러운 상황에 처하게 될 가능성도 있다는 시각을 소개함. 또한 동 기사는 미국이 GULF 지역에서 완전한 목표 달성을 위한 군사작전능력에는 한계가 있다는 점과 , 금번 사태가 장기화될 경우 재정적자문제, 제 3 세계에 대한 미국 개입에 대한 반대론등 국내정치 여건으로 인해 미군 개입의 효용성에 대한 의문이 제기될 수 있다는 견해를 표시함(미국인들의 인질화 가능성 우려)

　　3. 한편 BUSH 대통령과 BAKER 국무장관은 최근 수일간 기자회견을 통해 이락-쿠웨이트 내 미국인들이 인질상태는 아니라는 점을 강조, 미국인들의 소개를 위한 미측의 노력에 손상을 미치지 않으려는 자세를 보였음., 또한 미 행정부의 주요인사 들은 쿠웨이트의 원상회복을 위한 금수 조치의 성공가능성에 대한 자신감을 표시 하였음.

　　4. 8.12. 현재 다국적군 군성, 대이락 제재조치의 실효화 노력등 미 행정부의 주요 외교 노력은 대체로 성공적 결과로 보이고 있는바 미 행정부측 관련 조치 상세 추보 예정임.

미주국	장관	차관	1차보	2차보	중아국	통상국	정문국	영교국
청와대	안기부	건설부	노동부					

PAGE 1   90.08.13   13:37

(대사 박동진-국장)
예고:90.12.31. 까지.

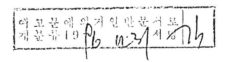

PAGE 2

	분류번호	보존기간

발 신 전 보

WUS-2677   900813 1855 DP

번   호 : _____   종별 : _____

수   신 : 주 미 대사. 총영사

발   신 : 장 관 (미북) 기협)

제   목 : 이라크.쿠웨이트 사태

    1. 금번 이라크의 쿠웨이트 침공과 이에 대한 미국정부의 강력한 대응, 국제적인 경제제제 조치 및 군사적 움직임 등 일련의 사태는 그 심각성으로 인해 향후 동 사태가 진정된 이후에도 세계경제 및 정치정세에 다대한 영향을 끼치게 될 것으로 사료됨

    2. 본부로서는 현재 이라크.쿠웨이트 사태가 향후 상당기간 가변적이 될 것으로 사료되나, 아국의 중장기 정책수립에 참고코저하니 우선 현재까지 밝혀진 미국 정부의 입장, 학계 및 전략문제 전문가들의 다각적인 견해, 언론 해설 등을 예의분석하여, 앞으로 사태 종결후 예상되는 중동정세 및 세계정세의 변화 등에 관하여 가급적 조속 보고바람.

    3. 본건과 관련하여서는 앞으로도 미국 정부의 입장, 각계 의견을 예의 관찰, 분석하여 수시로 보고바람.   끝.

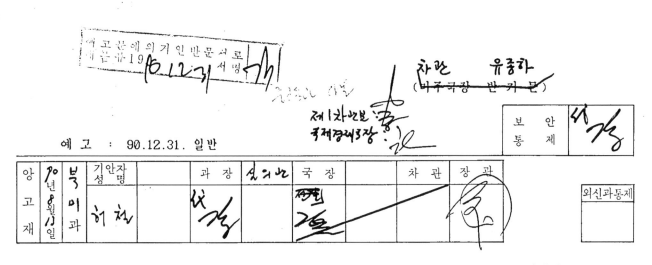

예고 : 90.12.31. 일반

외 무 부

종 별 :

번 호 : USW-3719　　　　　　　　　　일 시 : 90 0813 1805

수 신 : 장 관(중근동, 미북,통일, 해운항만청)

발 신 : 주 미 대사

제 목 : 페르시아만 대 이락 해운 수송 검색

　　1.8.13. 미 정부는 쿠웨이트 망명 정부의 요청에 의거, 유엔의 대이락 경제 제재 PPA 치의 효과적 시행을 위한 대이락, 쿠웨이트 하비상 검색 (SHIPPING INTERDICTION)노력을 개시할것임을 공식 발표 하였음.

　　2.당관 김성수 해무관이 국무부 해운, 육운담당관실에 확인한바에 의하면, INTERDICTION 의 시행을 위한 절차등 GUIDANCE 는 명일 발표될 예정이며, 동조치의 주내용은 유엔 안보리 결의에 의거 수출입이 금지된 (단, 의약품 및 인도주위적 식량은제외) 화물 수송 의혹이 있는 폐만 통항 선박에 대해 미 해군이 동 선박에 승선점검활동 및 필요시 회항 조치등이 될것으로 예상됨.

　　3.한편 미측은행상 검색 이외에도 외국정부에 대해 이락.쿠웨이트와의 항공. 육상 화물 수송을 중단할것을 촉구 하였는바, 국무부 발표 보도자료등 별첨 보고함.

　　(대사 박동진- 국장)

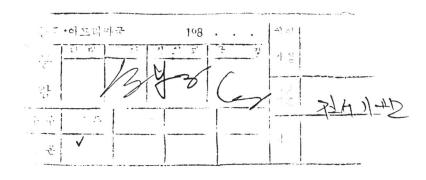

중아국　　2차보　　미주국　　통상국　　안기부　　해항청

PAGE 1　　　　　　　　　　　　　　　　　90.08.14　　09:15 WG

외신 1과 통제관

0109

USW(미)-1793
수신: 장관 (국조동, 미걸, 통인, 가주, 안반심)
발신: 주미대사   USW~1719 회부

INTERDICTION

--THE GOVERNMENT OF KUWAIT HAS REQUESTED THAT THE UNITED
STATES PARTICIPATE IN AND COORDINATE MULTINATIONAL NAVAL
OPERATIONS TO INTERDICT MARITIME TRADE WITH IRAQ AND KUWAIT THAT
IS PROHIBITED BY UN RESOLUTION 661.

--WE ARE COMMENCING INTERDICTION EFFORTS IN ACCORDANCE WITH
ARTICLE 51 OF THE UN CHARTER, WHICH RECOGNIZES THE INHERENT RIGHT
OF INDIVIDUAL AND COLLECTIVE SELF-DEFENSE.

--WE ARE CONTACTING OTHER NATIONS ALREADY ASKED BY KUWAIT TO
PARTICIPATE IN THIS MULTINATIONAL INTERDICTION EFFORT TO WORK OUT
MODALITIES AND PROCEDURES.

--THERE HAVE BEEN NO INTERDICTIONS SO FAR.

--I UNDERSTAND THAT AN IRAQI TANKER SEEKING TO TAKE ON IRAQI
CRUDE OIL FROM TANKERS IN SAUDI ARABIA WAS UNABLE TO DOCK BECAUSE
SAUDI TUGBOATS WERE UNAVAILABLE TO SERVICE IT.   UNITED STATES
FORCES WERE NOT INVOLVED IN THAT INCIDENT.

IF ASKED WHAT OTHER NATIONS HAVE BEEN REQUESTED TO PARTICIPATE:
--I WOULD PREFER TO LET OTHER NATIONS SPEAK FOR THEMSELVES.

IF ASKED ABOUT A BLOCKADE

--THIS IS NOT A "BLOCKADE" AS THAT TERM IS TRADITIONALLY
USED.   WE ARE TAKING LIMITED MEASURES TO ENSURE THAT TRADE
PROHIBITED BY THE UN SANCTIONS DOES NOT TAKE PLACE.

1793-1

0110

PRESS GUIDANCE

MONDAY, AUGUST 13, 1990

" BLOCKADE "

-- PRESIDENT BUSH SAID HE IS NOT PLAYING A SEMANTICS GAME. WE
ARE WORKING WITH OTHER COUNTRIES TO SEE THAT THE U.N.
SANCTIONS ARE IMPLEMENTED. THE PRESIDENT HAS DECIDED THAT
THE U.S. WILL DO WHATEVER IS NECESSARY TO SEE THAT RELEVANT
U.N. SANCTIONS ARE ENFORCED.

-- WE ARE GOING TO TAKE WHATEVER STEPS ARE NECESSARY AND
PROPORTIONATE. (MEANS WHATEVER ACTIONS ARE APPROPRIATE
UNDER THE CIRCUMSTANCES)

-- PRESIDENT BUSH: "I CONSIDER INTERDICTION OF SHIPPING TO BE
IN ACCORD WITH U.N. ECONOMIC SANCTIONS."

-- PRESIDENT BUSH: THE U.N. - APPROVED EMBARGO, "GAVE US BROAD
AUTHORITY, WORKING IN CONJUNCTION WITH OTHERS, TO DO
WHATEVER IS NECESSARY TO SEE NO OIL GOES OUT."

-- SECRETARY BAKER: THE U.S. WOULD BEGIN "ALMOST INSTANTLY TO
TAKE MEASURES THAT ARE NECESSARY AND PROPORTIONATE IN ORDER
TO ENFORCE THE U.N. SANCTIONS."

1793-2

0111

PRESS GUIDANCE

MONDAY, AUGUST 13, 1990

REFUSING TO STOP

-- ANY VESSEL SUSPECTED OF CARRYING PROHIBITED CARGO THAT
REFUSES TO STOP WILL BE INTERDICTED;
WILL DO WHAT IS NECESSARY AND PROPORTIONATE.

FOOD SHIPMENTS

-- U.N. SECURITY COUNCIL RESOLUTION 661 PROHIBITS IMPORTS AND
EXPORTS TO AND FROM IRAQ AND KUWAIT EXCEPT THOSE "INTENDED
STRICTLY FOR MEDICAL PURPOSES AND, IN HUMANITARIAN
CIRCUMSTANCES, FOODSTUFFS."

AIR AND LAND SHIPMENTS

-- WE WOULD EXPECT THE GOVERNMENTS IN THE COUNTRIES FROM WHICH
LAND AND AIR SHIPMENTS ORIGINATE OR ARE TRANSSHIPPED
DESTINED FOR IRAQ AND KUWAIT TO BE RESPONSIBLE FOR ENSURING
THAT SUCH SHIPMENTS ARE STOPPED.

--WE WILL DO WHATEVER IS NECESSARY TO ENFORCE U.N. SANCTIONS.

1793-3 (E-N7)

0112

외   무   부

종   별 : 긴 급

번   호 : USW-3729   일   시 : 90 0813 1931

수   신 : 장관(미북,중근동,기정)

발   신 : 주 미 대사

제   목 : 이락크-쿠웨이트 사태(한미 협조)

대:WUS-2677

연:USW-3713

1. 금 8.13. 당관 유명환 참사관은 DOUGLAS PAAL 백악관(NSC) 아시아 담당 보좌관을 접촉, 이락-쿠웨이트 침공에 대한 현재 NSC 의 분위기를 탐문한바, 동 보좌관의 주요 반응 다음 보고함.

가. 대이락 정책 방향

-현재 백악관으로서는 이락의 사우디 침공기획를 봉쇄하고, 제재조치의 실효적 시행을 위한 기반을 구축하였다는 점에서 제 1 단계 상황이 끝나고, 이제 2 단계 조치가 강구되어야 한다고 생각함.

-이와관련, BUSH 대통령은 명 8.14(화) 잠시 백악관에 복귀, 2 단계 조치에대한 내부 전략회의를 가질 예정임.

미국은 금번 사태가 장기화될수록 많은 문제점이 발생할것임을 잘알고 있으며, 대이락 경제제재 조치가 실효를 거둘수 있도록 강력한 방안을 강구할것임.

-현재 많은 동맹국들의 자발적 참여와 신속한 판단에 의해 제재조치가 효과적으로 개시되었으나, BUSH 대통령은 일부 무임승차국들에 대한 경각심을 주입하는 방안을 고려하고 있음.

(최근 미국내 인사들은 일본, 서독 및 여타 서방국들이 미국보다 중동원유 의존도가 높다는 사실을 지적, 미국의 과도한 부담에 불만을 표시하고 있다함)

나. 관계국간의 협조 내용

(1) 미국 정부는 일본 정부에 대해 해상 검색 조치에 구체적으로 어떤 기여를 하도록 요청하지는 않았음.

(2) 호주의 외국함대 동참결정은 BUSH 대통령과 HAWK 수상간 직접 통화후 호주측이

미주국 장관   차관   1차보   2차보   중아국   통상국   정문국   정와대
안기부 국방부

PAGE 1

자발적으로 취한 조치임.

(3) 미측은 8.2. 침공 사태직후, 중국측에 대해 분명한 입장을 취할것을 요청하고, 특히 중국이 동 사태와 관련, 이락과 교역(무기판매) 을 계속할 경우, 향후 서방과의 경제 협력 기회를 상실할 뿐 아니라(미국의 경우 당장 MFN 지위 상실 가능), 국제사회에 책임있는 일원으로서의 위치가 훼손될 것임을 지적한바 있음.

현재 미측은 중국의 대이락 금수조치가 분명히 취해지고 있다고 판단하고 있음.

다. 한. 미간 협조 방향

-미행정부로서는 <u>다국적 군사조치와 관련 아국에 대해 어떠한 구체적 내용을 요청할 것은 현재로서는 고려하고 있지 않음.</u>

다만, 개인적 견해로는 미국으로부터 한국에 대한 어떠한 요청이 나오기전에 한국정부가 가능한 방안을 검토하고 있다는 점을 미측이 인지 토록 한다면 좋을것으로 봄(예로서, 주한 미군 사령관과의 긴밀한 협의등)

라. 북한이 금번 사태관련 미국 및 이락을 공히 비난한것이 특기할만하며, 북한이 대이락 무기수출을 할 가능성이 있으나 해상 검색을 통하여 이를 효과적으로 봉쇄할수 있을것으로 봄.

2. 이에 대해 유참사관은 금번 아국정부의 제재조치의 내용과 중동지역에서의 아국의 정치적 특수성(북한의 공작관련)을 설명하고, 한미 양측이 가급적 긴밀히 협의를 지속해 나갈것을 언급 하였음.

(대사 박동진-국장)

예고:90.12.31. 일반

외　무　부

종　별 : 긴급

번　호 : USW-3731　　　　　　　　　일　시 : 90 0813 2002

수　신 : 장관(미북,기협, 중근동, 봉일,기정)

발　신 : 주미대사

제　목 : 이락-쿠웨이트 사태 전망

　　대:WUS-2677

　　대호관련, 이락-쿠웨이트 사태에 관해 현재의 상황을 아래 요지 종합 보고함(경제정세 전망은 별전 보고)

　　기타 상세에 대해서는 그간의 당관 보고를 참조 바람.

　　1. 현 중동 사태의 배경

　　가. 이락의 후세인 대통령이 쿠웨이트를 전격 침공, 합병선을 하게된 직접적 동기는 다음과 같은것으로 보임.

　　-쿠웨이트를 합병함으로써 원유수출에 절대 필요한 항만 시설 확보(이락의기존 해안선은 약 30KM 미만)

　　-쿠웨이트의 풍부한 유전지대확보(역사적 연고권 주장 및 실현)

　　-아랍권 지도국으로서의 위상확립

　　나. 그러나 금번 사태의 근저에는 아랍권의 전통적인 반이스라엘, 반외세 감정, 일부 산유국 집권층의 "부" 의 독점 및 친서방 태도에 대한 비판 심리등도작용한것으로 보임.

　　다. 또한 전쟁을 자신의 정치적 목표 달성을 위한 하나의 수단으로 간주하는 훗세인 대통령의 호전적 태도도 금번 쿠웨이트 침공을 일으킨 가장 직접적인 동기로 볼수 있음.

　　다만 훗세인 대통령 자신도 이락의 쿠웨이트 침공이 현재와 같은 범세계적 차원의 규탄과 경제제재, 그리고 미군의 사우디 파병과 같은 엄청난 반향을 불러일으킬 것으로 예기치 못했을 가능성이 큰바, 이러한 점에서 훗세인 대통령이 오판을 범한것으로 분석하는 당지 중동 전문가들도 많이 있음.

　　2. 미국의 기본전략

미주국	장관	차관	1차보	2차보	중아국	경제국	통상국	정문국
청와대	안기부							

PAGE 1

가. 미국은 금번 쿠웨이트를 침공한 이락군의 사우디 침공 가능성을 중점 부각시킴으로써 사우디측으로 부터 미군 주둔 허가를 얻고, 즉각 파병 조치를 실시한바 우선 이락의 대사우디 진격을 억지하는 전략적 성과를 거두었음.

즉, 현상황하에서 이락의 사우디 침공은 곧 대미 선전 포고를 의미한다는 점을 이락측에 중점 인식시킴으로써 TRIP-WIRE 효과에 의한 억지 전략을 구사하고 있음.

나. 한편, 외교적으로 유엔을 통한 이락의 쿠웨이트 침공 규탄 결의안 및 쿠웨이트 합병 무효선언 결의안 채택등을 통해 이락의 국제적 고립화를 추구하고있고, 경제적으로는 유엔 안보리의 대이락 경제제재 결의 및 소련을 포함하는 범세계적 차원의 경제제재 동참을 유도함으로써 소위 대이락 질식(CHOKE) 전략을구사하고 있음.

(미국은 이락이 여사한 질식 전략의 고통을 느끼기 시작하는데에는 약 1 개월이 소요될것으로 예상하고 있으며 3-4 개월이 경과하게 되면 심각한 정도의 고통을 받게될 것으로 기대하고 있음)

다. 전술한 바와같은 군사적 억지 전략, 외교적 고립화 전략 및 경제적 질식 전략을 통해, 미국은 이락을 상대로 일종의 지구전(WAITING GAME) 을 전개하고있는바, 미국 자신도 사우디 파병의 기본 성격이 방어적이라는 점을 수차에 걸쳐 분명히 밝힘으로써 여사한 지구전 태세를 갖추고 있다는 점을 간접적으로 시인한바 있음.

라. 미국으로서는 여사한 전략이 이락을 무력화 시킴으로써, 궁극적으로 이락군의 무조건적이고 전면적인 쿠웨이트로 부터의 철수를 통한 전전 상태의 회복이 이루어질것으로 기대하고 있으며, 한편으로는 이락지도층 내부의 반란이나 민중 봉기에 의한 훗세인 정권의 전복도 기대하고 있는것으로 보임.

마. 이러한 미국의 전략 수행에 긍정적 기여를 하고 있는 환경적 요인으로는 다음의 세가지를 지적할수 있음.

1)미소 관계가 소위 탈 냉전 시대에 접어들게 됨에 따라, 제 3 세계에서의 지역분쟁 발발시 통상 미국이 느껴오던 소련과의 경쟁적 부담을 지지 않아도 되는점.

2)이집트 주도하에 개최된 아랍 정상회담이 범 아랍군의 사우디 파병을 결정한점(따라서, 미국으로서는 자국의 사우디 파병이 아랍제국에 심어줄수도 있는 소위 "제국주의자" 적 인상을 어느정도는 탈색할수 있게 되었으며, 또한 금번사태를 미국 대이락의 대결 뿐만이 아닌 아랍권 내부의 분열로도 인식시키는 효과를 거두게 되었음.)

3) NATO , 일본, 한국등 기존 우방국들 뿐 아니라 중공도 대이락 제재조치

PAGE 2

0116

시행등에 있어 거의 완전히 보조를 맞추고 있는점.

이하 USW-3733 으로 계속됨.

PAGE 3

관리 번호	PO-410

외 무 부

종   별 : 긴 급

번   호 : USW-3733

일   시 : 90 0813 2002

수   신 : 장관(미북)

발   신 : 주미대사

제   목 : USW-3731 계속분

바. 그러나 여사한 미국의 지구전 전략은 이락과의 군사적 대결이 교착된 상태하에서 시간이 지나면 지날수록 그결과가 점점 더 미국이 불리한 방향으로 전개될수 있으며, 이점 미측도 잘인식하고 있는것으로 보임.

즉, 지금 당장은 미국민들이 정치적 성향에 관계없이 미군의 사우디 파병을지지하고 부쉬 대통령의 대응 방안을 높이 평가하는 입장을 견지하고 있으나, 11 월 중간선거, 12 월 크리스마스등이 다가옴에따라 소위 "BRING OUR BOYS HOEM"을 주장하는 철군론이 대두할 가능성도 크며, 또한 미국을 제국주의자로, 사우디를 아랍 내부에 외세를 끌어 들인 시온주의자로 규정짓는 이락의 심리전 전술이 소기의 성과를 거두는 경우 아랍 민족주의를 바탕으로 하는 외세 배제론이 아랍권내에서 강력히 주창될 가능성도 배제키 어려움.

이러한 경우 부쉬 대통령은 문자 그대로 진퇴양난에 빠질 것임.

3. 이락의 기본 전략

가. 미국이 사우디 파병 미군 병력을 TRIP-WIRE 로 이용, 이락의 군사행동 확대를 억지하고 있는반면, 이락은 이락과 쿠웨이트에 억류된 것과 다름없는 약 3,500 명의 미국인들을 사실상의 볼모로 잡고, 파나마나 그레나다 에서와 같은 미군의 전격 기습 전략이나 리비아에서와 같은 공중 폭격 가능성을 억지하고 있다고 볼수 있음.

따라서, 미국내 일각에서는 전기 미국인들의 출국이 실현되기 까지는 상당시간이 소요될것으로 조심스러운 예측을 하고 있기도 함.

(미국 행정부에서 이들 미국인을 "볼모"로 호칭하지 않기 위해 노력하고 있다는 사실 자체가, 역설적이기는 하나 이들이 실질적인 볼모임을 입증하고 있음)

나. 또한 이락군은 공공연히 미국의 관찰이 가능하도록 대 이란전 및 쿠르드족 살상시에 사용된 화학 무기 배치를 실시하고 있는바, 미측은 여사한 화학전에

미주국	장관	차관	1차보	2차보	중아국	경제국	통상국	정문국
정와대	안기부							

90.08.14   10:21

외신 2과 통제관 CW

0118

완벽하게 대비하고 있다고 하기는 하나, 이락측의 화학무기 사용가능성 불배제도 어느 정도의 대미 억지 효과를 거두고 있는것으로 봄.

4. 정세 전망

가. 요약컨데, 현재의 중동정세는 미국과 이락 양국간의 상호 억지 전략을 통한 군사적 교착상태로 요약할수 있음.

나. 또한, 이러한 군사적 교착상태는 일종의 소모전 성격을 띄면서, 미국이지구전 전략을 계속 이행하고 이락이 체면을 지키면서 후퇴를 할수 있는 방안이 없는한 상당기간 지속될 것으로 전망됨.

다. 미 행정부의 입장에서는 적어도 11 월 중간선거 까지는 현재의 전략을 계속 추구할 가능성이 큰 것으로 예측되는바, 동 전략을 수행해 나가면서 후세인대통령 전복 가능성등 이락의 국내 정세를 예의 주시할것으로 전망됨.

라. 현재 미측이 요구하고 있는 이락군의 즉각적이고 무조건적인 쿠웨이트로 부터의 철수가 훗세인 대통령의 입장에서 볼때 국내정치요인등을 감안시 절대수용할수 없는 조건인것 처럼, 이락측이 쿠웨이트로 부터의 철군 조건으로 내세우고 있는 WEST BANK 및 GAZA 지구로부터의 이스라엘군 철수도 미측으로서는받아들일수 없는 조건인바, 이처럼 현 상황이 ZERO- SUM GAME 의 성격을 띄고 있기 때문에 당분간은 타협의 여지가 있는 중도적 해결 방안을 모색하기 어려울것으로 봄.

마. 한편 전술한 미국의 대이락 억지 전략은 서구적인 기준에서볼때 이락도RATIONAL ACTOR 라는 대전제하에서 수립된 전략인바, 만약 이락이 이미 선전 포고한 "성전(JIHAD)" 을 실행으로 옮겨서 이스라엘에 대한 군사적 도발을 할경우 사태는 더욱 심각한 국면에 빠질 가능성도 희박하나마 배제할수는 없음.

바. 현재까지의 중동사대 관련 미 행정부의 대응은 미리 준비된 계획에 따른 단계적 전략 이행이라기 보다는, 주어진 여건에 대한 상황 대응의 성격이 강한바, 조만간 미 행정부는 경제제재 조치의 효과를 극대화 시키기 위해 보다 더 구체적인 MANEUVER 방안을 천명 할것으로 봄.

(대사 박동진-차관)

예고:90.12.31. 일반

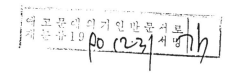

PAGE 2

0119

외 무 부

종 별 : 지 급

번 호 : USW-3751

수 신 : 장관(미북,중근동)

발 신 : 주 미 대사

제 목 : 부쉬 대통령 동정(재정적자 문제)

일 시 : 90 0814 2025

중근동 관서가관

1. 부쉬 대통령은 예고된바와같이 금 8.14 KENNEBUNKPORT 로부터 워싱턴에 일시 귀환, 백악관에서 기자 회견을 가졌음.

2. 동 대통령은 기자 회견이 모두 성명시 예산문제에 관한 자신의 입장을 밝히면서 민주당 지배 의회가 자신의 예산 타협 제안에 대해 응답하지 못하고 과도한 예산 배정 결의만 봉과시키고 있다고 비난하였음.

3. 부쉬 대통령은 현재 의회의 예산 심의 구조가 근본적으로 잘못되어 있으며, 특히 민주당 지도부가 전혀 필요한 조치를 취하지 못해 왔다고 전면적인 정치 공세를 개시하였는바, (부쉬 대통령은 지난 3 개월간 민주당 지도부와의 타협입장 표명과 함께, 민주당 비난을 자제), 이는 의회의 휴회 종료, 중간 선거등 중요 정치 일정을 앞두고 예산및 조세 문제에 있어 민주당측에 대한 기선을 제압하기 위한 전략으로 관찰됨.

3. 최근 미 정계는 경기 침체 조짐, 재정적자 해소의 구조적 어려움, 선거를 앞둔 현 시점에서 증세 조치의 비 인기성등 제반 어려운 사정하에서 -예산 정상회담-의 중요성에 주의를 기울여 왔으나, 이락의 쿠웨이트 침공 사태로 인한 원유가 상승, 파병에 따른 재정 지출 증대 가능성등으로 경제적 위기감이 일반 국민간에 증대되고 있음.

4. 한편, 최근 의회 일각에서는 중간 선거를 앞두고 각종 예산의 삭감을 피하기 위해 그라함. 레드만. 홀링스 법안의 의무를 회피하는 방안이 모색되고 있다는 관측이 있는바, 향후 민주, 공화 양측은 상호 삭감을 원치 않는 항목의 현상 유지(공화는 국방 예산, 민주는 사회 복지 예산)를 위해 공방을 벌이게될것으로 예상됨.

5. 동 대통령의 이락 사태 관련 언급과 관련 주요 동정 별전 보고함

첨부 USW(F)-1815

미주국	차관	1차보	2차보	중아국	청와대	안기부

(대사 박동진-국장)
예고:90.12.31 까지

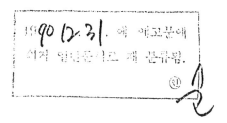

: USW(F)- 1815
: 장   관(1개,총리실)   발신 : 주미대사   [동지]
: Bush 대통령 기자 가자회견 (예산, 이약문제) (10 매)

PRESS CONFERENCE WITH PRESIDENT BUSH

THE WHITE HOUSE
WASHINGTON, DC

TUESDAY, AUGUST 14, 1990

.STX

PRESIDENT BUSH: Excuse the slight delay on the timing. I've
just -- on the phone with Mr. Mandela. Let me -- let me just say I
have a statement here on the -- (general laughter) -- it's that kind
of world, I'll tell you.

Q   What did you talk about?

PRESIDENT BUSH: And with your forebearance, I'll make a
statement here at the beginning. Bear with me, it may be a tad
longer than we're used to in this press room, but I want to get in
focus the question of the budget.

I know that the focus of the media attention today, and
understandably, is on a crisis 6,000 miles away. But there's
another important, well known, long standing crisis at home and
that's the failure of the budget process to produce a solution to
this nation's deficit -- terrible deficit. And even while we
address our critical international obligations, we must address that
persistent real need. And therefore, I want to just take a few
minutes to -- to talk about that.

Our current budget, or lack thereof, constitutes a real threat
to the economic well-being of this country. And in this case, the
problem is a lack of action on the part of the Congress, an
abdication of responsibility that endangers our economic vitality
and the jobs that go with it. It is no secret to the American
people that the congressional budget process has broken down.

Over the last couple of decades, we've seen the real problems
of overspending. And we've seen the stalemate in budgeting, which
is the result of internal congressional conflicts and a committee
system that is so complex that not only have the hard decisions been
postponed or avoided, but today nearly all budget decisions are
being finessed.

Previous presidents have urged fundamental reform, fundamental
budget reform. And we can all remember President Reagan slamming
down that massive continuing resolution. And yet Congress has
failed to straighten out this procedural monstrosity. As a result,
the deficit continues to grow. And with the growing threat, such
deficit spending poses, I took the initiative in May in calling on
the Democratic congressional leaders to join me in a bipartisan
summit on the budget, and the success of this summit is essential to
ensure the economic health of the nation, to resolve once and for
all the deficit dilemma, and, in doing so, to avoid the painful
sequester cuts which will occur without an agreement.

1815 - 1

0122

As the talks flagged, I acted to jump-start them, and you're all familiar with that. When the Democrats sought to hold the talks hostage over new revenues, I made a very difficult decision: to put everything, including taxes, on the table to make those budget talks succeed. And to keep those budget talks going, the administration kept -- I feel I kept my share of the bargain. The administration refrained from divisive rhetoric. We worked in earnest. We held meeting after meeting without any preconditions and emphasized the need, above all, for progress to put a budget package together. We offered billions in additional spending cuts, even as congressional committees were voting out spending bills that would bust the budget.

On July 26th, both sides agreed to put budget plans on the table. We again had a complete

proposal ready for negotiation. And after weeks of good faith negotiating, we expected -- we honestly believed there would be a specific democratic plan in exchange. And while the summit failed to move forward with specific solutions, the Congress continued with counterproductive legislation.

For example, the House has already passed 10 appropriations bills; 8 of which exceed my request for discretionary spending by $14 billion, and are 25 billion [dollars] higher than the budget for last year.

And the Senate is asking the taxpayer now [to] put up another $150 million to finance election campaigns of Congress. And let me be clear on that one, I oppose adding this kind of taxpayer financing of Congressional elections, and I'm going to veto any such bill that appears on my desk.

Congress is now on recess. And 100 days after I called on Democrats and Republicans in the Congress to work with me toward a bipartisan solution, I note, frankly in sadness, that after three full months the Democrats have yet to offer one single proposal at the budget summit.

And I've been reluctant to go public in this manner. We've dealt in good faith with the leaders. We have played by the rules. And now it is up to the Democrats who control Congress, it is up to the Democrats in Congress. And I stand ready to work on this process as long as it takes to get a five year package which solves the problem. And I've postponed what I think was a very important September trip to Latin America so as to focus on this issue.

And there are, however, a number of specific realities to be noted. First, it's the Congress that has the responsibility to pass a budget. And while they have the power of the purse, like any power of the President I got the power of the veto pen. And I will use that pen to veto any and every spending bill that busts the budget.

And second, if no budget is reached -- no agreement is reached, that means a sequester on October 1st

of about $100 billion. And as painful as such deep cuts would be, I must uphold the law. I'm determined to manage them as best I can, knowing that I've done all in my power to avoid them.

1815-2

0123

And so, the Democrats in Congress should know that if it comes to sequester they will bear heavy responsibility for the consequences.

And third, if the Congress really wants economic growth and increased government revenues, the place to start is not with tax increases but with incentives for growth, investment and jobs. And again, I cite the capital gains area as one that would stimulate and be investment-oriented.

And fourthly, the Congress must recognize the utter failure of their budget process to control spending. It's got to be reformed; the process has to be reformed.

And fifth, our budget must maintain a defense posture consistent with the demands on American leadership in the world and in the dangers we face.

And finally, the Democratic leadership of Congress must understand that the American people expect them to get that job done, to come forward with concrete proposals to cut the deficit. I, and the members of my administration, stand ready to work with them in meeting these obligations. And I know that it's a complicated time for our country, but it is essential that the American people focus, as they are now, on international matters, also focus on the domestic problems we face in terms of budget. And that's why I'm doing this today. Congress will be back soon. I hope we can rejoin these talks and get this budget deficit under control once and for all.

Now I'll be glad to take some questions. Who is the first?

Q   Helen.

PRESIDENT BUSH: Helen?

Q   Mr. President, I have a two-part question. After successfully internationalizing opposition to the Iraqi aggression through the UN, why did you jump the gun and unilaterally order a blockade upsetting other members? And two, is the US policy against the annexation of captured lands in the Middle East an across-the-board policy with the US?

PRESIDENT BUSH: Upsetting -- I don't think we've upset members on our policy of interdiction. We are acting within our legal rights, and I don't think -- I think the world wants to see these Chapter 51 sanctions carried out, and that's the role that the United States is trying to do.

Q   But you didn't -- you didn't go through the step by step of Chapter 7.

PRESIDENT BUSH: Well, we're doing it the way our attorneys and others around the world recommend, and I think we're doing it properly, and I hope we're doing it to the degree that all ships will turn back if they're in contravention of the UN action.

Q   And how about the last, there?

PRESIDENT BUSH: The last was -- what was that?

0124

Q   Opposition to annexation of conquered lands is our policy across the board.

PRESIDENT BUSH: Well, I can only address myself in the current -- currently. I don't know whether there are any exceptions or not. But I know that annexation, if this is what one calls this invasion of Kuwait, is unacceptable and that it won't stand.

Q   Mr. President, Jordan says that it's abiding by the UN sanctions, yet truckloads of goods are rolling through Jordan into Iraq coming from the port of Aqaba. Do you think that Jordan is subverting the sanctions, and what will you do about it?

PRESIDENT BUSH: Well, before I have a chance -- before I answer your question, I ought to let King Hussein tell me whether -- you know, what is happening. And if a country is not -- is permitting a flow of commerce, it would be in violent -- violation of the sanctions. But I -- you know, he's coming here, and I'll have a chance to talk to him and explain the US view, though I'm pretty sure he understands it clearly.

Q   Let me ask you, what do you think about King Hussein's charges that the American forces in the Persian Gulf have created an explosive situation?

PRESIDENT BUSH: I don't know what he means by that, but I don't agree with that. I think we are there not to have the situation explosive but to supplement fully what the United Nations has done in condemning this outrageous aggression. So we'll discuss that one, too. It's going to be an interesting conversation, I see, if you're writing his agenda for him. (Laughter.)

Q   Why is King Hussein coming, when he called to ask you that he'd like to come? And his brother has told reporters in Jordan that one of Jordan's problems is it would suffer so economically if it
abided by the sanctions; that they complained that they had no guarantees or assurances from the West to Jordan. What can you offer --

PRESIDENT BUSH: Maybe that's what he's -- maybe that's what he wants to talk about. I hope it is. Because, clearly, we've always been a friend of Jordan. We've helped them in the past. We'd help them in the future -- if they fulfill their obligations here. But I -- I'll -- Ann, I can just tell you what he told me on the telephone yesterday when he called. He said he'd like to come over and talk about the whole situation. There was no agenda. There was no discussion of any support for action of that kind.

Q   But you are willing to support him economically or have other countries in the region help him?

PRESIDENT BUSH: I think we would, provided Jordan joined these other countries in fulfilling these obligations under the sanctions.

0125

Q   Mr. President, is there any hope at all of a diplomatic
solution to this crisis?

PRESIDENT BUSH: I don't see it right now. But as the
sanctions begin to take effect, and it's going to take a while, I
would hope there would be a diplomatic solution to this crisis.

Q   Well, sir, like the other day when Saddam Husayn offered
his proposal, which I realize was totally unacceptable to you, I
mean, could that serve as a basis for perhaps some type of
negotiation?

PRESIDENT BUSH: I don't think just any proposal serves as a
basis for negotiation. No. I couldn't -- I don't see enough
positive elements there to think that that would be a basis for a
negotiation at all. It was bringing in extraneous problems, and it
did not address itself to the fundamental problem, which is that
they took over Kuwait and that they've got to get out of Kuwait and
they've got to let the rightful rulers return to Kuwait. So I don't
see that as a -- you know -- possibility to negotiate from that --
those proposals at all.

Q   Mr. President, you have ambassadors coming to the State
Department presumably to discuss a UN multinational quarantine or
interdiction -- whatever word you want. Is it now the policy of the
United States to potentially submit to a joint UN command or to
reflag US ships under a UN command?

PRESIDENT BUSH: That is not the plan right now, but we are
talking to see how we can make this naval presence most effective.
But that, what you said there, is not the policy of the United
States.

Q   Well, sir, may I ask, do you consider in any way -- there
were reports out of the UN that there is some criticism that you
have acted unilaterally and perhaps outside your legal authority in
the de facto blockade that's going on.

Do you consider that you've had your hand slapped, or do you think

PRESIDENT BUSH: No! I don't think so at all.

Q   Do you think you're --

PRESIDENT BUSH: And I think we are acting legally. And I --
so, this little meeting that was called by Cuba yesterday, it
doesn't disturb me in the least. I mean, let -- there can be
differences, people can discuss them, but I am convinced we're doing
-- acting properly, and we are determined to continue to act in that
manner. You see, Perez de Cuellar apparently talked about only the
UN through resolutions can decide about a blockade. But he also
said every country has a right to bring up Article 51, and as
Secretary General, I have nothing to say against it. And we have
good opinions that we are acting properly, and I have no intention
to change at all. I think it's important that others join in and do
their part, which most of them are doing in their determination to
see that commerce does not continue.

1815-5

0126

Q   Mr. President, given the staggering -- given the staggering number in the deficit and the cost of the military operation in the Gulf and in Saudi Arabia, doesn't it make sense that some of the countries that are reliant on us will pay some of the cost? I'm thinking, of course, of Japan, Germany, France, Italy. Shouldn't they pay some of the cost of our troops over there?

PRESIDENT BUSH: I think that we will find a very cooperative spirit in that regard from countries. I am convinced from a good talk I had, I think it was yesterday, with Prime Minister Kaifu that the Japanese are more than ready to entertain proposals along those lines. I have not talked to Kohl about that recently. France, of course, has vessels and are spending funds on their own right now. But I think you'll -- I think we'll have a cooperative -- cooperative effort here, some on the financial side, some on the military and shipping side.

Q   What about the Saudis themselves? They're the most direct beneficiaries.

PRESIDENT BUSH: Yes, I think the Saudis will do their -- do their part in helping out along the way. I'm confident of that. And I also would say -- the question hasn't yet been asked --

in terms of the peaceful resolution to the problem of how you eliminate apartheid. I talked to him a little bit about the -- the joy we felt in the progress that's been made on releasing prisoners, and I -- that was about it -- congratulating him, and Mr. de Klerk yesterday, on the same progress. It's very exciting what's taking place there.

Ann?

Q   Mr. President, the Iraqis have now held Americans for 12 to 13 days. Are you willing to sacrifice those Americans should it come to direct military action?

PRESIDENT BUSH: Never willing to sacrifice the life of any American -- sacrifice. No.

Q   Do you believe the Iraqis are using those Americans as a shield against potential American military action?

PRESIDENT BUSH: I don't have that -- I don't have that -- that feeling now, and I hope I never come to that, because you see difficulty of others getting out. And so it's a -- but it's a troubling situation. When people are held against their will or delayed in -- from leaving, it troubles me.

Q   What's their status, in your view?

PRESIDENT BUSH: Status is inconvenienced people who want to get out. And it's not only them, but a lot of others. And I hope it -- that it doesn't become more than that. I have no reason to think at this juncture that it will. But the more we talk about it and the more we speculate about it, the less helpful it is, I think. But I'd like to -- I'd like to feel that all foreigners who want to leave Kuwait or want to leave Iraq would be free to do so. And there have been some encouraging statements -- you heard from their

1815—6

0127

Ambassador this morning -- that make me say, "Well, let's see, let's wait and see on that one."

Frank?

Q   Mr. President, your June 26th statement had specifically said that the (points in it were jointly agreed ?) by the Democrats and Republicans. Why do you suppose that the Democrats have not made any proposals other than that, and what other proposals have the Republicans offered?

PRESIDENT BUSH: Well, we had a proposal that happened to ease into the public domain there against my best judgment. I would like to say I have no control over those leakers and it got out there and we were still prepared to hand over that proposal in all its detail to the Democrats in accord with their handing us one. But that didn't materialize. And I think there was some politics in it. I'm not going to accuse Tom Foley of this or Dick Gephardt of this. But I think there were some saying, "Hey, we think we got the President over a barrel here. We've made him back away and give and give and give and get nothing." And my view is, "Well, fine, if that's the game that some up there want to play." But I think the American people understand it is the Congress that has to pass this budget. They're the ones that have the power of the purse and I sat there and played by the rules, didn't comment on this proposal or that proposal, just as I said, and others did, and -- frankly, some Republicans as well as Democrats did. But I think what I'm trying to do now is to put it in focus so the American people will understand that it is the Congress that must move now to bring this deficit under control.

Yeah, follow-up?

Q   Yes, sir, other than sequestration, do you have any tools at your disposal to get anything done on this?

PRESIDENT BUSH: Well, sequestration is a pretty strong one, and veto is a helpful one.

Q   -- where you stand on it publicly?

PRESIDENT BUSH: No, not now. I still have hopes that we can resume this kind of summitry that is essential if you're going to get a deal. And I felt that way when we entered into the deal and I still feel that way in spite of the fact that I think -- I do think there has been some politics rearing its head.

Q   Mr. President, assuming that Saddam Hussayn were to work out some face-saving way to withdraw from Kuwait, he would still be there with a very large army, still, presumably, intimidating to his neighbors having invaded once. Given all that, do you think it is possible for this crisis ultimately to be resolved without removing Saddam Husayn from power; and if so, how?

PRESIDENT BUSH: I -- all I want to do is see it resolved the way that the world opinion wants it resolved, and then we will worry about the rest of that later on. But the main thing is to have the -- have the withdrawal and the restoration of the rulers to their -- to their responsibilities. And so, it's too hypothetical for me to.

18/15-7

0128

go into what happens beyond that, but yes, I'd like to -- I'd like to feel that that can still happen. And the economic sanctions are just beginning to -- Marlin says "pinch," I'd say "bite." And I think that they're going to be quite effective, more so than in the past. I certainly hope so. So, let's just see how all that works.

Jerry.

Q   Mr. President, if I can go back to the naval interdiction effort for a second. The Soviets apparently are proposing some kind of a joint Security Council command to control the naval interdiction effort. Are you pursuing that in any way with the Soviets, and are you interested in the idea at all?

PRESIDENT BUSH: Well, there was a -- there was originally a -- I think that was raised to Jim Baker by Shevardnadze, and I -- I don't have any objection -- any problem with talking to the Soviets about that. I think it would be a very good thing to have an active Soviet presence to enforce these UN resolutions. All I'm saying is I don't think it is essential that you have a UN flag in order to -- carry -- for countries to carry out their responsibilities. But I'd -- I'd be somewhat open-minded to talk further along those lines.

Q   Do you think it will be necessary at some point to stop ships going into Aqaba because that is a potential lifeline --

PRESIDENT BUSH: I think at some point it might well be. If it's a -- if it's a -- if it's a hole through which commerce flows in (an otherwise?) tight net, I would certainly think that Aqaba should be closed to Iraqi commerce.

Q   I have a question about the budget, Mr. President. After 100 days of negotiations, don't you think the "I'll show you mine, you show me yours" strategy is getting a bit silly? And why not just as president show some leadership and put your proposal and say, "Here's where I want to go"? This is the --

PRESIDENT BUSH: You know, we got one out there and it wasn't totally on the table, it was kind of oozed out on the side, and all we did was have a bunch of Democrats going after me, going to every special interest raising hell. And now it is time that the Congress, who has to pass the budget, must pass the budget, get going! I'm still here in a nice tranquil mood -- (laughter) -- wanting to discuss it with them. And I will discuss it with them.

But I'm using this -- you see, we had this kind of a truce on this abiding by the Marquess of Queensberry's "no comment" rules. And so, we got -- during this period of truce I'm going to put the focus where it belongs and where the American people year after year know it belongs, and that is on the party that controls the United States Congress. And then I'll be here in a reasonable mode come September saying, "Well here, here's our proposals, what's yours? Let's go." But it doesn't do any good. I -- they've been laughing all the way to what they think is the electoral bank, saying everytime we show a -- throw up a proposal they gun it down and rush off and tell a special interest of one kind or another "we're going to protect you. Ha Ha!" Now it's time for them to come forward and we will be more statesmanlike and try to resolve this national problem.

Q129

Q   Isn't it also true that when that proposal oozed out, as you say, it was Republicans who were involved in the (fight/flight ?).

PRESIDENT BUSH: That's why I was very careful of how I said who leaked)t.

Yes?

Q   They led the fight from that plan in revolt, I think.

PRESIDENT BUSH: Which one?

Q   The proposal that oozed out as you say.

PRESIDENT BUSH: Listen, one -- if you're ever going to -- I can't find anybody elated over any facet of taxes, Democrat or Republican. They want to stick it to the other guy a little bit. But what I'm saying is we had a proposal, people know what was in it; we had an original proposal with detail. They've had none. And the deal was they were to have a proposal. Now, let's come forward with it and set aside politics because it's getting tough now. It's getting right down to the crunch. And

the American people know that the Congress appropriates every single dime and tells us how to spend every single dime. Now they ought to get on with doing something about budget reform, process reform. Nobody's interested in the jurisdiction of this committee or another. The American people want the deficit down!

Q   Sir?

PRESIDENT BUSH: And they don't want to have these -- these delaying arguments about, "Well, I can't move because the chairman of this committee hasn't passed a continuing previous resolution and seconded the motion." Nobody cares about that.

Q   Mr. President?

PRESIDENT BUSH: They want the deficit -- I can't hear you, Sarah. Yeah, right in the middle. (Laughter.)

Q   Mr. President, you called -- you called the President --

Q   Mr. President --

PRESIDENT BUSH: I'm coming -- let me -- just a second.

Q   Mr. President, should the American people look forward to an ongoing American presence in Saudi Arabia over a period of years?

PRESIDENT BUSH: I don't know about a period of years, but certainly we're going to be there long enough to get the job done. But I can't -- I'd like to give you a time frame but I can't.

Yeah?

Q   Mr. President, you called the President of Venezuela to ask him for some help with the oil. Did you talk numbers with him at all?

/ᵃ/ᵣ-ᵖ

0130

PRESIDENT BUSH: No, I called him to thank him for what I understood was a Venezuelan willingness to step up and increase production -- they can still do it at a reasonably efficient rate, I'm told -- and to thank him for his approach on this. He told me that he'd sent his Foreign Minister to various capitals to coordinate all of this.

And I had a couple of other matters to discuss with him, too, that were unrelated to the Persian Gulf, mainly -- I can give you a little hint -- on Central America, an area where he and I stay in very close consultation and touch on this. But I didn't have a -- if your question was, did I have a specific request of him, no, I didn't.

Last one.

Q   Follow up. Just a second. Are you satisfied with the offer of Mexico as far as oil -- 100,000 barrels a day?

PRESIDENT BUSH: I -- I haven't the slightest way of knowing how -- you know, whether it ought to be more or less, but I'm very, very pleased with Mexico's cooperation in all of this. President Salinas [is] a courageous man, and I'm very pleased that he is willing to pitch in and help. I can't help you with the exact numbers, whether it ought to be 100,000 or something else, but when we heard that, I said, "That's good."   We've got a good relationship now with Mexico.

Thank you.

All right. Here's the last. This is. I really do have to run.

Q   Thank you, Mr. President. Just very briefly. You have called repeatedly for the Iraqis to be out of Kuwait, to withdraw unconditionally and completely and you've helped put sanctions in place to try and force them to do that. How important is that withdrawal? Is it important enough that if the sanctions don't seem to work after a short period that you will promise to use military force to force Saddam Husayn out?

PRESIDENT BUSH: That is too hypothetical a question. We have a plan and the plan is to implement fully the United Nations sanctions and also part of our plan is to -- arrangement with King Fahd is to help protect Saudi Arabia in a part of a multinational force now of quite a few countries against aggression from Saddam Husayn, the same kind of aggression that took over Kuwait. So that's where we are. That's the plan and I just can't help you by going in a hypothetical sense any further.

Listen. I hate to run. But I do have an appointment in here and thank you very much.

END

/815-10

0131

관리 번호	f0-1543

원 본

외 무 부

종 별 : 지 급

번 호 : USW-3756

일 시 : 90 0814 2034

수 신 : 장관(미북,중근동)

발 신 : 주 미 대사

제 목 : 부쉬 대통령 동정(이락 사태 관련)

연: USW-3751

1. 부쉬 대통령은 명일 워싱턴에 도착 예정인 HUSSEIN JORDAN 국왕을 KENNEBUNKPORT 로 초청, 8.16 회담을 갖을 예정인바, 부쉬 대통령은 금일 기자 회견시 HUSSEIN 국왕이 8.13 전화를 걸어 미국 방문을 희망하였으며, 자신은 JORDAN 의 제재 조치 참여시 JORDAN 에 대한 경제 지원을 포함 모든 문제를 논의할것이라는 입장을 밝힘.

2. 동 대통령은 또한 HUSSEIN 국왕이 SUDDAM HUSSEIN 이락 대통령의 멧세지를 휴대할것이라는 보도와 관련, 8.12 HUSSEIN 대통령의 제안에 대해 타협의 소지가 없는 제안이라는 입장을 표시하였음.

3. 또한 동 대통령은 미국측의 일방적인 해상 단속 조치(INTERDICTION)가 유엔 안보리에서 비판을 받았다는 질문에 대해, 미국으로서는 헌장 51 조에 따른 개별적 자위권에 의거 합법적인 조치를 취한것으로 믿는다는 입장을 강조하고, 미측 조치가 당장 이락행 화물선의 회항 효과를 거두고 있다고 답변함(미해군 활동이 반드시 유엔 FLAG 하에 들어갈 필요가 없다는 입장도 표시)

4. 한편 금 8.14 KIMMIT 국무차관은 유엔 안보리 상임 이사국 회원국 대사들을 초치, 다국적군 활동을 유엔안보리 군사위 통제하에 두려는 쏘련측 제안을 포함, 다국적군 활동에 유엔 권한을 부여하는 문제를 논의하였음.

(대사 박동진-국장)

예고:90.12.31 까지

미주국	장관	차관	1차보	2차보	중아국	정문국	정와대	안기부

90.08.15   10:52

외신 2과   통제관 CW

0132

외　무　부

종　별 :

번　호 : USW-3760　　　　　　　　　　일　시 : 90 0815 1247

수　신 : 장 관 (중근동,미북)

발　신 : 주 미 대사

제　목 : 이락 -쿠웨이트 사태 (부쉬 대통령 연설)

　　1. 부쉬 대통령은 금 8.15 오전 현 중동제세에 대한 국방부 브리핑에 참석후 국방부 인사들을 위해 행한 연설을 통해, 시리아, 모로코등 아랍국가가 대이락 제재에 동참함에 따라 사담 후세인이 아랍권으로부터 완전 격리, 고립되었음을 강조하고, 미국은 이락군의 무조건 철수, 쿠웨이트 정부의 원상회복, 사우디등 중동지역의 안전보호등을 위해 우방국과의 협력을 바탕으로 대이락 제재조치를 강화할 것이라고 재 천명했음.

　　2. 동 연설문 내용은 FAX 송부함.

　　첨부: USW(F)-1825

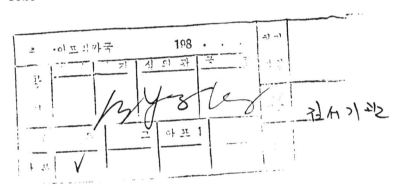

중아국　　1차보　　미주국　　정문국　　안기부　　2차보　통상국　대책반　차관　장관

PAGE 1

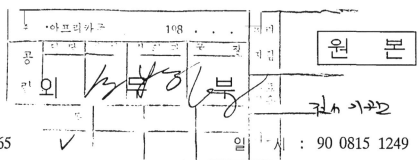

종   별 :

번   호 : USW-3765

일   시 : 90 0815 1249

수   신 : 장 관 (중근동,미북,통일,기협)

발   신 : 주 미 대사

제   목 : 중동 사태

이락-쿠웨이트 사태관련 금 8.15 당지 언론보도 요지 아래 보고함 (기사 전문은 별전 FAX송부함)

① CNN 방송은 09:00 뉴스를 통해 사담후세인 이락 대통령이 이란에 대해 군대철수, 전쟁포로 교환, 국경조약 체결등 전면화해를 제의했다고 보도했는바, 이는 시리아의 대이락 제재동참에 따라 고립상태에 빠진 이락이 이란과의 화해를 통해 현재 이란-이락전에 개입되어 있는 이락군을 이동시켜 쿠웨이트내 점령군을 증강시킬수 있는 전술로 평가되고 있음.

2. 미국 정부는 요르단의 AQABA 항구가 이락에 대한 물품반입에 이용되고 있다고 비난하면서 동항구의 봉쇄가능성을 시사했으며, 또한 사우디내 미군증강을 위해 20만명 규모의 예비군의 동원계획을 검토중인 것으로 알려졌음.

한편 금일 아침 워싱턴에 도착한 후세인 요르단국왕은 명일 부쉬 대통령과 메인주 휴가소 (캐니벙커포트)에서 회담할 예정임.

③ 대이락 제재조치에 대한 아랍국가들의 동참과 관련, 미국정부는 이집트에 1억불 이상의 무기판매를 결정했으며, 요르단이 동 제재에 동참할 경우 요르단에 대한경제지원도 고려하고 있다고 알려졌음. 또한 사우디, 오만, 바레인, UAE, 모르코등에 대한 무기판매 확대문제도 검토중인 것으로 보임.

4. NYT, WP 는 금일자 사설을 통해 미국이 취한 일방적인 해상단속이 유엔헌장의규정에 따른 적법한 조치라 할지라도, 안보리 상임 이사국인 소.불 등의 반대에 유의, 유엔안보리등에서 강대국과의 긴밀한 협의를 통해 실시할것을 촉구했음.

5. 한편 당지 전문가들의 분석에 따르면 미국은 금번사태가 장기화될 경우 제반상황이 미국측에 불리하게 전개될 것으로 판단, 대규모병력 파견을 통해 대 이락 압력을 강화함으로서 이락이 스스로 협상에 응해오던지, 아니면 이락의 대 사우디

중아국   1차보   미주국   경제국   통상국   정문국   안기부

90.08.16   07:23 FC

외신 1과 통제관

0134

침공 또는 이락군 내부의 반란에 의한 후세인의 몰락을 예상하고 있다함.

(대사 박동진-국장)

외 무 부

종 별 :

번 호 : USW-3788　　　　　　　　　　　일 시 : 90 0816 1934

수 신 : 장 관(미북,중근동,봉일,기협)

발 신 : 주 미 대사

제 목 : 요르단 국왕 방미

연: USW(F)-1843,(2)USW(F)-1842

1. 부쉬 대통령은 현재 방미중인 요르단의 훗쎄인 왕과 금 8.16 메인주 KENNEBUNKPORT에서 정상 회담을 가졌는바, 동 정상 회담후가진 기자회견에서 부쉬 대통령 주요 언급 요지 하기보고함 (기자 회견 전문은 연호 (1)송부)

가. 금일 회담을 통해 금번 중동 사태 관련 미-요르단간의 이견이 좁혀졌는바, 특히 훗쎄인 왕은 대이락 경제 제재 조치에의 동참 입장을 재천명하였음.

나. 훗쎄인 왕은 AQABA 항을 통한 대이락 수출입의 금지를 약속하였음 (단, 요르단 측은 식량등 인도적 상품도 경제 제재 대상 품목인지에 대해 유엔측의 의견을구하고 있는 상태임)

다. 또한 금일 회담시 후세인 왕의 최근 이락 방문 결과에 관해서는 언급이 없었는바, 이락측이 쿠웨이트로 부터 철수 하리라는 느낌은 받지 못했음.

라. 한편 후쎄인 왕은 현재 미-이락간에 여하한 중개자 역할도 하고 있지 않음.

마. 미국으로서는 이락 골비화 정책을 계속 추구할것이며, 자국만의 경제적 이익을 위해 전 세계적차원의 경제 제재 조치를 위배하는 CHEATERS를 계속 경계할것임.

2. 또한 전기 정상 회담후 후세인왕은 기자들과 간단한 질의 응답을 가졌는바 동인 주요 언급 요지하기 보고함 (기자 회견 전문 연호(2) 송부)

가. 요르단 정부는 유엔 안보리의 대이락 경제 제재결의를 존중해 왔음. 다만 SANCTION 의 구체적 의미에 관해서는 유엔측의 의견을 구하고 있는중임.

나. 금번 방미시 이락측으로부터 여하한 MESSAGE 도 가지고 오지 않았음.

다. 현재 AQABA 항을 통한 대이락 수출입 상품은 없음.

(대사 박동진-국장)

미주국	1차보	중아국	경제국	통상국	안기부			

PAGE 1　　　　　　　　　　　　　　　　　　　　　90.08.17　　10:23 WG

외 무 부

종 별 :

번 호 : USW-3810　　　　　　　　　　　　　　일 시 : 90 0821 1422

수 신 : 장관(통일,중근동, 미북, 해운 항만청)

발 신 : 주미대사

제 목 : 대 이락.쿠웨이트 해운 검색

　　연: USW- 3719

　　연호 미국의 대이락.쿠웨이트 봉항 선박에 대한 해상 검색 (INTERCEPTION
OPERATON) 에 관한 미국방부 발표문 (GUIDANCE 및 상세 문답 포함) 및 국무부의 대
선박회사 통고문을 별첨 송부함.

　　첨부: USW(F)- 1869 (5 매)

　　(대사 박동진- 국장)

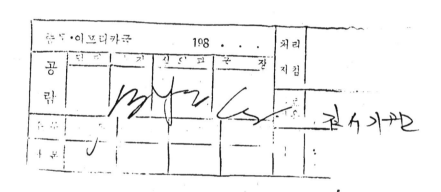

통상국　　미주국　　중아국　　해항청　　대책반　　1차보　　2러방　　한기부

PAGE 1　　　　　　　　　　　　　　　　　　　　　90.08.21　　05:05 DA

　　　　　　　　　　　　　　　　　　　　　　　　외신 1과　통제관

　　　　　　　　　　　　　　　　　　　　　　　　　　　　　　0137

UNCLAS SECTION 01 OF 07
SUBJ: PUBLIC AFFAIRS GUIDANCE - MULTINATIONAL MARITIME OPERATIONS
CHUSMTM RIYADH SA PASS TO CENTCOM PUBLIC AFFAIRS FORWARD
1. FOLLOWING IS THE APPROVED PUBLIC AFFAIRS GUIDANCE FOR THE SUBJECT
INTERCEPTION OPERATIONS. THE DEPARTMENT OF DEFENSE MADE THE
FOLLOWING ANNOUNCEMENT AT APPROXIMATELY 1930 (EDT) ON 16 AUG 1990
IN WASHINGTON:

(QUOTE) FOLLOWING THE INVASION OF KUWAIT BY IRAQ, THE GOVERN-
MENT OF KUWAIT REQUESTED THE UNITED STATES GOVERNMENT ACT WITH KUWAIT
IN EXERCISING THE INHERENT RIGHT OF INDIVIDUAL AND COLLECTIVE SELF
DEFENSE, AND TO TAKE SUCH MILITARY AND OTHER STEPS AS ARE NECESSARY
TO ENSURE THAT ECONOMIC MEASURES DESIGNED TO RESTORE KUWAIT'S
SOVEREIGN RIGHTS ARE EFFECTIVELY IMPLEMENTED. THE GOVERNMENT OF
KUWAIT REQUESTED THAT THE UNITED STATES GOVERNMENT ACT AS COORDINATOR
OF TE SHIPS PARTICIPATING IN THIS MULTINATIONAL EFFORT.

ACCORDINGLY, THE PRESIDENT OF THE UNITED STATES HAS AUTHORIZED
U.S. FORCES TO PARTICIPATE IN A MULTINATIONAL MARITIME EFFORT

PAGE 03 RUEKJCS1215 UNCLAS
THAT WILL INTERCEPT SHIPS CARRYING PRODUCTS AND COMMODITIES THAT ARE
BOUND TO AND FROM IRAQ AND KUWAIT. THIS ACTION IS CONSISTENT WITH
U.N. SECURITY COUNCIL RESOLUTION 661, WHICH IMPOSED MANDATORY
SANCTIONS ON TRADE WITH IRAQ AND OCCUPIED KUWAIT.

INTERCEPT OPERATIONS WILL BE CONDUCTED BY SHIPS OF THE PARTICIPA-
TING NATIONS IN SPECIFIED ZONES IN THE PERSIAN GULF, THE GULF OF
OMAN, AND THE RED SEA. OPERATIONS WERE AUTHORIZED TO BEGIN
TODAY. (END QUOTE)
2. THE ABOVE ANNOUNCEMENT AND FOLLOWING QUESTIONS AND ANSWERS ARE
PROVIDED FOR USE IN RESPONSE TO QUERY ONLY.
Q1: WHAT IS THE SPECIFIED INTERCEPT ZONES?
A1: THE PRIMARY AREAS OF OPERATIONS ARE IN THOSE INTERNATIONAL
WATERS OF THE PERSIAN GULF SOUTH OF 77 00N LATITUDE, THE GULF OF
OMAN, AND THE RED SEA NORTH OF 21 00N AND EAST OF 034+10E LONGITUDE.
Q2: WHAT VESSELS WILL BE INTERCEPTED?

PAGE 04 RUEKJCS1215 UNCLAS

A3: IN THIS CONTEXT, IT MEANS MAKING CONTACT WITH A SHIP TO DETER-
MINE WHETHER IT MUST BE TURNED AWAY OR OTHERWISE DIVERTED, AND DIVER-
TING THAT SHIP IF REQUIRED.

Q4: WILL ALL SHIPS IN THE RESTRICTED AREAS BE STOPPED?
A4: NOT NECESSARILY. FOR EXAMPLE, IF A SHIP CAN SATISFY US THAT IT
IS NOT CARRYING PROHIBITED MATERIAL FROM IRAQ OR KUWAIT, OR IT IS NOT
BOUND TO OR FROM PORTS OF OTHER COUNTRIES WITH PROHIBITED MATERIALS
DESTINED FOR OR ORIGINATING IN IRAQ OR KUWAIT, OR IF A SHIP SIGNALS
ITS INTENTION TO PROCEED TO PORTS OTHER THAN THOSE IN IRAQ OR KUWAIT,
THEN THE SHIP MAY BE ALLOWED TO PROCEED. IF THE SHIP FAILS TO
PROCEED ON ITS STATED OR PRESCRIBED COURSE, OR IT ATTEMPTS TO PROCEED
TO IRAQ OR KUWAIT, IT MAY BE STOPPED AND BOARDED.

Q5: WHAT WILL HAPPEN TO SHIPS THAT ARE STOPPED?
A5: WE MAY BOARD AND SEARCH THEM. IF THESE SHIPS ARE NOT CARRYING
PROHIBITED MATERIAL, THEY SHALL BE PERMITTED TO PROCEED TO THEIR
DESTINATIONS. HOWEVER, VESSELS DESTINED FOR KUWAIT/IRAQ WILL BE
DIVERTED.

Q6: HOW WILL A SHIP BE INFORMED TO STOP?
A6: THE COMMANDER OF THE INTERCEPTING SHIP WILL USE ALL AVAILABLE
COMMUNICATIONS, INCLUDING INTERNATIONAL CODE SIGNALS, FLAG HOISTS,

PAGE 05 RUEKJCS1215 UNCLAS
BLINKING LIGHTS, RADIO, LOUD SPEAKERS, AND OTHER APPROPRIATE MEANS.

Q7: WHAT IF A SHIP REFUSES TO STOP AFTER THESE EFFORTS TO
COMMUNICATE HAVE BEEN MADE?
A7: WE WILL THEN USE MEASURES NECESSARY TO ENSURE COMPLIANCE.
TO THE MAXIMUM EXTENT POSSIBLE, WE WILL CONDUCT OPERATIONS WITHOUT
THE USE OF FORCE. THE ON-SCENE COMMANDER IS, HOWEVER, AUTHORIZED TO
USE THE MINIMUM FORCE NECESSARY.

Q8: WHAT IS "MINIMUM FORCE"?
A8: THAT WILL DEPEND ON THE CIRCUMSTANCES, WHICH ARE COVERED BY THE
RULES OF ENGAGEMENT. WE DO NOT DISCUSS RULES OF ENGAGEMENT.

Q9: WHAT ARE "PROHIBITED MATERIALS"?
A9: ALL COMMODITIES AND PRODUCTS FROM IRAQ OR KUWAIT, AND ALL
COMMODITIES AND PRODUCTS TO IRAQ AND KUWAIT EXCEPT FOR SUPPLIES
INTENDED STRICTLY FOR MEDICAL PURPOSES.

Q10: WHAT IS THE LEGAL BASIS FOR THE INTERCEPT OPERATION?
A10: THE OPERATION IS BASED ON THE RIGHT OF INDIVIDUAL AND COL-
LECTIVE SELF DEFENSE RECOGNIZED IN ARTICLE 51 OF THE U.N. CHARTER,
THIS OPERATION HELPS TO GIVE EFFECT TO THE U.N. SECURITY COUNCIL'S
RESOLUTION 661, WHICH IMPOSES MANDATORY SANCTIONS ON TRADE WITH IRAQ
AND KUWAIT.

1265 - 2

0139

Q11: WHAT OTHER NATIONS ARE PARTICIPATING IN INTERCEPTING VESSELS?
A11: CONSULTATIONS ARE ON-GOING REGARDING PARTICIPATION. WE UNDER-
STAND THAT THE GOVERNMENT OF KUWAIT HAS INVITED THE OTHER PERMANENT
MEMBERS OF THE U.N. SECURITY COUNCIL (FRANCE, PRC, USSR, U.K.), ALONG
WITH EGYPT, AUSTRALIA, AND MOROCCO TO JOIN. NAVAL SHIPS FROM A
NUMBER OF COUNTRIES, INCLUDING THE UNITED KINGDOM, AUSTRALIA, CANADA,
AND FRANCE ARE ON THEIR WAY TO THE REGION.
Q12: ARE WE INTERCEPTING AIRLIFTED SUPPLIES?
A12: NO, BUT AIRLIFTED SUPPLIES ARE ALSO PROHIBITED UNDER U.N.
SECURITY COUNCIL RESOLUTION 661.
Q13: HOW CAN THE U.S. GOVERNMENT JUSTIFY THE INTERCEPTING OF FOOD?
A13: OUR INTERCEPTION OPERATIONS ARE LAWFUL AND CONSISTANT WITH U.N.
SECURITY COUNCIL RESOLUTION 661. SEE A10.

Q14: WHAT IS THE DIFFERENCE BETWEEN A "BLOCKADE" AND AN "INTERCEPT"?
A14: THE PURPOSE OF THIS OPERATION IS TO INTERCEPT BY DIVERTING
SHIPS BOUND TO OR FROM IRAQ AND KUWAIT, AND OTHER SHIPS WITH PRO-
HIBITED CARGO. A BLOCKADE IS A BELLIGERENT ACT WHICH COULD INVOLVE
THE DELIBERATE AND UNPROVOKED CAPTURE AND EVEN DESTRUCTION OF SHIPS
RUNNING THE BLOCKADE.
Q15: WHAT ARE THE NAMES OF THE SHIPS PARTICIPATING IN THE INTERCEPT

OPERATION?
A15: ALL U.S. NAVY SHIPS IN THE REGION EXCEPT THE HOSPITAL SHIPS ARE
CONSIDERED TO BE PARTICIPATING IN INTERCEPT OPERATIONS. YOU WILL
HAVE TO ASK THE INDIVIDUAL ALLIED AND REGIONAL COUNTRIES ABOUT THEIR
SHIPS THAT ARE PARTICIPATING.
Q16: IS THE UNITED STATES COMMANDING THE FORCES INVOLVED IN THE
INTERCEPT OPERATIONS, BOTH U.S. AND FOREIGN?
A16: AT THE REQUEST OF KUWAIT, THE UNITED STATES IS COORDINATING
THE MULTINATIONAL EFFORT; NAVAL FORCES PARTICIPATING IN THAT EFFORT
REMAIN UNDER THEIR NATIONAL CONTROL. THE U.S. CENTRAL COMMAND IS
DIRECTING THE U.S. FORCES INVOLVED IN THE OPERATION.
Q17: WHAT WILL HAPPEN TO SHIPS DESTINED FOR IRAQ OR KUWAIT?
A17: UNLESS THEY ARE CARRYING EXCLUSIVELY CARGO INTENDED STRICTLY
FOR MEDICAL PURPOSES, THEY WILL BE DIVERTED TO A NON-IRAQI/KUWAITI
PORT, AS THE OWNERS OR MASTER MAY ELECT.
Q18: WHAT IF A SHIP REFUSES TO BE SEARCHED, OR REFUSES TO TURN AWAY?
A18: IF THE ON-SCENE COMMANDER HAS REASONABLE GROUNDS FOR SUSPECTING
THE VESSEL IS CARRYING PROHIBITED MATERIALS, HE MAY TAKE THE SUSPECT
VESSEL INTO CUSTODY USING MINIMUM FORCE, AND DIVERT IT TO A DESIG-
NATED PORT OR ANCHORAGE FOR DISPOSITION.

0140

Q19: HOW WILL MARINERS KNOW THE INTERCEPT OPERATION IS IN EFFECT?
A19: NOTICE WILL BE PUBLISHED IN INTERNATIONAL NOTICE TO MARINERS
AND BE PROMULGATED IN OTHER APPROPRIATE CHANNELS, INCLUDING LOCAL
MARINE BROADCASTS.
Q20: HOW LONG WILL THESE INTERCEPT OPERATIONS CONTINUE?
A20: FOR U.S. FORCES, AS LONG AS THE PRESIDENT DIRECTS. YOU
WILL HAVE TO ASK THE OTHER COUNTRIES FOR THEIR POLICIES ON
THE LENGTH OF THESE OPERATIONS.
Q21: WILL OTHER NATIONS FOLLOW THE SAME RULES OF ENGAGEMENT AS U.S.
FORCES, AND THE SAME PROCEDURES DESCRIBED IN PREVIOUS ANSWERS ABOVE?
A21: YOU WILL HAVE TO ASK THOSE NATIONS.
Q22: WHERE, SPECIFICALLY, WILL U.S. AND THE OTHER PARTICIPATING
NATIONS' FORCES INTERCEPT FORCES OPERATE?
A22: SEE ANSWER 1. WE CANNOT DISCLOSE SPECIFIC OPERATIONS.
Q23: WHAT WILL BE THE STATUS OF CARGO ON SHIPS THAT ARE DIVERTED OR
DETAINED? CAN THE CARGO BE SEIZED?

PAGE 03 RUCKJCS121G UNCLAS
A23: THE PURPOSE OF THE OPERATION IS TO DIVERT CARGO BOUND TO OR
FROM IRAQ OR KUWAIT, NOT TO SEIZE IT.
Q24: WILL U.S. SHIPS BE ALLOWED TO DAMAGE UNARMED SHIPS NOT COMPLY-
ING WITH THE U.N. SANCTIONS?
A24: U.S. FORCES ARE AUTHORIZED TO USE MINIMUM FORCE NECESSARY TO
ENFORCE THE U.N. SANCTIONS.
Q25: HAS THE U.S. EVER CONDUCTED A SIMILAR OPERATION?
A25: ALTHOUGH THE CIRCUMSTANCES WERE DIFFERENT, A SIMILAR ACTION WAS
TAKEN DURING THE 1962 CUBAN MISSILE CRISIS.
7. FOR QUESTIONS BEYOND THE SCOPE OF THIS GUIDANCE, OASD (PA) POC FOR
PLANS IS MAJ. K. CERSHANECK, USMC, A/V 223-1075, COMM (202) 693-1075)
POC FOR MEDIA QUERIES IS LTCOL STUART WAGNER, USMC, A/V 227-5131,
COMM (202) 697-5131.

1. Request you publish the following international NTM.

SPECIAL WARNING TO MARINERS NO. 80

In response to requests from the legitimate Government of Kuwait and in exercising the inherent right of collective self-defense recognized under Art. 51 of the UN Charter, United States forces will, in cooperation with regional and allied forces, conduct a maritime operation to intercept the import and export of commodities and products to and from Iraq and Kuwait that are prohibited by UN Security Council Resolution 661.

Affected areas include the Strait of Hormuz, Strait of Tiran, and other choke points, key ports, and oil pipeline terminals. Specifically, Persian gulf interception efforts will be concentrated in international waters south of 27 degrees north latitude; Red Sea interception efforts will be conducted in international waters north of 22 degrees north latitude.

All merchant ships perceived to be proceeding to or from Iraqi or Kuwaiti ports, or transshipment points, and carrying embargoed material to or from Iraq or Kuwait, will be intercepted and may be searched.

Ships which, after being intercepted, are determined to be proceeding to or from Iraq or Kuwait ports, or transshipment points, and carrying embargoed material to or from Iraq or Kuwait, will not be allowed to proceed with their planned transit.

The intercepting ship may use all available communications, primarily VHF channel 16, but including international code signals, flag hoists, other radio equipment, signal lamps, loudspeakers, and other appropriate means to communicate his directions to a ship. (Safe navigation may require vessels to be diverted to a port or anchorage prior to conducting a search.)

Failure of a ship to proceed as directed will result in the use of the minimum level of force necessary to ensure compliance.

Any ships, including waterborne craft and armed merchant ships, or aircraft, which threaten or interfere with U.S. forces engaged in enforcing this maritime interception will be considered hostile.

Doc. #4418K

0142

외 무 부

종 별 : 긴 급

번 호 : USW-3823   일 시 : 90 0820 1833

수 신 : 장 관 (미북, 중근동, 미안, 통일)

발 신 : 주 미 대사

제 목 : 부쉬 대통령 연설 (중동사태 관련)

연: USW (F)-1877

1. 금 8.20 부쉬 대통령이 볼티모어에서 개최된 CONVENTION OF THE VETERANS OF FOREIGN WARS 에서 행한 연설중, 중동사태 관련 주요 언급내용 요지를 아래 보고함. (연설문 전문은 연호 FAX 송부)

가. 금번 중동사태는 미국인의 인내와 개인적 희생을 요구하는 위기상황임.

나. 미국은 미국 자신의 국가안보뿐만 아니라 관련국 전체의 국익을 위해서 이들국가와 공동으로 금번 사태에 대처하고 있음.

다. 이락측이 현재 억류하고 있는 사실상의 인질 (HOSTAGES)들을 국제법과 유엔안보리 결의 664호에 따라 즉각 석방 (RELEASE) 할것을 촉구함.

라. 현재 억류상태에 있는 미국민들의 안전에 대해서는 이락측에 책임이 있다는점을 다시한번 상기 시키는 바임.

2. 지금까지 미측은 인질이라는 용어의 사용을 피하면서 이락측에 대해 이들 억류 외국인의 출국허용을 촉구해 왔었는바, 금일 연설시 부쉬대통령이 인질이라는 용어를 사용한 점을 당지 일각에서는 미국이 이락측에 대해 보다 더 강경한 자세를 취할조짐으로 해석하고 있음.

(대사 박동진-국장)

| 미주국 | 1차보 | 미주국 | 중아국 | 통상국 | 정문국 | 안기부 | | |

PAGE 1

번호 : USW(F) - *1877*

수신 : 장   관 (미북,중근동,미안,동아)발신 : 주미대사

제목 : 부시 대통령 연설 (중동사태관련)   (*6* 매)

보안
통제

REMARKS BY PRESIDENT GEORGE BUSH TO THE
CONVENTION OF THE VETERANS OF FOREIGN WARS

BALTIMORE, MARYLAND

MONDAY, AUGUST 20, 1990

.STX

        PRESIDENT BUSH: Thank you all. Thank you very much. Thank
you so much. Please be seated.

        And it's a privilege to join you, and a deep personal pleasure
to renew old ties, greet new friends. And my thanks to all of you,
but especially, Walter, to you, Walter Hogan, doing a great job as
Commander in Chief. And following the likes of Larry Rivers isn't
easy. We all know that. But Walter's done the VFW proud. And I
also know we're looking forward to the same kind of strong
leadership from James Kimmery (ph). And let me offer my thanks
again to another old friend, Cooper Holt (ph), a real legend, who
gave so many years of service to the VFW. (Applause.) Cooper, we
welcome you. (Applause.)

        And next, I want to thank my outstanding Veterans' Secretary, a
fellow VFW member, Ed Derwinski. (Applause.) Ed's got so much
going on, but I'm especially happy to see the work he's doing to
improve these veterans' hospitals. And his department is intent on
serving you, much as you have served America. (Applause.) I'm glad
to see the Secretary of the Army with us today, an old friend of
mine and a friend of yours, Mike Stone.

        And let us remember those who could not be with us. Our
administration will not forget our POWs and MIAs, as well as those
brave
men and women -- (cheers and applause) -- as well as those brave men
and women who gave what Lincoln termed "the last full measure of
devotion." Again, my acknowledgement to Mike Stone (sp) and also to
Baltimore's mayor, who courteously came to greet me, Kurt Schmoke --
glad to see you here, sir. And finally, today's -- also let me
single out today's honorees -- Bud Dudley (sp) and my own United
Nations -- our own United Nations ambassador, Tom Pickering, who is
doing an outstanding job up there in the United Nations for the
United States of America. (Applause.) Both Bud and Tom [are] being
honored appropriately by you tonight.

        Apologies for keeping you waiting. There are some events going
on around the world, and I was on the telephone to a good friend of
the United States, President Ozal of Turkey, and also to another great
friend of the United States, Prime Minister Thatcher of the United
Kingdom. And I must say, I'm proud of the support -- (applause)
-- that we are all getting around the world.

1877 -1

0144

You know, as a veteran I want to salute this organization on its 91st year. By supporting our nation's veterans, the VFW has enriched America, and I'd like to take a moment to ask your support for man whom I'm convinced will also enrich America. I want to work in a strong plug, and I'm talking about our Supreme Court nominee, Judge David Souter. (Cheers and applause.) I see the New Hampshire delegation is here -- (laughter). And -- well, they know something we all know, and that is that he is an exceptional jurist and a brilliant legal mind and he will be a voice of excellence on the nation's highest court, and I call on the Senate to confirm him without delay.

But this morning I'm also grateful to have this special opportunity to discuss an issue of great concern to all Americans, the crisis in the Persian Gulf. A crisis that will require American planning, patience, and yes, personal sacrifice. But a crisis that we must and will meet if we are to stop aggression, help our friends, and protect our own interests in the peace and stability of countries around the globe. (Applause.)

Eighteen days ago these beliefs prompted me to take action in the Middle East, to restore the sovereignty of Kuwait and deter those who threaten friendly countries and the vital interests of America. And I acted knowing that our cause would not be easy, but that our cause is right. And that while one should not underestimate those who endanger peace, an even greater mistake would be to underestimate America's commitment to our friends when our friends are imperiled -- (applause) -- or our commitment to international order when that too, is imperiled.

Today the outcome is not yet decided. Hard choices remain but of this we are certain, America will not be intimidated. And when some ask, "Where does America stand?" Our answer is America stands where it always has, against aggression, against those who would use force to replace the rule of law. (Applause.)

And who better than this group know that throughout history we've learned that we must stand up to evil. It's a truth which the past 18 days have reaffirmed. And its lessons speak to America and to the world.

The first lesson is as vivid as the memories of Normandy, Caisson, Pork Chop Hill. We've been reminded again that aggression must and will be checked. And so, at the request of our friends, we have sent US forces to the Middle East, reluctantly, but decisively, knowing, as Teddy Roosevelt said, that America means many things, among them, equality of rights, and therefore, equality of duty and obligation. And yet we are not acting alone but in concert; hoping to protect our own national security interests, as well as those of the broader community of nations.

1877-2

0145

Which brings me to the second lesson reaffirmed by the past 18 days. By itself, America can do much; together with its friends and allies, America can do much more for peace and for justice. Think back with me to World War II when together allies confronted a horror which embodied hell on Earth. Or Korea, where United Nations forces opposed totalitarianism.

Today, once again, many nations -- many of them Muslim -- have joined to counter aggression, and thus to restore the peace. And our Saudi friends, under the wise leadership of King Fahd, ask for our help in deterring further aggression by Iraq. And I salute the many countries who have courageously responded to Saudi Arabia's request. I also salute those governments who are responding

to the Emir of Kuwait's call for the full enforcement of United Nations sanctions. We must not delude ourselves. Iraq's invasion was more than a military attack on tiny Kuwait, it was a ruthless assault on the very essence of international order and civilized ideals.

And now, in a further offense against all norms of international behavior, Iraq has imposed restrictions on innocent civilians from many countries. This is unacceptable -- (applause) -- and that's why the United Nations Security Council voted unanimously Saturday night to condemn Iraq's action, just as it earlier voted to condemn the invasion itself. They know as we do, that leaders who use citizens as pawns deserve and will receive the scorn and condemnation of the entire world. (Applause.)

And so to the leaders of Iraq I'll now make two points clear: In moving foreign citizens against their will, you are violating the norms of your own religion. You are going against the age-old Arab tradition of showing kindness and hospitality to visitors.

And so my message is: Release all foreigners now. Give them the right to come and go as they wish. Adhere to international law and UN Security Council Resolution 664. (Applause.)

We've been reluctant to use the term "hostage," but when Saddam Husayn specifically offers to trade the freedom of those citizens of many nations he holds against their will in return for concessions, there can be little doubt that whatever these innocent people are called, they are in fact hostages. (Applause.)

And I want there to be no misunderstanding. I will hold the government of Iraq responsible for the safety and well being of American citizens held against their will! (Applause.)

Let me also take a moment to thank President Gorbachev for his recent words condemning the Iraqi invasion. He has shown, if anyone doubted it, that nations which joined to fight aggression in World War II can work together to stop the aggressors of today. (Applause.)

1877 -3

0146

A third lesson has also been reaffirmed by the last 18 days. As veterans it won't surprise you, the steadfast character of the American will. Look to the sands of Saudi Arabia and the waters offshore where brave Americans are doing their duty just as you did at Anzio, and Inchon, and Hamburger Hill. And think of the men and women aboard our planes and ships, young, alone, and so very far from home. They make us humble. They make us proud. And I salute the finest soldiers, sailors, airmen, and marines that any nation could possibly have! (Applause.)

And moreover, I pledge to you we will do whatever it takes to help them compete their mission. (Applause.)

This means realizing the fourth lesson reaffirmed by the past 18 days. Although the size of America's armed forces in the years ahead will be smaller because the threat to our security is changing, future American defense capacity must be even more a lean, mean, fighting machine. And by 1995 we estimate that our security needs can be met by an active force 25 percent smaller than today's, the lowest level since 1950.
And yet we must ensure that a reduction of numbers does not mean a reduction in American strength.

Operation Desert Shield proves vividly that instead of relieving past contingencies, we must prepare for the challenges of the 1990s and beyond.

By ensuring that our troops are ready and trained, we can exert our presence in key areas and respond effectively to crisis, and this is readiness measured in days and hours, not weeks and months, and Operation Desert Shield has underscored the need to be able to get our soldiers where they are needed and when they are needed. This kind of responsiveness will be critical in the crises of the future.

Recently, our outstanding Chairman of the Joint Chiefs, General Colin Powell, spoke to this when he praised the finest peacetime military in the history of America. We will be smaller in troop strength and restructured, but we will remain purposeful, proud, and effective.

Just look at the last 18 days. Desert Shield has been a classic case of America's military at its best. I think, for instance, of Airman 1st Class Wade West (ph), home on leave to be married. On August 7, he was called up, and within an hour, he had the ceremony performed and left for the Middle East. He's now stationed over in Saudi Arabia. You talk about a guy that gets things done. (Laughter.)

But, I would like to emphasize, with his bride -- wherever she may be. (Laughter.)

And another example -- seven years ago, Diana Kroptivich (ph) worried at home while her husband, Walter, steamed off the Lebanon coast on the USS New Jersey defending the marines. Today, their roles are reversed. Retired, Walter is at home with their 5-year-old son, and Diana serves aboard the destroyer USS Yellowstone. (Laughter and applause.)

1899 —4

Here -- here's an Army couple. Today, Paratrooper Joseph Hooter (ph) of the 82nd Airborne Division is serving in Saudi Arabia, and his wife, Nurse Dominique Allen (ph) of the 44th Medical Brigade, will be deployed there within the next two weeks.

And finally, recall the 8 year old who, watching her dad leave for the Mediterranean, spoke truth from the mouths of babes. "I just think," she said, "that they shouldn't let daddies go away this long, but they still have to, to keep the world safe."

These profiles show the true caliber of America and the vital essence of our mission. What's more, they remind us of the fifth and final lesson, reaffirmed by the past 18 days, the need for a continued strong defense budget to support American troops. (Applause.) Or, as George Washington said in his first inaugural address, "To be prepared for war is one of the most effectual means of preserving the peace." History has shown the wisdom of his words, especially in our century. What Desert Shield has shown is that America can ensure the peace by remaining militarily strong.

And now, I know that we're operating in a time of budget restraint. We have limited resources. We must use them wisely. And the budget deficit is a threat to our vital interests at home and won't be made easier by today's threat abroad. Everyone realizes that the deficit is too large and that it's got to be brought down, and the Congress must act courageously and immediately when it returns from recess. (Applause.)

But here's the point. We cannot attack the deficit by attacking the very heart of our armed forces, committed men and women who are motivated and ready. And last week I asked Congress to do what we have done, produce a budget proposal, including defense, that is both responsive and responsible and, most of all, fair. And when they do, I will listen; listen, but not break faith with the troops who are defending our nation. (Applause.) Make no mistake, to prevent aggression, to keep America militarily prepared, I will oppose the defense budget slashers who are out of tune with what America needs to keep freedom secure and safe. (Applause.)

You know, most Americans know that when it comes to national defense, finishing second means finishing last. And so they reject what the House Armed Services Committee recently suggested -- unacceptable cuts from our defense budget for fiscal year 1991. Most Americans know, too, that giving peace a chance does not mean taking a chance on peace, and so they endorse giving the military the tools to do its job -- the peacemaker (sic), the Midget Man, the B-2 and the Strategic Defense Initiative. Americans want arms negotiations to succeed, but they know that even a START treaty will not help our security if we disarm unilaterally.

And let us never forget that our strong national defense policies have helped us gain the peace. We need a strong defense today to maintain that peace. And I will fight for that defense, and I need your help. So help me convince the Congress, given recent events, to take another look into adequately defend -- (correcting himself) -- to fund our defense budget. (Cheers, applause.)

1877-5

0148

Let me tell you a little story about why I feel so strongly.   I
was talking to some of the young soldiers who liberated Panama.   We
invited them to come with General Thurman and others to the Cabinet
Room for a briefing for me.   And I asked one of them, a medic, about
the operation.   Corporal Roderick Ringstaff (ph) spoke of combat,
and he spoke of the heroics of others, but not of his own.   And next
to him was his commanding officer.   And so his commanding officer
filled in the rest.   This medic had been wounded but repeatedly
braved fire to rescue other wounded, pulling soldier after soldier
to safety.   For that he was awarded the Silver Star for bravery.
And listening, I thought to myself,

I will never send young men and women into battle with less than the
very best that this nation can provide them.   (Applause.)   I will
never -- I will never ever let Americans like this down.

August 1990 has witnessed what history will judge one of the
most crucial deployments of allied powers since World War II.   Two
weeks ago, I called for the complete, immediate, and unconditional
withdrawal of all Iraqi forces from Kuwait.   Second, the restoration
of Kuwait's legitimate government.   Third, the security and the
stability of Saudi Arabia and the Persian Gulf.   And fourth, the
safety and protection of American citizens abroad.

And today, I say those objectives are and will remain
unchanged.   (Applause.)   And will it take time?   Of course, for
we're engaged in a cause larger than ourselves.   A cause perhaps
best shown by words many of you remember, words spoken by one of
the greatest Americans of our time to allied soldiers, and sailors,
and airmen: "The eyes of the world are upon you," he told them.
"The hopes and prayers of liberty loving people everywhere march
with you."   And then he concluded with this moving prayer, "Let us
all beseech the blessing of almighty God upon this great and noble
undertaking."

Fellow veterans, more than half of all VFW members fought in
World War II.   Many of you serving under the man who spoke those
words, Dwight David Eisenhower.   And you know how America remains
the hope of liberty loving people everywhere.

Half a century ago, the world had the chance to stop a ruthless
aggressor and missed it.   And I pledge to you, we will not make that
mistake again.   (Applause.)   Together -- for you see, together we
can successfully oppose tyranny and help those nations who look to
us for leadership and vision.

Thank you for your support and your prayers and may God bless
the land we deeply love, the United States of America.   Thank you
all and God bless you.   (Applause.)

END

1877-6

0149

기록물종류	일반공문서철	등록번호	2012090521	등록일자	2012-09-17
분류번호	772	국가코드	US/XF	보존기간	영구
명 칭	걸프사태 : 미국의 대응, 1990-91. 전6권				
생 산 과	북미과/안보과	생산년도	1990~1991	담당그룹	.
권 차 명	V.2 1990.8.22-10월				
내용목차					

0001

외 무 부

종 별 :

번 호 : USW-3863　　　　　　　　　　일 시 : 90 0822 1927

수 신 : 장 관(미북, 중근동,통일,아일)

발 신 : 주 미 대사

제 목 : 중동사태 관련 부쉬 대통령 기자회견

연: USW(F)-1905

금 8.22 부쉬 대통령은 메인주 KENNEBUNKPORT에서 기자회견을 가졌는바, 주요 언급요지 하기 보고함. (기자회견 전문은 FAX 편 연호 송부)

1. OPENING STATEMENT 주요 내용

- 미국의 사우디 파병 과정은 순조롭게 진행되고 있음.

- 금번 사태는 미국과 이락 양자간의 문제가 아니라 이락과 전세계 공동체간의 문제임. (금번 사태해결을 위한 다국간 협력의 중요성을 재삼강조)

- 현재 예비군 동원에 필요한 절차를 밟고 있는바, 행정부의 조치에 대한 의회 지도층의 지지를 고무적으로 생각함.

(USW(F)-1896 으로 보고한바와 같이 부쉬 대통령의 사우디 파병은 여론조사결과 약 77 푸로의 지지를 받고있는 것으로 나타났는바, 금번 중동사태로 인해 국내경제문제등에 대한 미국인의 관심이 상대적으로 저하됨에 따라 이러한 높은 인기도를 얻게된 것으로 봄)

2.질의응답시 주요 언급내용

유엔이 대이락 무력 제재등에 관해 명시적 입장을 표명해준다면, 미국으로서도 도움이 될것임.

- 미국인들이 유류 절약에 힘써줄것을 촉구함.

그러나 충분한 양의 유류공급에는 문제가 없을것임 (GUARANTEE AN ADEQUATE SUPPLY OF PETROLEUM)

- 현재 일본정부가 대이락 경제제재 조치로 인해 불가피하게 타격을 받을수도 있는 몇개 국가를 돕기위해 BIG DIPLOMATIC INITIATIVE 를 취하고 있는 것으로 알고있음.

훗세인 요르단 왕의 이락 재방문관련, 미측이 특별히 전달 요청한 멧세지는 없음.

| 미주국 | 1차보 | 2차보 | 아주국 | 중아국 | 통상국 | 안기부 | 대책반 | 차관 |

- 이락군을 쿠웨이트로부터 축출하기 위한 무력사용 가능성에 대해서는 있다고도, 없다고도 밝힐수 없음.

(대사 박동진-국장)

PAGE 2

0003

PRESIDENT BUSH PRESS CONFERENCE, KENNEBUNKPORT, MAINE
WEDNESDAY, AUGUST 22, 1990

PRESIDENT BUSH: Let me make a brief opening statement, and
then I'll be glad to take any questions.

First, Secretary Cheney and General Powell have just given me a
very full and, I would say, encouraging briefing on the status of
our deployment to the Persian Gulf. This has been a very
complicated mission, calling for precision, calling for maximum
coordination with Saudi Arabia and the other nations providing
forces. The process has gone smoothly, and we've now moved what
amounts to a medium-sized American city, completely capable of
sustaining itself, all the way over to the Middle East.

And the Secretary reports that the men and women in the armed
forces have performed with extraordinary ability. Their morale is
high and they've accepted the challenge of their mission with
extraordinary dedication to duty. And I'm very proud of each and
every single one of them. And I want them to know that the American
people are behind them 100 percent, supporting them strongly.

And it's also crucial that everyone understand we are not in
this alone. We stand shoulder to shoulder right there in the Middle
East with the armed forces of 22 other nations, from the Middle
East, from Europe and around the world.

Secretary Dick Cheney reports an impressive alliance of
multinational forces
that stands behind the United Nations resolve that Iraq completely
and unconditionally withdraw from Kuwait, with the restoration of
the legitimate government in that country. The United Nations has
provided enormous leadership to the whole world community in
pursuing this objective and voting the sanctions necessary to
carrying it out.

And let's be clear, as the deployment of the forces of the many
nations shows, and as the votes in the United Nations show, this is
not a matter between Iraq and the United States of America. It is
between Iraq and the entire world community -- Arab and non-Arab
alike, all the nations of the world lined up that oppose
aggression.

And as our forces continue to arrive they can look forward to
the support of the finest Reserve components in the world. We are
activating those special categories of Reservist's that are essential
to completing our mission. The United States considers its Reserve
forces to be an integral part of the total military command. These
essential personnel will soon be joining the cohesive organization
required to support the military operations in and around the Arabia
Peninsula and I have the highest confidence in their ability to
augment the active forces in this operation. We continue to pursue
our objectives with absolute determination.

1905-1

0004

I might add that I talked to the four leaders of Congress today and I am very pleased that they are giving us the strong support they have been -- Speaker, Senator Mitchell, Senator Dole, Congressman Michel. And the world simply cannot waiver in its opposition to the threat that Iraq has placed on the doorstep of all nations who cherish freedom and the rule of law.

Now what I plan to do is take some questions. And then I know you'll have more questions for Secretary Cheney and General Powell. And then the discussions that we've had with these two gentlemen and with Secretary Eagleburger and General Scowcroft, our Chief of Staff and Bob Gates, will continue for a little while this afternoon before they return to Washington.

But, Dick, I am
very grateful to you for your mission -- successful mission. And both to you and Colin, my sincere thanks for the superb leadership you are giving the United States military, the superb leadership you are showing in working with other countries as we pursue these moral -- high moral objectives.

Q   Mr. President, the Soviets have voted with us in the Security Council for the economic sanctions, but we learned today that they have 193 military advisors still advising the Iraqi army on how to use Soviet-built weapons against the allied forces. Do you call upon them to pull those people out?

PRESIDENT BUSH: Well, I'm -- I think that -- frankly, I'd like to see Iraq do what is civilized and permit foreigners who want to leave leave. But I'm not going to comment on that, because I don't have this information that you're telling me about. Maybe Dick Cheney can comment on it later.

Q   Sir? May I just follow, sir?

PRESIDENT BUSH: Yeah.

Q   You've talked to a least a dozen world leaders right from here in the past week and a half. Have you called Secretary -- President Gorbachev, and will you call President Gorbachev for his help in the crisis?

PRESIDENT BUSH: Secretary Baker talked to -- to Foreign Minister Shevardnadze less than two hours ago, and we are in close touch with the Soviets. At this point, I can say we are getting superb cooperation from the Soviets. There may be some differences. In fact, I think it's fair to say we've been discussing some of them regarding the timing of certain further UN action. But I have no argument with the way in which they have cooperated, and I would expect that Secretary Cheney would agree on that point.

Q   Could I follow on that, sir?

PRESIDENT BUSH: Yes. Yes.

Q   Talking about the UN -- the action that you would hope to have, the US forces fired across the bow of a ship that then was allowed to continue on and is now in Yemen. Why did they not pursue that farther? Do you want to wait until you now have that UN authority?

/905 -2

0005

PRESIDENT BUSH: W███, you know, we feel we ██ all the authority we need, and ██ ██ world leaders I've tal██ to, particularly Francois Mitterrand and Margaret Thatcher, agree that

we have all the authority we need. We have been trying, and I think prudently so, to work with other countries around the world. And the more unanimity we get out of the United Nations, for example, the better.

So we are prepared to intercept shipping, but where I stand now is I'm talking to my top advisors here and have been on the phone to Secretary Baker a couple of times in the last two hours talking about should the United Nations -- should we give the United Nations more time to take more productive action? And it has taken productive action, obviously. The Chapter 7 was a significant step. So I think we've made clear to the shipping

that they can be stopped, and that we have the forces to stop them right now. And I believe that General Powell would back me up on what I've just said.

So my question is, how much more United Nations action is required? And so I'm going to continue the discussion asking for the advice of my officials here. But at this juncture, I'm not prepared to say whether we're going to insist on UN action before we go further. But I think the record -- the signal must go out to the world that many countries are prepared to fully enforce these sanctions, and if there's some UN action that will help, so much the better.

Q   How long will you wait for that UN action?

PRESIDENT BUSH: We haven't made a determination. I think the signal is out there as we pursue certain vessels and clearly have superior -- have the demonstrated ability to board these vessels, that we can do it. So now the question is, how much more UN action is beneficiary -- benefits this idea of the world staying more closely together? And I might be prepared to give a little time -- speaking just for the US, we're only one country there, important one though it may be -- in order to get more collective action. But, on the other hand, I need more advice in terms of the logistics, where these ships are, what the -- what the signal would be if we go ahead and take action to stop them, which we could confidently do.

Yeah?

Q   Mr. President, despite demands from the Iraqis that the US and other countries close their embassies in Kuwait and remove all their diplomatic personnel, the State Department announced today that the US would not do that. Why have you decided to take that course of action, and how can you possibly enforce that?

PRESIDENT BUSH: Because the occupation of Iraq (sic) is illegal under international law, and other countries agree totally that we must not take the position that this illegal regime can shut down legitimate embassies at -- as a result of their aggression, that's why.

Q   But with this -- but with Iraq in military control of Kuwait, how can you possibly hope to enforce that?

1905 -3

0006

PRESIDENT BUSH: ██ell, my view is let's wa██ ██nd see what happens. I don't g██ ██to these hypothetical q██████ons. I'd like to explain this because I know there's a lot of them out there, as to what I might not or might do under certain circumstances. But here -- I think most countries that I'm aware of -- and I'd defer to Secretary Eagleburger -- would agree that they will not go along with the -- with agreeing to this kind of affirmation of Iraq aggression, aggression that has been thoroughly condemned by the United Nations.

Yes?

Q   I'd like to ask, please, about your hostage policy. You were very firm the other day in warning Saddam not to harm the Americans, but I wonder, as Commander in Chief, sir, do you consider the US has been provoked right now?

PRESIDENT BUSH: Consider what?

Q   Has it been provoked? Has the United States been provoked now?

PRESIDENT BUSH: I don't think it's a question of the United States, I think it's a question of the whole world is being provoked by this illegal action, outrageous action.

Q   Do you have a plan for getting --

PRESIDENT BUSH: I don't discuss hypothetical contingencies. But I would reiterate, it is of grave concern to all the countries whose leaders I've talked to.

Q   Mr. President?

PRESIDENT BUSH: Yeah --

Q   Will the United States give safe haven to our citizens in Kuwait and Iraq if -- in the embassies if --

PRESIDENT BUSH: If citizens came to the embassy seeking -- seeking support and help, clearly we would do that.

Yes?

Q   Mr. President, do you have plans --

PRESIDENT BUSH: Let me just work right down the line here, if that's agreeable.

Q   Do you have plans to drawdown the number of Americans in our embassy in Kuwait?

PRESIDENT BUSH: I'd like to defer that question to Secretary Eagleburger when I continue this. There has been talk of it. Indeed, I think we're talking about taking down some personnel, but I'd like to ask him to be a little more definitive.

Yes?

Q   Mr. President, how constrained do you feel by the Americans trapped in Kuwait as you make your decisions?

/905-K

0007

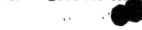

PRESIDENT BUSH: How -- ?

Q   How constrained do you feel as you make your decisions by
the plight of the Americans in Iraq and --

PRESIDENT BUSH: I think any decision-maker in the United
States or in any of these countries is concerned about the lives of
innocent civilians, innocent people.   And so you weigh that very
thoroughly against -- against your actions.   Having said that,
international law, in this case the Chapter 7 sanctions, must be
enforced.

that part of what we're fighting for -- standing for in the desert
is our way of life.   Part of our way of life is heavy usage of
energy, much more so than any other industrialized country.   We
haven't really heard you call upon Americans to conserve as part of
this crisis --

PRESIDENT BUSH: I call upon Americans to conserve.

Q   Do you want to elaborate?

PRESIDENT BUSH: No, I think we ought to conserve in times like
this.   On the other hand, we're doing everything we can to guarantee
that we don't panic Americans and that there will be an adequate
supply of hydrocarbons.   But I think it is a good time to conserve,
so I'm glad you reminded me of that and I would call upon Americans
to conserve.   And I think that doesn't mean that life screeches to a
halt, and therefore I would say that.   But I also think that we're
going to be able to guarantee an adequate supply of petroleum.

Yes?

Q   Why is --

Q   Mr. President, how many Reserves are going to be called
up as a first step?

PRESIDENT BUSH: I will defer that question to -- to Secretary
Cheney.

Q   Mr. President, do you sense any frustration or even
desperation in the recent statements we've been hearing out of
Iraq?

PRESIDENT BUSH: I certainly sense a sense of isolation.   I
sense -- I think the urgency in these statements and the high --
high immoderate tone is due to worldwide isolation.
And I think that's very clear and I think he's trying to whip up
support and make this Iraq versus the United States.   Indeed, it is
Iraq versus the rest of the world.   And I talked to leader after
leader after leader; talked at length to Helmut Kohl today, and he's
been making just that point and will continue to make that point.
But yes, I think there is some of that feeling, that as they become
isolated from their Arab brothers -- and they are -- and as they
become isolated from traditional trading partners -- and they are --
there is a sense of -- of irrational urgency there.

Q   How seriously do you take his public threats?

1905-5

0008

PRESIDENT BUSH: The United States won't be threatened.

Q   Mr. President, the other day you called on Americans for personal sacrifice, but you didn't really elaborate. Were you talking about economic deprivation or were you --

PRESIDENT BUSH: No, I was not particularly talking about economic deprivation. I'm think of families whose plans have been severely altered by this. I'm thinking of -- of more of that kind of thing when I made the statement.

Q   What --

Q   Are you preparing -- are you preparing Americans for the possibility of war and American deaths?

PRESIDENT BUSH: I think any time you move American forces and any time you are up against what most of the world now considers to be an outrageous violator of international law, that the best thing is to be prepared.

Yes, Charles?

Q   Mr. President, King Hussein today in **Jordan** suggested that perhaps you moved too precipitously, in his words, that if there had not been this buildup that we might not be in the situation we're in and that Saddam Husayn might have withdrawn. Was there ever any signals, anything that suggested that that might have been in the case?

PRESIDENT BUSH: No. And the King, regrettably, did not have much support in the Arab world for that position. You recall the vote at the Arab -- Arab summit. He certainly had no support for that position in the United Nations and as the United Nations moved toward Chapter 7.

And I would simply remind people who hear that allegation that it isn't just the United States, it's the rest of the world. But when we are invited by a friend to help defend it against aggression that has recently taken place and that threatens to take place again, we're going to respond, and that's a good signal to send to friends around the world.

And I might say, the request for support was not taken without reason. The Saudis were very much concerned -- and let me just recite the history for the American people here. He had said -- Saddam Husayn had said -- "We're withdrawing." I believe it was on a Sunday. And they had a picture of one truck, people frantically waving goodbye to the beloved brothers in Kuwait as they went north. And at the same time, there was truckload after truckload of armor and mechanized equipment moving south.

Now, we're not dumb when we see that, nor are the Saudis, nor are the other countries that are rejoicing, as Dick Cheney will tell you, in the fact that we moved. But I think it's important to keep reminding people of why the Saudis felt threatened and probably today still feel threatened.

Q   If I could follow up, sir --

1905-6

0009

PRESIDENT BUSH: Let Charles follow up. I'll be right over, Ann.

Q   --- with another sense of the enormity of this buildup... The reports have come during the Secretary's visit that the Saudis wanted --- preparing to send them the most advanced fighter, the F-15Es. Is that, in fact, the case? And isn't there a political problem with that?

PRESIDENT BUSH: I will let Secretary Cheney address it --- himself to it. But, the Saudis have been threatened. A neighboring country has been aggressed against --- international law has condemned it. We should do all we can to help the Saudis arm themselves against aggression. And so, he can talk about 15Es or some other weapon system. I want to do everything I can, and I hope there would be no political problem because the world clearly sees that the --- the Saudis have been strongly threatened, Charles.

Yeah?

Q   Prince Bandar is on his way into Moscow. King Hussein says he's going back to Baghdad. Is there a new stage of diplomacy that's beginning now?

PRESIDENT BUSH: There's a lot of activity, Ann, going on --- a lot of diplomatic activity. I am continuing to conduct a good deal of it; Secretary Baker is. I mentioned his recent call with Shevardnadze. Other countries are reaching out to friends, trying to be sure that we're all --- that we all stay together in this.

And indeed, the Japanese, I might say, have a very big diplomatic initiative going now, and I must say once again that I think Prime Minister Kaifu's willingness to help some of these countries that might be victimized by a full enactment of the sanctions is very good. The Turks, as I've told you, have been heavily involved. I talked to the --- Mr. Mitsotakis in Greece today --- who've (sic) been cooperative. So, there's an awful lot of diplomatic activity behind the scenes.

Q   And does it help to have King Hussein going back to Baghdad?

PRESIDENT BUSH: I have no feelings about that. I --- I'd --- I have no --- no, there was no message or anything of that nature. As you remember there was a lot of speculation that the King was coming here bearing a message. And I can tell you unequivocally there was no request on my part for a message to go back --- other than one: Our determination to stay joined up with others to see that this aggression is reversed and that the rightful rulers of Kuwait are returned.

Yeah, Jim?

Q   Mr. President you mentioned concern for the families here in the United States a few minutes ago. Traditionally, those families have been able to rely on open press coverage of young men and women who were sent into the breech, such as they've been now. Despite their earlier hospitality, the Saudis are now restricting press coverage and are saying that they will probably order foreign

1905-7

0010

press out of the country perhaps by the end of this week.   Is there anything you can do to ensure that Americans will have free, complete and open press coverage of their young men and women abroad?

PRESIDENT BUSH: We are -- we are the guests of Saudi Arabia in their country.   I think Dick can address himself to that question because it has been discussed.   And the more coverage the better as far as we're concerned.   However, when people travel to countries like Iraq and countries of that nature, I hope the press --- the press coverage will be totally objective, just as it is right here in this marvelous setting.

Q   Well, are you saying then that we're at the total mercy of Saudi Arabia, that there's nothing we can do to --

PRESIDENT BUSH: No, I'm not saying that.   I'm saying I'll let the Secretary address himself to this question.

Q   Has the --

Q   Mr. President --

PRESIDENT BUSH: But I'm saying I hope the same -- tough questions are asked in every country as they are in this country, and I'm speaking of Iraq, particularly.

Yes?

Q   Is that a criticism of the press coverage?

PRESIDENT BUSH: No, that's no criticism, Jim.   I've learned long ago that you've got the loudest mike and I just am standing here.   So I'm not criticizing.   Don't be so sensitive about it. (Laughter.)   American people know what the American people see, and so all I'm simply saying is don't be sensitive, it's not a criticism, it is an objective statement.

Yeah?

Q   Mr. President, why is Iraq still being allowed to receive supplies through Jordan?

PRESIDENT BUSH: I'm not sure they are and I hope they're not. And very little is going into the Gulf of Aqaba these days. (Aside) Don't be sensitive.   (Returning)   And so it is a question though, that if it -- if it is going in it clearly violates not only the sanctions but what King Hussein told me.

Q   Is it your understanding that it's been stopped?   I mean, many of our colleagues at the border say --

PRESIDENT BUSH: Yeah, there is a difference of view on it and I'm not sure I know the total facts on that, because we were discussing it a few minutes ago.

STAFF: A final question, please.

PRESIDENT BUSH: Yeah, Michael?

rPo5-8

0011

Q   When you said -- when you made the announcement that you were sending US troops to Saudi Arabia, you said their mission was not to kick the Iraqis out of Kuwait. Do you still rule out the use of US military force to kick --

PRESIDENT BUSH: I don't rule in or rule out the use of military force. And I learned long ago not to tie oneself down by stating what I will or will not do in that regard.

Q   Mr. President --

PRESIDENT BUSH: These two last and then I'll go peacefully -- (inaudible).   One and Two.

Q   Mr. President, we asked you last week if you saw any hope of a diplomatic solution. You said, "I don't see it right now." Do these statements from Baghdad that they are willing to put their cards on the table increase the hopes there will be a diplomatic solution?

PRESIDENT BUSH: If they're willing to put all their cards on the table, that's good. I didn't hear that, but if they're willing to put them all out there, including complying with international law, that would be good. And in terms of readiness to talk, we've got a very able person there in Baghdad who is prepared to talk. And they came in the other day and said they'd like to talk -- well there he is, available to talk.

But please don't tell us that they're going to talk with conditions that are unacceptable under international law because that is not -- that's not the way it would work. And the world community has made a strong statement, a very strong statement, and I don't sense any view in the world community that it's going to back
away from that statement. And that statement included removal of Iraqi forces from Kuwait and the restoration of the rulers.

Yeah, Charles, last one.

Q   Mr. President, somebody's got to ask the tough question. You talked about conservation. Does that include Fidelity?

PRESIDENT BUSH: I'm going to keep using my boat, and I hope the rest of America will prudently recreate. I don't think we've reached the point where I want to call on everybody in the recreation industry to shut it down or everybody that's taking a vacation in American to shut it down.

So, it's not a tough question. It's a very fair question. And I would simply say that there's a lot of industry, a lot of people that have been looking forward to vacations in this country, and I would not suggest that the situation at home requires they stay at home now, or that they don't use their recreational facilities.

Yeah?

Q   In what condition are those --

Q   So we're not in any energy --

/805-9   0012

PRESIDENT BUSH: Not now we are not.

    Q   In what condition are those 54 missing Americans, have you been told? And is the number still 54?

    PRESIDENT BUSH: I can't answer the question about the condition, and I -- maybe Larry can expand on this later on. He says we don't know.

    Thank you all very much. And now I will turn it over, again with a vote of thanks to Dick Cheney and to Colin, who are doing a superb job, and to both of whom the American people owe a strong vote of thanks, and people around the world, too.

    All yours.

                          END

19.5-10

0013

외 무 부

종 별 :

번 호 : USW-3864   일 시 : 90 0822 1927

수 신 : 장 관 (미북, 중근동)

발 신 : 주 미 대사

제 목 : 중동사태 관련 미 국방장관및 합참의장 기자회견

연: USW(F)-1904

금 8.22. CHENEY 미국방장관 및 POWELL 합참의장은 부쉬 대통령 기자회견에 이어 기자들과 질의, 응답을 가졌는바, 주요 언급 요지 하기 보고함.(질의응답 전문은 연호 FAX 편 송부)

1. 금번 사태 관련 예비군 동원 규모를 언론에서는 4만명으로 추측하고 있으나 현재로서 확정된바 없으며 법정 최대 동원가능 인원인 20만명보다는 훨씬 못미치는 수준이 될것임.

2. 현재 미군이 보유하고 있는 F-15 중 일부를 사우디측에 대해 추가로 판매할 계획임.

3. 사우디 파병 미군에 대한 작전지휘권은 미측이 보유하나, 작전수행 지침등에 대해서는 사우디측과 긴밀히 협의할것임.

4. 현재 사우디-쿠웨이트 국경 북부지역에 16만 여명의 이락군 및 다수의 탱크 야포등이 집결되어 있는바 CAPABILITY 의 차원에서 여사한 이락군이 공격 수행능력을 보유하고 있는것은 틀림없으나 DEPLOYMENT 의 차원에서 이들이 공격태세를 갖추고 있는지의 여부는 불분명함.

5. 사우디파병 미군의 성격은 방어적임.

(대사 박동진-국장)

미주국	차관	1차보	2차보	중아국	정문국	안기부	국방부	대책반

PAGE 1   90.08.23   09:23 WG

외신 1과 통제관

0014

전보 : USW(F)- *1904*
수신 : 장 관 (미봉,즉) ████   발신 : 주미대사 ████   보안 용제   P.001   02

제목 : 중동사태관련미 국방장관및 합참의장 기자회견 (6 매)

PRESS BRIEFING BY SECRETARY OF DEFENSE DICK CHENEY AND GENERAL COLIN POWELL, CHAIRMAN OF THE JOINT CHIEFS, WEDNESDAY, AUGUST 22, 1990

SEC. CHENEY: We'd be happy to entertain a question or two.

Q   Would you answer the F-15E question? What are the Saudis going to get?

SEC. CHENEY: The -- the instructions of the President -- I've been asked to sort of do three things, defense. One is to deploy forces to deter aggression; secondly, be prepared to defend if deterrence should fail; and third is to look at how we can best enhance the indigenous defense capabilities of the forces in the region so that they can do more in the future for themselves. Part of that is to see that we deal with their emergency requirements given the crisis they are now faced with and the large number of Iraqi forces on their border.

There has been a report that we plan to provide F-15E aircraft. For the uninitiated, that's the latest model of the F-15. It's -- basically, it's got both air-to-air and air-to-ground capability, long-range. We have not yet completed the buy for our own forces on the F-15E. So, what's currently coming off the line will come to US forces. What we have talked with the Saudis about is really a two-stage process. Stage one would be meeting their emergency requirements. Stage two would be a more comprehensive plan that dealt with the long term.

In terms of emergency requirements, we are looking at transferring to the Saudis from our own forces, our own inventory, a number of existing F-15s. They would not be the E model; they would be the C or D model, basically designed for air-to-air combat, although they have some ground attack capability as well.

The report that we're going to provide F-15Es immediately simply isn't valid. That's the kind of thing we'd work in the longer-term package.

Q   Secretary Cheney, we were told that --

Q   Secretary Cheney --

SEC. CHENEY: Charles?

Q   Do they even need them? And don't you run into a problem with the Israelis if you give them to them?

SEC. CHENEY: Well, I think first of all that the situation in the Middle East and in the Gulf region has changed dramatically, and the argument over the years has been that we wanted to help our friends in the region, including the Saudis, satisfy their legitimate security requirements. I would argue that a

1904-1

0015

million-man Iraqi army, 160,[000] to 200,000 Iraqi soldiers, 1,000 Iraqi tanks poised ●● the northern border of S●● Arabia is a legitimate security need, and that in light of that, it is appropriate for us to work with the Saudis within the confines of existing authority that the President has to see to it that we help meet their most urgent requirements, and then we will also work long term. But I don't think this is a situation that presents any threat whatsoever to Israel, and I would not expect there to be any opposition in that quarter to our efforts to help the Saudis and our other friends in the region deal with what is a threat to their very existence.

Q   Secretary Cheney, the order the President signed on the Reserves was open-ended. It vests you with the authority to call them up. We're told that there will be 40,000 called up by the end of August. Is that correct? And how many more will there be after that?

SEC. CHENEY: Well, the services are looking at and working right now preparing their proposals. I have, working with the chairmen, asked them to scrub those proposals, and they'll be presented to me in detail tomorrow at a briefing scheduled at the Pentagon on a service-by-service basis by the service chiefs and the service secretaries. I expect that we will not use the full 200,000 authority that's in the statute, that the President's authorized to call up. It will be considerably short of that. But it is important for us to move forward because many of these key requirements in special areas have for years been built into the Reserves. We've always assumed the Reserves would perform those missions, and we need to have those missions performed now in light of the deployment to the Middle East.

Q   So is 40,000 the right ballpark figure?

SEC. CHENEY: I wouldn't want to put a figure on it at this point because I haven't reviewed the plans in detail. I would expect that the number will obviously increase the longer period of time goes by. But again, I think the ultimate call-up will be significantly below the 200,000 that's there. And as soon as we have got some specific plans approved and we know which units are involved and we know how many people will be asked to come back for service, we'll be happy to make that public. It's just that we have not yet finalized the plans, and I am reluctant to speculate on what the exact number is until I personally review and approve those plans.

Q   Mr. Secretary, on the F-15Cs and Ds, you said "transfer." Do you mean that we're going to give those jets to the Saudis?

SEC. CHENEY: The Saudis would pay for them. But the point is, we'd take them out of existing inventories, not future procurement.

Q   But they will remain in Saudi Arabia once this operation is --

SEC. CHENEY: That's correct.

Q   Okay, and on the press question, the President asked me to defer this question to you --

1904-2

0016

SEC. CHENEY: I noticed that., (Light laughter.)

Q   Yeah. Will the American people be able to rely on free, open and complete press coverage of their American men and women deployed overseas or are we going to be restricted?

SEC. CHENEY: Well, I suppose you get into a debate here over definition of terms. And what you mean by "free and unrestricted" might be different than what the Saudis think of as free and unrestricted.

The fact of the matter is, we are in their country at their request. They've asked us to come help defend their nation, as have many other countries. They are a very traditional society. They've got certain standards and norms, certain ways of doing business; they're very private in their personal lives and I think we have to respect their culture just as they respect ours.

By the same token, I think it is important that we have an adequate flow of information to the American people about what our young men and women are doing in Saudi Arabia and I'm hopeful that we'll be able to arrange that. I do not have the final authority over what kind of access the government of Saudi Arabia grants to our press.

We have, to date, I think been able, working under difficult circumstances, to provide pretty good coverage. I think the pool system at the Pentagon worked to initiate that process. I know, having been there the last few days myself, that there are a lot of stories being filed out of Saudi Arabia.

I think we'll work with the government of Saudi Arabia to provide as much access as we can. In the final analysis, they'll make the decision, but obviously, we will be advocates for the concept that there should be significant coverage of US forces in Saudi Arabia available to the American people.

Q   As you can understand, the American people look at the Saudis asked us to come over there and help -- and have the US help protect them and we're expending our blood, sweat and tears, that the American people would think that we should have open access to what is going on.

SEC. CHENEY: I'm -- there may be a little bit of a difference, Jim, between what the American people think qualifies as open access and what the press thinks qualifies as open access. I don't want to get into that kind of a debate. But the fact is that -- I'll come

back again to the proposition, we think that a good, steady flow of information about US forces' operations over there is an important part of the existing arrangement.

We also think that we have to recognize and honor the requests and the desires of the Saudi government. And we'll do the best we can. This affects not only the press. I mean, there are other areas where our presence there forces, if you will, debate over different ways our two societies do business. Women play a very prominent role in our society, they play a very prominent role in our military; in Saudi society, a very different role. And having the two societies come together raises questions that have to be addressed, and we've done that successfully in a number of areas and I'm confident we can do it with respect to the press as well.

/9au-2

0017

Q   Mr. Secretary on that same -- on that ● thing, who will be in ultimate control or command of the American forces over there? Would that also be the Saudis?

. SEC. CHENEY: No. The way the process works is that under our constitutional principles, the chain of command runs from the President to myself, to General Powell, to General Schwarzkopf, who's our CINC in the area, and that constitutional principle is honored in our current arrangements. It's also true, though, that we work very closely with the Saudis and that we coordinate very closely with them in terms of overall strategic guidance. We have parallel arrangements worked out between our forces and Saudi forces, that our people on the ground have arrived at, and it seems to be working very smoothly. And this is not unusual. We do this in nations all over the world.

Q   On that point, the President said there are armed forces from 22 countries involved in this operation. Has the issue been resolved in terms of command of this multinational force, particularly if combat were to occur?

SEC. CHENEY: I don't really have anything to add to what I've already offered. That is to say that the Saudis, obviously, are the host for the operation. They've asked the rest of us to participate and I'm confident that we will have adequate command arrangements to deal with --

Q   Will there be a --

SEC. CHENEY: -- whatever situation might arise.

Q   -- unified command at some point, or are we going to have to waste a lot of time with units negotiating back and forth over who moves where?

SEC. CHENEY: We've not wasted a lot of time now. We've moved very rapidly and very aggressively, and I'm satisfied with the current arrangements that we can do whatever we're called upon to do.

Q   General Powell, can you tell us anything about reports that there's a large buildup of missiles, SCUD missiles and the like, along the -- along the border of Saudi Arabia?

GEN. POWELL: I've seen those reports but I can't verify them or confirm that those large buildups are taking place.

Q   But we have, I would suspect, adequate intelligence to tell us that.

GEN. POWELL: I have adequate intelligence and I think we have an extremely good picture of what the situation looks like on the ground north of the Kuwaiti/Saudi border, and, without telling you how good that picture is, let me just say that I cannot confirm the reports you refer to.

Q   General, the President said we've sent a medium-sized American city over there. The Pentagon talked about forces the size of Jefferson City. Without looking at our atlases, how many people do we have over there now?

1904-4

0018

GEN. POWELL: About ██ he size of a medium-size ██ erican city.
(Laughter.)

Q   (Inaudible).

GEN. POWELL: I'm not going to give the exact number of troops
who are in-country, I think I will just rest on what we have been
saying, that it's an adequate force that's being moved over there to
accomplish the mission given to us by the President, and it has been
a very impressive performance on the part of all the branches of the
armed services for them to have delivered this force some 8,000
miles to the Saudi desert over a period of two weeks.

Q   Are no longer undermanned by the 160,000 or so Iraqis in
Kuwait?

GEN. POWELL: I'm not trying to match them man-for-man.

Q   Are you satisfied then that the current force is
sufficient to handle any contingency?

GEN. POWELL: "Any contingency" is a very broad statement, Jim,
not -- let me just say that the mission given to us was to deter
initially and then be prepared to defend. And with each passing day
I am more and more confident of our ability to accomplish that
mission.

Q   General, how would you characterize --
Q   Are the naval ships that are shadowing some of the
tankers and freighters in the area under orders now to just shadow
and no longer fire across the bow --

GEN. POWELL: They're performing the mission given to them by
the President, which was to perform those monitoring functions you
described, and we're just -- we're tracking.

Q   General, how would you characterize the Iraqi deployment
now? Offensive? Defensive?

GEN. POWELL: It's ambiguous, frankly. As the Secretary
pointed out, there are 160,000 or more Iraqi soldiers north of the
Saudi-Kuwait border. There is a large number of tanks, there are
artillery formations there, there is some buildup. And when you see
that kind of a force you have to give it the capability of either
defending or attacking.

And so, I'm not prepared to say which one they're going to do.
I always assume the worst in our planning, but I really can't
ascribe an intent to Mr. Saddam Husayn. But it is a very capable
force that does have the capability to go on the offense.

Q   General, logistically, when you call up the Reserves --

Q   Presumably ours have the same dual capability?

GEN. POWELL: Excuse me?

Q   Logistically, what happens now when you (call up ?) the
Reserves?

190X-5

GEN. POWELL: After the service Secretaries and service Chiefs
brief the Secretary of Defense tommorrow morning and get approval of
their plans, then the call-ups will begin. Selected units will be
called up as they are needed and when they are needed. So you
will not see a sudden rush, but individual units will be called up
and told at what time to report to their mobilization station and
whether or not they are going overseas or whether they'll be used
just to backfill for units who have left the United States.

STAFF: Thank you very much.

Q   Thank you.

GEN. POWELL: Thank you.

Q   (What about your mission that was clearly offensive
now?)? You've put significant offensive capabilities on the ground
there and I wonder if you could explain that.

GEN. POWELL(?): Our mission there is to defend.

                              END

0020

관리
번호 PO-1814

외 무 부

종 별 :

번 호 : USW-3877   일 시 : 90 0823 1948

수 신 : 장관(미북,중근동,연기)

발 신 : 주 미 대사

제 목 : 미국의 대이락 정책

당관 김영복 서기관은 국무부 정책기획실 RICHARD HARRMAN 중동담당관을 접촉, 최근 이락사태와 관련한 미측 실무의견을 청취하였는바, 요지 참고로 다음 보고함.

1. 미소 협의

- 현재 소련측은 유엔 안보리에서의 실효적 봉쇄(최소의 무력사용)결의안 통과를 주저하여왔는바, 소측은 동결의안 통과 자체에는 반대치 않으나, 시기적으로 너무 빠르다는 입장을 미측에 표시해 왔음.

- SHEVARDNAZE 외상이 8.22. BAKER 국무장관에게 전화, 여사한 입장을 표시하고 유엔 안보리 결의안 통과를 며칠간 지연시킬것을 요청한것이 사실임.

- 미측은, 소련측 입장을 이해하나, 국제사회가 HUSSEIN 에게 필요시 무력을 사용해서라도 봉쇄가 시행될 것이라는 점을 이시점에서 분명히 하는것이 중요하다는 점을 강조했음.

-소측이 여사한 주저를 보이는것에는 물론 소련측의 전략적 이해(이락과의 관계 완전 손상방지, 아랍의 민족주의에 대한 소련의 지지 표시등)가 개재되어 있는것이 사실이나, 소측은 여사한 전략적 이해 보다는 소련국민들의 안전한 소개등 보다 전술적 고려때문에 여사한 지연을 희망하는것으로 관찰되고 있음.(소련도 현재의 국제질서 유지에 이해를 갖고 있음.)

-미측은 소련측이 이락측의 침략행위가 POST-COLD WAR 시대에 있어 매우 부정적인 선례가 된다는점을 충분히 이해하고 있는것으로 평가하고 있음.

2. 미국의 향후 정책 대안

- 미국으로서는 향후 사태 진전과 관련 몇가지 대안을 마련해 놓고 있는것은 사실이나, 최소한 당장 목표물 공습등 이락에 대한 직접적 군사행동을 계획하고 있다고 생각치 않음.(HARRMAN 담당관은 자신의 레벨에서는 알수 없는 일이라고하면서,

미주국 대책반	장관	차관	1차보	2차보	중아국	외연원	정와대	안기부

PAGE 1

OPTION 은 OPEN 되어 있다고 사견을 표시)

- 현재 미언론, 학계등에서 미-이락 대치가 장기화되면 미국으로서 불리하며 특히 BUSH 대통령의 입지가 약화될 것이라는 분석과, 최근 이락측의 미, 영국인들의 사실상 인질화, 쿠웨이트내 대사관에 대한 강제 집행등과 관련, 미국과 이락이 전쟁상태로 가고 있다는 시각(KISSINGER 등)에 기본 적으로 동의함.

- 이락군과 다국적군 사이에 군사행동이 본격화될경우, 이락은 미국뿐아니라, 요르단, 이스라엘등을 TARGET 으로 삼을수 있으며, 군사전술상의 가상적상황은 매우 복잡함. 다만, 미국의 사우디 파병은 어디까지나 HUSSEIN 의 쿠웨이트 철군을 유도하기 위한것이지, 직접적 군사 대결을 위한것은 아님.(예비군동원등 주사우디 병력증강은 공격목적이기보다는 이락에 대한 심리적 압박과 미군의 안전 확보의 목임)

- 현재의 교착상태를 타개하고 보다 장기적인 안정과 평화를 보장하기 위해서는 보다 포괄적인 평화안이 필요하다는 의견 (CARTER, BREZEZINSKI)의 당위성은 인정하나, 현재 미국으로서는 여사한 방안을 바로 이니시에이트 할수 없는 입장임.

(동 PROCESS 를 제안할경우, 이는 HUSSEIN 의 주장을 인정하는 결과가 될뿐더러, 미국은 상금 이스라엘로하여금 점령지 철수, 포괄 평화안 수락등을 유도할만한 정치적 의지가 있다고는 생각치 않음.)

- 만일 소련이 금번 사태 해결을 위해 기존의 중동평화에 관한 국제회의 제안을 들고 나올 가능성과 관련, 미국으로서는 이락군의 쿠웨이트 철수, 쿠웨이트정부 회복을 위한 소련의 협조가 선행되어야, 동 지역에서의 소련의 역할을 긍정적으로 고려할수 있다는 입장을 갖고 있음.

- 미국으로서는 우선 이집트-시리아와의 관계개선, 미국-시리아 관계 증진과 이를 바탕으로한 이스라엘-시리아간 새로운 관계 모색등 가능한 목표를 착실히 추진해 나가는것이 바람직하다고 생각함.

(현재 특정 채널을 통한 미-이란간의 상호 조치 통보외에, 미,이란관계 개선을 위한 특별한 움직임은 없는 것으로 암)

3. 향후 전망

- 미국으로서는 BUSH 대통령의 조치에 대한 국내적 지지 확보 뿐아니라, 대이락 제재에 대한 국제적 단결 유지에 계속 중점을 두어 나갈것임.

- 사태의 중장기화의 경우, 비용문제가 예산문제와관련 최대의 국내적 관심사가 될전망인바, 경제적 사정이 좋은 동맹국들에 대한 분담요구가 더욱 커질것으로

PAGE 2

0022

예상됨.

   - 현재로서는 금번사태가 전반적인 국제관계에 갖는 영향을 판단하기는 아직
시기상조라고 생각함.

    (대사 박동진-국장)

    예고:90.12.31 일반.

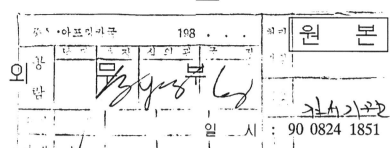

종 별 : 긴 급

번 호 : USW-3893

수 신 : 장 관 (중근동,미북)

발 신 : 주 미 대사

제 목 : 중동사태에 대한 미정부 브리핑

일 시 : 90 0824 1851

연: USW (F)-1939(1), 1940(2)

1. 금 8.24. 실시된 백악관 및 국무부 정례브리핑시 언급된 중동사태관련 사항을 아래 보고함.

0 미국은 주쿠웨이트 대사관을 철수하지 않을 방침이며 쿠웨이트 및 이락내 외국인의 자유로운 출국을 허용할 것을 이락정부에 재촉구했음.

0 주쿠웨이트 미국대사관 인원감축 계획에 따라 쿠웨이트를 떠나 이락에 체재중인 미국 외교관 및 가족 약 100명에 대해 이락정부는 출국불허조치를 내렸음. 동조치는 현재 쿠웨이트내에 공관을 계속유지하고 있는 모든 나라의 외교관들에 대한 출국을금지하는 것으로 알려졌으나, 실제 미국이외의 여타국가 외교관에도 적용되는지 여부는 상금 확인되지 않고 있음.

0 주쿠웨이트 대사관에 비치되었던 미해병 SECURITY GUARD 는 전원 철수했으며,현재 이락군이 주쿠웨이트 대사관 주위를 포위, 대사관 출입을 통제하고 있음.

0 BAKER 장관은 세바르나제 소련 외무장관과 무력사용에 관한 유엔결의안 통과문제등에 관해 계속 전화 협의중이며, 서독, 이집트, 사우디, 이태리 외상들과도 접촉했음. 한편 MULRONEY 카나다 수상이 중동사태 논의차 8.27 KENNEBUNK PORT로 부쉬대통령을 방문할 예정임.

2. 동 브리핑 내용 연호 FAX 송부함.

(대사 박동진-국장)

중아국   1차보   미주국   정문국   안기부   1차보 통상국 미책반 차관 장관

PAGE 1

90.08.25   08:18 FC

외신 1과 통제관

0024

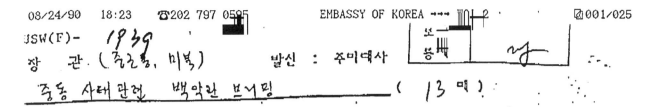

THE WHITE HOUSE REGULAR BRIEFING, KENNEBUNKPORT, MAINE
BRIEFER: MARLIN FITZWATER/ FRIDAY, AUGUST 24, 1990

MR. FITZWATER: The Iraqi government has reneged on its
explicit commitment first made on 9 August, and reiterated just
yesterday, to allow American diplomats and their families in Kuwait
and Iraq to depart. Iraqi authorities have denied permission to
leave the country for a convoy of over 100 American men, women and
children that had departed our Kuwaiti embassy yesterday on their
way to Turkey. These Americans are now in our embassy in Baghdad.
They are safe and they're being handled there by our embassy staff.

As was announced on August 22, the United States will maintain
its embassy in Kuwait with a small staff headed by Ambassador
Nathaniel Howell to look after the interests of the American
community there, and as a symbol of our rejection of Iraq's illegal
occupation and annexation of Kuwait. We call upon Iraq to observe
international agreements protecting the activities and persons of
diplomatic establishments in Kuwait.

The United States once again calls upon Iraq to comply with UN
Security Council Resolution 664 and its demand that Iraq permit and
facilitate the immediate departure from Iraq and Kuwait of the
nationals of foreign countries and grant immediate and continuing
access of consular officials to such nations. The United States
also reminds Iraq that it will be held responsible for the safety
and well-being of American citizens being held hostage.

That's the conclusion of my statement on that subject, if you
want to take some questions.

Ann?

Q   Marlin, what's the condition around the embassy in Kuwait
right now? Do you keep an open telephone line from Ambassador
Howell, and does he (say he has ?) instructions on what to do should
the Iraqi soldiers come and ask him to leave the building?

MR. FITZWATER: We have communications with Ambassador Howell
and with his staff. They are trying to perform consular duties as
best they can in terms of staying in touch with Americans that are
in Kuwait and helping to facilitate their departure wherever that
might be possible.

The military situation is that Iraqi forces of one kind or
another are around the embassy. They have not made any moves
against the embassy or intruded in any fashion, but they are
nevertheless present. It would appear that people are not being
allowed to enter or leave the embassy, but that's as precise as our
description is on the outside at this point.

Michael?

Q   What is your understanding of this deadline? We've had
several different times given. And what have the Iraqis told us
will happen at that deadline?

1539 ⌐   0025

MR. FITZWATER: Well, the -- I don't know that there's any specific time. This, of course, has happened today. The situation is pretty much the same regardless of the hour, so we continue to watch it, to implore Iraq to live up to the international plea from all the countries which have citizens in Kuwait and in Iraq and who have embassies operating there. And the fact is that the United Nations has concluded that the annexation of Kuwait is in violation of international law and those embassies should be allowed to continue to operate.

David?

Q Marlin, any indication that the Iraqis have moved to cut off water or electricity or anything of that sort to the embassy?

MR. FITZWATER: It's my understanding that the embassy still has electricity and water and those facilities.

Q Marlin, the US Embassy's not the only one affected. Are there any consultations under way with US allies or the UN on the current situation or a possible response?

MR. FITZWATER: We are in consultation with the other countries that have citizens in Kuwait. As we reported yesterday, most other nations have indicated that they are keeping their embassy open and they are pursuing a course very similar to ours. All of the countries of the world want to be able to help facilitate their citizens as much as possible. The degree of drawdown is different with each country, but we are in consultation with all of them concerning the best course.

Q Any idea -- any prospect for some kind of unified response at this point?

MR. FITZWATER: Well, the unified response at this point is through the United Nations and through our conversations with Iraq and our joint and unified appeal to them to abide by UN sanctions. Charles?

Q It's my understanding that there have been some Iraqi troops at the embassy for some time. Is this now an enhanced force? Can you describe it in any sense of how big it is?

MR. FITZWATER: Well, there have been Iraqi forces in the area of course virtually since the country was invaded. And the reports differ on the size of that force and exactly what their location is. But I think it's fair to say that there are more Iraqi forces there today than there have been in the past. There does appear to be a pattern of focus on the embassy that would suggest that as their purpose. But I can't be more specific than that.

Q Well, they have not actually (halted ?) anyone. They have not pulled anyone out. There have been no confrontations --

MR. FITZWATER: I don't believe there's been any direct contact, although it is our conclusion that they are not allowing people to enter or to leave.

Q And how do you come to that conclusion, Marlin?

MR. FITZWATER: Wyatt, go ahead.

/849 - 7

0026

Q   The -- I missed whether or not you are contact with Ambassador Howell.

MR. FITZWATER: We are in contact with the Ambassador, yes.

Q   Can we switch up to Baghdad a second? Can you be -- give us more details about how the Americans were stopped? And does -- and was the barring of these Americans from leaving, the diplomats from leaving, Iraq explicit? I mean, how explicit was it from the Iraqi government that they could not leave?

MR. FITZWATER: Well, these diplomats and dependents from our embassy in Kuwait went by car convoy to Baghdad, where they went to the US Embassy and they are now located. So they were not stopped or detained in that sense; that they have reached the embassy. On the other hand, they have not allowed -- been allowed to depart on for Turkey or to leave Iraq; that is, by notification to our officials there that their credentials and so forth would not be processed in a way that would allow them to leave.

John?

Q   Has the President been in personal communication with Ambassador Howell? And what is he doing today with the swirl of events in the Middle East?

MR. FITZWATER: The President, of course, met this morning with General Scowcroft and with Andy Card for his normal intelligence update and briefing on other White House activities in the days ahead. I have a number of things I'll go through with you in a moment. He is now meeting with General Scowcroft and probably will be for the rest of the morning. Also, General Scowcroft went with him on the Fidelity. So they are in discussions, I would think, for the rest of the morning.

Q   Marlin, does the President regard this as a new escalation of Saddam's violations? Is this something that will require an even more immediate response from us?

MR. FITZWATER: Well, it certainly is another troublesome element in the overall pattern of harassment and hostage-taking kinds of activities that Saddam Husayn has been engaged in. He has rounded up citizens in some instances and located them in one location or another. He has issued verbal threats to citizens of all countries and asked them to congregate in various locations. Now we have this action against the diplomats. Prior to this point, Iraq had been promising to live up to the international commitment to our diplomatic envoys and to allow them to leave the country, even though he was not allowing US citizens to leave. So, this rejection is -- is, indeed, a further step in the harassment that he has undertaken.

Q   Does the President fear for Ambassador Howell's life or his safety?

MR. FITZWATER: We are always concerned about the safety of diplomats and citizens. That has been the case from the very beginning. There is, of course, a high degree of danger there. We have urged citizens not to go to Iraq or Kuwait. We have advised everyone there to leave by any -- as they can. And we would like to get our people out for the obvious reasons of personal safety.

/939-2   0027

MR. FITZWATER: Craig?

Q   Was there no other way for the diplomats to leave Kuwait City? Is that why they went to Baghdad? They couldn't -- they would not be allowed to go south or any other way? This was the only way out for them?

MR. FITZWATER: This was considered the safest and most promising route, yes.

Owen?

Q   What are Howell's instructions if Iraqi troops were to move toward the embassy?

MR. FITZWATER: Well, I can't get into specific instructions, but he is staying there to help out as he can. And force has not been applied. Should he be subject to that, he will have to act accordingly, but those are judgments that he is authorized to make in many cases. And beyond that, I couldn't -- I couldn't go into specific discussions we have had with him.

Q   There are no military forces there any more, as you said yesterday, right?

MR. FITZWATER: That's right.

Q   So there are no Marines, there's no security guard at all.

MR. FITZWATER: That's correct.

George?

Q   Marlin, can you give us an update on the talks with the Soviets concerning the UN resolution?

MR. FITZWATER: Ambassador Pickering continues to consult at the United Nations with the other Security Council members. The United Nations Security Council Resolution 661 called for comprehensive sanctions against Iraq, and the world community has undertaken a concerted effort to enforce them. However, Iraq continues to attempt to violate the sanctions. Ambassador Pickering has outlined at the United Nations the various efforts being undertaken by Iraq to circumvent the sanctions.

It is important that the sanctions be effective and comprehensive. In this regard, the United States is continuing work in the Security Council for steps which will enhance their enforcement. Progress has been made. We remain confident that a resolution concerning enforcement measures will be arrived at soon. The United States continues to shadow a number of Iraqi and other vessels which are enroute to ports that may be used to transship goods to Iraq. We are pleased by the Yemen government announcement that it will abide by the United Nations sanctions and not allow tankers to offload. We continue to consult on this matter.

Q   Have there been any further talks between Baker and Shevardnadze?

1939 -4

0028

MR. FITZWATER: There were discussions yesterday. I don't know about today. But we continue to be in close contact, obviously, with the Soviets and the other permanent members of the Council.

Ann?

Q   There's a report from the British this morning that an Iraqi tanker was, indeed, allowed to either offload or take on Iraqi cargo at Yemen, and they said that was a clear violation of the embargo. Has it been broken?

MR. FITZWATER: We don't want to comment on specific tanker situations. We are monitoring all of them. This is a very complex matter in the sense that judgments have to be made about whether the oil is being stored and where it's being shipped, whether it's being transshipped, how it's being used, what the ports have indicated they intend to allow the ships to do. And so we will have to make judgments along those lines, but at this point we are not willing to comment on any specific tanker situation.

Q   Marlin?

MR. FITZWATER: David?

Q   When you refer in your statement to Pickering giving details of Iraqi attempts to evade the sanctions, are those attempts mostly the attempts to get those tankers into Aden? Is that primarily what we're talking about when we say that they're trying to circumvent the sanctions?

MR. FITZWATER: That's just one of many areas. Prominent other ones would include aviation shipments into Baghdad of one kind or another; materiel -- military materiel that appears to be coming in through some routes; and also the procurement of chemical warfare products which we have great concern about, and that appears to be taking place from some other countries as well. So there are any number of issues of great concern and the ambassador laid those out for the UN yesterday.

Q   Could you expand a bit on that last item -- the chemical warfare agents? Where do they seem to be getting them? How are they getting them in?

MR. FITZWATER: We -- we're not willing at this point to identify the sources or the avenues because we're still working to resolve the matter and to put an end to this, and we simply can't discuss it publicly until we've been able to deal with it effectively.

Q   Marlin?

MR. FITZWATER: Yes, Charles?

Q   The Soviets have said that they would cut off military shipments to Iraq. Are you confident that the Soviets have done so?

/939 -5   0029

MR. FITZWATER: We think the Soviets have been very helpful and responsive. And I can't comment on individual cases or shipments. But suffice to say that, overall, the Soviet response has been very helpful.

Q   If I could follow, you just said that -- expressed concern about military materiel coming in on some routes. The major supplier historically has been the Soviets. If you could be specific on that, I think it would be quite helpful.

MR. FITZWATER: I just cannot be specific, but I would guide you away from that course of thinking.

Yes?

Q   Two questions. Are you now considering the **diplomats** and the dependents **hostages** since they can't leave Iraq?

MR. FITZWATER: We, from the beginning, have been very reluctant to attach names to categories of people for obvious reasons, that it makes it more difficult to deal with. I think suffice to say that the President has been very clear in saying that -- that we consider all Americans and, indeed, all -- all foreign nationals, of which there may be two [million] or three million people from countries around the world, as hostages to the aggressive ambitions of Saddam Husayn.

Yes?

Q   And secondly, are you considering any action against the Iraqi Embassy in Washington in retaliation for what's going on?

MR. FITZWATER: No, we're not.

Q   That is the question.

Q   Why not?

MR. FITZWATER: Pardon, Joe?

Q   That was my question.

Q   Why not?

MR. FITZWATER: Oh, that was your question?

Q   Marlin ---

MR. FITZWATER: We don't think that it's appropriate.

Q   Well, what can you do if even more Americans are now taken hostage and the embassy unable to conduct business easily in Kuwait City? What will you do?

MR. FITZWATER: We, again, are talking with any number of countries, bringing pressure to bear at the United Nations and through our many allies in the **Arab** world as well as here, to ensure the safety of our citizens and to assure that -- to try to continue to get them to be released.

/939-6

0030

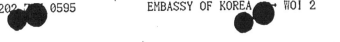

Q   If the Iraqi troops go in, as it seems they might, will you consider it as invasion of US territory?

MR. FITZWATER: Well, I can't speculate on hypothetical cases.

Gene?

Q   Marlin, a couple of days ago, the President suggested he was prepared to wait a few more days before using force to enforce the sanctions. You said earlier this morning that the United States was confident we would soon have a resolution that would make implementation of the sanctions more effective. Is it still the US position that we'll -- we'll wait before using force?

MR. FITZWATER: We are continuing to talk and continuing to seek a UN resolution, but we would not want to forecast judgments that may have to be made down the road.

David?

Q   I'd like to go back just a moment to when you were talking about the ways that they have tried to evade the sanctions. You mentioned aviation shipments into Baghdad. Are we considering expanding the interdiction to go beyond Iraqi shipping to include Iraqi air traffic?

MR. FITZWATER: Well, we won't comment on specific military operations or interdiction efforts,

again for obvious reasons.

Ian?

Q   Do you know if the other embassies are surrounded and if people are prevented from coming and going at those premises?

MR. FITZWATER: It's my understanding that this situation is duplicated at other embassies. I don't know how many but that it is duplicated at other embassies.

Q   (Off mike) -- any countries at all?

MR. FITZWATER: I wouldn't want to name them. I'd want -- let them report for themselves on their status.

Kevin?

Q   Marlin, can you bring us up to date on the phone calls the President's made yesterday evening, last night and this morning? Has he made any to foreign leaders or received any?

MR. FITZWATER: The President called President Hawke of Australia. I don't know the exact time -- anyway, yesterday evening to discuss the situation with him. As you know, he had talked earlier in the day with Chancellor Kohl and also with some US officials, Secretary Brady, Secretary Mosbacher. I don't believe he's made any calls today, but I'll have to check.

Q   Did he call Kohl yesterday and the day before?

1839-7

0031

MR. FITZWATER: I -- I don't -- I think it was yesterday.

Jim?

Q   Marlin, back to the embassy in Kuwait. You said it appears that no one is being allowed to enter or leave. Is it just because the presence of the troops is such an intimidating factor that nobody has attempted, or has there been an actual confrontation of some kind where somebody was either turned away or forced back into the embassy?

MR. FITZWATER: I'm not aware of any confrontations. It just has not happened. Let me -- I'm sorry, go ahead.

Q   Has Iraq formally notified the United States that -- that diplomatic credentials, privileges, immunity, has been revoked?

MR. FITZWATER: Well, that has been the notification that's gone to -- to our embassy officials in Baghdad, yes.

Let me go through the schedule here. We have a number of other things. We've about exhausted this. Yes?

Q   Can I follow just on that thread?

MR. FITZWATER: Yeah.

Q   You said the -- there was notification to our officials in Iraq that their credentials wouldn't be -- would not be processed in a way to let them leave. Did they say you couldn't leave for seven days? Did they say, we'll put these at the end of the list? Or what exactly were we told about their status?

MR. FITZWATER: Well, I don't have a description of the exact language and we would want to be very circumspect in that case anyway, because we continue to talk with Iraq and continue to seek them to allow us to leave. So we'll --

Q   Marlin?

MR. FITZWATER: -- continue to work on it.

Wendell.

Q   May I follow up on my question, please?

MR. FITZWATER: Wendell.

Q   Marlin, give us some idea of the international support for keeping the embassies open in Kuwait. Can you tell us -- I know you've got five dozen embassies there, but can you give us some idea how many others are joining in the US protest?

MR. FITZWATER: I don't have a complete list, but I would say the vast majority, I've -- I -- almost every embassy I've heard of is following that course.

Q   Would you describe it then as saying only a handful have decided to comply with the order to close?

MR. FITZWATER: No. I'd leave it the way I said it.

1939-8

0032

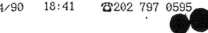

Q   Marlin, could I --

MR. FITZWATER: Let me just --

Q   I don't mean to belabor this, but is it our understanding that the government of Iraq now does not recognize that the US Embassy in Kuwait exists?

MR. FITZWATER: I can't answer that question. They have not given us any definitions of their motivation. They simply have not allowed it to happen.

Q   No, I --

MR. FITZWATER: Yes?

Q   In other words, they haven't informally -- or formally informed the United States that they consider that the embassy no longer exists? They haven't done that officially?

MR. FITZWATER: Well, I'm describing the situation, but I won't go into details of conversations.

     Charles?

Q   It would seem that by going from Kuwait to Baghdad, they've sort of gone from the frying pan into the fire. Have any diplomats gone out the other way, through **Saudi Arabia**, since individuals and groups seem to be able to get out that way? And if not, why not? Was that -- why was that not --

MR. FITZWATER: I assure you, this represents the thorough analysis and consideration of the United States government and the authorities in the **Middle East**; that we obviously have been working every route out of both of those countries. You have all interviewed people who have gone out through Jordan into Saudi Arabia by various means, some by car, some by desert vehicle, through the embassies. But I assure you that this course of action was well considered and thought to be the safest and most-effective way of doing it.

     Pierre? Yes, Pascal. I'm sorry. (Laughter.)

Q   Is the President going back to Washington on Tuesday?

MR. FITZWATER: Pierre was his predecessor.

     I'm sorry. Go ahead.

Q   Is the President going back to Washington on Tuesday?

MR. FITZWATER: Let me go through that. Secretary Brady, after flying into Sanford Airport, should have arrived at Walker's Point

1939-10

0033

by this time in preparation for a meeting this afternoon on the budget and other matters. However, due to weather closure of Boston's airport, Director **Darman** will -- his arrival will be delayed, and so their meeting will now be some time around 2:00 to 3:00. We'll have a photo release of that meeting.

On a related matter, Prime Minister **Mulroney** and his family are scheduled to arrive at Pease Air Force Base at 11:30 Monday from Ottawa. They will then helicopter to Walker's Point and arrive at 12:00 noon. We'll have expanded photo coverage on arrival.

The two leaders will have extensive discussions, but no other scheduled activities have been planned during the Prime Minister's 24-hour stay. The Prime Minister and his family are scheduled to depart Walker's Point at 11:30 Tuesday for Pease Air Force Base for Ottawa, and we will again have expanded pool coverage upon departure.

The President will return to Washington Tuesday afternoon, following the **Prime Minister's** departure. And he will meet that afternoon with congressional leadership, House and Senate Foreign Affairs and Armed Services Committee members, and it hasn't been determined yet whether we will return to Maine on Tuesday night or Wednesday morning.

The President has had conversations with the leadership of the Congress by telephone in the last few days. There have been extensive consulations with individual members and committees by the Pentagon, by Secretary **Cheney** and others, and it is our purpose and intent to keep the Congress fully informed, and this special trip back to Washington is for that purpose.

Q   We may have gone over this yesterday, and I don't remember, but Ambassador **Howell**, and the people remaining behind, are they volunteers, or were they ordered to stay, or what is their status given the danger to them?

MR. FITZWATER: They are United States **diplomats**. They face danger as our diplomats do in all parts of the world. The Ambassador obviously is in charge of the embassy in making decisions about who will stay, including himself.

Q   So he was given the choice of whether to stay or go?

MR. FITZWATER: The Ambassador's in charge of the embassy. He makes those decisions.

Q   Can you give any specifics, Marlin, about the -- how the decision was made to remove the Marine guards from the embassy?

MR. FITZWATER: I don't have a great deal of details under that -- except to say that the Ambassador is in charge of the embassy. He makes decisions that he feels are in the best interest of the safety of all the personnel that are leaving as well as the personnel that were staying. And it was his judgment and the judgment of the **State Department** that that was the best course of action to take.

Q   Why is it the best course of action?

1839 - 11   0034

MR. FITZWATER: Because we were drawing down our personnel to a bare minimum that could help US citizens. We're not -- our purpose is not to create a confrontation or create a threat at that point. And the Marines are not essential to the conduct of the mission, which was to help US citizens.

Q   The President -- I think you -- we've passed this in one way, but the President did say two days ago he was going to give a little more time to the UN. Can we assume that that interlude will be over by Tuesday?

MR. FITZWATER: What do you mean "interlude in time"? What do you mean?

Q   Before we enforce the sanctions ourselves. -.

MR. FITZWATER: Oh. I wouldn't try to apply a timetable to this.

Gene?

Q   Marlin, back on the aerial delivery of war materiels to Iraq, how extensive is that?

MR. FITZWATER: Well, there again, we are not willing to give definition to these kinds of matters. We are monitoring them on a continual basis, but it is crucial, as we begin to consider these kinds of problems in the UN and other places, that we be able to discuss these with some degree of confidence. So I could not give definition to you. Ambassador Picking -- Pickering has extensive information in this regard. He is sharing it with other members of the United Nations who are having to consider this matter, and we are hoping for a united UN policy in facing up to this issue.

Q   Has this been discussed among this group of five -- the session, these consultations --

MR. FITZWATER: Well, it was discussed yesterday in the Perm 5 consultations, yes.

All the way in the back.

Q   Yeah, what's on the agenda for the Mulroney visit?

MR. FITZWATER: The discussion will undoubtedly focus on the situation in the Persian Gulf. Canada, of course, is one of 22 countries that is providing forces to the multinational effort going on in the Gulf. Prime Minister Rooney -- Mulroney is also a valued advisor to President Bush. They have talked many times by telephone, as well as personally. The Prime Minister has many contacts in the Arab world and discussions that he would also like to explore. So I'm sure that they will have extensive discussions, but primarily on that problem.

Craig?

Q   Can I try for a little definition on both war materiel.

1939-12

0035

and chemicals? Are these in any way coming from people -- from
nations we consider to be allies?

        MR. FITZWATER: That information is classified, Craig. I
simply cannot discuss that.

        Doug?

        Q   Marlin, there seems to be some confusion about whether
the President specifically asked Prime Minister Kaifu for -- to open
up the Japanese "checkbook" to aid in the Middle East. Did he
specifically ask the Japanese to do this? And does the President
plan to do this with other nations as well?

        MR. FITZWATER: The President talked to Prime Minister Kaifu as
well as any number of other nations about the situation, about their
helpfulness, and many nations are contributing in various ways,

whether it be financial resources or increased oil production or
medical supplies or military equipment. Japan has been very
forthcoming and helpful in this matter, but I would not want to go
into personal discussions.

        Mike?

        Q   There were -- there were reports yesterday that the
Kuwaitis have offered to pay the cost of the Middle East operation
from the funds that have been frozen around the world. Have they
made any formal offer to the United States and, if so, what are we
doing about it?

        MR. FITZWATER: We are discussing these kinds of matters with
all of the -- the alliance that is involved in the Persian Gulf.
Again, we have 22 nations that have forces there. There are
continuing discussions with the Arab countries and with others about
shared responsibilities, shared costs, and so forth. Those
discussions go forth. We are quite pleased that many nations have
offered to help in one way or another, but I wouldn't want to
specify -- it's up to them to define what they want to do.

        Q   But have we received a -- a formal offer from Kuwait,
though?

        MR. FITZWATER: I refer you to Kuwait.

        Q   Well, Marlin, will we know at -- when this deadline that
we believe is either 4:00 or 5:00 Eastern passes, will we be able to
find out from you what has happened to Ambassador Howell?

        MR. FITZWATER: Well, we'll -- we'll pass along any information
we have when we have it. That's the best I can do.

        ALL: Thank you.

        MR. FITZWATER: Thank you.

                                END

                        /P39_12   0036

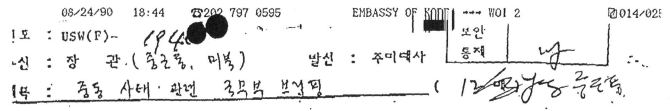

STATE DEPARTMENT REGULAR BRIEFING/ BRIEFER: RICHARD BOUCHER
1:17 P.M. (EDT)/ FRIDAY, AUGUST 24, 1990

MR. BOUCHER: Good afternoon, ladies and gentlemen. I'd like to start out by reviewing the situations in Iraq, Kuwait, and the plight of displaced people who are on the Iraqi border with Jordan. If you'll indulge me, I'll go through several pages of stuff.

Today, we have another stark example of Iraqi duplicity. Our diplomatic convoy from Kuwait is being held in Baghdad and denied permission to leave Iraq. In addition, a small contingent of Iraqi soldiers has taken up positions at various points around the embassy compound in Kuwait. They control entry and exit from the compound. They have permitted at least one private American to depart, but they have blocked entry to the compound by an embassy vehicle.

The embassy's primary mission remains the safety of the American community. Ambassador Howell and his team will continue their efforts as much as circumstances allow. In Kuwait, we are still in contact with Americans outside the embassy by telephone. Such communication is difficult, not only because telephone service is sporadic, but because of restraints put on movement by the embassy staff in general in terms of contacting Americans, and because we know that the Iraqis are monitoring the embassy's local telephone calls in an attempt to locate American citizens.

For that reason, our telephone conversations with the American community are very short, and the information passed is that they are well and safe, and in some cases, that they have moved location, but never saying where they have moved to.
We gave our wardens yesterday some instructions on how to proceed in the event that our normal communications with them is disturbed. We have also established a backup warden system with other friendly countries in Kuwait.

Now back to the situation of the personnel who tried to leave from Kuwait through Baghdad and onward; they were planning to go out to Turkey.

The personnel and dependents from our Kuwait embassy are now resting in Baghdad. It remains our intention to try to move these people out of Iraq by the best available means as soon as possible.

In that regard, late last night, that is, early morning Baghdad time, just as we were preparing to move our Kuwaiti embassy personnel out of Baghdad, we were informed in Baghdad that a new set of regulations prohibits travel from Iraq of personnel from embassies representing countries which have refused to close their missions in Kuwait. During a series of telephone calls between Iraqi Ambassador [Al-] Mashat and Deputy Assistant Secretary David Mack, Ambassador [Al-] Mashat requested and received the information from Foreign Minister Tariq Aziz in Baghdad that basically confirmed this new regulation and that our personnel from Kuwait would be prevented from leaving Iraq.

1940 - 1

0037

Q   (Off mike.)

MR. BOUCHER: These were in the middle of the night.

In addition, at 1:00 a.m., Washington time, Charge Wilson met with the Iraqi Ministry of Foreign Affairs. The Charge reminded ministry officials of the Iraqi government's obligation to provide the US government with a list of those Americans being held and to provide consular access. At that meeting, again, Charge Wilson was told that the diplomats of countries that had not closed their embassies in Kuwait were no longer free to leave Iraq.

Q   Did you say with the "ministry" or the "minister"? Excuse me.

MR. BOUCHER: I said the "ministry". It was an official; I don't remember exactly which one.

We have strongly protested to the Iraqi government this outrageous breach of international law and its violation of repeated Iraqi commitments to allow travel of our diplomats from Kuwait out of Iraq. We are insisting that our American diplomats and their families receive the full protection and freedoms accorded them under international law and by the norms of civilized behavior.

At the present time, the individuals who left Kuwait yesterday are staying at embassy residences in Baghdad. They include over 100 people, including approximately 30 children.

Now, to move on to some other subjects. On the Secretary -- he's been keeping in touch with Acting Secretary Eagleburger and Undersecretary Kimmit. In addition, he's made several phone calls to foreign ministers. If I can list to you the ones he made yesterday -- he spoke with Foreign Minister Abdel Meguid of Egypt, Foreign Minister Saud of Saudi Arabia, Foreign Minister De Michelis of Italy, and with Foreign Minister Shevardnadze.

Today, the Secretary has spoken twice to the President. He has spoken at least once with Foreign Minister Shevardnadze. And he spoke with Foreign Minister Genscher of Germany.

Q   A relaxing vacation.

MR. BOUCHER: Yeah. At the United Nations, active consultations continue among the representatives of the Permanent 5 members on the text of an enforcement resolution, which we hope will lead to a full Council session and a vote as soon as possible.

The Council on August 6 adopted Resolution 661, imposing sanctions. Now is the time to ensure effective enforcement of these sanctions. As Marlin said this morning, Iraq continues its attempts to violate the embargo, including attempts to procure chemical weapons products. It is abundantly clear that Iraq intends to evade the sanctions, if possible.

For example, its ships are at sea carrying cargo which was loaded after August 6, the date the sanctions were imposed. In light of Iraq's record, it is ever more urgent for the Council to send a clear message to Iraq that the international community will not tolerate attempts to circumvent international law.

1P40 - 2

0038

And, finally, I'd like to point to what we're doing about the plight of the many, many people who are at the border between Iraq and Jordan. We recognize the burden on Jordan caused by tens of thousands of persons who are fleeing Iraq and Kuwait.

The United States is making available $1 million to help meet these urgent humanitarian needs. Within this $1 million, we are making funds immediately available to our embassy in Amman to assist locally, and we are making arrangements to immediately fly 500 tents to Jordan for shelter needs.

We're in discussions with the International Committee of the Red Cross, which is working with the Jordanian Red Crescent in the border area where the immediate needs are the greatest. Other governments are also providing assistance. We're in touch with them and with the United Nations and other international organizations to provide additional assistance in the most effective and coordinated manner. The US is certainly prepared to do more as the needs require.

With that update, I'd be glad to take your questions.

Q   Richard, can you give us any idea how many people are in the US Embassy in Kuwait?

MR. BOUCHER: Jim, I can't really do that. You can do the math. We've said that over 100 were in the convoy. We've said before that about 120 official personnel were at our embassy. But I'm afraid we still think that, for the safety and welfare of the people at our embassy there --

Q   Well --

MR. BOUCHER: -- it's better to leave the numbers a little bit fuzzy.

Q   When I said "people," I didn't mean --

MR. BOUCHER: I know.

Q   Okay.

Q   Richard?

Q   The Iraqi soldiers -- did you say how many are outside the embassy?

MR. BOUCHER: There's a dozen or less.

Q   A dozen. Now, are they -- in the past you've said they've been out there -- soldiers have been out there. Is this the largest -- how do you compare this to what's been --

IP40-3

0039

MR. BOUCHER: I think in the past what we've reported is various military activity in the area, in the vicinity near our embassy. These are people who arrived to take up specific positions at various points around the compound and who have done that in order to control the entry and the exit from the compound.

Q   This -- the -- this current situation?

MR. BOUCHER: This group that got there --

Q   To the best of your knowledge, have Iraqi authorities in Kuwait communicated directly with the embassy, telling them that the embassy is no longer an embassy or that there is a specific deadline? There are now at least three deadlines out there. Has there been communication between authorities on the ground and that embassy?

MR. BOUCHER: I'm not aware of any specific meetings like that. The question of deadlines is a little unclear to me right now frankly, because I think we told you that we'd heard both midnight and noon. We had word, and I am not exactly sure where from, today in Kuwait that the deadline would be noon. But, in fact, the controls on the entry and exit were imposed even before them.

Q   Richard, what time?

Q   But --

MR. BOUCHER: I think about 11:00 their time.

Q   -- there's controls, but you still don't know whether the embassy is regarded by the controlling government as an embassy. Is that right?

MR. BOUCHER: They have made various statements to that effect. They have repeated them I think many times publicly. You saw Ambassador Al-Mashat a day or two ago saying that they would consider it that way. For our part, we don't consider the precise moment that they change their attitude that important. The whole thing is null and void as the UN declared.

Q   Richard, other than these various acts of intimidation, putting soldiers outside the gates, have the Iraqis made any move themselves to enter the embassy complex?

MR. BOUCHER: No. They have not made any attempt. They have made no effort to enter the compound.

Q   Richard, is --

Q   Who is in the --

MR. BOUCHER: Go ahead.

Q   Can you give us an idea in terms of jobs -- who is left behind at the American embassy, like is the DCM there and political officer --

1140-4

0040

MR. BOUCHER: I'm not in a position to go into great detail. Ambassador Howell, of course, is there as the head of the team that's at the embassy. The chief consular officer is there. And there are other officers and people who we thought were necessary to maintain there to carry out this essential function of seeing to the safety and welfare of American citizens, and continuing to press whenever possible for the right of departure.

Q   Do you expect -- are you calling in the Iraqi Ambassador today? Would you expect him here?

MR. BOUCHER: I don't -- (pauses) -- let me check on that. I may have something on that. (Pauses.) Well, I don't think I have anything specific on that. The phone calls -- the contact during the middle of the night was by telephone, and I would expect we would be -- continue to be in touch with him as necessary. But

I guess I'm not aware of any specific meetings.

Q   Could you tell us, at least approximately, how many embassies have remained open and how many have closed?

MR. BOUCHER: I can't confirm the status of every embassy or foreign national group in Kuwait and Iraq. We know that most governments have announced that they intend to keep their embassies in Kuwait open. I saw one list that had at least 20 countries on it, but I have no idea if that's the total or if that's only part of it.

A few governments have decided, for various reasons, to close their embassies. I think what is clear to us is that Iraq has tried in a most callous way to barter the security of foreign citizens for concessions on the presence of diplomatic missions in Kuwait and that most countries are resisting this blatant violation of diplomatic practice and international law.

Q   Richard, are diplomats from other countries being detained in Baghdad under the same restrictions?

MR. BOUCHER: I think you'll have to ask the other countries. I don't -- I don't really know.

Q   You don't have any indication from the Iraqis?

MR. BOUCHER: Well, other than that the -- when they explained why this American group could not leave, they didn't say it applied just to Americans. They said that diplomats from countries who maintain embassies in Kuwait will not be permitted to leave, and therefore, I would assume that this order is -- that they're trying to apply it to all the countries who are maintaining embassies in Kuwait, and as I just said, that could be quite a number.

Q   You say the Iraqis are controlling the entry and exit. How is that considered? Is that considered part of the effort to shut it down or is that just considered harassment? How would you characterize it in those terms?

MR. BOUCHER: Well, it's certainly harassment and it's certainly an attempt to make it difficult for the embassy to carry out its functions, and as I said before, that function is primarily

1P40-5

0041

to stay in touch with the American community and see to their safety
and welfare. That would constitute a -- you know, a violation of
consular access and other things. But as to how to characterize it
at this point, I don't want to be -- try to speculate on what else
they might try to do, so I don't know quite what picture it might
fit into.

Q   But you're not characterizing it as attempting to shut
the embassy down right now as -- in terms of what they've done so
far?

MR. BOUCHER: Well, I think I'd just characterize it the way
I've characterized it.

Q   Could you comment [on] the trip of Austrian President
Waldheim to Baghdad, please?

MR. BOUCHER: No, I'm afraid I don't have anything on that.

Q   Have there been some contacts before his trip between
Washington and Vienna? Do you know that?

MR. BOUCHER: I know that we've been in touch with the Austrian
government, as we've been in touch with many, many governments about
the Iraqi invasion, the sanctions, the status of foreigners, the
status of the diplomatic community in Kuwait. I have no idea if
we've talked about any specific trip.

Q   Richard, the Spanish diplomat -- a Spanish diplomat in
Madrid was quoted as saying that he had heard of a tommorrow morning
deadline, combined with a threat that troops would be moved in.
Have we received any other deadline or any other threat?

MR. BOUCHER: I'll have to check on that and see.

Q   Have you received any --

Q   Have you got any information on how the diplomats made
the trip, what it was like from Kuwait to Baghdad?

MR. BOUCHER: I don't have a detailed read-out. It took
approximately 19 hours -- they, I think had a couple breakdowns of
vehicles. They spent a lot of time at the border processing papers.
But they got there safely.

Q   Richard, this morning Marlin Fitzwater was asked if the
United States is considering any retaliation against Iraqi diplomats
in this country, and he said, no, it would not be appropriate. Why
would it not be appropriate?

MR. BOUCHER: I'm afraid I don't have any guidance that goes to
that level of detail or any knowledge that does. We're certainly ---
we're monitoring developments closely to see what happens out there.
We are continuing to try to press the Iraqis to stick to their
promises that they've made, that our diplomats will be allowed to
depart. And at this point, I don't really have any specifics of the
various options that might be considered.

Q   The Iraqis say that American diplomats in Baghdad cannot
leave that group. Are they still referring to them as diplomats?

1140-15

0042

Do they still regard them as having diplomatic status and are treating them as such, or are they regarding them as some other category?

MR. BOUCHER: Frankly, I don't know.

Q I mean that's a very important distinction.

MR. BOUCHER: Well, I don't think the distinction is that important, John, because the departure of these specific peole, in the way that they attempted to depart, was the subject as I've made clear over the last few days of detailed conversations with the Iraqi government, and whatever their diplomatic status as seen by the Iraqi government, the fact is that what we have here is a clear violation of specific commitments made about these idividuals and their ability to depart.

Q Can you --

Q Richard, are there any plans for Secretary of State Baker or any of the other top members of his staff who are now on leave to return early from vacation?

MR. BOUCHER: You'll probably be pleased to hear that Margaret Tutwiler told me yesterday afternoon that she would come back and do the briefings next week. I'm not aware of any changes in the plans of Secretary Baker at this point, but don't hold me to that more than a little while.

Q Richard, will this --

MR. BOUCHER: I mean, I just don't know on that.

Q Let's pursue that a bit, because it's beginning to get a little attention in the press, his being out there while this is going on. The day you've described all those telephone calls, that hardly can be called a vacation, so I'm beginning to be mystified why he would not do this in Washington. He's either spending the bulk of the day working on this problem or he's not. If he is, why do it out there? Isn't it easier to consult here?

MR. BOUCHER: I haven't really asked him, Barry. He is in very close touch with us. We talk to him frequently. He calls in and gets updates from the operations center. He's been talking to foreign ministers. As I said, he's been talking to various people in Washington, but he's doing it from Wyoming.

Q Can the United -- the US State Department assure all of us here that Secretary Baker has spent all of his days and hours in Wyoming throughout the whole process, [that] he has not gone out of Wyoming and gone to somewhere else?

MR. BOUCHER: Uh, yes.

Q You said that the Iraqis appear to be monitoring telephone conversations in an effort to locate Americans. Could you be more specific on what you mean by that?

MR. BOUCHER: No.

1P40 -7

0043

Q   Are you — do you have any concern that the Iraqis maybe
will round them up, or search house-to-house, you know, to round
them up?

MR. BOUCHER: Well, I mean, clearly that would be a matter that
would be of great concern to us.   At this point, there have not been
any more roundups of Americans.   We don't have any new reports of
Americans being taken into custody by the Iraqis, nor do we have
reports of harassment of Americans.   And we've not heard any reports
of personnel from embassies in Kuwait being rounded up.

Q   Richard, does Iraq know where most of the 3,000 Americans
in Kuwait and Iraq are?

MR. BOUCHER: Sorry, you'll have to ask them.

Q   Well, if they do not, does time then work against the
Americans, the longer that this thing is a stalemate, the longer
Iraq has to find out exactly where they are?

MR. BOUCHER: That would be totally speculative on my part.

Q   Richard, have you received any assurances since yesterday
when you mentioned the problem of the Soviet military advisors in
Iraq?   Any new developments there?

MR. BOUCHER: I'm not aware of any new developments, no.

Q   Has there been contact between the — between Howell and
the general of the occupying authority?   Has he been told why those
men are at the gate and what they intend to do?

MR. BOUCHER: I'm not aware of any contact, Mark.

Q   So far as water, et cetera, Fitzwater was asked and he
really didn't answer the question, he said there are adequate
supplies.   But the question really is, have the Iraqis cut off the
flow of material to the embassy?   You could have —

MR. BOUCHER: Barry, I — I don't think that's a subject I
really want to talk about.   I mean, I think that relates directly to
the safety and health and welfare of people who are at the embassy.

Q   Richard, on that question, are they denying entry to
people trying to go into the embassy at this point?

MR. BOUCHER: That's my understanding, yes.   I said they've
stopped at least one embassy vehicle trying to come in.

Q   But is it everyone they're denying entry to, or just
selected people?

MR. BOUCHER: Uhm — my understanding is that no one has come
in —

Q   (Inaudible.)

MR. BOUCHER: This embassy driver in a vehicle made the attempt
to come in and they were stopped.

Q   Other than the one civilian who was allowed to leave, has
anyone tried to leave and been told not to?

                        /P40 _ d

                                                    0044

MR. BOUCHER: Well, I said there was at least one. I'm not sure if there's -- if there were -- what? -- a couple of other people with him, who had gone out, a private citizen, a private American citizen.

Q   Richard --

MR. BOUCHER: I'm not aware of any other people who've been able to -- been allowed to leave.

Q   Were they stopped? Were they questioned? Were they -- what happened?

MR. BOUCHER: I don't have the full details on each of these things. The guards are controlling the entry and the exit from the compound. They're at various points around there, such as the gate, and they're just not letting anybody through.

Q   What kind of --

MR. BOUCHER: Except for the exceptions.

Q   This exception about these people that left, were there -- was there anyone that was actually denied exit from the embassy?

MR. BOUCHER: Again, I don't know in a specific case, but it's clear to us that they are barring the exit of people from the compound, with the exceptions -- you know, with some exception. And it's not clear that there's any pattern yet.

Q   The vehicle that were stopped did not contain an American diplomat who's now outside the embassy?

MR. BOUCHER: Uh -- no.

Q   You said there are 500 --

Q   .Richard, about **Jordan** and the money for Jordan, would the decision to give all this money to Jordan in any way -- did Jordan open its border before or after you made the announcement you were going to give it this money? Did it reopen the border, that's the first thing?

MR. BOUCHER: I don't -- I don't know exactly what the status of the border is or when it was said. I think this -- this money is -- if you're hinting that it's some sort of quid pro quo, I think I would dissuade you from that.

Q   What about **Aqaba**?

MR. BOUCHER: It is a very difficult humanitarian situation there. There are tens of thousands, if not several hundred thousand, people on one or the other side of the border.

Q   What about Aqaba? What do you know about Aqaba at the moment? Is -- are goods still getting through Aqaba on their way into Iraq?

MR. BOUCHER: I don't have any change from the way I described it yesterday.

1940-9

Q   Has the government of Jordan told you that they need 500 tents, or this is something that you offered out of --

MR. BOUCHER: We have been in close touch with the government of Jordan. I would assume that this was worked out with them or in the contacts with the various groups of governments or relief agencies that are indentifying needs and trying to find supplies.

Q   When do you think that they will arrive there -- in that area?

MR. BOUCHER: I don't know exactly. The arrangements are still being made.

Q   Richard?

Q   Do you know about embargo violations in Yemen? The British government says there have been in the last 24 hours violations off-loading oil. And also, do you have any more evidence that Americans are being used as a shield -- or do you have any evidence?

MR. BOUCHER: I think you have the information on the tanker that was partially off-loaded the other day. I have that; let me start with that. There's another piece of paper that's useful about this, too.

The Iraqi tanker Ins Allah (ph) began to off-load a portion of its cargo at Aden on August 21st. The Yemenis, however, have assured us that the off-loading stopped before it was completed. We do note that the Ins Allah (ph) pulled into Aden before the Yemen government's pledge to adhere to the UN sanctions on August 21st. We, of course, welcome that Yemeni pledge and we will press the government of Yemen to honor it fully.

Beyond that, I'd just say that we are monitoring developments with regard to adherence to the sanctions in various countries, including in Yemen, and that we don't really have a final assessment on specific country at this point.

Q   And Americans in the shield -- you said you had evidence that there were some nationals being moved to various locations --

MR. BOUCHER: You're talking about people --,

Q   Yes, people in refineries and --

MR. BOUCHER: Okay. Well, as before, we note that there are credible reports that some Westerners had been moved to Iraqi industrial and military installations. However, we still cannot confirm this, nor do we -- are we able to speculate as to the validity of some of these reports. There was a report, I think sourced to Polish workers, that they had seen some Westerners, but we really can't confirm whether the Westerners that they saw were American citizens.

Q   Is there any --

Q   Filing break.

IP40 -10

0046

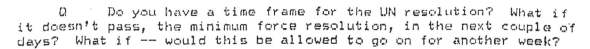

Q   Do you have a time frame for the UN resolution? What if
it doesn't pass, the minimum force resolution, in the next couple of
days? What if -- would this be allowed to go on for another week?

MR. BOUCHER: Well, I think I just have to stick to the time
frame I stated. We're in active consultations with other members of the
United Nations. We've been in contact with individual countries, and in
meetings such as one that will be held today, the -- the informal
consultations of the Perm 5, and that we are pressing for a
resolution as soon as possible.

Q   Filing break --

MR. BOUCHER: Filing break.

Q   Richard, could you tell us any -- or give us any details
about $1 million going to Jordan? Is that a cash payment to them to
use as they see fit for the circumstances, or is it in supplies?

MR. BOUCHER: It -- it will be divided up into various ways and
probably, you know, not just for one organization. I said portions
of this money will be made available to our embassy to spend
locally to buy what they can or supply services, whatever they --
they can find locally that -- that can help these people. And other
than this --

Q   But is any of it going to the government?

MR. BOUCHER: I'm not -- I don't think we've made that kind of
final arrangement on all the money. I only have the -- the idea
that one portion will be allotted to our embassy to use as best they
can locally.

Q   Richard --

Q   Poland is another country that's complaining about
economic losses because of the sanctions. Was the meeting of the
Polish charge d'affaires with Eagleburger today related to that, or
can you tell us what it was about?

MR. BOUCHER: No, I'm afraid I can't. I didn't get a readout.
I'll see if I can get you one.

Q   Richard, there were -- Marlin said in his briefing that
there are reports of chemical weapons stocks continuing to flow into
Baghdad. Can you tell us where those are coming from, and
specifically, are any of them coming from Germany?

MR. BOUCHER: Well I -- I mentioned it in my statement as
well, as Marlin has said. But I'm afraid we're not in a position to
provide any more detail.

Q   Richard?

Q   You mean you don't know, or you just don't want to?

MR. BOUCHER: I don't -- we don't want to. It relates to the
source of the information.

1040 -11

0047

    Q   On the question of what's going into the embassy, can you tell us whether the utilities are still turned on, whether there's power or water still going into the embassy?

    MR. BOUCHER: Yeah, as Marlin said, the water and electricity are still -- they're still available in the compound.

    Q   Thank you.

    Q   At what point --

    MR. BOUCHER: I guess we got one more.

    Q   At what point will you consider this harassment or menacing by the Iraqi troops, essentially a blockade of American territory -- a military blockade?

    MR. BOUCHER: I -- I really am not going to speculate in those terms. As the President said the other day, let's wait and see.

    Q   Richard, can you confirm the report that commercial banks are open now in Kuwait and giving Arab citizens there 30 dinar a day?

    MR. BOUCHER: I've seen a few scattered reports that there were some banks opening. I'm not -- I don't think I have anything that would deal with the breadth or how much was available.

    Well, can we say thank you and leave?

                    END

IPKO_12   0048

키신저, 브레진스키와의 ABC 인터뷰(90.8.26)

1. 키신저 입장

   ○ 이라크를 쿠웨이트로부터 축출하지 않은 상태에서 페르시아만 지역의 안전과
     안정적 원유공급 확보는 생각할 수 없음. 왜냐하면 금번 사태가 이라크의
     쿠웨이트 병합 및 미군의 사우디 주둔으로 종결된다면 사우디와 걸프만
     국가들의 보호를 위하여 미국은 방대한 군사력을 계속 주둔시켜야 할
     것인 바, 이는 미국으로서 감당하기 어렵기 때문임. 따라서 미국은 강대한
     군사력으로 이라크를 쿠웨이트로 부터 철수 시켜야 하며(무력 과시로
     관철되면 다행이나 안되면 무력 행사 불가피 시사), 국제적 압력으로 상기
     목표를 달성하지 못할 경우 미군이 절대 철수해서는 안됨.

   ○ 중동 지역에서 장기적 평화 확보를 위해서는 이라크 군사력의 감축 특히
     화학전 능력의 제거가 극히 바람직함.

2. 브레진스키의 입장

   ○ 석유의 안정적 공급 확보와 이라크의 쿠웨이트로 부터의 철수는 별개의 문제임.

   ○ 미군의 사우디 주둔이 장기화 되더라도 미국이 단독으로 이라크를 쿠웨이트로
     부터 축출키 위해 무력 사용을 해서는 안됨. 이 경우 아랍의 반미 주의가
     촉발되고, 중동 산유국 정부들이 불안정하게 되어 결국 원유 공급이 위태로워
     질 것이기 때문임.

   ○ 집단적인 국제적 압력을 계속 유지하면 중재자의 해결책이 나올것임.

0049

ABC "THIS WEEK WITH DAVID BRINKLEY"
WITH HOST, DAVID BRINKLEY
JOINED BY SAM DONALDSON AND COKIE ROBERTS
INTERVIEW WITH:

ZBIGNIEW BRZEZINSKI, FORMER NATIONAL SECURITY ADVISER

HENRY KISSINGER, FORMER SECRETARY OF STATE

SUNDAY, AUGUST 26, 1990

.STX

MR. BRINKLEY: Mr. Kissinger and Mr. Brzezinski, we're delighted to have you with us today. Thank you for coming.

MR. BRZEZINSKI: Nice to be with you.

MR. BRINKLEY: Now, I have a remarkably easy question for each of you, beginning with Mr. Kissinger. If you were President Bush right now, what would you do? Mr. Kissinger?

MR. KISSINGER: Well, I would stick to the policy that President Bush has been pursuing. I would state the two objectives that he put forward: withdrwal from Kuwait and restoration of the government, and -- which the United Nations has endorsed and for which we have now sent 100,000 troops into the area. And I would be prepared to start withdrawing our troops if those conditions are achieved.

MR. BRINKLEY: Mr. Brzezinski?

MR. BRZEZINSKI: I think the President has succeeded in deterring Iraq from moving against Saudi Arabia. He has resisted the temptation to act alone and unilaterally, and he now has the opportunity to bring to bear the collective pressure of the international community, thereby making possible some form of a regional solution along the lines that, I thought, very intelligently, was being recommended by the Crown Prince of Jordan.

MS. ROBERTS: Mr. Kissinger, you've written that the United States has crossed the Rubicon here, that it simply cannot lose, cannot be perceived as losing, but that time is not on our side. What does that argue for, in your mind? Does that argue for a quick military strike?

.ETX

FEDERAL NEWS SERVICE 202-347-1400

0050

        MR. KISSINGER: No, I think that the President has to balance
a variety of elements: maintaining international support, as
against the possibility of achieving the fundamental objective,
which he stated and which the United Nations has unanimously
endorsed. I do not believe that the problem of the Gulf can be
segmented into a Kuwaiti problem and into a Gulf problem, certainly
not after the actions that have been taken and that have been
correctly taken. And the President has to decide when to strike
that balance.

        My basic point is we cannot, after the deployment into the
Gulf, march out of the Gulf without having achieved these
objectives. And when the time has come to take other measures, that
is not for me to say. And I hope that sanctions will work, and I
hope that international pressure will work. And if that does work,
we will have had a great success, but if it doesn't work, we -- the
consequence of a setback would be disastrous.

        MS. ROBERTS: Mr. Brzezinski, you have separated the two, from
the problem of protecting the oil and the problem

.ETX

CONTINUED ON PAGE 2-1

0051

of getting, as you've said, disgorging Iraq from Kuwait. Why do you think there's a difference here between the two of you on this?

    MR. BRZEZINSKI: Well, over the years I have tended very much to agree with Henry Kissinger's views. I think on the large issues we have tended to stand together. But on this issue, I guess we have a different perspective. My judgment is that time is working on our side, that collective international pressure will work, and that in any case the costs of unilateral and solitary American military action would be disproportionate to any possible achievement. I think it would explode the Middle East; it would turn not only the Arab community against us, but much of the international community. And it could even jeopardize our vital interests.

    In fact, I think this is the first post-Cold War crisis in which America has the unique opportunity to fashion a new form of leadership, leadership which is genuinely supported by the international community, and gives us its moral sanction. And that entitles us to exercise prudence and patience.

    MR. DONALDSON: You know, although unstated by the President, Washington seems to feel that one of our objectives either is or ought to be the destabilization of Saddam Husayn himself, that is, toppling him from power in Iraq. Mr. Kissinger, do you believe that ought to be our objective?

    MR. KISSINGER: I think for a long-term outcome in the area and for the peace of the area, a reduction of the Iraqi military capability would be extremely desirable. And in fact, the New York Times editorial today has a number of conditions that I strongly favor: The elimination of their chemical capability, but these have not been stated as formal objectives of the United States.

    MR. DONALDSON: Should they be? Should they be objectives?

    MR. KISSINGER: I put these in the category of highly desirable. What I put in the category of essential is the achievement of the objectives that the United Nations has unanimously endorsed, which is the withdrawal of Iraqi forces from Kuwait --

    MR. DONALDSON: I'm curious. How -- how do you reduce, sir, the Iraqi military and perhaps their chemicals, without military action?

.ETX

0052

     MR. KISSINGER: Well, it could be -- well, one is by military
action, the other would be if the sanctions are as effective as the
advocates maintain, that the sanctions are maintained until the
chemical facilities are either dismantled or put under United
Nations supervision, which is one of the proposals that was made
today in the newspaper.

     MR. DONALDSON: Mr. Brzezinski, what about the question of
whether the destabilizaton
.ETX
                    CONTINUED ON PAGE 3-1

of Saddam Husayn ought to be one of our objectives?

    MR. BRZEZINSKI: I will put it this way. The defense of Saudi
Arabia is such a vital American interest that we should pursue it
unilaterally. The expulsion of the Iraqis from Kuwait is a general
interest which I think the international community can achieve by
sustained pressure. The toppling of Saddam Husayn can only be
achieved by force. That force could only be pursued by the United
States. I believe we would be alone, and therefore, it is not worth
it.

    MR. KISSINGER: May I -- may I make one point. My view is, and
it apparently is the view of the administration as well. But
at any rate, my view is that if this crisis ends with Iraqi forces
in possession of Kuwait and American forces in Saudi Arabia, that
the protection of Saudi Arabia and of the Gulf states will not be
possible over an extended period of time, that it would be possible
only by the presence of a very large American force permanently
which would be a constant irritation, and that therefore, you cannot
separate the future of Kuwait from the future of the Gulf area, and
that if it --

    MS. ROBERTS: So that sounds like what you're saying is that
you have to invade, that you have to take military action?

    MR. BRZEZINSKI: May I come in? May I come in on this?

    MR. DONALDSON: Please.

    MR. KISSINGER: I'm not saying you have to invade. I believe
these -- Iraqi must be made to withdraw from Kuwait which most
people seem to think the sanctions can accomplish, and that I --

    MR. BRZEZINSKI: Okay what I would like -- if I may come in on
this?

    MR. KISSINGER: -- and I'm saying that if they -- if the
sanctions don't accomplish it, then we will face the problem that
Zbig has mentioned, namely the protection of Saudi Arabia by -- by
other measures, but I'm --

    MR. BRZEZINSKI: Henry?

    MR. KISSINGER: I'm not recommending that for now.

    MR. BRZEZINSKI: Henry, could I come in on this?

    MR. DONALDSON: Come in now.

.ETX
                                                              0054

    MR. BRZEZINSKI: It seems to me that of course the disgorging
of Kuwait by Iraq is desirable, but if the choice is a prolonged
American presence in Saudi Arabia with all the complications that
Henry rightly mentions, or a solitary and larger unilateral American
military effort to throw Iraq out of Kuwait, then I prefer the
former to the latter. I prefer to sit in the sands in Saudi Arabia
then to have American soldiers fighting through the streets of the
City of Kuwait, taking very heavy casualties, and precipitating an
Arab anti-American explosion which could even destabilize the
governments that we're seeking to protect, and thereby in the end
even deprive us of the oil that we so vitally need.

    MR. DONALDSON: I -- I'd like to put you on the spot with a
very quick answer if I may. Apart from the views which you've both
expressed this morning very eloquently, looking at the situation in
total, do you

.ETX

CONTINUED ON PAGE 4-1

0055

.STX

expect that there will be major military action?   Mr. Kissinger?

    MR. KISSINGER: I believe that Saddam Husayn is looking for
some way out, and I think if we remain firm and if we keep open the
prospect that we will not stop, he will settle.

    MR. DONALDSON: Mr. Brzezinski?

    MR. KISSINGER: There will not be military action.

    MR. DONALDSON: There will not be.   Mr. Brzezinksi, very
quickly, what's your view?

    MR. BRZEZINSKI: I think if we sustain collective international
pressure, with the United States actively involved, there will be
some form of an intermediary regional solution as discussed by Crown
Prince Hassan.

    MR. BRINKLEY: Mr. Brzezinski and Mr. Kissinger, thank you
both very much.   Interesting discussion.   Glad you were able to be
with us.

    MR. BRZEZINSKI: Thank you.

.ETX

                              END

                                                           0056

William Safire의 평론에서 키신저에 관한 언급 내용

ㅇ 키신저는 미국의 전략 목적을 후세인의 세계에 대한 위협에 종지부를 찍는
것으로 명확히 하지 않았음.

ㅇ 키신저는 국무장관이나 취할법한 조심성을 가지고 이야기 하였는 바, 후세인이
쿠웨이트를 계속 약탈하고 수많은 서방 인질들을 붙잡아 놓았는데도 협상의
구도를 제시한 NYT지의 사설속에 칭찬할만한 내용이 많이 있다고 언급함.

0057

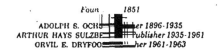
Squeeze — and Contain — Iraq

The United States has forged two potent weapons against Iraq, a worldwide diplomatic alliance and a swelling army in the Saudi sands. Some analysts fear the alliance cannot long hold, however, and impatiently urge that force be used immediately to quell Iraq's grandiose ambitions once and for all. But there's a solid chance that the alliance and its trade embargo will force Saddam Hussein to negotiate.

If so, what terms could the United States and its allies possibly trust to contain so dangerous and untrustworthy an adversary?

Consider first how much the diplomatic weapon has already accomplished. Saddam Hussein is bereft of allies. Unable to sell his oil, he is without income. He has now surrendered to Iran the fruits of an eight-year war. Construction of his military arsenal has ceased. His dreams of empire and influence have been shattered. The only realistic goal now left to him is survival.

He may thus be driven to serious negotiations. If so, he must not only leave Kuwait as the United Nations has demanded, but must agree to a series of conditions that would prevent Iraq from presenting a continuing threat to regional stability and the world's oil.

☐ Iraq must withdraw entirely from Kuwait, but its territorial claims could be adjudicated by the World Court. This would afford Saddam Hussein a fig leaf.

☐ An interim government of Kuwait should be established, probably under U.N. auspices, to allow Kuwait's future to be decided. The United States could thus avoid unseemly commitment to the automatic return of the Emir of Kuwait, an absolute monarch.

☐ Iraq must destroy all its chemical weapon stockpiles and submit to international inspection of its industrial plant and chemical and nuclear facilities.

☐ The international embargo on selling arms and military-related technology to Iraq must remain in place indefinitely.

☐ A continuing international force, perhaps under U.N. auspices, must remain in the region by invitation of all countries concerned. These forces would be stationed in Saudi Arabia and Kuwait, and in Jordan and Syria, too, if these countries desired.

☐ In return, the embargo on non-military trade would be lifted, and Syria and Iran would agree not to attack Iraq. *No Israel?*

A package of this kind would defang Saddam Hussein, puncture his ambitions and remove him as a threat to neighboring countries and the world's oil. It offers a credible alternative to force, and is indeed the best conceivable solution to the crisis since it avoids harm to troops, hostages, oil fields and American standing in the Arab world.

How likely such a solution may be is another matter. Trade embargoes, even as tight as this one, take a long time to work; Saddam Hussein can probably feed his population for months. But the world can afford to wait too, particularly if Saudi Arabia increases oil production.

In the United States, which bears the principal burden of a sustained confrontation, support for the President shows no sign of faltering. The chief danger at present stems, rather, from impatience.

Some Hasty Hawks, in and out of the Pentagon, urge an immediate strike for military reasons, or because they fear domestic support is perishable. In another view, America does not dare allow a stalemate to develop. And in any case, if the public should be sufficiently outraged by Saddam Hussein's abuse of hostages and irritated by rising gas prices, it might clamor for action.

These pressures can be resisted only if there's a credible and desirable alternative to the use of force. There is one, if Saddam Hussein has a strong enough survival instinct to take it.

When Children Shoot Children   0058

The kids don't have .38's anymore. They have Uzis. — Jose Resto, resident of a crime-plagued Bronx community after neighbors stabbed a robbery suspect to death.

The sad, alarming trend seems apparent enough to police and residents of many cities: More murderers, and victims, are kids. New data confirm the impressions. Beyond hand-wringing about family values, there's an obvious way to respond: Disarm adolescents.

According to the Crime

"since guns are demonstrably more lethal than other weapons." And indeed, the dramatic surge of teen-age homicides after 1984 coincides with the development of thriving illicit urban markets for semiautomatic firearms capable of spraying indiscriminate fire.

This arms traffic appears to have grown up with the crack trade, as drug profits lined the pockets of young gangsters. Disputes once settled with fists, chains and knives now develop

Americans Murdered

ESSAY | William Safire

Return of the Doves

WASHINGTON

Longtime doves of the left, joined by anti-Israelites of the far right — plus sober second thinkers who want to give pacifism a chance — have combined forces to try to stop the worldwide momentum aimed at driving Saddam Hussein from power.

You could see the not-so-fast crowd out in strength in the Sunday papers and on the talk shows. ABC's Sam Donaldson, fresh from a star turn at the desert front, suggested on the Brinkley show that these bellicose types calling for a strike at the dictator's nuclear plants were personal cowards unless they volunteered to do it themselves.

The intellectual guru was Zbigniew Brzezinski, arguing for a long-term "squeeze" to induce Iraq to disgorge Kuwait. He posits that time is on our side — as if a blockade would not be fun; as if television interviews with starving hostages would not squeeze us to supply all Iraqi food needs; as if the world's nations united in crisis would not soon separate during a long siege.

Zbig out-certituded Henry Kissinger, who could not bring himself to define our strategic purpose as ending Saddam Hussein's threat to the world. Instead, Henry spoke with the caution of a Secretary of State (a position apparently now unfilled); he found much to praise in a New York Times editorial yesterday, that offered a formula for a negotiated settlement even while Mr. Hussein continues to rape Kuwait and seizes ever more Western hostages.

The Times is an institution whose style dictates I loyally obey. (Notice the required "Mr. Hussein" above; until our stylebook conforms to the general usage of "Saddam," which avoids confusion with the little Hussein, I will retaliate by conferring an honorific on "Mr. Hitler.") But editorial-page readiness to split the difference with organized evil I am here to help offset.

It is one thing for Kurt Waldheim to treat with the hostage-taker — symbols of Nazism then and now flock together — but it is hardly helpful, with Mr. Hussein's gun to our heads, to begin offering a way-out way out.

The Times's suggested capitulation to aggression includes (1) adjudication of Iraq's claims on Kuwait by the World Court, which would surely be amended to an Arab League court, which would hand over half the country; (2) the overturn of the present Emir in a replay of JFK's early Vietnam mistake; (3) a world embargo on arms to Iraq, sure to be undermined in a few months, and (4) self-destruction of poison-gas stocks and inspection of nuclear facilities, a nice

idea that would be the first sacrificed in any negotiation.

In return for these so-called concessions, the dithering deal calls for a promise from Syria and Iran not to attack the new regional superpower, freeing Mr. Hussein to develop his nuclear missiles in secret and to choose his next target undistracted.

Before negotiating with ourselves to see who can come up with the sweetest deal for the aggressor and hostage-taker, we should re-examine our purposes:

The aim of doves is to limit our involvement to a U.N. force to defend Saudi Arabia. They want no risky rollback of Kuwait, whose deposed Government they only recently recognized as a corrupt dictatorship unworthy of collective defense. Stern message to aggressor: Only one conquest at a time.

The U.N. purpose is both to defend the Saudis and to nullify the conquest of Kuwait. This puts at risk thousands of hostages trapped but not yet

How to dissolve resolution.

rounded up, and accepts war as a possibility.

The goal of the realists is to rid the world of the danger of a proven war-starter before he takes more hostages next week and before he gets nuclear missiles in four years. This goal — held privately by almost all the world's leaders, but too impolitic to state publicly — requires the use of overwhelming force quickly.

Which purpose will prevail? Mr. Hussein's defeat will cost lives now; his undishonored survival will inspire a holocaust of Americans later. He has wasted a million lives in one war, introduced poison gas to the repression of dissent and turned mass hostage-taking into a conventional weapon; the new Mr. Hitler's appetite will not be assuaged by appeasement now.

If we slip into a period of "phony war," our resolution will dissolve in the acid commentary of talk shows. We can hope that Mr. Bush and Arab leaders seize the moment, but the man realists count on at this moment is in Baghdad. His arrogance and foolish slyness can provide the spark to ignite his own destruction; Mr. Hussein may bring hawks and doves together.

0059

외 무 부

종 별 :

번 호 : USW-3897   일 시 : 90 0826 1110

수 신 : 장 관 (중근동,미북,봉일)

발 신 : 주 미 대사

제 목 : 중동사태 관련 언론보도

1. 이락-쿠웨이트 사태 관련, 당지 언론보도 내용을 아래 보고함.

0 당지 시간 8.26(일) 10:00 현재 미국, 영국, 이태리, 불란서 대사관을 포함
쿠웨이트 주재 각국 대사관이 이라크군에 의한 출입봉제, 단전, 단수상태가
계속되고있으며, 일체의 물품반입이 허용되지 않고 있음.

0 사담후세인은 현 중동위기의 해결을 위한 케야르 유엔사무총장과의
회담제안을수락했음.

0 바그다드에 체류중이던 미국 공관원 및 가족등 55명에 대한 출국이 허용되어 현
재 터키 국경으로 이동중임.

0 OPEC 회의가 비엔나에서 긴급 개최, 석유증산안을 통과시킬 것으로 보임
(이락대표 불참예상)

2. 관련기사 별첨 FAX 송부함.

(대사 박동진-국장)

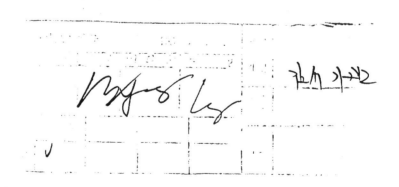

중아국   미주국   통상국

외 무 부

종 별 : 지급

번 호 : USW-3898   일 시 : 90 0826 1200

수 신 : 장관(미북,미안,중근동)

발 신 : 주 미 대 사

제 목 : 미국의 대이락 정책

연:USW-3877

BUSH 대통령의 예비군동원 결정, 이락측의 쿠웨이트 외국공관에 대한 단전,유엔안보리 해상봉쇄시행(적절한 실력 행사 허용)결의안 통과등 사태진전과 관련한 최근 미국 조야의 대이락 정책 검토동향에 대한 당관 관찰을 다음 보고함.

1. 미행정부의 목표와 조치

- 미행정부는 상금까지 이락군의 쿠웨이트 철수 및 합법정부회복이라는 기본목표를 고수하고 있는 것으로 보임.

- 이를 위해 행정부는 정치.외교 수단및 군사적 수단을 복합적으로 동원하고 있으며, 특히 이락측이 미국의 무력사용가능성에 대해 압박을 느껴, 굴복해오도록 하는데 중점을 두고 있는 것으로 보임.

0 GULF 만 군사력의 대대적 증강(동원예비군 50,000 을 포함 200,000 규모로병력 증강, 기존의 공군력외에 F-1 11 장거리 폭격기 편대 증파)

0 유엔 안보리의 실력행사 허용 결의안 통과를 위한 외교적 노력 집중 (BUSH 대통령의 정상간 친분및 BAKER 국무장관의 광범위한 접촉 능력 총동원)

- 여사한 상황에서 미언론, 학계등 조야는 미국의 이락에 대한 전면적 무력사용 여부에 비상한 관심을 집중하고 있음.

2. 미국의 대이락 무력공격 가능성

- 현재 미국의 대이락 무력공격가능성은, GULF 만 위기가 장기화될 경우, 미국 특히 BUSH 대통령에 정치적 실패가될 가능성이 있다는 전략적 우려를 바탕으로 하고 있으며, HUSSEIN 측의 서방인 인질화등 적대적 행위의 표시에 따라 그개연성이높게 논의되고 있음.(이락측의 핵능력, 화학무기 보유, 국토 회복주의등에대한 선례적 단속 필요성)

미주국 안기부	장관 대책반	차관	1차보	2차보	미주국	중아국	외연원	청와대

PAGE 1

- 특히 키신저, 헤이그 등 전 공화당 정부 국무장관들은 사태가 장기화될 경우, 현 미행정부정책에 대한 국내 외적 지지가 급격히 감소되고, 이란인질사태시와같이 BUSH 대통령이 인질석방문제로 정치적 손실을 입을 가능성을 지적하고 있음.

- 또한 BUSH 대통령은 미국인 인질 문제가 사태의 중심에 등장, 문제의 본질을 흐리고, 행정부의 군사적 대안을 축소하게될 가능성을 방지하기 위해 미국인 인질과 자신의 이미지를 직접 연결시키는것을 의식적으로 피하고 있는것으로 관찰됨. (여사한 태도도 미국의 대이락 공격을 추측케하는데 일조하고 있는 것으로 관찰)

3. 직접적 무력공격에 대한 제약 요소

-그러나 현재 BUSH 행정부로서는 이락에 대한 직접적 무력사용에 있어 여러가지 제약 요소를 앉고 있는것으로 보임.

1) 국내적 요인

- 이락측이 미국인 인질에 위해를 가하고 미군에 대해 선제공격을 가해오지않는한, 미군에 의한 대이락 선제공격은 BUSH 정책에 대한 미국내 지지도를 급속히 저하시킬 가능성이 있음. (대의회, 국민설득에 어려움:제 2 의 월남전에 대한 반감 증대)

2)군사적요인

- 현재 미측은 전면적 군사대결시 군사적 승리를확보할수 있는 능력을 거의확보해 놓고 있는것으로 관찰되고 있으나, 이락측의 화학무기 사용 가능성, 대이스라엘 공격 가능성 시사등과 관련, GULF 만에서의 군사대결이 매우 복잡한 양상을 띄고, 대규모 인명살상을 초래할 가능성이 있다는 전문가들의 견해가 제시되고 있음. (해공군력에 이락이 굴복치 않을경우, 사막 참호전에서 미군이 불리)

3)국제 정치적 요인

- 국제여론이 미국의 무력사용에 절대적 지지를 보낼정도의 환경이 조성되지 않은상태에서 미국의 대이락 공격은 현재의 국제적 지지를 급속히 와해 시킬 가능성이 있음.

- 또한 대다수 중동문제 전문가들은 미국의 대이락 무력공격과 이락정권의 문리적 붕괴는 중동에서의 세력균형을 파괴할뿐 아니라, 아랍의 강경민족주의를 부추겨서 중동에서의 미국의 지위를 급속히 훼손하게될 가능성을 경고하고 있음. (전쟁에서는 승리하고 정치에서는 패퇴할 가능성:1956 SUEZ 사태,1982 레바논 사태등)

- 특히 아랍연합국 뿐아니라 많은 NATO 동맹국들도 이락과의 직접적 군사대결은 바람직하지 않다는 입장을 갖고 있는 것으로 분석됨.

PAGE 2

- 기타 미국의 전면적 무력사용시 중동정세가 오히려 더욱 혼돈에 빠질가능성도 거론됨(JORDAN 의 붕괴, 이스라엘의 개입등)

4. 전망

-여사한 상황하에서 미행정부는 당분간 대이락 봉쇄를 실효적으로 실시하고,이락측에 대한 군사적, 정치적 압박을 가하는데 최우선의 중점을 두어나갈것으로 예상됨.(대부분의 전문가들은 BUSH 대통령의 국제적 지지, 단결확보노력을 높이 평가하고, 동 대통령이 당분간 여사한 노력을 지속해 나갈것을 권고)

- 다만, 미행정부로서도 사태가 여하히 진전되어 나갈지 판단키 어려운 입장에 있는것으로 보이는바, 현재로서는 일단 가능한 모든 대안을 수립, 유사상황에 대비하고 있는것으로 보임.(BUSH 대통령, CHENEY 국방장관, POWELL 합참의장등은 GULF 만의 미군의 목표는 대이락 공격이아니라고 언명하는 일방, 전면적 무력대결에 대비한 군사력 증강 조치 계속)

- 단기적으로 의회가 9 월초 개회키로되어 있는 점도 하나의 고려요인이될수 있는바, 주요한 국내외 정책에 있어 초당적 지지를 중요시해온 BUSH 팀으로서는 주요한 군사활동 이전에 의회 지도자들의 지지확보 노력이 긴요함.(일방적 무력사용 결정시, EXECUTIVE POWER 를 제한하자는 반대여론 비등가능성 및 보수진영내 고립주의자들의 반발 가능성)

- 대부분의 당관 접촉, 미측 인사들은 군사적 대안의 사용여부에 대해 자신들로서도 알수 없다는 입장을 표시하고 있는바, 현상황에서 여사한 가능성을 구체적으로 예측하기는 어려운것으로 보임. 다만 국내외 적으로 충분히 납득이 될만한 사태의 발전 또는 사건이 발발한경우(해상봉쇄, 단속시 이락측의 공격등)경우, 미국의 대이락 공격을 배제할수 없음.

- 장기적으로 키신저등은 미국의 사태의 진정 이후에도 상당기간 미군의 사우디 주둔이 동 지역 안정상 필요하다는 입장을 보이고 있고, 몇몇 전직 행정부 고위 책임자 들도(TURNER 전 CIA 국장, HAIG 전 국무장관)도 여사한 의견에 동조하고 있음을 참고 바람.(대사 박동진-국장)

예고:90.12.31 까지

관리
번호 PO/14f5

외 무 부

종 별 : 지 급

번 호 : USW-3905   일 시 : 90 0827 1836

수 신 : 장관(중근동,미북)

발 신 : 주 미 대 사

제 목 : 주미 이락 공관원 활동 제한 조치.

연:USW-3899

1. 미국무부는 금 8.27(월) 정례 브리핑을 통해 주미 이락 대사관에 대한 연호 제한 조치를 발표하였는바, 전문 별첨 FAX (USW(F)-1954)송부함.

2. 동 발표문에 따르면 이락 공관원 감축 대상자 36 명(작일 소집된 연호 외교단 회의시 현원을 26 명으로 발표했으나 금일 55 명으로 수정 발표)에는 상무관등 외교단 7 명이 포함된다함.

3. 또한 이락 공관원에 대한 25 마일 활동 범위 제한 조치는 주워싱턴 대사관에만 해당되고, 주유엔대표부 직원은 이에 구속되지 않는다함.

(대사 박동진-국장)

예고:90.12.31 까지

1990 12.31 . 에 예고문에
의거 일반문서로 재 분류됨.

중아국 대책반	장관	차관	1차보	2차보	미주국	정문국	청와대	안기부

PAGE 1

90.08.28   08:37
외신 2과 통제관 CW

0064

신호 : USW(F)- 1954
수신 : 장 관 (중근동, 미북)   발신 : 주미대사   보안
                                                    통제
제목 : 주미 이락 공관원 활동 제한 조치 (첨부) (2 매)

STATE DEPARTMENT/REGULAR BRIEFING/BRIEFER: MARGARET TUTWILER
1:55 P.M. EDT/MONDAY, AUGUST 27, 1990

Since its brutal aggression against Kuwait on August 2nd, Iraq
has demonstrated a blatant disregard for international law and the
norms of civilized society through a series of acts, including: the
military occupation of Kuwait; overthrow of the legitimate
government of that country; establishment of a wholly illegitimate
puppet government; purported annexation of Kuwait; denial of the
essential right of departure of tens of thousands of foreign
nationals in Kuwait and Iraq, including diplomats from the United
States and other countries; forcible removable of a large number of
detained foreign nationals, including American citizens from Kuwait
and Iraq; denial of consular access to those detained; institution
of a large-scale hostage policy using foreign hostages, including
American citizens as human shields. Iraq has ordered the closure of
all remaining foreign embassies in Kuwait, including the American
embassy. In brazen defiance of mandatory United Nations Security
Council resolutions, the Iraqi authorities have cut off electricity
and water to our embassy, among others.

In response to all of these actions, but in particular the
illegal order to close our embassy in Kuwait, the United States has
decided to take the following measured steps, all in strict
accordance with US and international law: The number of authorized
Iraqi personnel at Iraq's embassy in Washington will be reduced from
the current 55 to 19. Among the 36 leaving are seven accredited
diplomats, including all those who deal with commercial affairs.
The travel of personnel assigned to Iraq's embassy in Washington
will be limited to the area defined by a 25-mile radius from that
embassy. All Iraqi diplomatic visas will be changed from multiple- to
single-entry. New procedures will be instituted for handling
applications for non-official US visas by Iraqi nationals over the
age of 16. Use of Iraqi embassy funds for students and other
allegedly humanitarian needs will be closely controlled.

The United States is urging other governments, particularly
those whose embassies have been affected by Iraqi actions in Kuwait,
to consider taking similar actions against Iraq's official and
non-official presence in their countries. The governments that we
have consulted with are as concerned as we are about Iraqi actions
in Iraq and Kuwait. A number of them have indicated that they will
be taking actions similar to our own.

Iraqi Ambassador Mashat was summoned to a meeting with Acting
Secretary of State Lawrence Eagleburger this morning at 9:00 a.m. to
receive the information I just gave to you. It is our intention
that these new restrictions take effect as expeditiously as
possible. A diplomatic note is currently being prepared by the
Department, which will spell out for the embassy how these
restrictions will take effect, including timing. We will have more
information later on the specifics of the restrictions.

0065

As I said, 36 of the 55 Iraqi nationals at the embassy are
being told to leave the United States. This includes seven
accredited diplomats and 29 non-diplomatic staff members. Nineteen
diplomatic personnel will be allowed to stay in the United States.
This roughly two-thirds reduction was considered to be an
appropriate reduction at this time.

Dependents are not specifically mentioned, but I would note
that the visa status of dependents is derived from the visa status
of the employee. Therefore, dependents would be expected to leave
with the head of family who is leaving.

I will not, at this briefing, have anything further for you on
reductions or further steps.

Last night, Deputy Assistant Secretary of State David Mack
spoke here at the Department to representatives of 34 embassies
whose governments are attempting to maintain their embassies in
Kuwait. He briefed them on the measures which the United States was
planning to take against the Iraqi embassy in Washington this
morning. We have consulted closely, as I said earlier, with our
allies and others on this issue, and initial response indicates that
other governments are studying further steps in response to specific
Iraqi actions against their respected (sic) embassies. The 34
representatives who met with the Deputy Assistant Secretary included
all the members of the Security Council Permanent Five members,
Egypt and the Gulf Cooperation Council countries.

We understand that at least 25 embassies in Kuwait are open and
staffed. A number of others are considered to be open by their
governments, but have withdrawn their diplomatic personnel. And as
far as what the other governments are going to do, obviously, I have
to refer you to them.

As far as why did we do this now, we have looked at a range of
options from the beginning of this crisis, and we have a number that
remain under review. In this circumstance, we find that now was the
appropriate time to take this step for a number of reasons, not the
least of which was continued Iraqi reneging on commitments with
regard to safe passage of Americans, including our diplomats. Iraqi
diplomats at the United Nations are not included in these
restrictions. It has been decided that they will not be included
this time due to the obligations which we have under our host
country agreement with the United Nations. At the present time,
Iraqi diplomats are restricted to Washington, DC, Virginia, and
Maryland, and must obtain permission to travel from outside those
areas. There are no restrictions on Iraqi diplomats in New York at
the United Nations.

1954-2   0066

외 무 부

종 별 : 긴 급

번 호 : USW-3953   일 시 : 90 0830 1855

수 신 : 장 관(미북,미안, 중근동)

발 신 : 주 미 대사

제 목 : 미국의 대이락 정책(BUSH 대통령기자회견)

연: USW(F)-2000

1.금 8.30 부쉬 대통령은 백악관에서 걸프만 사태에대한 특별 기자 회견을 갖고,이락의 쿠웨이트 침공과 관련, 유엔 결의안에 반영된 미국의 기본목표를 재확인하고, 일본,한국,서독,사우디, UAE 쿠웨이트 망명정부(발언순)등 여러국가에게 여사한목표 실현을 위한 비용 분담을 요청할계획이라고 발표하였음.

2.동 대통령 발표에 따르면, 금번 대이락 제재조치의 시해에 따른 피해 국가(터키, 이집트,동구국가)의 지원, 각국의 비용 분담 문제등에관한 전략이 8.29 NSC에 보고 되었다고 하고, 동 문제와 관련, 미정부 고위 사절단이 걸프만,유럽,아주 지역에파견될것이라고 밝힘(BAKER국무장관과 BRADY 재무장관이 대표단을이끌도록 지시함)

3.한편 동 대통령은 행정부내의 강경파(후세인 대통령 제거)와 유화파(중동 평화국제회의소집)의 대립이 있다는 질문에대해, <u>현재미국의 당장의 목표는 쿠웨이트에서의 기존 질서 재확립이며, 전반적인 중동 평화의 달성은 장기적 목표가</u> 될수 있으나국제회의의 소집은 목표가 될수 없다고 답변하였음(중동평화 문제관련 기 보고 전문 참조)

4.동 대통령 기자 회견 전문은 별전 FAX송부함.

첨부: USW(F)-2000

(대사 박동진-국장)

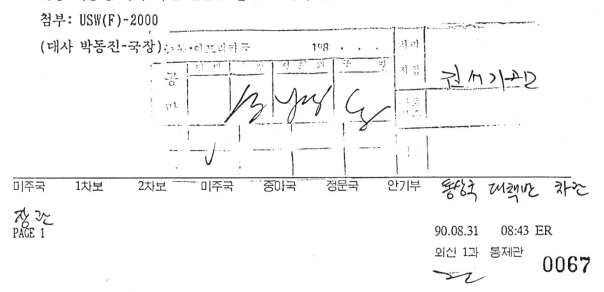

미주국	1차보	2차보	미주국	중아국	정문국	안기부

전쟁에 대한 미국민의 지지성향 분석

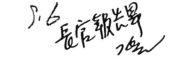

(9.2. W.P 지 기사요약)

1. 전쟁에 대한 미국민의 지지성향 관련, 6가지 신화(myth)

    신화 1 : 전쟁에 따라 미국민의 지지도가 달라진다.

    신화 2 : 교착 상태가 되면 지지도는 급속히 감소된다.

    신화 3 : 전시에 미국민은 초당적으로 단결한다.

    신화 4 : 미국민은 전쟁 개입에 대한 강력한이유를   요구하는 경향이
            있는 바, 현 중동사태에서는 그러한 이유를 발견하지 못하고 있다.

    신화 5 : TV 시대에는 실제 전쟁을 수행할 수 없다.

    신화 6 : 미국민은 침략자가 되길 싫어하며 따라서 미국이 이라크에 대해
            공격을 감행하므로써 야기되는 전쟁을 용인하지 않을 것이다.

2. 60여년에 걸친 실제 여론 조사 결과 (한국전 및 월남전시 조사결과 포함)

    가. 전쟁에 대한 미국민의 반응은 놀라울 정도로 일관성을 유지하고 있는
        바, 미국의 여론 향배에 가장 결정적인 요소는 총 사상자수(casulaty
        total)임.

    ┌──────────── 사상자수의 증가에 따라 지지도 감소율 ────────────┐
    │ - 사상자수가 100에서 1,000으로 증가시 : 초기 지지도에서   │
    │   15% 감소   │
    │ - 사상자수가 1,000에서 10,000으로 증가사 : 지지율 15%   │
    │   추가 감소   │
    │ - 사상자수가 10,000에서 100,000으로 증가시 : 지지율 15%   │
    │   추가 감소   │
    └──┘

0068

나. 고착상태시 지지도 급속 감소 신화는 역사적으로 근거가 없음.

따라서, 가까운 장래 전투가 개시되지 않더라도 부쉬 대통령의 대 페만
조치에 대한 지지도가 급격히 감소 되지는 않을 전망(단, 미국경제가
깊은 침체의 늪에 빠지거나 작전상 실패가 나타날 경우는 별 문제)

다. 미국민은 위기상황에서 대통령을 중심으로 단결하나 상황이 더욱 악화
되면 소속정당에 따라 견해차가 발생하기 시작하고 국민적 단결에
군열이 생김.

라. 미국민은 특징적으로 전쟁초기 단계에서는 어느 전쟁을 박론하고 높은
지지를 보내는 경향이 있음.

마. TV가 대중의 지지도에 결정적 영향을 미친다는 주장의 과학적 근거 빈약.

바. 대부분의 미국민은 별 지식이 없거나 강한 이해관계가 없는 경우,
대통령의 대외정책 결정을 그대로 수용하는 경향이 높으며, 전쟁의
타당성 등에 크게 좌우되지 않음.

3. 현 페만 사태와 관련한 여론조사 결과의 의미

o 미국민은 정부의 대외정책을 지지하고 따르는 경향 있는 바, 부쉬
대통령이 이라크에 대해 공격을 하지 않고 방어적 태세를 취하고 있는
현 정책을 계속 지지할 것임.

o 그러나, 장차 부쉬 대통령이 그럴듯한 이유를 들어 이라크에 대해 공격을
가할 경우, 미국민은 동결정도 지지할 것임.

o 이 경우, 부쉬 대통령의 이라크 공격에 대한 국민적 지지도는 사상자수가
증가함에 따라 급격히 감소될 것임.   끝.

0069

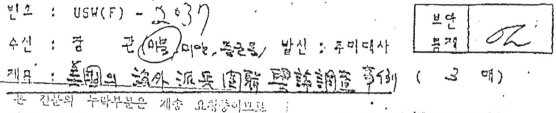

How Much War Will Americans Support?

By Richard Morin

THE SHOWDOWN in the sand is not yet a month old and already there are muttered doubts inside the Beltway and beyond: How long will American public opinion support our massive military presence in the Persian Gulf—and war, if it comes to that?

Six decades of polling suggest an answer to that question. This research also serves to dispel several myths that currently misinform much of the debate about our role in the Middle East. Here are six of these myths:

Myth 1—Every war is different.

Actually, our reaction to wars is surprisingly consistent: Public support appears to rise and fall in remarkably predictable ways. This is particularly true of limited wars fought in distant parts of the world.

The evidence comes from extensive analyses of data collected during the Vietnam and Korean wars. Studies of public attitudes toward those two seemingly different wars have produced a remarkable finding with decidedly unexpected implications.

Of all the complex variables governing public opinion, the single overwhelming factor is the casualty total. As the number of dead, wounded and missing in action rose, support for both wars fell at an identical rate. Moreover, this simple relationship explained virtually *all* of the change in attitudes during both wars—suggesting that initial support for the war, the vagaries of domestic politics, different levels of public dissent and a host of other factors have little to do with shifting public attitudes.

"Casualties were easily the most important variable," said John Mueller, professor of political science at the University of Rochester and author of the groundbreaking book, "War, Presidents and Public Opinion." "We found that as casualties rose from 100 to 1,000, support for the war dropped 15 percentage points. As casualties rose from 1,000 to 10,000, support declined by another 15 percentage points." Should casualties increase to 100,000, the model suggests, support would drop another 15 points.

Of course, ideological predisposition also affects the national mood; and in that regard, support for the Gulf crisis could erode faster. Korea and Vietnam were wars that initially sounded "right" to Cold War America. Whether protecting access to Mideast oil would play as well as the Red card did in Korea and Vietnam is an open question: "Going to your death for stable oil prices might be difficult for the public to accept," Mueller argues. 'He died for $25-a-barrel-oil'—you don't put that on somebody's tombstone."

Myth 2—Stalemates quickly become stale.

If the shooting hasn't started—and it hasn't yet—there is little historic evidence to suggest that support for Bush's desert gambit will weaken substantially in the near future.

The United States has kept troops in South Korea for four decades with hardly a whimper from the body politic. In 1979, as the U.S. military prepared to celebrate its 30th anniversary in South Korea, just a third of those interviewed in a Gallup poll favored withdrawing troops.

Moreover, this country currently maintains 320,000 soldiers in Western Europe and the public seems in no particular hurry to bring them home. The U.S. contribution to NATO, for example, is running about $160 billion annually (a somewhat misleading figure since some of these forces would be based elsewhere even if we left Europe). By contrast, the estimated annual cost of Operation Desert Shield is $10 billion to $15 billion.

Of course, there are circumstances under which support could shift dramatically. Operational blunders could turn Desert Shield into a Johnny Carson punch line. Iraq could commit atrocities that would further steel public support and perhaps lead to calls for massive retaliation. Or America's currently soft economy could plunge into deep recession—perhaps the single greatest threat to public support for a costly Mideast buildup.

But until the killing starts or the economy dies, it's a good bet that reporters and soldiers sweating it out in Saudi Arabia will tire of a stalemate long before the public.

Myth 3—In times of war, we aren't Republicans or Democrats, we're Americans.

The public does rally around the president in times of crisis. But when the going starts getting tough, the opposition party gets going.

0070

2 ○〕〕-/

90 /9 /2

Polls conducted during the Korean and Vietnam eras suggest that party membership dramatically affects individual perceptions of the overall success and failure of the war effort. Gallup data from the Truman and Johnson administrations shows that Democrats were less likely than Republicans to be pessimistic about the progress being made in each war.

Trend data collected during Vietnam discloses that support for the war among Democrats and Republicans abruptly shifted when LBJ moved out of the White House and Nixon moved in. Before 1969, a larger percentage of Republicans than Democrats opposed the war. Thereafter, however, Republicans were more inclined to support the war than were Democrats.

"It's the 'my team' effect, and you see it again and again in a number of areas, but frequently in foreign policy," said political scientist Everett Ladd, who directs the Roper Center for Public Opinion Research at the University of Connecticut. "There is a section of the public, and not a trivial section, more inclined to grant consent when it is the president of their party who is carrying out the activity."

Ladd suggests that partisan differences may therefore be among the first cracks to appear in Bush's solid shield of public support, as strong Democrats begin responding to the first discouraging words from their party leaders. Those words may begin to be heard next week when Congress returns from its summer vacation.

Myth 4—Americans need a strong reason to believe in a war, and they don't yet have one in the Middle East.

(Actually, this is a near myth.) It would be nice to think this is so, but history indicates otherwise. Public opinion of recent wars—even those the populace doesn't completely understand and will later reject—typically starts high.

The currently popularity of the reason-to-believe myth can be traced to Vietnam. In 1967, Gallup asked Americans this question: "Do you feel you have a clear idea of what the Vietnam war is all about—that is, what we are fighting for?" Fewer than half—48 percent—thought they knew.

To many, this result suggested that the government had failed to justify the war to its citizens. That could be true. But there may be another explanation: Americans typically are puzzled by or simply ill-informed about foreign relations, including war policy. Thus the 48-percent figure may reflect acknowledged ignorance.

Consider what happened when Gallup asked the same question six months after the Japanese attacked Pearl Harbor. Barely half—53 percent—of those interviewed said they had a clear idea of why the United States was in World War II. (The percentage did rise considerably later in the war.)

Anyway, worries about a befuddled public may be moot: According to a new Washington Post poll completed last week, 70 percent of those persons questioned said they had a clear understanding of why Bush sent troops to Saudi Arabia.

Myth 5—You can't fight a real war in the television age.

Some researchers argue that this is one of the longest-lived myths of the Vietnam war—one that should have expired 15 years ago when studies began showing that increases in casualties had almost precisely same the effect on public attitudes toward Vietnam—America's first TV war—as they did for Korea, perhaps our last newspaper war. (This apparent mathematical fact of life has been confirmed and amplified by numerous studies.) If television had a pronounced effect on attitudes, the rate of decline during the Vietnam War should have been greater, Mueller and other social scientists say.

"War, after all, is a singularly unsubtle phenomenon, and the assumption that people will know how they feel about it only if they see it regularly pictured on their television screens is essentially naive and patronizing," Mueller has written.

There even is some admittedly shaky evidence that watching television news accounts of the fighting and dying in Vietnam may have momentarily increased support for the war. A 1969 Harris Poll asked: "Has the television coverage of the war made you feel more like you ought to back up the boys fighting in Vietnam or not?" This somewhat loaded question produced a hawkish 83 percent affirmative response. Even those unwilling to dismiss the impact of TV acknowledge that evidence for its effect is, as Ladd says, "very, very hard to find."

And even assuming that televised protest did play a significant role in determining public support, it is unlikely that the always-photogenic peace demonstrations of the Vietnam era would occur in these days of an all-volunteer army.

Myth 6—Americans don't like being the aggressors and won't tolerate an offensive war against Iraq.

That's what the public seemed to be clearly saying to pollsters immediately after Bush sent troops to the Gulf. But it probably isn't what they meant. In fact, Bush probably has more publicly acceptable policy options than the first polls may suggest.

2037-2   0071

Except in extraordinary circum——ces, most Americans dutifully follow the ——and-er-in-chief on matters such as foreign relations where the public has little knowledge or firmly held views. Remarkably, this tendency persists even when Americans initially may have doubts about the direction in which they are being led.

A classic example occurred just last year. An October Gallup survey for Newsweek asked respondents whether they favored or opposed using "U.S. military forces to invade Panama and overthrow Noriega." Only 26 percent supported committing troops.

Barely two months later, Bush did precisely that. And the reaction was immediate: 80 percent of those questioned in a Gallup Poll days after the invasion supported Bush's actions; just 13 percent were opposed.

Panama was, at best, a war writ exceedingly small. Vietnam, however, provided equally graphic examples of how the public in the early years of the war, when casualty levels were still tolerable, readily accepted official war policy.

In October 1967, a Gallup poll found that about two out of three Americans opposed de-escalation of the war in Vietnam and a slightly smaller majority rejected withdrawing troops. But in another poll taken three months later—when those options were presented as an official change in policy—opinion followed policy.

Gallup asked: "If our government were to decide at this time that the best thing for us and the Vietnamese to do would be for the United States to stop the bombing and the fighting and gradually withdraw from Vietnam," nearly six out of 10 said they would approve of this new policy and barely a third said they would oppose such a plan.

Likewise, when Harris asked in September 1965 if the administration was right or wrong not to bomb Hanoi or Haiphong, just 30 percent approved. A scant 10 months later—but after the bombing began—85 percent said the administration was right.

Similar effects may have been at work in the Civil War and World War I, said Mark Lorell, a senior defense analyst at the Rand think tank and co-author of "Casualties, Public Opinion and Presidential Policy during the Vietnam War," a 1985 study for the Air Force. Lorell said each conflict was preceded by widespread public protests in the countries involved. Yet the eventual declaration of war was immediately met with equally ubiquitous support.

What does all this suggest for ||I||rrent conflict? It would seem to imply that Americans now support a defensive crouch in the Persian Gulf and oppose an invasion of Iraq because that's what their president has done. Should Bush decide tomorrow to invade Iraq and offer a plausible explanation to justify this decision, he could expect support "until the casualties start coming back," Lorell said.

Set against the public's historic predisposition to follow and support official policy—wherever it leads—it may be grimly comforting to note the inevitable braking effect that body counts seem to have on public opinion and, eventually, on public policy. It may also be discomforting to note that this lesson was known but ignored in the first years of the Vietnam war.

The relationship between casualties and public support for the war was specifically discussed before the National Security Council on July 21, 1965. Undersecretary of State George Ball, quoted in Rand's study for the Air Force, recalled what he said at that meeting:

"In a long war, I said the president would lose the support of the country. I showed him a chart I had prepared showing the correlation between Korean casualties and public opinion, as our casualties during the Korean war had increased from 11,000 to 40,000. The percentage of those Americans who thought that we had been right to intervene had diminished from 65 percent in 1950 to a little more than 30 percent in 1952. Moreover, as our losses mounted, many frustrated Americans would demand that we strike at the very jugular of North Vietnam with all the dangers that entailed."

Ball recalls telling President Johnson directly: "Look, you have a lot of support right now, but once you get a lot of casualties, this thing is going to change." But, Ball recalled, "nobody really focused on the consequences of a lot of casualties."

2037-3
(END)

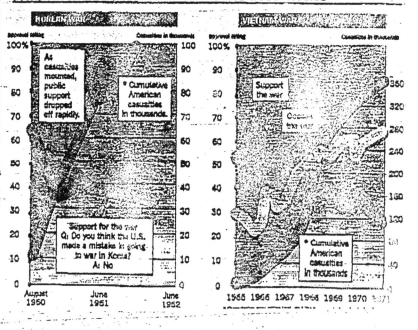

PUBLIC SUPPORT FOR U.S. WARS

KOREAN WAR — As casualties mounted, public support dropped off rapidly. * Cumulative American casualties in thousands.

"Support for the war. Q: Do you think the U.S. made a mistake in going to war in Korea? A: No"

(Approval rating 100%–0; Casualties in thousands 100–0; August 1950, June 1951, June 1952)

VIETNAM WAR — Support the war. * Cumulative American casualties in thousands.

(Approval rating 100%–0; Casualties in thousands 360–40; 1965 1966 1967 1968 1969 1970 1971)

0072

"어려울때 도와주지 않는 우방들"

(Tom Wicker)

o 서독은 미군의 사우디 파견이 미국.사우디간 쌍무 합의에 의한 것이고, 헌법상 구라파 이외 지역에서의 군사관계에 참가할 수 없다는 이유로 수송기와 선박 몇척만 지원하는 매우 미온적인 반응을 보이고 있는바, 서독이 제2차 세계대전 이후 미국의 갖가지 혜택을 받고, 최근에 콜 수상이 미국의 통독 지원에 사의를 표명한 바 있으며, 서독 헌법에도 현금 지원을 금지하지는 않았음.

o 일본도 지난 45년간 미국의 혜택을 많이 받은 부국이면서 일본 경제의 원동력인 석유공급을 보호하는데 실질적인 현금지원은 없음.

o 반면에 영국은 2,000명 군대, 선박 및 항공기를 사우디에 파견 하면서도 군사 작전 비용의 일부를 부담하겠다고 약속하였음.

o 현재 대 이라크 공격에 대한 찬반 논의가 있으나 아래 이유로 반대함.
  - 독.일이 미국의 단독적 대 이라크 공격을 반대할 가능성이 있음.
  - 전쟁은 현재의 작전 및 경제 제재 비용보다 더 많은 비용이 소요됨.
  - 대이라크 공격이 장기화되고 사상자를 많이 내며 지원을 받지 못하면서 실패할 가능성도 있는바 이경우 비용이 훨씬 더 들고 미국민은 물론 세계 여론의 지지를 상실할 것임.
  - 미국의 대 이라크 공격은 새로운 중동 집단 안보체제의 가능성을 무산시킬 것임.
  - 미국의 대 이라크 공격이 단기적으로 이스라엘을 기쁘게할 수 있으나, 아랍 대 미국.이스라엘 전쟁으로 확산되면 장기적으로 미.이스라엘 양국에 좋을 수 없음.

0073

USW(F)- 2/08

장 관 (마북 총(한동)) 밖신 : 주미대사

"돼" 관 책啓 미병方 수방策 태도 評價 (매)

IN THE NATION | Tom Wicker
Fair-Weather Allies

West Germany, after decades of benefiting from American policies, including military protection, has offered the flimsiest of excuses for shirking a fair share of the costs of the shield American troops are providing in Saudi Arabia for German oil supplies.

Bonn cannot financially support that shield, German officials told The Washington Post, because it represents only a bilateral arrangement between the United States and the Saudis. As if the American deployment of troops and weapons to prevent an Iraqi invasion had nothing to do with protecting oil for the factories of the Ruhr!

This shameful exercise in pinchpenny rationalization overrode what the officials said was Chancellor Helmut Kohl's "gratitude" for U.S. support of German unification. Some gratitude!

The affluent Germans point out that their Constitution prohibits their participation in military efforts beyond Europe. But it doesn't prevent them from sending cash, if they want to. And if it salves the German conscience, it hardly repays American sacrifices that Bonn says it may provide a few ships and planes (but only if necessary) to help move someone else's troops — the U.S.'s, naturally — to the Middle East.

Japan, another wealthy beneficiary of U.S. policies and protection over the last 45 years, has joined the Soviet Union in professing support for collective security in the Middle East. Thanks a lot, Tokyo; now how about putting up some real yen to give meaning to that profession, as well as to help protect the oil that fuels the Japanese economy?

Compare the meager contributions of Germany and Japan with that of hard-pressed Britain. Prime Minister Thatcher's Government not only has sent a 2,000-member force but also ships and planes to Saudi Arabia, and has committed itself to sharing the overall costs of Operation Desert Shield — which may reach $50 billion for the first year.

The spectacle of principal allies and primary beneficiaries looking the other way when Washington justifiably seeks their help does underscore a point too easily overlooked in the U.S. If Germany and Japan will do little or nothing to help an international operation that's clearly in their own interest, they will do nothing — they probably would oppose — a unilateral American attack on Iraq designed to disarm it and overthrow Saddam Hussein, and which would destroy rather than preserve oil production.

Such an attack is hotly debated among American conservative spokesmen, although neither the Bush Administration nor Mrs. Thatcher now contemplate so dubious a military adventure. Self-proclaimed hard-liners who favor it argue that a nuclear-armed Iraq may someday threaten not only the Middle East but the world. Erstwhile hardliners who oppose an aggressive war in the desert believe the U.S. interest is only to defend Saudi Arabia from invasion and to use economic pressures to try to force Saddam Hussein out of Kuwait.

Patrick Buchanan, Robert Novak and others in the latter group may be discomfited to find themselves

But opposing an attack on Iraq would be justifiable.

aligned with some they deride as liberals; and in a few cases it may be the other way around; but prudence and common sense alike argue against a preventive U.S. war against Iraq — a war that probably would cause even faithful Britain to stand aside.

That's not anti-Semitism or isolationism or cowardice, or any other -ice or -ism that the hawkier conservatives are throwing at opponents. Wars cost more than holding operations or boycotts; and if the holding operation on the Saudi border, together with the boycott of Iraq, already costs the U.S. more than it can easily afford, a long, bloody, unsupported, perhaps unsuccessful war against Iraq would cost far more — in American and world public support as well as dollars.

If such a war against its most-feared antagonist would please Israel in the short run, that war would turn the rest of the Middle East and the Arab world against the U.S. and Israel, and that can't be good for either in the long run. A U.S. attack on Iraq also would destroy the new possibilities for collective security in a post-cold-war world, either to free Kuwait or to contain Iraq in the years to come.

And what, no hard-liner has yet had the foresight to say, would the U.S. do if it did conquer Iraq? Occupy it? Install a government chosen in Washington? Turn it over to Yitzhak Shamir? Man the oil derricks with marines? □

Sept 7, 1990
NYT

0074

War Powers and the Iraq Crisis

THE RETURNING Congress cannot avoid being called on to address the Iraq crisis, which blew up while it was in recess and which is in a politically sensitive phase now. Almost everyone agrees that a president can dispatch forces for certain emergency or short-term purposes, as President Bush has done in the Persian Gulf. But now the question arises of whether and how Congress will insist that they cannot stay for any greater length of time without its approval. This is the mandate inscribed in law when Congress passed the War Powers Resolution of 1973. It was meant to circumscribe war-making powers that, the chastened and angry legislature of the day felt, successive presidents had abused. The purpose was to ensure that the solemn decision of commiting the nation's forces along the spectrum of risk, battle and war would be shared by the two branches in an agreed constitutional way.

Except that, from the start, there was no agreement. Mr. Nixon vetoed the bill, and his successors have insisted it infringes unconstitutionally on, among other things, the president's powers as commander in chief; there have been objections on less exalted but weighty pragmatic grounds too. On the 22 occasions since Vietnam when the resolution might somehow have come into play, presidents have picked their way around it, commonly—as Mr. Bush did on Aug. 9 in respect to Iraq—reporting to Congress as the resolution demands but insisting they were doing so outside its purview. Presidents have been particularly scrupulous in avoiding the provision that compels a president, 60 days after he moves in armed forces, to withdraw them unless Congress votes otherwise. In the avoiding, they have usually done what Mr. Bush did on Aug. 9—pretend blandly that "involvement in hostilities" is not "imminent." Like him in this crisis, they have tried to meet the resolution's requirements of consultation, as of reporting, not in the resolution's terms but in their own—by, for example, inviting members to be briefed at the White House.

There is a case for these circumlocutions and deceits, and it is that the War Powers Resolution, even when presidents skirt its provisions, forces a degree of consultation and openness that otherwise might never be achieved. But this is not a persuasive case. How can the evasive presidential habits that are bred by this resolution and—this is almost worse—that have come to be blinked at or only mildly griped at by Congress possibly build respect for either this law or the Constitution itself? The 60-days-and-you're-out provision is especially worrisome: this "lesson" of Vietnam imposes a procedure that could too easily invite misunderstanding in a crisis.

Looking at the War Powers Resolution, some conclude that it is right and better and enough that a president be guided by his political instincts than that he be locked in the grip of an inevitably rigid and anachronistic legislative dictate. But to undo the resolution entirely could send presidents a dangerous anything-goes signal and would amount to a historic surrender of powers and responsibilities by Congress. The idea of shared responsibility remains valid and essential.

What is necessary is to flesh out this idea in terms that provide a fair balance of executive flexibility and congressional control and that command reasonable consensus in both branches. The Constitution's separation of powers has aptly been described not as a formula for agreement but as an invitation to struggle. A certain amount of push and pull is even desirable. But it should not be disabling, and in the instance of the awkward 60-day provision, it should not look like Rube Goldberg was one of the Founding Fathers.

One proposal that has been floating around for a while deserves a closer look now—S. 2, introduced in 1989 by Sens. Byrd, Nunn, Warner and Mitchell. It replaces the automatic requirement for withdrawal of troops after 60 days with expedited procedures for a joint resolution authorizing the action or requiring disengagement. Further, it fills a void in the War Powers Resolution's terms on consultation by creating a standing congressional core group with which the president would regularly consult.

This proposal would not guarantee smooth politics or wise policy, but it acknowledges evident flaws in existing legislation and procedure. Further, it calls into play the genius of American constitutional government—to bring the judgment of one branch to bear on the judgment of the other in a realm where the most vital national interests are engaged and to ensure that the decisions that result enjoy national support. The Iraq crisis is only the latest passage where the advantages of this approach are apparent.

September 4, 1990   WP

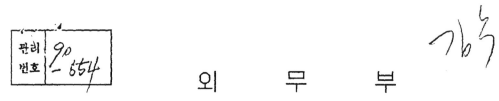

외 무 부

관리
번호 90 -654

종 별 : 긴 급

번 호 : USW-4037   일 시 : 90 0905 1857

수 신 : 장관(중근동,미북,미안)

발 신 : 주 미 대사

제 목 : 걸프 사태 전망

대 WUS-2937

연 USW-3634(1),3731(2),3877(3),3898(4)

대호 관련, 이락의 쿠웨이트 침공 이후 걸프 지역내 국제 관계의 정치, 군사적 역학 구조는 기본적으로 연호(2) 보고 내용에서 크게 일탈하지 않고 있는바, 동 보고 이후의 전술적 사태 발전을 중심으로 한 표제 전망등을 하기 보고함(기타 관련 상세에 대해서는 그간 매일 본부로 송부한바있는 주요 일간지의 보도,논설 및 주요 인사 기자 회견 내용등 당관 보고를 참조 바람)

1. 최근 주요 동향

가. 미측 동향

-사우디 파견 미군 전력의 지속적 강화(사막전의 승패에 결정적 영향을 끼칠 것으로 보이는 최신형 M-1 탱크등 배치)를 통해 계속 군사적 해결 가능성 으로서 대이락 압력을 가중시키고 있음(실제로 전부를 개시할수 있는 병력, 장비및 물자의 배치를 완료하는데에는 앞으로 1 개월 정도가 더 필요하다고함)

-병력 및 군수물자의 대 사우디 신속 수송을 위한 병참 지원을 중심으로한 예비군 동원(8.22)

-이락측이 제시한 주 쿠웨이트 대사관 철수 시한(8.24)이 경과 했음에도 공관 계속 유지

-소위 ECONOMIC ACTION PLAN 을 통해 우방국과의 대이락 고립화에 따른 비용 분담 요청(8.30 부쉬 기자 회견 발표)

-9.9 헬싱키에서 미소 정상 회담 개최, 걸프 사태 집중 논의 예상

나. 이락측 동향

-전쟁 포로 교환등 대이란 유화 조치 제의

중아국 안기부	장관 대책반	차관	1차보	2차보	미주국	미주국	정문국	정와대

-훗세인 대통령, 미군이 걸프 지역에서 철수하는 경우 이락및 쿠웨이트 내 외국인 인질의 석방 의사 표명(8.19)

-이락측, 미측 공격을 억지키 위한 인간 방패(HUMAN SHIELDS)로서 주요 군사, 산업 시설에 외국인 인질 배치 개시(8.20)

-미, 영 등의 주 쿠웨이트 대사관 계속 유지를 "AN ACT OF AGTGRESSION" 으로 간주, 단수, 단전등의 조치를 취하면서도, 무장 군인 부입등 강제 폐쇄 조치는 적극 자제

-이락측, 자국 선적 상선에 대해 미군등 다국적군의 해상 검색 조치에 저항하지 않도록 지시

-훗세인 대통령, 외국인 부녀자 및 아동의 출국 허용 발표(8.28)

-이락측, 일부 주요 식료품등의 배급제 실시중

다. 관련 국제 동향

-부쉬 대통령과 훗세인 요르단 국왕간의 회담(8.16), 유엔 사무총장과 이락외상간의 회담(8.31)등 걸프 사태 해결을 위한 외교적 노력의 성과 별무

-유엔 안보리, 대이락 경제 제재 이행을 위한 무력 사용 허용 결의안 통과(8.25)

-쿠웨이트 침공 직후 이락의 여타 아랍국에 대한 대미 성전 참여 촉구에 대한 아랍권 내부의 반응 미온적

2. 미국의 대응 방안

가. 여사한 상황하에서, 미국은 작 9.4 하원 외무위 청문회 증언시 베이커 국무장관이 재천명한바와같이 부쉬 대통령이 8.8 대국민 연설에서 밝힌 금번 사태 해결을 위한 4 대 원칙(쿠웨이트로부터 이라크군의 즉각적이고 무조건적인 전면철수, 쿠웨이트 합법 정부의 복구, 중동 지역의 안정과 안전 유지, 동 지역내 미국민의 안전 확보)을 지속적으로 일관되게 견지하고 있음(부쉬 대통령 연설 관련 사항은 연호 (1)참조)

나. 즉, 현재 미 정부는 대이락 공격을 통한 사태의 즉각적 해결 보다는 연호(2) 2 항으로 보고한 대이락 질식 전략을 계속 구사하고 있는바, 다음과같은 요인들이 미국의 대이락 군사 행동을 제한하고 있는것으로 보임(대 이락 무력 공격 가능성을 포함하는 관련 상세에 대해서는 연호 (4)참조요)

-최소한의 인적, 물적 COST 만을 지불하면서 전쟁을 승리로 이끌기 위해서는 상대방에 대해 BLITZKRIEG 을 가하는것이 긴요한바, 이락측이 외국인 인질들을 주요

PAGE 2

군사, 산업 시설등에 배치한 현 상황하에서 미측이 일방적으로(즉, 이락의 도발을 받지 않고) 기습 공격을 감행한다는것을 인명 피해가 너무큼(이러한 점을 고려, 일부 전문가들은 이락의 쿠웨이트 침공 직후 미국이 이락에 대해 막강한 공군력을 동원, 기습 공격을 가하지 않으므로서 실기한점을 비판하고 있으나, 미측으로서는 지상 병력이 열세인 상황하에서 여사한 기습공격을 감행하기는전술적으로 어려웠을것임. 즉 사태 발생 직후 부쉬 대통령이 사우디 파병의 성격을 방어적이라고 규정한점등을 감안할때 미국으로서는 100 만 병력을 갖고 있는 이락에 대해서 기습 공격을 감행할 의사가 별무 했던것으로 추측할수 있음)

-한국 전쟁 및 베트남 전쟁 당시의 여론 조사 결과에 따르면, 전쟁으로 인한 미군 사상자의 수와 정권의 인기도는 반비례하는것으로 나타났는바 미군이 대이락 공격을 감행하므로서 주요 군사 시설등에 배치된 외국인 인질들이 목숨을잃고 또한 이락의 화학 무기 사용으로 인해 미군측에도 다수의 사망자가 발생하는경우 부쉬 정권의 인기도는 현재와같은 지구전을 감행하는 경우 보다 훨씬 더 저하될 가능성이 큼(당지 일부 언론에 따르면 미국이 대이락 전면 공격을 개시하는 경우 최초 단계에서 만도 약 2-3 만명의 인명 손실을 입을 가능성이 있다함)

-또한 미국의 대이락 공격은 이락이 대미 성전을 선언한점등을 감안할때 한국 전쟁과같은 제한 전쟁으로 종료될 가능성은 거의 희박함. 따라서 전투가 지속될경우 중립적인 여타 아랍국가도 반미 감정의 고조로 아랍권의 단결이 와해 될가능성이 크며, 그 경우 미국과 전체 아랍권과의 대결 구조도 상황이 변동될 가능성이 큼(일단 전투가 개시되면 이락은 이스라엘을 공격함으로 전쟁의 성격을바꾸려고할것임)

다. 이상의 요인등을 고려시 미국의 대이락 고사작전은 앞으로도 상당기간 지속될것으로 전망되며, 또한 이러한 맥락에서 베이커 국무장관은 작일 의회 청문회시 미국인들의 인내를 촉구한것으로 보임.

라. 특히 부쉬 정권으로서는 현재 사우디 파병등 미국의 대중동 정책이 국내적으로 70 프로 이상의 인기도를 계속 유지하고 있고 또한 금번 사태를 미국과이락간의 대결이 아닌 전세계 인류 공동체와 이락간의 대결로 부각함으로서 국제적으로도 이락 고립화 정책을 성공적으로 전개하고 있는 상황인바, 여사한 상황을 변동시킬수 있는 전략의 선택을 통해 얻을수 있는 실익이 별무한것으로 판단하고 있는것으로 보임.

마. 또한 미측은 상기 4 대 원칙의 고수를 주장하면서 이락과의 타협 가능성을 배제하고 있는바, 현재의 상황이 미측에게 불리한것이 없는 만큼 이락을 계속 죄어

나가면서 WAIT-AND-SEE 의 태도를 추구코저 하는 입장인것으로 봄.

3. 이락의 대응 방안

가. 이락으로서는 대규모의 미군 병력이 사우디에 주둔하고 있는 이상 대 사우디 공격을 감행하기는 현실적으로 불가능한것으로 보이는바, 특히 미국을 도발할수도 있는 무력 행사를 자제함으로서 미국에게 CASUS BELLI 를 제공하지 않기 위해 노력하는 군사적 수세에 처해 있음(예컨데 현재 이락측은 자국 전부기의행동 반경을 자국 영공내로 엄격히 제한하고 있음)

나. 즉, 이락측은 현재 군사적으로는 RATIONAL ACTOR 로서 미국등 서방권의조치에 대응하고 있는것으로 보이며, 이러한 태도를 견지하는한 대 이스라엘 공격등의 군사적 모험을 감행할 가능성은 상당히 희박할것으로 봄.

다. 다만, 훗세인 대통령으로서는 외국인 인질의 일부 석방, 외국인 인질과의 대화 장면 TV 방영등 대 서방 심리전을 전개함으로서 서방측의 분열을 꾀하고있는것으로 보임.

즉 훗세인 대통령으로서는 서방권이 분열되는 경우 외교적 타협을 통한 사태 해결 압력이 가중되므로서 미국이 전기 4 대 원칙에서 후퇴하는 국면이 도래하는것을 기대하고 있는것으로 보임.

4. 결론

가. 기본적으로, 당분간은 연호 (2)의 정세 전망이 그대로 적용될것으로 예상됨. 특히 부쉬 대통령은 GORBACHEV 쏘련 대통령과의 긴급 정상 회담을 제안함으로서 대이락 금수 조치의 강화및 제반 외교 수단을 통한 문제 해결 방안을 선택하고 있음을 표하고 있음.

나. 즉 미국의 대응 방안에 대한 지금까지의 높은 국내적 인기도와 국제적호응도 및 대이락 군사 조치가 어느면에서 TIMING 을 실기한점등을 감안할때 미국으로서는 대이락 고립화 전략에 대한 광범위한 국제적 동참을 유도하면서 이락 국내 정세등을 예의 주시할것으로 전망됨.

다. 한편, 미측은 금번 사태로 인한 아랍권 내부의 REGROUPING 동향및 반 HUSSEIN온건 아랍 세력의 영향력 확대등을 통해 장기적으로는 중동 역내의 구조적 안정을 확보하기 위한 지역 안보 기구의 수립등을 모색할 가능성이 높은것으로 봄(KISSINGER 등 일부 보수학계에서는 지역정세의 안정을 위한 미군의 사우디 장기 주둔이 필요할것이라는 견해를 제시)

PAGE 4

0079

라. 9.9 헬싱키 미소 정상회담 관련 사항은 추보 예정임.

(대사 박동진-국장)

일반문예공 90. 12. 31 까지

Baker Proposes New Alliance To Contain Iraqi Aggression

By David Hoffman
Washington Post Staff Writer

Secretary of State James A. Baker III told Congress yesterday the United States and Arab nations should establish a new "regional security structure" for the Persian Gulf similar to the post-war Atlantic Alliance to "contain" and "roll back" Iraqi President Saddam Hussein and his pursuit of weapons of mass destruction.

In testimony to the House Foreign Affairs Committee, Baker said that even if Iraq withdraws from Kuwait there should be a long-term effort to restrict Saddam's "aggressive tendencies" and that such an effort could require a sustained U.S. naval presence in the region. He suggested this concept of a gulf regional security organization could resemble the North Atlantic Treaty Organization (NATO), the post-World War II effort led by the United States in Western Europe to contain Soviet communism.

"There was no question about the aggressive Joseph Stalin, and we developed a regional ... security strategy that worked," Baker said. "And I don't doubt for one minute that we can do it here."

Baker added that the administration is not interested in any negotiations with Saddam until Iraq pulls out of Kuwait and that Saddam has "shown no signs" of being serious about a diplomatic solution.

Also yesterday, the U.S. Navy boarded and commandeered the first Iraqi vessel that tried to run the multinational naval blockade with a load of tea bound for the Iraqi port of Basra in the gulf. No shots were fired, and the ship, under the command of a 14-member boarding party from the guided missile destroyer USS Goldsborough, was diverted to the Omani port of Muscat.

Two planeloads of Western women and children flew out of Iraq, and busloads of German and British citizens were evacuated from occupied Kuwait in arduous overland convoys to Baghdad.

Also yesterday, the Kremlin called for fresh United Nations efforts to resolve the crisis in the gulf, including the rapid convening of a Middle East peace conference to settle the Arab-Israeli conflict.

The administration announced that President Bush will ask Congress to forgive Egypt's $7 billion debt to the United States for military aid. White House press secretary Marlin Fitzwater said the gesture was in response to Egypt's "leadership" in the gulf crisis. Baker said the debt "has basically been unrepayable" because of Egypt's troubled economy. Fitzwater said the move would add $750 million to the current federal budget deficit.

House Minority Leader Robert H. Michel (R-Ill.) expressed reservations at the move, saying, "That comes off the wall without our prior knowledge." He said it "may be a little premature for us to say we're going to forgive this one big item." Michel said he would "like to have a full accounting of what is our status with other countries around the globe" before he takes a position on the Egyptian debt.

Israeli Finance Minister Yitzhak Modai said if Congress approves Bush's request to forgive the debt to Egypt, Israel will demand most of its $4.6 billion debt from previous arms sales also be erased. Fitzwater said the United States would "entertain" forgiveness for other nations besides Egypt.

The debt announcement came as Treasury Secretary Nicholas F. Brady began a European and Asian tour to drum up billions of dollars in international assistance for the campaign against Saddam. Brady went first to France and planned later visits to Great Britian, Japan and South Korea. Baker is to depart today for the Middle East in a related mission before joining Bush and Soviet President Mikhail Gorbachev in Helsinki this weekend.

In his testimony yesterday, Baker said the State Department has put Iraq back on the list of states that sponsor terrorism. Iraq was taken off the list in 1982, amid much controversy, when the United States was seeking closer ties with Saddam to counter Iran in the region; at that time, some terrorist groups were expelled from Baghdad. U.S. officials believe a number of

60. P
9/5/90

2074 -1

0081

international terrorists have made their way to Baghdad since the invasion of Kuwait.

Baker said the action to return Iraq to the list of terrorist states was taken following statements by Iraqi Foreign Minister Tariq Aziz "that Iraq was free of any moral obligations to proscribe acts of terrorism against Americans, British and French interests."

Administration officials said the action was approved over the weekend by Deputy Secretary of State Lawrence S. Eagleburger. It was under consideration before the Aug. 2 invasion of Kuwait, officials said, but the taking of Americans and other foreigners hostage tipped the balance. Officials said the decision will have little practical impact, however, because of the international economic sanctions and arms embargo already in place against Iraq. However, if the Kuwait crisis is resolved, Iraq could not be removed from the list without a presidential decision.

Other nations on the list are Iran, Libya, Syria, Cuba, North Korea and Yemen. Since the formation of a new government there, the status of Yemen has been under review, officials said.

In his testimony, Baker sought to answer criticism that the United States has not articulated its long-term objectives in the Persian Gulf crisis and that the administration has failed to outline the stakes to the American people.

Baker said the crisis is a "political test of how the post-Cold War world will work," an era "in which ethnic and sectarian identities could easily breed new violence and new conflict" and "threats could erupt as misguided leaders are tempted to assert regional dominance long before the ground rules of a new order can be accepted." He added, "The current crisis is a first opportunity to limit such dangers."

He also noted the dangers of a wider conflict in the Middle East and said "we must help demonstrate that Saddam Hussein's violent way is an anachronism, rather than the wave of the future."

Some members of Congress have questioned whether U.S. soldiers and sailors should be put at risk in an action some characterize as a defense of cheap gasoline. Baker said, "We're not there in order to keep the price of gasoline low." Instead, he sought to define the issue in terms of global security. "It is . . . about a dictator, who, acting alone and unchallenged, could strangle the global economic order, determining by fiat whether we all enter a recession or even the darkness of a depression." He noted that the emerging democracies of Eastern Europe and other developing countries would be particularly hard hit by an energy crisis.

Baker reiterated Bush's four objectives in the gulf: complete and unconditional withdrawal of Iraqi troops, restoration of the "legitimate" government of Kuwait, protection of Americans and stability in the region. Asked whether the United States is trying to overthrow Saddam, Baker said this goal "is not one of those stated objectives." But he added, "It would not make us terribly unhappy if the people of Iraq decided they wanted a new leader."

He said Bush's goals include restoration of the emir of Kuwait and the government "as it existed on the date of the invasion."

Baker rejected suggestions that Saddam be offered a face-saving exit from Kuwait. "We don't buy this idea that some are pushing today that you've got to find a way to give Saddam Hussein a face-saving way out, give him something that would, in effect, reward him for his aggression," Baker said. "We think that's totally unprincipled."

Baker did not offer details about the concept of a new regional security structure. But he said resolution of the crisis "should also become a springboard for a sustained international effort to curb the proliferation of chemical, biological and nuclear weapons and ballistic missiles" in the region. Saddam has the Third World's largest stockpile of chemical weapons and is known to have been seeking nuclear arms.

Rep. Stephen J. Solarz (D-N.Y.) pressed Baker on whether it would be possible to eliminate Saddam's nuclear, chemical and biological weapons programs "without destroying them" in a military strike. Baker, while cautioning that he did not want to rule out any option, said, "It's not possible to eliminate them without destroying them." However, he added, it might be possible to create a "security structure that would make it so clearly to the detriment" of Saddam to use such weapons "that there would be very little risk that they would be used."

Baker praised the cooperation of "an enlightened Soviet leadership" in the gulf crisis, and, referring to "the new thinkers and reformers in the Soviet Union," said that "partnership is replacing conflict in that relationship." Questioned about the 193 Soviet military advisers who reportedly remain in Iraq, Baker said there was some uncertainty about whether they were free to leave. But if they are, he added, it is "inappropriate" for the Soviets to be providing any military aid to Baghdad.

The interception of the Iraqi vessel occurred at 6:30 a.m. local time in the Gulf of Oman when the USS Goldsborough hailed the small cargo ship Zanoobia, whose captain ignored orders to turn around or sail for a neutral port, Pentagon spokesman Pete Williams said.

Navy officials said they could not detail how the boarding party got aboard the Zanoobia, which refused to stop but which allowed the U.S. Navy and Coast Guard personnel to take over the ship without opposition. Yesterday's action marks the first forced boarding of an Iraqi vessel since Iraq ordered its commercial shipping fleet not to resist enforcement of the U.N. trade embargo against Iraq.

Also yesterday, the U.S. military's top commander in the Middle East denied a Washington Post report that a dispute exists between him and the Saudi government over who controls the decision to launch U.S. offensive military operations from Saudi Arabia. U.S. Army Gen. H. Norman Schwarzkopf said, "I absolutely have no disagreement whatsoever with any agreement that exists between Saudi Arabia and the United States." Schwarzkopf said he did not complain when Saudi commander Lt. Gen. Khalid bin Sultan told reporters last week that any decision to use U.S. forces deployed in the kingdom for offensive operations would have to be preceded by consultations between Bush and Saudi Arabia's King Fahd.

At a news conference last week, Schwarzkopf called the Saudi commander's statement "a great simplification of the arrangements that exist."

In a telephone interview yesterday, Schwarzkopf said, "Every agreement that has been reached between Saudi Arabia and the United States about anything was already run by me. I participated in the formation of the agreement."

He said the initial details of the command and control of U.S. and Arab forces was forged when he and Cheney visited King Fahd days after the Iraqi invasion of Kuwait. "There have been a million questions from everybody," said Schwarzkopf. "But, from our situation, not now nor has there ever been . . . any dispute about how it would work."

Staff writers Patrick E. Tyler, Ann Devroy and John E. Yang in Washington and Molly Moore in Saudi Arabia contributed to this report.

201X - 2

0082

The Troops in the Desert

AMERICAN TROOPS are not in the Saudi desert to defend $1-a-gallon gasoline. Neither are they there to defend democracy, for that term applies to none of the Persian Gulf states. But the United States and its allies in the desert have clear and compelling reasons to be there.

An oil crisis alone—a soaring price and the threat of shortages—would be unlikely to push the United States to the point of war. The price of oil is somewhere around $27 a barrel. In early 1981 it went over $35—in today's dollars, that's well over $50 a barrel—and there was no impulse to send aircraft carriers to the Gulf. But oil is certainly part of the calculation that makes Iraq's invasion of Kuwait dangerous to the rest of the world.

Iraq's aggression is the central fact that has created the alliance of Arab, European and U.S. forces that now surrounds the aggressor. There have been other cases of aggression in recent memory that the world has let pass with a less decisive response. But the circumstances in Iraq's case would make complaisance there intolerably costly.

Suppose that the United States and the others had not sent troops and ships or shut off Iraq's trade. Saudi Arabia, finding itself isolated and wholly vulnerable to attack, would—under the *best* of circumstances—have had little choice but to accommodate Iraqi demands for higher prices. These might not necessarily have been high enough to produce a catastrophe in the industrial world; if they weren't, but were, say, as high as prices were six or seven years ago, Iraq's oil revenues would have tripled. What do you suppose it would have used that money for? Clinics? Schools?

The present Iraqi regime has for years funneled vast resources of oil wealth—its own and subsidies from its neighbors—into armaments and its military ambitions. With a huge increase in those revenues, won by armed conquest, it would move into an entirely different category of power. Iraq, according to careful estimates here, could develop nuclear weapons in perhaps five years. It already possesses medium-range missiles, and the technology to extend their reach is for sale. By its use of poison gas, Iraq has already demonstrated that it feels no need to observe its treaties.

Secretary of State James A. Baker, testifying before Congress, emphasized a hope that the present crisis will launch a new international effort to bring under control the proliferation of nuclear, biological and chemical weapons, including missiles, in the Middle East and worldwide. He spoke forcefully of the need for a new security structure for the Persian Gulf. Clearly the presence of American forces is going to be a necessary element in that security structure for a long time.

The Saudi desert is not a pleasant place to spend time, but the troops gathering there are doing a crucially valuable job. If you doubt it, consider what would be happening in their absence.

w. P
a/5/90

2074-3

0083

EGYPT DEBT ERASED

Navy Seizes Iraq-Bound Freighter in the Gulf — First Such Act

By THOMAS L. FRIEDMAN
Special to The New York Times

WASHINGTON, Sept. 4 — Secretary of State James A. Baker 3d told Congress today that the Administration intends to maintain a long-term military presence in the Persian Gulf area even if Iraq agrees to withdraw from Kuwait.

In the first appearance before a Congressional committee by any Administration official since Iraq invaded Kuwait on Aug. 2, Mr. Baker outlined what he called "a new regional security structure" that the Administration is considering to counter Iraq's chemical, nuclear and conventional arms potential. [Excerpts, page A14.]

The proposal was far different from one offered by the Soviet Government today. Foreign Minister Eduard A. Shevardnadze renewed the Kremlin's longstanding proposal for an international conference on the Israeli-Palestinian struggle and other Middle East problems. [Page A17.]

Egypt's Debt Forgiven

Mr. Baker's appearance before the House Foreign Affairs Committee came after President Bush formally announced a proposal to forgive the $7 billion that Egypt owes the United States for military aid. This would relieve Egypt of onerous interest payments, but Mr. Baker indicated that Washington had long ago given up hope of recovering the principal.

Mr. Baker suggested that a new Middle East security structure might deter Iraq just as the North Atlantic Treaty Organization for decades deterred the Soviet Union.

He said it would most likely combine some type of continued international arms boycott of Iraq, a concerted buildup of the armies of the pro-American Arab gulf countries neighboring Iraq, and a long-term American naval or land force in the Persian Gulf.

Iraqi Freighter Seized

In the first seizure of Iraqi bound cargo under the United Nations trade embargo, the Defense Department announced today that the United States

Navy intercepted, boarded and seized an Iraqi freighter in the Persian Gulf. The Pentagon said it was carrying tea from Sri Lanka.

Mr. Baker's remarks appeared intended to answer arguments that the only way to make sure Iraq never threatens its neighbors again is to destroy Iraq's military structure. The Administration has made it clear in recent days that it is reluctant to attack Iraq unless provoked.

The proposed alignment would also indicate to the Iraqis that Washington would not accept any deal by which the United States would pull its forces out of the region in return for Baghdad's evacuation from Kuwait, an idea floated by Arab intermediaries.

Mr. Baker said that in view of the Administration's desire for a new alliance in the region, he could not predict how long the United States might have to remain in the Persian Gulf.

"If we're going to build a new regional security structure, what role should the United States play in that new regional structure?" Mr. Baker asked. "Certainly we ought to play some role, and therefore there would be some presence, some continuing presence there. Maybe it wouldn't be a

A freighter with Sri Lankan tea is intercepted and seized in the gulf.

ground force presence. Maybe it would be a naval presence."

"I think we will have to give consideration to working with others to create a new security structure for the region," Mr. Baker added. "I think that's likely to be required even if there is a pullback from Kuwait."

Mubarak's Role Praised

In announcing the Egyptian debt relief proposal, President Bush spoke of his appreciation for the leading role played by President Hosni Mubarak in putting together the Arab alliance against Iraq.

Initial reactions to the President's debt forgiveness proposal from some key lawmakers, such as Patrick J. Leahy, Democrat of Vermont and chairman of a Senate foreign aid subcommittee, and Robert H. Michel of Illinois, the House Republican leader, suggested that while there is great sympathy for Egypt, there is also great

concern on Capitol Hill that such a move would invite a whole series of similar requests for debt forgiveness, which could cost American taxpayers billions more.

Israel's Finance Minister, Yitzhak Modai, declared today that if Egypt's military debts were erased by Washington it would be "ridiculous" if Israel's $4.6 billion debt was not wiped out also.

The Pentagon said that the Iraqi freighter Zanubia had been boarded and seized by naval and Coast Guard forces. The boarding was accomplished without incident at about 6:30 A.M. in the Gulf of Oman, the Pentagon said.

A Defense Department spokesman, Pete Williams, told reporters that an armed boarding party of Navy and Coast Guard crewmen from the guided missile frigate Goldsborough boarded the Zanubia and took over its helm.

No Force Used

"It refused orders to either return to the port of origin or to a nonprohibited port," he said. "No warning shots were fired or force used. That was not necessary."

The ship was reportedly taken to the Omani port of Muscat, although the Pentagon declined to specify its destination.

The Administration has acknowledged that it is widening its security umbrella in the Persian Gulf to cover not only Saudi Arabia but also the neighboring Arab gulf nations of Qatar, Oman, Bahrain and the United Arab Emirates, where American warplanes have recently been deployed.

Asked whether the Administration's commitment to protect Saudi Arabia also included the four other countries, Mr. Baker said, "We are of the view that our commitment is one to preserve stability and security of the gulf, and that of necessity would involve some of the other states along the fringes of the Persian Gulf."

Moscow Pressed on Advisers

Defense Secretary Dick Cheney, in an interview on the ABC television program "Good Morning America," was asked if the presence of American forces in these four other gulf countries represented an implicit intent to defend them. "I think it clearly does," he replied.

Mr. Baker said that the United States was asking Moscow to remove its mili-

N.Y.T
9/5/90

2074-K

0084

0085

tary advisers from Iraq, but that the Soviets had responded that the advisers would not be withdrawn until their contracts had expired at some unspecified date.

"I've had a number of conversations with my colleague Mr. Shevardnadze about this," said Mr. Baker. "The Soviets have roughly 190, or had 8,900, citizens in Iraq and Kuwait when this crisis began. About 1,960 of these Soviet nationals are involved in some sort of military-related tasks in Iraq, primarily training and maintenance. One hundred and ninety-three of that 1,900 are actual military people. The Soviets have said that these people, 193, are going to remain until their contracts expire. We think that frankly it's inappropriate to be providing any military assistance to Iraq at the present time, and we will continue to talk to the Soviets about the 193."

Justifying the President's decision to wipe out Egypt's military debt to the United States, Martin Fitzwater, the White House press secretary, said it

was stimulated "by Egypt's leadership in resisting Iraqi aggression," which has been "an essential component of the ongoing U.S. contribution to the current situation in the Persian Gulf."

Egypt Takes the Lead

President Mubarak took the lead in first getting a majority of the Arab League to condemn the Iraqi invasion of Kuwait and in assembling an Arab peacekeeping force to stand alongside American and Saudi troops. Although that force still includes only units from Egypt, Syria and Morocco, it has provided a critical patina of Arab legitimacy for the deep American military intervention in the Gulf, and deprived President Hussein of the argument that the conflict is simply between Iraq and the United States.

The Egyptian military debt has been incurred largely over the last decade as the United States steadily increased sales to Cairo after it signed the Camp David peace treaty with Israel in 1978. The interest on the loan alone re-

quired the Egyptian Government to make a payment of $750 million this year, which will now have to be added to the Federal budget deficit. Today's decision does not wipe out Egypt's entire debt to the United States. Egypt still owes the United States $6 billion in nonmilitary loans.

If approved by Congress, the debt forgiveness should increase pressure on Japan and West Germany to increase their financial aid for the multinational effort in the gulf. Several Congressmen complained to Mr. Baker about the paltry support of some of America's wealthy Western allies.

As Representative Ted Weiss, Democrat of New York, said the Secretary: "If there's been one area of concern that has been expressed to me by constituents over and over again, it's in the area of what, you would call responsibility sharing. For Japan, which is almost totally dependent on foreign oil, Middle East oil, to suggest a $1 billion contribution, and then seem to renege on that, that just doesn't seem to be appropriate."

Bush's Actions Explored

A dozen members of the Senate returned from a fact-finding mission to the Persian Gulf today with a unanimous endorsement of President Bush's actions.

"The delegation is convinced that the President's decision to send forces to the Persian Gulf area was an essential response to Iraqi aggression," said Senator Claiborne Pell, Democrat of Rhode Island and chairman of the Foreign Relations Committee.

The Senators met with the heads of state of Saudi Arabia, Bahrain, Egypt

and the United Arab Emirates.

"We were told by everyone we talked to that the critical point was to make the embargo tight," said Senator John Glenn, Democrat of Ohio. Mr. Glenn and others said that the United Nations forces appear to be capable of imposing a sea and a land embargo.

The Senators also noted that they had been promised by King Fahd of Saudi Arabia that the Saudis and other Arab oil-producing countries would provide sufficient financial support for the defensive effort in the gulf.

"King Fahd said that they are working out a financial proposal that will be forthcoming any day," said Senator Daniel Patrick Moynihan, Democrat of New York. Mr. Moynihan said that specific amounts were not discussed but that they would be considerable.

NYT
9/5/90

2074-5

Soviets Renew Call For Broad Mideast Peace Conference

By Michael Dobbs
Washington Post Foreign Service

MOSCOW, Sept. 4—The Kremlin called today for fresh United Nations efforts to resolve the crisis in the Persian Gulf, including the rapid convening of a Middle East peace conference to settle the Arab-Israeli conflict.

The calls by ranking Soviet officials for a diplomatic solution to the crisis came five days before a U.S.-Soviet summit meeting in Helsinki. They appeared designed to preserve Soviet influence in the Arab world while reiterating Moscow's strong condemnation of Iraq for the invasion of Kuwait.

In a speech in the Soviet Far Eastern city of Vladivostok, Foreign Minister Eduard Shevardnadze predicted that the Helsinki meeting between Presidents Bush and Mikhail Gorbachev would mark a "major milestone on the road toward resolving the crisis in the Persian Gulf." He said the world faced a "highly critical, emergency situation that had made necessary extraordinary action in the form of a special meeting between the Soviet and U.S. presidents."

Shevardnadze stopped short of directly linking a solution of the gulf crisis to the tackling of broader Middle East issues, including self-determination for the Palestinians and Syria's occupation of Lebanon. An attempt by Iraqi President Saddam Hussein to tie the fate of Kuwait to a resolution of the Arab-Israeli conflict has already been rejected by the United States and other Western countries.

But by speaking of a set of "highly complex, interlocking problems" in the Middle East and reviving a longstanding Soviet proposal for a U.N.-sponsored peace conference, Shevardnadze was in effect taking a symbolic step in Baghdad's direction. He was also staking out an independent Soviet position in a potential diplomatic marathon as international pressure builds on Iraq to withdraw from Kuwait.

"Unless peace comes to the Middle East, we shall continue to pay a huge price for its wars," said Shevardnadze, who will accompany Gorbachev to Helsinki. "It is time that we acted now in the interests of the world."

In Washington, Secretary of State James A. Baker III also raised a vague connection between the crisis in the Persian Gulf and a settlement of the Arab-Israeli dispute. Without referring to the Sheverdnadze speech, Baker told the House Foreign Affairs Committee that "resolution of today's threat . . . . can become a springboard for revived efforts to resolve the conflicts" that fuel regional arms races, "including the festering conflict between Israel and its Palestinian and Arab neighbors."

Shevardnadze hinted that Moscow would consider establishing diplomatic relations with Israel—broken off after the 1967 Arab-Israeli war—if the Israelis agreed to the convening of a Middle East peace conference. He said any Israeli move would meet with a response by Moscow, including "a fresh look at the issue of Soviet-Israeli relations."

In Jerusalem, Israeli Prime Minister Yitzhak Shamir reiterated his government's opposition to a Middle East peace conference, saying, "We have our position about an international conference around the solution of the Israeli-Arab conflict. We will not participate in such an international conference."

In a separate briefing in Moscow, presidential press spokesman Vitaly Ignatenko said Gorbachev was ready to discuss in Helsinki "ways of stepping up further U.N. activity aimed at unblocking the crisis in the Persian Gulf." The Soviet Union has already supported five Security Council resolutions condemning Baghdad's invasion of Kuwait and enforcing an economic blockade of Iraq.

Ignatenko said Gorbachev would fly to Helsinki on Saturday evening and meet with Finnish President Mauno Koivisto prior to a full day of talks with Bush on Sunday. He said Gorbachev and Bush would hold a joint news conference Sunday evening, following a precedent set in Malta last December and Washington in June.

Apparently setting the stage for the line that Gorbachev is likely to pursue in Helsinki, Shevardnadze praised the "unanimity and firmness" with which the international community had responded to Iraqi "aggression" against Kuwait. He added, however, that it was "essential to pursue our objective through non-military means and in a way that would remove the military presence of other countries."

Western and Arab diplomats here expect that Gorbachev could press Bush for guarantees that the United States will withdraw its troops from Saudi Arabia once the crisis is over. Soviet military commanders have expressed concern that the U.S. military buildup in the gulf could disrupt the East-West strategic balance.

Shevardnadze said the Soviet Union would not "acquiesce in any option that would fall short of restoring the sovereignty, territorial integrity and legitimate government of Kuwait." He said that one possible solution to the crisis would be for Iraqi troops in Kuwait to be replaced by a U.N. peace-keeping force, with an inter-Arab contingent replacing U.S. troops in Saudi Arabia.

Arab diplomats here said the proposal for a reciprocal withdrawal of Iraqi and U.S. forces had originally been broached by Libyan leader Moammar Gadhafi and Palestine Liberation Organization Chairman Yasser Arafat.

W.P
9/5/90
2075-2

0086

이라크 사태가 군축에 미치는 영향

================================

90. 9. 5
C S M

1. 이라크 사태는 모처럼의 세계적 군축 진전을 저해할 가능성이 큼

   가. 미국내 군비증강 논의 대두

   o 부시 대통령은 하원에서 권고한 금년 국방비 10% 감축을 받아들일 수 없다고 일축

   o 중동전과 무관한 대소전략용 Stealth 폭격기 생산과 SDI 부활 논의 대두

   나. 미쏘 군축 진전 지연 가능성

   o 미국이 중동전에 몰두, 금년말 목표로 추진중이었던 START, CFE 회담 금년내 타결 가능성 약화

   o 추가 후속조치 회담 개최시기도 더욱 미뤄질 가능성

2. 미 행정부의 제3세계 국지전 대비용 군사력 보강 필요성 주장에도 불구, 군축 계속 가능

   o 최근 군축논의 진전 배경은 쏘련의 군사적 후퇴, 동구의 변화, 미국의 재정적자등이며 이런 요인은 계속 존재

공	안보과	90년 9월 7일	담 당	과 장	심의관	국 장
			김수권			

0087

o 쏘련에 대응키 위한 중부유럽 군사력 유지비가 미국방예산의 50%
  이상을 차지. 따라서 제3세계 국지전에 대비한 군사력 보강
  조정에도 불구, 대대적 군축가능

o 제3세계 국지전 대비에 적합한 군사력 증강을 위해서는 MX미사일,
  Midgetman미사일, Seawolf잠수함등 전략무기의 감축 필요

3. 최근 제3세계의 군비 증강은 무기선진국으로부터의 수입에 의한 것인
   바, 제3세계 무기 수출입을 통제하므로서 국지전의 강도 약화 가능

o 이라크 보유의 고성능 무기는 프랑스, 쏘련, 중국등지에서 수입된
  것이며, 여기에는 미국의 묵시적 동의도 작용해 왔음

o 이번 중동사태를 계기로 제3세계 무기수입 통제를 위한 국제적
  방안 마련 중요성 부각

4. 최근 일련의 불리한 사태 진전에도 불구, 세계는 미.쏘관계 호전과
   이에따른 대대적 군축 실현 가능성을 최대한 활용하여야 할 것임

끝.

0088

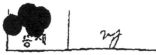

By Lee Feinstein

WITH United States and Iraqi forces eyeball to eyeball in the Middle Eastern desert, back in Washington it has become apparent that whatever the outcome, two casualties of the Persian Gulf confrontation will be the peace dividend and progress toward arms control and disarmament.

In a toughly worded speech before the Veterans of Foreign Wars last month, President Bush called "unacceptable" the modest but significant 10 percent cut in military spending recommended

by the
House Armed
Services Committee.
The president told the veterans that he will "oppose the defense budget slashers who are out of tune with what America needs to keep freedom secure and safe."

The largest mobilization of US forces since Vietnam now costs $46 million a day beyond the expenses of normal operations, according to the Pentagon. The Defense Department has indicated that it will seek a "supplemental appropriation" to this year's military budget.

Added to the tab for transporting troops to Saudi Arabia may be the expense of formerly endangered weapons systems that could survive due to the perceived needs generated by the Gulf confrontation. Among the programs that may benefit are the C-17 transport aircraft, whose production the Senate voted to delay, and the V-22 Osprey tilt-rotor aircraft, which the Defense De-

partment has tried to stop. New arguments are also being offered to justify costly weapons originally designed for nuclear war with the Soviet Union, including the B-2 "stealth" bomber, which a House committee refused to fund beyond the 15 aircraft already paid for, and the Strategic Defense Initiative, which both the House and Senate cut sharply.

The mobilization of forces to the Gulf, however, does not justify rejecting cuts in military spending. The driving forces behind most of the reductions voted by Congress – Soviet military retrenchment, political change in Eastern Europe, and US budget deficits – are unchanged.

Even if the United States decides to tailor its armed forces for third-world "contingencies," that would not be reason to abandon budget cuts, since the military forces needed to meet a Soviet threat in central Europe – which accounted for 50 percent or more of annual US military spending – should now be drastically reduced. Reorienting US military forces toward potential third-world conflicts should actually intensify the trend toward cuts in strategic weapons, including the MX and Midgetman nuclear missiles and the SSN-21 Seawolf attack submarine.

Even as the Gulf confrontation quickens defense spending, it will probably slacken the already slowed pace of arms control and disarmament talks. The marathon START negotiations and the Conventional Forces in Europe talks were already mired in minor but nettlesome disputes between East and West. As the president devotes more of his attention to dealing with the military face-off

in the Middle East, rather than on the number of SS-18 flight tests or land-based naval aircraft to permit the Soviet Union, the chances of completing START and conventional forces treaties by year's end, as both Bush and Gorbachev have pledged, may fade. In addition, efforts to negotiate deeper reductions in nuclear and conventional forces in follow-up negotiations will be pushed still further into the future.

Meanwhile, the impact of the Gulf crisis on the chemical disarmament talks in Geneva will be more direct in light of Baghdad's renewed threats to use poison gas if attacked. Like the START talks, these negotiations were moving slowly before the Aug. 2 invasion of Kuwait, as the US and the Soviet Union – the states with the largest chemical arsenals – were preoccupied with completing protocols to a separate bilateral agreement signed in June. Concern among Middle Eastern states about whether key nations in the region would adhere to a global ban had also been a persistent complication in the talks. Now those nations may grow less interested in the negotiations while one of the regional powers is threatening to use poison gas.

Iraq's all-too-credible chemical threats, however, may yield an unintended benefit for the talks. In recent statements, US officials have virtually ruled out responding in kind to a chemical attack from Baghdad. "I cannot conceive of a situation in which the United States would want to use chemical weapons," was the way Defense Secretary Dick Cheney put it recently.

Secretary Cheney's position, supported by the Air Force chief of staff, would seem to undercut the Bush administration's insistence in the Geneva talks on retaining a "deterrent" stockpile of 500 tons of chemical agent even after a global ban enters into force. The US demand to keep such stockpiles until all "chemical-capable" states adhere to a treaty has gained no support in the negotiations and has been a major impediment to progress. With the US all but ruling out retaliation with chemical weapons, this obstructionist negotiating position may ultimately fall away.

The crisis in the Persian Gulf may also affect the just-opened review conference of the Nuclear Non-Proliferation Treaty (NPT). Until the invasion of Kuwait, the Geneva conference to review the NPT, aimed at preventing the spread of nuclear weapons and reducing the size of already existing arsenals, was expected to be relatively uneventful. The review was also expected to benefit from a number of encouraging developments: progress in US-Soviet arms control; the possibility that South Africa, a traditional "problem" state, would sign the treaty; and greater openness and cooperation between Brazil and Argentina, both of which pursued

nuclear weapons options in the past.

Though Iraq is a member of the NPT, with its reactors subject to international inspections, the Gulf confrontation and recent evidence of Iraqi efforts to smuggle US-made nuclear trigger components may focus attention on Iraq's still nascent nuclear-weapons program, and on undeclared nuclear-weapon states such as India, Israel, and Pakistan (which have not signed the treaty). Such controversy may give greater urgency to the work of the conference, but it also could make it more difficult for the delegates to settle on a final consensus document, the key aim of the month-long meeting, and could precipitate an Iraqi walkout, or Baghdad's eventual withdrawal from the pact.

THE Gulf confrontation also points to the need to begin serious multinational efforts to control the transfer of sophisticated non-nuclear weapons to the third world. At present, no international rules govern the multibillion dollar flow of weapons from the developed to the developing world. The current strength of the Iraqi military is due primarily to military aid and supplies provided by France, the Soviet Union, and China with the decade-long ac-

quiescence of the United States. That buildup, in turn, was fueled by the US arming of the Shah of Iran until the 1979 revolution. Secretary of State James Baker recently acknowledged that "we should have been more concerned about all of this, perhaps going further back," adding that the current confrontation in the Gulf "may provide a good lesson in that regard."

While third-world states are increasingly building an independent capacity to stock their arsenals with lethal conventional weapons, the intensity of regional conflicts would be reduced substantially by constraints on exports from the developed world and ultimately international controls on all sales and transfers.

It is inevitable and appropriate that the confrontation in the Persian Gulf consume the attention of the administration – especially now while some small prospect for resolving the conflict short of full-scale military confrontation may remain. But in the longer run, developments in the Persian Gulf underline the importance of aggressively pursuing arms control and disarmament. Intractable as the current situation may be, it would be far more ominous without the benefits of recent strides in arms control, improvements in US-Soviet relations, and the imperfect but useful efforts to stem the spread of nuclear and chemical weapons.

■ *Lee Feinstein is senior policy analyst at the Arms Control Association in Washington, D.C.*

CSM
9/5/90

2-077-2

0090

미국의 새로운 「중동안보구조」 설립 구상 분석, 평가

1990. 9

미 주 국
안 보 과

0091

새로운 「중동안보구조」 구상의 '윤곽'

o 새로운 「중동안보구조」(Regional Security Structure) 구상은, 9.4
베이커 국무장관의 하원외교위 증언에서 최초로 언급된 바, 동 장관은
청문회 질의 응답 과정에서,

   i) Hussein 대통령과 그의 대량살상무기 추구를 봉쇄(contain),
      패퇴(Roll-Back) 시키기 위하여

   ii) NATO와 유사한 형태의 지역안보구조 설립을 검토할 필요가 있다
      하였음

o 베이커 장관은, 9.5 상원외교위 증언에서도 새로운 지역안보체제 구축
필요성을 재강조 하면서, 동 기구의 목적은, 지역내 질서 구축과
침략저지, 특히 이라크의 팽창주의와 대량살륙무기 개발 저지에
있다 하였으나, 구체적 형태에 대해서는 검토된 바 없으며, 핵무기
균형을 전재로한 NATO와는 다른 형태가 될 수 밖에 없을 것 이라고
언급하여, 전날의 하원외무위 증언에서 약간 후퇴한 입장을 표명
하였음

o 베이커 장관은, 구상의 상세에 대해서는 설명하지 않았으나, 증언 벽두
발표문중 아래 부분들이 동 제의의 배경을 시사해 주는 것으로 보임

   - '전례없는 국제적 합의를 바탕 으로, 페르샤만의 장기적 안보와
     안정을 달성하기 위하여...'

   - '우리는 페르시아만의 보다 건실한 질서구축을 위해 역내, 외
     국가들과 협력 할 것이다. 역내 국가들의 침략억지 및 자체방어
     능력을 강화하여 미 병력의 파견 필요성을 축소 할 것이다'

0092

- '현사태 해결은 핵 및 생화학 무기와 탄도 미사일의 확산 방지 를 위한 지속적인 국제 노력의 계기가 될 것이며, 이스라엘-아랍간의 갈등등 보다 근본적인 분쟁의 해결 노력도 크게 활성화 시킬 것이다'

- 이라크의 쿠웨이트 철수이후에도 ... 동 지역에 대한 미 해군력의 계속 주둔이 필요할 수도 있다'

o 상기에 비추어, 미측이 구상하고 있는 「중동안보구조」 설립 계획의 '윤곽'은 대체로 아래와 같이 그려볼 수 있음

- 예상시기 : 이라크의 쿠웨이트 철수후, 지상군을 중심한 미군사력의 철수와 동시

- 구   성 : 페르시아만 국가를 중심하여, 일부 역외국가 포함

- 목   적
  . 단기적 : 이라크의 팽창주의 봉쇄와 역내 대량 살상무기 확산 억지 및 방지
  . 장기적 : 아랍-이스라엘 분쟁등 소위 중동문제의 보다 근본적인 해결 모색

- 미국의 참여 : 최소한 해군력의 장기적 주둔으로 기구의 실효성 보장

0093

미측 제의의 배경

o 베이커 구상이 상기와 같이 아직은 애매하여, 이를 제의한 미국의
   의도를 분명하게 분석할 수는 없으나, 아래와 같은 고려는 하였을
   것으로 보임

(냉전후 국제질서 및 평화유지 체제 개념)

o 베이커 구상은, 향후 국제질서 및 평화유지 체제구축에 대한 미측의
   개념이 쿠웨이트 사태를 계기로 하여 막연한 형태로나마 표시된
   것이라 볼 수 있음

o 쿠웨이트 사태에 대한 미국의 대응은 부쉬행정부의 새로운 국제주의적
   안보유지 개념을 보여주고 있는 바, 이는
   i)   미국의 영도하에,
   ii) 전 국제사회가 국제법과 보편적인 원칙을 기초로 단결하여,
   iii) 집단적으로, 특히 유엔을 통하여 평화와 안보유지 조치를 취하고,
   iv) 이를 위한 비용은 모든 국가가 형평에 맞게 분담한다는 것을
   주 내용으로 하고 있음

o 그러나, 부쉬의 새로운 국제주의가 효율적으로 운영되기 위해서는
   궁극적으로 미국의 독자적 결정권이 유엔의 집단적 결정권으로 대체
   된다는 것을 의미하고, 이는 미국의 전통적 국제정치 감각인 고립주의에
   배치되는 결과가 되어, 이것이 공식적인 정책으로 표명될 경우, 국내
   적으로 크게 논란이 제기될 소지가 있음

0094

o 따라서, 미국으로서는, 유엔을 중심한 단일 평화유지 체제보다는
세계를 여러개의 지역집단으로 구분하고, 그 각각에 대해 미국이
영향력을 행사, 평화 파괴자를 응징하는 체제가 보다 체질에 부합하는
것이며, 이러한 개념이 향후 중동안보유지체제 모색과정에서도
부지불식간에 적용되었을 것임

(중동지역 정치적 대립관계의 구조변경 모색)

o 쿠웨이트 사태는, 아랍-이스라엘간 대결이라는 중동지역의 기존 대립
관계를 이라크의 패권주의와 이의 견제라는 새로운 대립구조로 변경
시킴으로서, 당분간은 팔레스타인 문제에 대한 관심과 압력을 완화해
줄 것으로 보임

o 미국으로서는, 이라크의 쿠웨이트 점령과 팔레스타인 문제를 동일한
성격의 문제로 규정하기를 거부하면서, 새로이 형성된 아랍권 내부의
대결구도를 새로운 「중동안보구조」로 개념화, 제도화함으로써,
장기적으로 팔레스타인 문제의 해결은 용이하게 할 수 있을 것이며,
베이커장관이 상.하원 외교위 증언에서 아랍-이스라엘 문제를 언급한
것도 이러한 맥락에서 이해될 수 있음

o 「중동안보구조」가 실현되어, 반 이라크 연합전선이 구축된다면,
고립된 이라크의 자연적인 약화는 불가피할 것이며, 미국은 시간을
가지고 팔레스타인 문제의 해결을 모색, 전체 중동지역 정세의
안정과 평화를 도모할 수 있을 것임

0095

o 베이커 장관이 NATO형 「중동안보구조」를 제의한 하루만에 형태
  문제에 대한 입장을 후퇴한데서 알 수 있듯이, 「중동안보구조」
  설립이 결코 용이하지는 않을 것임

o 우선, 금번 사태에 대한 국제사회의 협조를 가능하게 하였던 유엔의
  역할문제, 유엔을 통하여 대미협조를 하였던 쏘련, 중국 및 일부
  여타 아랍국가의 협조확보와 역할보장 문제, 미국을 중심한 안보
  체제에 대한 아랍 민족주의의 반대문제, 그리고 팔레스타인 문제를
  위요한 아랍-이스라엘간 대립 해소문제등이 모두 베이커 구상 실현
  가능성에 의문을 갖게 하고 있음

o 따라서, 미국으로서는, 당면적인 문제인 이라크의 쿠웨이트 점령이
  일단 해결의 실마리를 보이게 되면, 보다 현실적인 대안으로 GCC의
  성격변화 및 강화를 모색해 나갈 것으로 보임

o 미국이 현 시점에서 베이커 구상을 공개적으로 제시한 이유는,
  당장 이의 실현을 추진할 계획에서라기 보다는, 페르샤만 사태가
  예상보다 장기화될 가능성이 높아짐에 따라, 페르샤만 파병을 보다
  적극적이고 체계적인 시각에서 정당화해야할 국내,외적 필요성에
  대응하려는 과정에서, 막연한 하나의 개념으로서 제시한 것으로
  평가해야 할 것임

0096

o 단, 미국이 전기한 여러 예상 문제점에도 불구하고, 「중동안보구조」
  설립 구상을 보다 적극적으로 추진할 경우, 이는 냉전후 세계질서와
  평화유지 체제구축 문제에 대한 미 정책방향과 관련하여 그 의미가
  클 것이며, 현재 논의가 시작되고 있는 동북아 내지 아.태 안보협의체
  형성에 대한 미국의 입장과 관련하여, 동건 진전 동향을 예의 주시할
  필요가 있음

<끝>

0097

관리 번호	Po-1P34

외 무 부

종 별 : 지 급

번 호 : USW-4056　　　　　　　　　　　일 시 : 90 0906 1936

수 신 : 장관(미북,미안,중근동)

발 신 : 주 미 대사

제 목 : 미국의 대이락 정책

　　1. 금 9.6 당관 김영목 서기관이 GERUMMON 정책 기획실 중동담당관, GREY 소련과 중동 담당관등을 접촉, 향후 미국의 대이락 정책 방향을 탐문한바, 동인들 반응 요지 다음임.

　　가. 미국의 정책 방향 개요

　　-대이락 제재 조치의 엄격한 시행, 국제적 단합 과시, 사우디 파견 미군의 계속적 강화로 요약되는 현 행정부 정책이 당분간 지속될것임.

　　-군사적 대안이 완전히 배제되었다고는 할수 없으나, 미국으로서는 금수 조치가 효과를 거둘수 있을것으로 기대함.

　　-사태가 장기화될 경우 미국내 지지가 급속히 감소하는등 미국에 불리하다는 분석도 있으나 부쉬 대통령이 금번 사태에 대한 미국의 대응은 미국 혼자만의대응이 아니라 전 세계적 동참과 우방국의 지원으로 이루어지고 있다는점을 미국민에 입증할수 있는한, 전기 현 행정부 정책에 대한 미국민의 지지가 크게 감소될것으로 보이지 않음(우방국들의 동참 필요성)

　　나. 금수 조치의 효과

　　-금수 조치가 이락측에 실질적 영향을 발휘하려면 최소 3-4 개월부터 그 이상이 되어야한다고 평가하나, 향후 어떠한 돌발 사태가 생길지 예측할수 없음.

　　-다만, 이락의 특수한 경제 사정과 전례없는 국제적 단합을 감안할때 금번 금수 조치가 분명히 효과적인 수단이라고 평가될수 있음.

　　다. 지역 안보체제 및 주 사우디 미군의 장래

　　-베이커 장관이 의회 증언을 통해 지역 안보 체제(SECURITY STRUCTURE)구상을 밝힌것은 현재 진행중인 아랍권내의 세력 재편성과 관련, 여사한 구조의 필요성에 대한 제안과 논의를 촉진코자 한것이며, 미측으로서 상금 구체적 복안이 있는것은

미주국　　차관　　1차보　　2차보　　미주국　　중아국　　정와대　　안기부　　대책반

PAGE 1

아님(아랍각국이 스스로 구체적 제안 마련 바람직)

   - 미국이 지역 안보 체제를 구상하고 있는것은 동지역 안정을 위하 미국의 부담을 줄이기 위한것은 아니나, 미 행정부로서도 대규모 미군을 장기간 사우디에 주둔시킬수도 없는것이 현실임.

   -사태의 종료 이후, 지역 정세는 더이상 사태 이전과 같을수 없는바, 사태 해결 이후 지역 안정을 도모하는 문제가 행정부의 과제로 등장하고 있음. 현재까지 정해진바는 없으나, 사태가 종료된다면 <u>미 지상군은</u> 완전히 철수 하거나 정치적으로 부담이 없을정도의 소규모가 잔류하고 <u>기존의 해군력과 공군력을</u> 강화하는선에서 미국의 PRESENCE 를 유지하는것이 바람직할것임(미국민의 일반적 분위기와 사우디등 아랍 제국의 입장을 감안)

   2. 전기 담당관들은 대체로 금번 미소 정상회담이 주로 정체적, 상징적 의미를 갖는것이지, 중동 평화안을 포함, 여사한 구체적 FORMULA 를 합의할 계기는되지 않을것이라는 의견을 표시하고, 특히 <u>지역 안보 체제 문제에</u> 관해서는 현재로서는 <u>극히 초보적 구상</u>에 불과하다고 하면서 매우 신중한 자세를 보였음.

   (대사 박동진-국장)

   90.12.31 일반

걸프지역에서의 미국의 장기적 역할 모색

(Christian Science Monitor 지)

90.9.10

o 금번 중동사태의 추이에 관계없이 미국은 앞으로 걸프지역에서 보다
  능동적 역할을 할 수 밖에 없는 입장임.

o 이러한 역할은 지역내 미군기지를 근간으로 하는 NATO형 협력기구가
  아니라 서방이 참여하는 걸프지역내 국가간 기구를 통하여 이루어져야 함.

o 단기적으로는 금번 사태로 형성된 이집트-사우디주축을 보다 공식화
  하므로서 걸프지역내 반 이라크 군사력을 구축하는 것임.

o 그러나 장래에는 바그다드 조약이나 CENTO의 경험에서 보듯이 강대국의
  군사동맹을 통한 중동지역 참여가 매우 어렵고 서방 군사력 주둔에 많은
  아랍국가들이 민감하게 반응하는 점등을 고려, 동지역 안보구조의 동인을
  지역내 국가에서 찾아야 할 것임.

0100

: USW(F)- 2146
: 장 관 (차관, 미국, 미안) 발신 : 주미대사
: 미국의 대 중동 정책   (1 매)

US Seeks More Long-Term Role In Gulf Region

White House is exploring idea of Arab alliance to guard against area aggressors

By Peter Grier
Staff writer of The Christian Science Monitor

WASHINGTON

SIX weeks after Iraq's invasion of Kuwait, one consequence seems clear: Whatever happens to Saddam Hussein, the United States is destined to play a more active role in the Gulf region for years to come.

The White House is quietly exploring the idea of more permanent ties with selected Arab states as a means of guarding against both current and future area aggressors. This may mean an expanded intra-Gulf council with Western participation, not NATO-in-the-desert and US bases in the Arabian Peninsula.

"Clearly, we want to begin to think about what kind of security arrangements will be appropriate once this crisis has passed," said Secretary of Defense Richard Cheney last week.

For the short term, the purpose of transforming the current anti-Saddam team into something more formal would be twofold. First, it would solidify the emerging Egypt-Saudi Arabia axis on which the opposition to Iraq has been based. Second, it could ensure the presence in the Gulf of a permanent military counterweight to Saddam Hussein.

Critics of the Bush administration's goals in the Gulf say that unless Saddam Hussein is removed and his nation's military capability destroyed, he will continue to intimidate his neighbors, even if he withdraws from Kuwait. A regional security structure could provide a "cage," in the word of one analyst, to permanently neutralize the Iraqi leader.

Even now, Gulf states are sensitive to the idea that US ground troops might dig in for a long-term stay.

Saudi Arabia is grateful to the US for its fast military response to the Iraqi threat – witness the multibillion-dollar Saudi commitment to pick up much of the tab. But Arab rulers know the idea of Western soldiers near Islamic holy sites does not sit comfortably with the man in the street, however threatening Iraq.

Secretary of State James Baker III first floated the concept of a regional security pact in a congressional hearing last week, and after his words were interpreted as a call for a NATO-like military deterrence infrastructure, he quickly played the idea down.

But administration officials continue to insist the concept has merit and say preliminary studies in the State Department and National Security Council have begun.

Mr. Baker discussed a regional pact with the Saudis before he arrived in Finland for Sunday's superpower summit, and reportedly the Saudis indicated interest. Kuwaiti leaders have been even keener on the subject.

While acknowledging regional sensitivities, the Bush administration obviously envisions an enhanced US military role in the future in the Gulf, through expanded naval deployments if nothing else. Due to the current crisis US-Arab military ties are closer than ever before, and out of that "will emerge new arrangements that will enhance the capability of governments in that part of the world to provide for their own security, but also cooperative arrangements that will allow the US to play a bigger role than we have in the past," said Secretary Cheney to a group of military analysts.

The petro-state Gulf Cooperation Council might be a starting point for a future regional alliance. Egypt, which has been the leader in rallying the now-fractured Arab League to oppose Iraq, would have to be included. Syria, which has also come to Saudi Arabia's aid.

"I can see some basis for a pretty long-standing alliance between Egypt and Saudi Arabia based on mutual interests," says Ambassador Walter Cutler, a former US envoy to Saudi Arabia. "Whether or not there is a long-standing commonality between Syria on the one hand, and Egypt and Saudi Arabia on the other, I think is more doubtful."

The difficulty of big powers striking up alliances with the Arab world is shown by the US experience with the Baghdad Pact, an attempt during the Eisenhower era to forge an anti-Soviet front of the US, Britain, Iraq, Iran, Pakistan, and Turkey.

Arab sensitivities to the legacy of British colonialism kept the Baghdad Pact from evolving into a real alliance.

Eventually, in 1959, the US and Pakistan, Turkey, and Iran formed Central Treaty Organization, but even that became moribund long before Iran withdrew following the overthrow of the Shah.

"The worst thing the US could possibly do is engineer a US replica of the Baghdad Pact," says Henry Berger, a historian of US Middle East policy at Washington University in St. Louis. The impetus for a regional security structure "should come clearly from within the Middle East" he says.

Sep 10

이라크 사태 해결을 위한 부쉬 대통령의 지도력 찬양

(9.10자 NYT지, Anthony Lewis)

o 부쉬 대통령은 최근 수십년간 미국의 대통령들에게서 보기드문 지혜와 노련함으로
  그리고 장기적 이해관계를 고려하여 이라크 위기를 잘 처리하고 있는바, 동
  사례들은 아래와 같음.
  - UN 안보리 결의 도출
  - 아랍 다수국의 후세인 비난 확보
  - 대 이라크 경제제재의 효율적 시행
  - 방대한 미군의 신속하고 안전한 사우디 파견
  - 사우디 및 쿠웨이트 정부가 대부분 미 군사 작전 비용을 부담 하겠다고
    동의
  - 냉전이후 최초로 국제분쟁에 미.쏘 공동 대처

o 일부에서는 쿠웨이트 정부의 복귀는 물론 후세인 전복 및 이라크 군사능력의
  무력화를 위하여 이라크의 쿠웨이트 침공 직후 대 이라크 공격을 주장했으나,
  미국의 군사적 승리가 그리 쉽지 않은 상황에서 상기 주장을 받아들이지
  않으므로써 부쉬 대통령은 현명한 판단을 하였음.

o 부쉬 대통령은 금번 사태 처리문제를 의회와 처음부터 협의 하였으며, 그레나다와
  파나마에서 드러난 일방주의와 불법성을 회피하였음.

o 부쉬 대통령의 정책은 이라크의 대 사우디 침공을 예방한 점에서 이미 효과를
  나타내고 있음.

o 다음 목표는 이라크의 쿠웨이트로 부터의 축출인바, 이는 쉽지 않은 일이지만
  미국민들은 부쉬 행정부의 정책을 자부심을 갖고 신뢰할 수 있음.

0102

SW(F)- 2148
장 관 (중고 미북 , 미북)   발신 : 주미대사
이락 사태 해결을 위한 부쉬 대통령의 지도력   (1 매)

ABROAD AT HOME | Anthony Lewis

Doing It Right

Bush's skillful leadership in the gulf.

BOSTON

There can be no assurance of how it will end. But so far President Bush has handled the Iraqi crisis with a wisdom, a professionalism and a care for long-term interests rare in recent decades of American leadership.

When Saddam Hussein sent his forces into Kuwait on Aug. 2, no one could have predicted what has actually been achieved since then in rallying the world against the aggressor:

• The United States and the Soviet Union are working together in a sensitive area where they were long in conflict: a new partnership symbolized by the Bush-Gorbachev meeting in Helsinki.

• The United Nations Security Council has acted vigorously against the Iraqi aggression, reviving the important principle of collective security through the U.N.

• A majority of Arab states have condemned the Arab aggressor.

• Iraq's oil exports have been totally stopped, and its imports of essential goods reduced to a trickle.

• The United States has moved an enormous military force to Saudi Arabia, with a minimum of mishap, in just five weeks.

• The Saudi and Kuwaiti Governments have agreed to cover most of the ongoing cost of the U.S. operation.

Those achievements are the measure of Mr. Bush's leadership. I say that as someone who has been no particular fan of his. I watched from vacation, skeptically at first, then with growing admiration for steps that were anything but easy to achieve.

The very idea of working together with the Soviet Union, for example, had met with loud resistance from the American right. Not so long ago conservative voices were warning that Mikhail Gorbachev's reversals of Soviet policy were all a trick. Even when the reality of the changes was unarguable, many cautioned that we should keep our distance from Mr. Gorbachev.

The partnership had to overcome strong objections in the U.S.S.R., too. The Soviet military, longtime Iraqi supplier and adviser, has been reluctant to cut that tie. It took great skill and patience on the part of Bush Administration officials to win a Soviet vote in the Security Council for the embargo in Iraq.

Mr. Bush and Mr. Gorbachev effectively seized the opportunity for a practical demonstration of how the post-cold war world could work. That has implications, profound and promising, beyond the immediate crisis.

Similarly, the use of the United Nations has long-term significance. The U.N. was founded on the premise that the great powers would act collectively against aggression. If that dusty hope is made reality now, it could provide a framework to resolve other conflicts, in the Middle East and elsewhere.

Along with the affirmative accomplishments of the last five weeks, Mr. Bush has to his credit a vital negative. He has resisted siren cries for an immediate military attack on Iraq.

Some commentators on the right began calling for war within days of the invasion of Kuwait. They set out sweeping objectives: not just the freeing of Kuwait but the overthrow of Saddam Hussein and the obliteration of Iraq's military capability. They talked, as usual, as if all this could be achieved neatly and easily by "surgical" measures, in Henry Kissinger's adjective.

What a disaster it would have been to follow that advice. The U.S. could not be ready for any military action at once. Bombing of Iraq, the strategy usually favored in such easy talk, would almost certainly not overthrow Saddam Hussein — it could increase support for him, if recent bombing examples are a guide. Serious military action, even for sensibly limited objectives, would involve ground forces and serious American casualties.

President Bush did not go down that road of folly. After some early rhetorical overkill he chose a measured, convincing policy. And he has the American people behind him — not just for the sake of cheap gasoline, as the cynics say, but for the principle of resisting aggression across international borders.

He has done this with respect for Congress, consulting it from the start. He has eschewed the unilateralism and the lawlessness of Grenada and Panama.

The policy has already worked to prevent an Iraqi invasion of Saudi Arabia. Some critics say that Saddam Hussein might not have invaded: a frail hope on which to rely against a move that would have changed the world. The next objective is to get Iraq out of Kuwait. That is hardly assured; but Americans can believe in their Government's policy, and be proud of it. □

Sept. 10, 1990
NYT

0103

원 본

외 무 부

관리 번호 : PO-2010

종 별 : 지 급

번 호 : USW-4159

일 시 : 90 0913 1250

수 신 : 장관(반기문 미주국장님)

발 신 : 주 미 대사(유명환)

제 목 : 업연

대:WUS-2999

대호 관련, 현지 언론 분석 및 국무부 관련 부서, NSC 관계관 접촉등을 통해 파악한바를 아래 보고드립니다.

1. 미측은 금번 중동사태 관련 최초의 대 국민 연설인 8.8. 부쉬 대통령 연설에서 "쿠웨이트 합법 정부의 복구(RESTORATION OF KUWAIT"S LEGITIMATE GOVERNMENT)"를 사태 해결 관련 4 대 원칙의 하나로 제시한 이래, 최근 9.11. 의회 연설을 포함 그동안의 각종 기자회견 및 연설등을 통해 동 원칙을 일관되게 계속 견지하는 입장을 취해 왔음.

2. 특히 9.9. 헬싱키 미소 정상회담 후 발표된 공동 성명에서도 "쿠웨이트 합법 정부의 복구"를 촉구하고, 보다 구체적으로는 "8.2. 침공이전 사태의 회복 (A RETURN TO THE PRE-AUG.2 STATUS OF KUWAIT)"을 강조한바 있음.

3. 전기 원칙을 천명하면서 미측 사용한 용어중 "LEGITIMATE" 라는 단어가 왕정이 아닌 민선 정부의 복구를 추구하는 느낌을 주기는 하나, 동 용어는 쿠웨이트 침공후 이락이 수립한 괴뢰 정권이 비합법 정부인데 반해 침공 이전의 왕정은 그렇지 않다는 취지에서 사용한 용어임.

4. 한편, 미국내 일각에서 진보주의적 입장을 취하고 있는 소수의 식자층은 금번 사태 해결을 위한 외교적 타협안의 하나로서 이락이 쿠웨이트로 부터 철군 하는대신 쿠웨이트는 총선에 의해 새로운 정부를 구성할것을 제의하고 있기도 하나, 여사한 의견은 현재 미국내 조야로부터 별다른 긍정적 반응을 얻지 못하고 있는 형편이며, 특히 이미 보고드린바와 같이 미 행정부는 대이락 고사 전략을 지속적으로 추구하는 과정에서, "쿠웨이트 합법정부의 복구"라는 당초의 목표를 계속 변함없이 유지하고 있음.

미주국

PAGE 1

90.09.14   04:38

외신 2과 통제관 DO

0104

5. 현 단계에서 미측은 동 목표가 <u>쿠웨이트 왕정의 복구를 의미하는것으로</u> <u>이해하여야 할것인바</u>, 다음과 같은 이유에서도 전기 외교적 타협안과 같은 구상은 생각키 어렵다는 반응임.

가. 미측의 목표가 쿠웨이트 왕정 복구를 반드시 의미하는것은 아니라는 점을 시사할경우, 사우디등 온건 아랍국의 지지를 배경으로 추구하고 있는 현재의 대 이락 전략에 차질이 생길 가능성이 있음.

(즉, 쿠웨이트 내 민선 정부 수립 문제는 쿠웨이트 일국만의 문제라기 보다는, 범세계적 민주화의 추세속에서도 상당수 국가가 전제 왕정이나 군사 독재체제를 유지하고 있는 중동지역 전체의 민주화 문제와 직결되는바, 이러한 일반론적 문제가 심각하게 대두될 경우 아랍권 내부의 분열이 초래됨은 물론 미국내 여론도 분열될 가능성이 큼)

나. 현 걸프 사태가 종결될후의 중동지역 역내 전반의 안전보장 장치 설치문제등 사후 처리 방식에 관한 미측 구상이 상금 확정적이지 않은것 처럼, 그보다 덜 중요한 문제라 할수 있는쿠웨이트 국내 정치 처리 문제에 관한 구상도 구정권 복구이외에는 미측으로서는 별무함.

다. 특히, 여사한 타협안을 수락함으써 이락이 쿠웨이트 에서 철수하는대신 쿠웨이트 에서 총선을 실시하는 경우, 쿠웨이트 거주 PLO 인등을 이용한 선거조작 등을 통해 이락이 친 이락계 세력의 합법적 권력 장악을 시도할 가능성도 큼.

라. 또한 상당 규모의 재산을 제 3 국 은행등에 유지하고 있는 쿠웨이트 왕정 세력이 미군의 사우디 파병 지원 의사등을 적극 개진하고 있는 상황이므로 , 결론적으로 현 단계에서 미측이 왕정 복구이외의 다른 대안을 추구한다는 것은 생각키 어려움

90.12.31. 일반

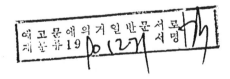

외 무 부

종 별 :

번 호 : USW-4194

일 시 : 90 0914 1940

수 신 : 장 관(미북,중근동,아일,구일)

발 신 : 주 미 대사

제 목 : 부쉬 대통령 기자 회견

연: USW(F)-2232

금 9.14 백악관에서 실시된 부쉬 대통령기자 회견 내용중, 걸프 사태 관련 주요언급 요지하기 보고함 (기자 회견 내용 전문 별첨 송부)

1.걸프 사태 관련 일본측의 추가 지원 결정에 대해 사의 표함 (동건 관련, 작일밤 가이후 수상과 통화시 개인적으로도 사의를 표한바 있음)

또한 금일 오전 영국 대처 수상도 영국측이 1개기갑 여단 및 헬리콥터, 항공기등을 사우디에 추가파견키로 결정하였다고 본인에게 전화로 알려왔음.

2.이라크군의 쿠웨이트 주재 불란서 대사 관저 칩입사건 관련, 폴란드 방문중인 미테랑 대통령과 방금 전화 통화를 하였는바, 무력 사용에 의한 보복 조치등 구체적 대응 방안을 협의친 않았으나 미국으로서는 이 문제와 관련한 프랑스측 입장을 적극 지지함.

3.미군의 사우디 파병은 사우디 정부의 요청에 따라 이루어진것인바, 이들 미군병력은 이들의 사우디내주둔이 더 이상 필요치 않거나 원치 않게되는 경우 (AS SOONAS THEY ARE NO LONGER NEEDED OR WANTED) 즉시 철수할것임.

(대사 박동진-국장)

미주국   1차보   아주국   구주국   중아국   정문국   안기부

PAGE 1

對 이라크戰 美軍戰略

(Dugan 空軍 參謀總長 인터뷰)

Washington Post
90. 9. 16

※ Dugan 참모총장은 아래 내용의 인터뷰에 대한 문책으로 9. 17
   동직에서 해임되었음

(對 이라크戰 美軍戰略)

o 對 이라크전 발발시 대규모의 바그다드 폭격을 포함한 공군 주도
   전략이 미국이 선택 가능한 유일한 효과적 전략 대안임

   - 이라크의 대규모 육군전력 감안시 공군 주도 전략만이 쿠웨이트의
     파괴와 대량의 인명 피해를 피할 수 있는 효과적 대안임(이에 대해
     중동지역 미군 고위 지휘관간에 의견일치를 보이고 있음)

   - 폭격은 집중적이고 대규모적으로 이루어져야 하며 특히 훗세인을
     살해하기 위한 공격목표 설정이 포함되어야 함

o 공격목표 우선순위는 이라크 공군기지, 중거리미사일기지, 지휘, 통신시설,
   원자, 화학 무기공장, 발전소, 도로, 석유 생산시설(유전 제외) 등임

   - 특히 이라크인에게 심리적 타격을 줄 수 있는 공격 목표를 설정할
     필요가 있으며, 이러한 목표 발굴을 위해 학자, 언론인, 전직
     군인들의 의견을 참조할 필요가 있음
     . 이스라엘 정보기관은 훗세인에게 타격을 줄 수 있는 최선의
       길은 그의 가족과, 경호원 그리고 情婦를 살해하는 것이라고
       조언해 왔음

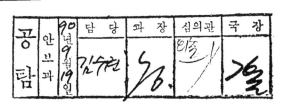

0107

(이라크 戰力 評價)

o 이라크군은 장비나 인원의 규모에 비해 운용능력이 빈약하여 실제
  전투력은 양적 위세에 크게 못미침

o 이라크의 대공방어 능력은 매우 부실하여 미 공군의 작적 수행에 큰
  위협이 되지 못함

(美 空軍 中東配置 現況)

o 전투기 및 폭격기 420대, 작전지원용 항공기 250대

o 중동배치 총 미군 150,000명중 30,000명이 공군 소속
  * 미국은 지난 5주동안에 냉전기간 동안 유럽에 배치한 전력과
    맞먹는 공군력을 중동에 집결 시켰음

o 미군은 최근 이스라엘로부터 24기의 해브납 미사일을 제공 받았음

(美軍戰略의 問題點)

o 일부 전략가들은 폭격만으로는 지상의 적을 섬멸하는데 불충분하다고
  주장

o 항공기등 군장비들이 거친 사막기후와 먼지에 노출되어 지능저하 우려

o 긴장상태하의 대치 장기화로 인한 피로 누적으로 군인들의 사기저하
  우려

0108

번호 : USW(F) - 22

수신 : 장   관 (중근동. ■■■ 북.(미안) 발신 : 주미대사   ■■ ■■

제목 : 이락 사태 관련 미공군력 사용 가능성   (3 매)
      (Dugan 공군참모총장 인터뷰)

U.S. to Rely on Air Strikes if War Erupts

By Rick Atkinson
Washington Post Staff Writer

DHAHRAN, Saudi Arabia—The Joint Chiefs of Staff have concluded that U.S. military air power—including a massive bombing campaign against Baghdad that specifically targets Iraqi President Saddam Hussein—is the only effective option to force Iraqi forces from Kuwait if war erupts, according to Air Force chief of staff Gen. Michael J. Dugan.

The cutting edge would be in downtown Baghdad. This [bombing] would not be nibbling at the edges," Dugan said in an interview. "If I want to hurt you, it would be at home, not out in the woods someplace."

Although U.S. ground and naval forces would play a substantive role in any military campaign, Iraq's huge army and tank force means "air power is the only answer that's available to our country" to avoid a bloody land war that would probably destroy Kuwait, Dugan said. That view, he added, is shared by the other chiefs and the commander of U.S. forces in the Persian Gulf region, Gen. H. Norman Schwarzkopf.

Consequently, the United States has in five weeks assembled in the gulf region a force of tactical air power roughly comparable to that deployed in Europe during the Cold War. Supplemented by Marine and Army aviators and three aircraft carriers, the Air Force has about 420 combat planes and 250 support aircraft operating from approximately 30 airfields in the area. Of more than 150,000 U.S. military personnel deployed as part of Operation Desert Shield, 30,000 belong to the Air Force.

Until two weeks ago, U.S. target planners had assembled a somewhat conventional list of Iraqi targets which included, in order of priority: Iraqi air defenses; airfields and war planes; intermediate-range missile sites, including Scud ground-to-ground missiles; communications and command centers; chemical, nuclear and munitions plants; and Iraqi armor formations. Other targets, Dugan said, would include Iraqi power systems, roads, railroads and perhaps domestic petroleum production facilities—though not the oil fields.

"That's a nice list of targets, and I might be able to accept those, but that's not enough," Dugan said. He asked his planners to interview academics, journalists, "ex-military types" and Iraqi defectors to determine "what is unique about Iraqi culture that they put very high value on. What is it that psychologically would make an impact on the population and regime in Iraq." The intent, he added, is to find "centers of gravity, where air power could make a difference early on."

Israeli sources have advised that "the best

See AIRPOWER, A36, Col 1

AIRPOWER, From A1

way to hurt Saddam" is to target his family, his personal guard and his mistress. Because Saddam is "a one-man show" in Iraq, Dugan said, "if and when we choose violence he ought to be at the focus of our efforts"—a military strategy known as decapitation.

The revised military targets now form "a better list," though it still contains all of the earlier targets; final targeting decisions will be made by Schwarzkopf and his staff in Saudi Arabia. Except for efforts to limit "collateral damage" to civilians, the military anticipates wide "latitude" in picking Iraqi targets. "I don't expect to be concerned" about political constraints, Dugan added.

However, the presence of Western hostages at or near potential bombing sites remains an uncertain factor. "I don't know what influence that consideration will have," said Lt. Gen. Jimmie V. Adams, Air Force deputy chief of staff for plans and operations.

The Air Force also has identified three "culturally very important" sites in Iraq—possibly religious centers—that the U.S. bombers would avoid. "We're not mad at the Iraqi people, and when this is all over we don't want the Iraqi people to be mad at us and the rest of the allies we've brought together," Dugan said.

Dugan's comments came in 10 hours of interviews with the chief and five of his senior generals on the U.S. air staff during a trip to and from Saudi Arabia last week. A tall, plain-spoken fighter pilot, Dugan commanded the U.S. Air Force in Europe before becoming chief of staff three months ago. Among other points made:

■ The Air Force is generally disdainful of the Iraqi armed forces. "Their air force has very limited military capability," Dugan said. "They did not distinguish themselves in the war against Iran," often missing targets by miles. Iraq possesses "an incompetent army," he added. "With 5,000 tanks one should have been able to do something" against Iran.

■ With the exception of some mobile, Soviet-made SA-6 surface-to

1237-1

WP
Sept. 16,
1990

0109

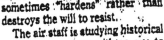
air missiles, Iraqi air defenses are considered no match for U.S. power. "I don't mean to tell you that we won't lose any planes," Adams said. "But I think it's a manageable risk." One concern is Iraq's capture in Kuwait of U.S.-made Hawk missiles. "We typically do not have any protection against Hawk missiles," Dugan said.

■ About 20 F-117 Stealth fighters based at a secret airfield in this region are flying training missions every night, with the exception of one daytime orientation flight. If an F-117 was shot down or crashed in Iraqi territory, "we'd probably go to some lengths, if we knew where the airplane crashed, to bomb the wreckage" in order to prevent the technology from reaching Baghdad, said Lt. Gen. Thomas R. Ferguson Jr., commander of the Aeronautical Systems Division, which is responsible for new Air Force technology.

■ Israel recently provided the United States with about two dozen new, Israeli-built Have Nap missiles intended for a comparable number of B-52 bombers now based at Diego Garcia in the Indian Ocean, according to an informed source. These "stand-off" missiles with a one-ton warhead permit the bombers to fire accurately at ground targets from 50 miles away, out of range of Iraqi defenses. The United States has designated a base closer to Iraq for the B-52s and is certain the host country will permit the move in event of war, although no formal request has been made yet. Officials would not identify the base.

■ In the past week, Iraq has dispersed some of its warplanes "in groups of three and four" to remote airfields in southern Iraq, apparently to make them less vulnerable to U.S. attack. In the past two weeks, Iraqi pilots have doubled their nocturnal flights, presumably in anticipation of night combat against a *U.S. force that prefers to fight in* the dark.

Some military strategists and historians are skeptical that air power is sufficient to dislodge an entrenched enemy; North Vietnam resisted intense U.S. bombing for years. The Air Force generals said they are aware of this view. "We often underestimate our enemies,"

Adams said, noting that bombing sometimes "hardens" rather than destroys the will to resist.

The air staff is studying historical bombing campaigns with an eye to applying lessons learned and "one of the lessons we got out of Vietnam was that gradualism doesn't work," Adams added. The full-scale air war envisioned now reflects the Joint

OPERATION DESERT SHIELD: THE AIR POWER
PARTICIPATING UNITS FROM THE U.S. AIR FORCE

Operation Desert Shield includes at least one squadron (typically 24 planes) of most aircraft on this list. The exceptions are the EF-111 and F-4G units.

■ F-15Cs and F-15Ds, 1st Tactical Fighter Wing, Langley AFB, Va.
■ F-15Es, 4th Tactical Fighter Wing, Seymour Johnson AFB, N.C.
■ A-10s, 23rd Tactical Fighter Wing, England AFB, La.
■ F-15s, 33rd Tactical Fighter Wing, Eglin AFB, Fla.
■ F-4Gs, 35th Tactical Fighter Wing, George AFB, Calif.
■ F-117a (Stealth fighter), 37th Tactical Fighter Wing, Tonopah Test Range
■ B-52s, 42nd Bomb Wing, Loring AFB, Maine
■ F-111s, 48th Tactical Fighter Wing, RAF Lakenheath, England
■ F-4Gs, 52nd Tactical Fighter Wing, Spangdahlem Air Base, West Germany
■ B-52s, 93rd Bomb Wing, Castle AFB, Calif.
■ RF-4G, 117th Tactical Reconnaissance Wing, Birmingham Air National Guard
■ C-130s, 317th Tactical Airlift Wing, Pope AFB, N.C.
■ A-10s, 354 Tactical Fighter Wing, Myrtle Beach AFB, S.C.
■ F-16s, 363rd Tactical Fighter Wing, Shaw AFB, S.C.
■ EF-111s, 366th Tactical Fighter Wing, Mountain Home AFB, Idaho
■ F-16s, 388th Tactical Fighter Wing, Hill AFB, Utah
■ F-16s, 401st Tactical Fighter Wing, Torrejon Air Base, Spain
■ E-3, 552nd Airborne Warning and Control Wing, Tinker AFB, Okla.

Also participating:
■ KC-10 and KC-135 air refueling aircraft
■ RC-135 reconnaissance aircraft from Offut AFB, Neb.
■ U-2 and TR-1 surveillance aircraft
■ C-141 and C-5 air transport planes, including many crewed by reserve and National Guard units.

A-10

F-15

Sept. 16, 1990
WP

0110

Chiefs' general approach brought to Desert Shield under Operations Plan 90-1002: a conviction that if U.S. power is committed, it should be fully committed.

"There are a lot of things that air power cannot accomplish," Dugan said. "We had great difficulty in driving people out of the jungle [in Southeast Asia]. But there's not much jungle where we're going."

Air power gives "a special kind of psychological impact," he added, and hopefully would soon persuade Iraqis that "Saddam and his regime cannot protect them." Although the Air Force can guarantee tremendous devastation in Iraq, whether raining destruction would effect the withdrawal from Kuwait or Saddam's ouster is a political conclusion that the president and others must make, Dugan said. There also is no guarantee that bombers would be able to find Saddam.

The Air Force generals declined to comment on whether U.S. chemical or nuclear weapons have been moved to the gulf region for use against Iraq.

Part of the focus on air warfare is the consequence of unpalatable alternatives. The Pentagon has decided that it cannot and will not match Saddam's ground forces, much less assemble the 3-to-1 advantage considered necessary for an offensive campaign. Air power plays to a U.S. strength while avoiding a protracted armor offensive or extensive urban fighting in Kuwait City, several generals said.

Marine and Army ground forces could be used for diversions, flanking attacks and to block an Iraqi counterstrike on Saudi Arabia. If major ground warfare is to be avoided, then the air war cannot be restricted just to Iraqi targets in Kuwait or "obviously, air power cannot achieve the goal" of dislodging Iraq, Ferguson said. Ground forces may be needed to reoccupy Kuwait, Dugan added, but only after air power has so shattered enemy resistance that soldiers can "walk in and not have to fight" house-to-house.

Unlike some of the U.S. ground forces, which may take another two months to reach their gulf destinations, the Air Force is virtually in place and has sufficient forces to fight an all-out war. Some additional aerial tankers have yet to arrive, but adequate supplies of munitions are on hand except for flares and chaff used to deceive anti-aircraft missiles. To fill out their war reserve kits, squadrons deploying to the gulf did considerable "cannibalizing" from squadrons left behind, which in turn have borrowed from reserve and Guard units.

Although Schwarzkopf recently said he was concerned about the impending overhaul of Air Force transport jets, Dugan said, "I'm not aware of any significant problems with the airlift. Yeah, we're going to have to replace some engines, but we replace engines" periodically anyway. A more pressing problem is to find rested pilots, for which more reserves might be needed.

The generals expressed great satisfaction with the Air Force deployment under Desert Shield. The Saudis have spent many billions of dollars building runways, hangars, repair shops and hardened subterranean aircraft bunkers that are the "finest I've ever seen anywhere," Adams observed. A new, still-unopened airport in the eastern portion of the country is "bigger than Dulles and JFK [airport in New York] combined," said Maj. Gen. Philip G. Killey, director of the Air National Guard. Airmen have made good use of materiel from Harvest Falcon, goods stored in Egypt, Oman, Turkey and elsewhere.

In general, aircraft used for defensive purposes—such as tank killers and air defense jets—have been placed closer to the Iraqi border while offensive planes—such as ground attack fighter-bombers—are at bases farther back, one general said. That deployment likely would change if combat begins. Six aircraft battle-damage repair teams have been deployed to the region.

"There's no doubt that heat affects our people and to some extent our equipment," Lt. Gen. Henry "Butch" Viccellio Jr., deputy chief of staff for logistics and engineering, said after visiting eight bases in four countries. "But I found that it's not substantially slowing down our operations." Crew members have shown ingenuity by making aircraft canopy covers—to protect cockpit instruments—out of bedsheets; small handheld "Dustbuster" vac-

cuums have also become very popular in this dusty environment.

One nagging concern is fuel. Although even without Kuwaiti supplies "we have far more refined fuel" on the Arabian peninsula than is needed, Viccellio said, "to sustain a high-tempo [combat] operation longer than a week you have to have a secure, reliable way to get it from the source to the base." Logisticians are working on the problem.

Another concern is morale. The prospect of an indefinite, tense, boring wait in a region with few amenities is a daunting problem for commanders. Though U.S. forces have performed admirably, Dugan said, "We've already started to see the bloom off the rose about the excitement of it all."

A related anxiety—and the subject of frequent questions from soldiers, sailors and airmen here—is the willingness of Americans to support Desert Shield indefinitely. "I think they'd support this operation longer than you would think," Dugan said during a brief meeting with more than 100 members of an F-15 squadron Friday. "The American people will support this operation until body bags come home."

Sept. 16, 1990
WP

2239-3

0111

이라크 事態와 이스라엘의 安保 問題

====================================

1990. 9. 16
Washington Post

1. 이라크 事態 以前의 이스라엘 安保 狀況

  o 중동지역에 대한 미. 쏘 양국간의 경쟁을 이용하여 안보 유지

    - 미국으로부터 고성능 무기를 지속적으로 도입, 對 아랍권
      군사력 우위 유지로 아랍권 국가들의 전쟁 도발 억지

  o 국내적으로는 1979 Camp David 협정 이후 West Bank와 Gaza 지구의
    장래 문제등 이스라엘 안보전략에 대한 논의 사실상 동결

    - 이스라엘 우익 연합의 계속 집권, 외교 문제 현상 유지 추구

2. 이라크 事態의 影響

  o 이라크 사태로 미국이 종전 적대관계를 유지하고 있던 아랍국가와
    對 이라크 연합전선 구축을 모색하고, 헬싱키 정상회담이후 쏘련의
    중동지역에 대한 역할 증대가 기대되자 점령지역의 장래 문제를 포함한
    이스라엘 안보전략 전반에 대한 재조정 필요성 대두

    * 그러나 현 집권 우익 연합은 외교문제에 매우 보수적이며
      변화에 소극적임

0112

o 이라크 사태의 영향에 대한 두가지 평가

(긍정적 영향)

- 미군의 중동배치 및 아랍권 국가와의 군사협력으로 아랍권
  국가들의 이스라엘 공격가능성 감소

- Jewish State의 존재를 부인하던 아랍권 국가들이 미국과
  對 이라크 연합전선에 참여하므로써 이들 국가들로부터
  Jewish State 실재에 대한 사실상 인정 획득 가능성

(부정적 영향)

- 對 아랍권 군사력 우위를 통한 안보전략에 차질 초래 가능성
  미국은 사우디에 수십억불 규모의 신형 무기를 제공하는 반면,
  이를 보상할 응분의 조치에 대한 이스라엘측의 요구에
  미온적 반응

- 중동문제에 대한 미. 쏘 공동대응 추진시 이스라엘의 점령지역
  철군을 요구하는 국제적 압력 가중 예상

3. 向後 展望

o 이스라엘은 향후 중동정세 변화에 대한 대응에 있어서 ① 미국과의
  정식 방위조약 체결로 기존 미. 이 안보 협력 강화를 통한 안보유지,
  또는 ② 미국과 아랍국가간 군사협력 구조에 직접 참여를 통한
  안보추구등 두가지 대안에 직면 예상

0113

o 현재 이스라엘의 최대 불확실 요소는 쏘련의 입장이며, 쏘련은
   팔레스타인 문제 해결을 위한 국제회의개최와 중동지역내 군비
   경쟁 완화를 위한 군비통제 추진등을 제시할 가능성이 크며 미국도
   군비통제 문제에 대해서는 다소 긍정적 반응을 보이고 있음

o 그러나 위 제안들은 이스라엘 집권당이 극력 반대하는 것으로서 향후
   이스라엘의 안보정책 문제에 대한 국제적 차원 뿐 아니라 이스라엘
   국내적 논의가 더욱 가열될 전망임

0114

Cold War's End, Gulf Crisis Shake Israel's Security Strategy

By Jackson Diehl
Washington Post Foreign Service

JERUSALEM, Sept. 15—The upheaval in the Middle East's political and strategic order caused by the crisis in the Persian Gulf now appears likely to force Israel to remake its strategy for security, and possibly to face the issue of its occupation of Arab territories after years of stalemate. |NEWS ANALYSIS|

From their position on the sidelines of Iraq's confrontation with a U.S.-led alliance, Israeli leaders until now have often seen themselves as among the prospective winners in the crisis, because of the likelihood that two major enemies—Iraq and the Palestine Liberation Organization—eventually will be defeated or discredited.

Still, the U.S.-Soviet summit meeting in Helsinki last weekend and the events that have followed it have made clear that Israel, too, faces an upheaval in its diplomatic and military standing as a result of the multinational effort to make the Middle East the testing ground for a new world order.

On the simplest level, the move by the Bush administration to forge a strong military and strategic alliance with Arab states in and around the gulf, and to provide them with tens of billions of dollars in new weapons, has threatened Israel's primacy as a U.S. regional ally and its traditional policy of maintaining qualitative superiority over its neighbors in military hardware.

But also, by his invitation in Helsinki for the Soviet Union to assume a greater role in Middle East affairs, President Bush implicitly prepared for a development Israeli leaders deeply fear: an eventual joint superpower effort to resolve the Israeli-Palestinian conflict. Such an initiative probably would result in the strongest pressure in years for Israel to withdraw from the West Bank and Gaza Strip.

Some Israelis believe the crisis also could encourage breakthroughs for the Jewish state, such as overt recognition of its existence by some Arab countries aligned with the United States. More likely, however, the country faces a struggle to find a secure position in the region's new diplomatic and military balance, and possibly a new domestic debate over what borders and alliances are needed for that security.

"I think the rules of the Middle East are likely to change radically, and a lot of the principles Israel used to live by are going to be viewed differently," said Gerald Steinberg, a political scientist at Tel Aviv's Bar-Ilan University. "It's going to take time for . . . Israel to adjust to it."

Although it has faced continual threats to its security, Israel benefited in many respects from the superpower rivalry that until now governed the Middle East. As Washington's chief client over the last two decades, Israel was assured a steady flow of advanced U.S. weapons that guaranteed its superiority over Soviet allies such as Syria and Iraq and moderate Arab states such as Saudia Arabia.

In a perverse way, the Cold War ensured a certain stability among the warring parties of the Middle East. "On one hand, the competition between the superpowers contributed to an arms race and eventually to armed conflict," said Yair Evron, a political scientist specializing in security issues at Tel Aviv University. "But on the other hand, it

See ISRAEL, A30, Col. 1

ISRAELI, From A25

was effective in preventing major outbreaks of violence, and stopping them when they started."

The Cold War also helped freeze diplomatic progress in the region following the 1979 Egyptian-Israeli peace treaty, leaving Israel in control of the West Bank and Gaza Strip. That suited the right-wing leaders who have dominated Israeli governments since 1977. Israel felt little pressure to resolve its own, potentially explosive domestic schism over what to do with the occupied lands, and papered the problem over with a series of "national unity" governments that endured from 1984 until early this year.

Despite the prospect of Soviet involvement raised at Helsinki, most Israelis continue to believe that a new Middle East order will be dominated by the United States. That is a double-edged prospect: While Washington is committed to Israel's security, its new role may make it less responsive to Israel's ambitions to sustain its regional military superiority and occupation of the West Bank and Gaza.

The erosion of Israel's position already can be seen as the Bush administration prepares to transfer tens of billions of dollars in new weapons to Saudia Arabia, a country whose hostility to Israel had, until now, limited its ability to obtain U.S. weapons. Israeli concern has been

least, to set up parallel arrangements with Washington.

Dore Gold, an expert on U.S.-Israeli strategic relations at the Jaffee Center of Tel Aviv University, said the new framework could resemble the "strategic consensus" that former U.S. secretary of state Alexander Haig aspired to create among Washington and Middle East states in the early 1980s. That would mean a series of parallel agreements between the United States, individual Arab states and Israel, with the common aim of deterring a mutual enemy. The difference is that Iraq would take the place of the Soviet Union as that enemy.

Other observers say Israel should seek to lock in its relationship with the United States by negotiating a formal defense treaty with Washington, a step that was once a primary objective of Israeli policy but has fallen from favor in recent years. While such a treaty would increase Israel's sense of security, past U.S. administrations have taken the position that its signing should be linked to a withdrawal from the occupied territories.

To some extent, Israel's ability to react to the rapidly changing situation is hampered by the nature of its right-wing government, which in addition to having a novice foreign minister in David Levy is headed by a prime minister, Shamir, noted for his reluctance to take new initiatives. "There is a policy dilemma,"

said Gold. "On the one hand, one wants to move actively and be part of establishing the new Middle East order. On the other hand, the Middle East is changing rapidly, and you don't want to, say, race ahead on the Palestinian issue when maybe that issue will soon take on a totally different dimension."

In the aftermath of Helsinki, perhaps the greatest uncertainty for Israel is the role the Soviet Union may eventually play in stabilizing the Middle East, and what influence Moscow may exert on the U.S. approach to the Israeli-Arab conflict. Soviet attitudes toward Israel clearly are changing yesterday in Moscow, Gorbachev met for the first time with members of the Israeli cabinet, including Science Minister Yuval Neeman, the leader of one of the country's most extreme right-wing parties.

Still, Soviet Middle East policy continues to focus on two strategies that the Israeli right staunchly opposes: an international conference to solve the Israeli-Palestinian dispute, and an arms control process to stop the region's weapons buildup. Although the United States does not yet appear ready to press Israel into participating in an international conference, Secretary of State James A. Baker III does appear to support an arms control initiative. "Arms control is one of the things that Israel is going to have to start thinking about," predicted Gold.

Even though some Israelis feel the U.S. military deployment in the Middle East protects Israel in the short term from any attack by Arab states, many Israeli strategists believe the country needs more substantial guarantees of security. Israel, they say, should aspire to become a direct part of any new network of alliances set up by the United States with its Arab allies—or, at

heightened by Washington's evident reluctance to immediately compensate Israel with its own new weapon supplies or a write-off of its military debts.

2275-2

Sept. 16, 1990

외 무 부

종 별 :

번 호 : USW-4220　　　　　　　　　　　일 시 : 90 0917 1841

수 신 : 장 관(미안,미북,중근동)사본:국방부장관

발 신 : 주 미 대사

제 목 : 미공군 참모총장 해임

1. 금 9.17 CHENEY 국방부장관은 기자회견을 통해 MICHAEL DUGAN 현공군참모총장을 해임하고, 후임으로는 태평양 지역 공군총사령관 (COMMANDER IN CHIEF, PACIFICAIR FORCES) 인 TONY MCPEAK 장군의 임명을 건의하였다고 발표함. (기자회견시 CHENEY 장관발표문은 별첨 FAX 편 송부)

2. 이러한 전격인사 조치는 작 9.16 WP 지에 실린 U.S. TO RELY ON AIR STRIKES IF WAR ERUPTS 제하의 기사에 인용된 DUGAN 참모총장의 인터뷰 내용이 군사기밀사항 (공습목표 선정 원칙, 미공군전력등)을 포함하고 있기 때문에 취해진 것이라함.

　첨부: USW(F)-2254

　(대사 박동진-국장)

미주국　　1차보　　미주국　　중아국　　정문국　　안기부　　국방부

PRESS CONFERENCE WITH SECRETARY OF DEFENSE RICHARD CHENEY
THE PENTAGON, WASHINGTON, DC/MONDAY, SEPTEMBER 17, 1990

    PETE WILLIAMS: Good afternoon, ladies and gentlemen. As you
know, the Secretary has answered some questions about the General
Dugan matter already at the White House, but in deference to those
of you who cover defense issues regularly, he agreed to come down
here and take your questions. He'll have a brief opening statement,
and then happy to respond to your questions. He has a 3:00 meeting
that he must go to, so we'll have to be finished by then. But when
you get to questions, if you'll raise your hand, then the Secretary
can point to you.

    Mr. Secretary.

    SEC. CHENEY: Thank you very much, Pete.

    This morning, I met with General Michael Dugan to relieve him
of his responsibilities as Air Force Chief of Staff. I took the
action after consultations with the President. Pending
confirmation of a successor, General Mike Loh, currently Vice Chief
of Staff, will act as chief of staff. I'm announcing today my
intention to recommend to the President that he nominate General
Tony McPeak as the new Air Force chief of staff. General McPeak is
currently serving as Commander in Chief, Pacific Air Forces, and had
been slated to take over Tactical Air Command in February.

    This was obviously a decision I did not take lightly. General
Dugan is a fine officer with an outstanding record of 32 years of
service to the Air Force and to the nation. This was not a pleasant
action for me to take, but under the circumstances, I felt it was a
necessary one. At this moment, we have over 150,000 military
personnel deployed in the Middle East for Operation Desert Shield.
They may face hostilities at any time, and we have put together a
very important, carefully built international coalition that's come
together in opposition to Saddam Hussein's aggression. Under the
circumstances, the conduct of US national security policy is an extremely
delicate task. The statements attributed to General Dugan in two
newspapers this weekend and as confirmed by him to me did not in my mind
reveal an adequate understanding of the situation and what is expected of
him as Chief of Staff of the Air Force and as a member of the Joint
Chiefs.

    I was concerned about the lack of judgment involved in wide-
ranging speculation about decisions which may or may not be made in
the future by the President. As a matter of policy, as you all
know, there are some things we never discuss. We never talk about
future operations such as the selection of specific targets for
potential air strikes. We never talk about the targeting of
specific individuals who are officials of other governments. Taking
such action might be a violation of the standing presidential
Executive Order.

2254-1

0118

I think it's important never to underestimate the strength of opposing forces. In a situation involving potential conflict, I think it's contrary to sound practice to reveal classified information about the size and disposition of US forces. And as a general matter of policy, I don't think we want to be demeaning the contributions of other services. General Dugan's statements, in my opinion, were not consistent with this policy and showed poor judgment at a very sensitive time. As a result I felt I had no choice but to relieve him as Air Force Chief of Staff. I'll be happy to take your questions.

225K-2

0119

Supporting the U.S. in the Gulf

1990.9.18

New York Times

WITH MIGHT

The international force confronting Iraq is dominated by more than
140,000 U.S. troops and naval personnel, with about 500 aircraft and
more than 40 warships. In recent days other countries, notably Britain,
France and Egypt announced major new deployments. Here is a breakdown
of non-American forces committed to the Persian Gulf region to date.

AUSTRALIA : Two guided-missile frigates and a supply ship

BANGLADESH : 2,000 troops in Saudi Arabia, 3,000 more to be sent soon

BAHRAIN : Army of 2,300 men, air force of 450 and a navy of 600. Britain
has based a squadron of Tornado fighters there

BELGIUM : Two minesweepers and a support ship

BRITAIN : Has ordered 6,000 troops and 120 Challenger tanks to the gulf.
The latest contingent will include the 7th Armoured Brigade
-the Desert Rats-which conquered Rommel's Nazi Panzer forces
in the North African desert. At least two squadrons of fighter
bombers in the region. Dispatch of 6,000 troops will bring
military personnel stationed in gulf to 9,000

CANADA : Two destroyers and a supply ship on way to gulf; has pledged
to send a squadron of CF-18 fighter planes and 450 military
personnel

0120

DENMARK : one corvette due soon in gulf

EGYPT : At least 5,000 troops in Saudi Arabia and 15,000 to follow in
next few days with tanks and air defense systems

FRANCE : Pledge of 4,000 more troops would raise number in or near gulf
to 13,100, including a 4,000 strong permanent garrison at
Djibouti. Fourteen ships in gulf and Red Sea, including an
aircraft carrier

GREECE : One frigate

ITALY : Two frigates and a supply ship in gulf region. A fourth warship
and eight Tornado fighters have been pledged

MOROCCO : About 1,200 men in Saudi Arabia, 5,000 in United Arab Emirates

NETHERLANDS : Two frigates

NORWAY : Military supply ship to leave for gulf soon

PAKISTAN : 2,000 troops in Saudi Arabia with 9,000 more to be sent in a
few days. Has 1,000 military advisers and technicians in
Saudi Arabia

SAUDI ARABIA : Army of 28,000, national guard of 56,000, plus 7,200 in
navy and air force of 16,500. Has 550 tanks, 180 combat
planes and eight frigates

SOVIET UNION : Two warships in gulf, not authorized to stop shipping

SPAIN : Two corvettes and a destroyer

SYRIA : 4,000 troops in saudi Arabia and United Arab Emirates. Diplomats
say Damascus will send 10,000 more and 300 tanks

TURKEY : 100,000 troops serve near the Iraqi border, backed by 35,000
para military and police officers

UNITED ARAB EMIRATES : 40,000 in army with more than 200 tanks, 1500-
member air force with 80 combat aircraft and a
1,500-member navy with 15 ships

0121

AND MONEY

The United States in recent weeks has carried out a compaign to persuade
other wealthy nations to share the burden of gulf costs. After visits
by Secretary of State James A. Baker 3rd and Treasury Secretary Nicholas
F. Brady to more than a dozen countries, here are the largest commitments
to date

GULF STATES : About $12 billion by the end of the year, including $5
                billion from the exiled Kuwait Government. Half is to
                support the U.S.-led military effort and half is for
                Middle Eastern nations adversely affected by the crisis
JAPAN : $4 billion, half to support the U.S.-led buildup and half in aid
        to Middle Eastern countries
EUROPEAN COMMUNITY : About $2 billion to aid nations hurt by the crisis
WEST GERMANY : $1.87 billion(excluding European Community Contribution),
                more than half to support the U.S. military including
                transport assistance and equipment to resist chemical
                warfare, the rest to aid Middle Eastern countries.

0122

美國의 對 이라크 軍事力 使用 可能性

1990. 9. 21
미 주 국
안 보 과

    최근 일부 미국 언론들은 미국의 대이라크 군사력 사용 가능성을
거론하고 있는바, 관련사항을 아래 보고드립니다.

背 景

o 미국은 이라크의 쿠웨이트 철수가 양보할 수 없는 우선목표이나 현재
   진행중인 경제봉쇄 조치로는 동 목적을 달성하기 어려우며, 제반
   여건 고려시 사태가 장기화될수록 상황이 미국에 불리해질 수
   있다는 가능성 감지(CSM 9. 18)

o 반면 훗세인은 시간이 흐를수록 아랍권 여론이 미국의 대중동 군사
   전략에 부정적인 방향으로 나가고, 결국에는 미국과 아랍권간의
   대결 구도로의 전환이 가능하다고 판단, 버티기작전 돌입(NYT 9. 19)

美國의 對 이라크 戰略目標 및 戰術代案

(전략 목표)

o 이라크군 쿠웨이트 철수 및 쿠웨이트 합법정부 수립

0123

o 중동지역에서 이라크의 패권 및 주변국가에 대한 위협을 제거할
  수 있는 항구적 중동 안보구조 확립

〈전술 대안〉

o 정보망을 통해 훗세인과 측근의 거처를 파악, 공중폭격으로 살해
  (WP 9. 16)

o 공군력 위주의 대규모 폭격으로 이라크의 군사기지, 산업시설 및
  교통 통신시설 파괴로 이라크 무력화 (WP 9. 16)

  ※ Dugan 미공군 참모총장은 WP와의 인터뷰에서 상기 전술대안
     언급에 대한 문책으로 동직에서 해입됨 (9. 17)

  向後 展望

o 제반 상황 감안시 군사력에 의한 훗세인의 붕괴만이 유일한
  해결책이며 이는 빠를 수록 미국에 유리 (U.S. News & WR 9. 24)

o 현재 미국의 중동지역 군사력 보강 진도에 비추어 볼때 공격에 필요한
  준비 완료시기는 대체로 10월 중순경으로 예상되며, 미국은 10월
  중순경부터 경제봉쇄 조치의 효과 및 여타 중동사태를 전반적으로
  재평가, 군사력 사용 여부에 대한 최종 결정을 내릴것으로 전망됨
  (CSM 9. 18)

0124

長官報告事項

報告畢

長信報告畢

1990. 9. 21

美 洲 局

安 保 課(35)

題 目 : 美國의 對 이라크 軍事力 使用 可能性

    최근 일부 미국 언론들은 미국의 대이라크 군사력 사용 가능성을
거론하고 있는바, 관련사항을 아래 보고드립니다.

背 景

o 미국은 이라크의 쿠웨이트 철수가 양보할 수 없는 우선목표이나 현재
  진행중인 경제봉쇄 조치로는 동 목적을 달성하기 어려우며, 제반
  여건 고려시 사태가 장기화될수록 상황이 미국에 불리해질 수
  있다는 가능성 감지(CSM 9.18)

o 반면 훗세인은 시간이 흐를수록 아랍권 여론이 미국의 대중동 군사
  전략에 부정적인 방향으로 나가고, 결국에는 미국과 아랍권간의
  대결 구도로의 전환이 가능하다고 판단, 버티기작전 돌입(NYT 9.19)

0125

美國의 對 이라크 戰略目標 및 戰術代案

(전략 목표)

o 이라크군 쿠웨이트 철수 및 쿠웨이트 합법정부 수립

o 중동지역에서 이라크의 패권 및 주변국가에 대한 위협을 제거할
   수 있는 항구적 중동 안보구조 확립

(전술 대안)

o 정보망을 통해 훗세인과 측근의 거처를 파악, 공중폭격으로 살해
   (WP 9.16)

o 공군력 위주의 대규모 폭격으로 이라크의 군사기지, 산업시설 및
   교통 통신시설 파괴로 이라크 무력화 (WP 9.16)

   ※ Dugan 미공군 참모총장은 WP와의 인터뷰에서 상기 전술대안
       언급에 대한 문책으로 동직에서 해임됨 (9.17)

向後 展望

o 제반 상황 감안시 군사력에 의한 훗세인의 붕괴만이 유일한
   해결책이며 이는 빠를 수록 미국에 유리 (U.S. News & WR 9.24)

o 현재 미국의 중동지역 군사력 보강 진도에 비추어 볼때 공격에 필요한
   준비 완료시기는 대체로 10월 중순경으로 예상되며, 미국은 10월
   중순경부터 경제봉쇄 조치의 효과 및 여타 중동사태를 전반적으로
   재평가, 군사력 사용 여부에 대한 최종 결정을 내릴것으로 전망됨
   (CSM 9.18)

0126

미국의 새로운 「중동안보구조」 설립 구상 분석·평가

1990. 9

미 주 국
안 보 과

0127

새로운 「중동안보구조」 구상의 '윤곽'

o 새로운 「중동안보구조」(Regional Security Structure) 구상은, 9.4
   베이커 국무장관의 하원외교위 증언에서 최초로 언급된 바, 동 장관은
   청문회 질의 응답 과정에서,

   i) Hussein 대통령과 그의 대량살상무기 추구를 봉쇄(contain),
      패퇴(Roll-Back) 시키기 위하여

   ii) NATO와 유사한 형태의 지역안보구조 설립을 검토할 필요가 있다
      하였음

o 베이커 장관은, 9.5 상원외교위 증언에서도 새로운 지역안보체제 구축
   필요성을 재강조 하면서, 동 기구의 목적은, 지역내 질서 구축과
   침략저지, 특히 이라크의 팽창주의와 대량살륙무기 개발 저지에
   있다 하였으나, 구체적 형태에 대해서는 검토된 바 없으며, 핵무기
   균형을 전재로한 NATO와는 다른 형태가 될 수 밖에 없을 것 이라고
   언급하여, 전날의 하원외무위 증언에서 약간 후퇴한 입장을 표명
   하였음

o 베이커 장관은, 구상의 상세에 대해서는 설명하지 않았으나, 증언 벽두
   발표문중 아래 부분들이 동 제의의 배경을 시사해 주는 것으로 보임

   - '전례없는 국제적 합의를 바탕 으로, 페르샤만의 장기적 안보와
     안정을 달성하기 위하여...'

   - '우리는 페르시아만의 보다 건실한 질서구축을 위해 역내, 외
     국가들과 협력 할 것이다. 역내 국가들의 침략억지 및 자체방어
     능력을 강화하여 미 병력의 파견 필요성을 축소 할 것이다'

0128

- '현사태 해결은 핵 및 생화학 무기와 탄도 미사일의 확산 방지 를
  위한 지속적인 국제 노력의 계기가 될 것이며, 이스라엘-아랍간의
  갈등등 보다 근본적인 분쟁의 해결 노력도 크게 활성화 시킬
  것이다'

- 이라크의 쿠웨이트 철수이후에도 ... 동 지역에 대한 미 해군력의
  계속 주둔이 필요할 수도 있다'

o 상기에 비추어, 미측이 구상하고 있는 「중동안보구조」 설립 계획의
  '윤곽' 은 대체로 아래와 같이 그려볼 수 있음

- 예상시기 : 이라크의 쿠웨이트 철수후, 지상군을 중심한 미군사력의
              철수와 동시

- 구   성 : 페르시아만 국가를 중심하여, 일부 역외국가 포함

- 목   적
    . 단기적 : 이라크의 팽창주의 봉쇄와 역내 대량 살상무기 확산
               억지 및 방지
    . 장기적 : 아랍-이스라엘 본쟁등 소위 중동문제의 보다 근본적인
               해결 모색

- 미국의 참여 : 최소한 해군력의 장기적 주둔으로 기구의 실효성 보장

0129

o 베이커 구상이 상기와 같이 아직은 애매하여, 이를 제의한 미국의
   의도를 분명하게 분석할 수는 없으나, 아래와 같은 고려는 하였을
   것으로 보임

(냉전후 국제질서 및 평화유지 체제 개념)

o 베이커 구상은, 향후 국제질서 및 평화유지 체제구축에 대한 미측의
   개념이 쿠웨이트 사태를 계기로 하여 막연한 형태로나마 표시된
   것이라 볼 수 있음

o 쿠웨이트 사태에 대한 미국의 대응은 부쉬행정부의 새로운 국제주의적
   안보유지 개념을 보여주고 있는 바, 이는
   i) 미국의 영도하에,
   ii) 전 국제사회가 국제법과 보편적인 원칙을 기초로 단결하여,
   iii) 집단적으로, 특히 유엔을 통하여 평화와 안보유지 조치를 취하고,
   iv) 이를 위한 비용은 모든 국가가 형평에 맞게 분담한다는 것을
   주 내용으로 하고 있음

o 그러나, 부쉬의 새로운 국제주의가 효율적으로 운영되기 위해서는
   궁극적으로 미국의 독자적 결정권이 유엔의 집단적 결정권으로 대체
   된다는 것을 의미하고, 이는 미국의 전통적 국제정치 감각인 고립주의에
   배치되는 결과가 되어, 이것이 공식적인 정책으로 표명될 경우, 국내
   적으로 크게 논란이 제기될 소지가 있음

0130

o 따라서, 미국으로서는, 유엔을 중심한 단일 평화유지 체제보다는
   세계를 여러개의 지역집단으로 구분하고, 그 각각에 대해 미국이
   영향력을 행사, 평화 파괴자를 응징하는 체제가 보다 체질에 부합하는
   것이며, 이러한 개념이 향후 중동안보유지체제 모색과정에서도
   부지불식간에 적용되었을 것임

(중동지역 정치적 대립관계의 구조변경 모색)

o 쿠웨이트 사태는, 아랍-이스라엘간 대결이라는 중동지역의 기존 대립
   관계를 이라크의 패권주의와 이의 견제라는 새로운 대립구조로 변경
   시킴으로서, 당분간은 팔레스타인 문제에 대한 관심과 압력을 완화해
   줄 것으로 보임

o 미국으로서는, 이라크의 쿠웨이트 점령과 팔레스타인 문제를 동일한
   성격의 문제로 규정하기를 거부하면서, 새로이 형성된 아랍권 내부의
   대결구도를 새로운 「중동안보구조」로 개념화, 제도화함으로써,
   장기적으로 팔레스타인 문제의 해결은 용이하게 할 수 있을 것이며,
   베이커장관이 상. 하원 외교위 증언에서 아랍-이스라엘 문제를 언급한
   것도 이러한 맥락에서 이해될 수 있음

o 「중동안보구조」가 실현되어, 반 이라크 연합전선이 구축된다면,
   고립된 이라크의 자연적인 약화는 불가피할 것이며, 미국은 시간을
   가지고 팔레스타인 문제의 해결을 모색, 전체 중동지역 정세의
   안정과 평화를 도모할 수 있을 것임

0131

o 베이커 장관이 NATO형 「중동안보구조」를 제의한 하루만에 형태
  문제에 대한 입장을 후퇴한데서 알 수 있듯이, 「중동안보구조」
  설립이 결코 용이하지는 않을 것임

o 우선, 금번 사태에 대한 국제사회의 협조를 가능하게 하였던 유엔의
  역할문제, 유엔을 통하여 대미협조를 하였던 쏘련, 중국 및 일부
  여타 아랍국가의 협조확보와 역할보장 문제, 미국을 중심한 안보
  체제에 대한 아랍 민족주의의 반대문제, 그리고 팔레스타인 문제를
  위요한 아랍-이스라엘간 대립 해소문제등이 모두 베이커 구상 실현
  가능성에 의문을 갖게 하고 있음

o 따라서, 미국으로서는, 당면적인 문제인 이라크의 쿠웨이트 점령이
  일단 해결의 실마리를 보이게 되면, 보다 현실적인 대안으로 GCC의
  성격변화 및 강화를 모색해 나갈 것으로 보임

o 미국이 현 시점에서 베이커 구상을 공개적으로 제시한 이유는,
  당장 이의 실현을 추진할 계획에서라기 보다는, 페르샤만 사태가
  예상보다 장기화될 가능성이 높아짐에 따라, 페르샤만 파병을 보다
  적극적이고 체계적인 시각에서 정당화해야할 국내.외적 필요성에
  대응하려는 과정에서, 막연한 하나의 개념으로서 제시한 것으로
  평가해야 할 것임

0132

o 단, 미국이 전기한 여러 예상 문제점에도 불구하고, 「중동안보구조」 설립 구상을 보다 적극적으로 추진할 경우, 이는 냉전후 세계질서와 평화유지 체제구축 문제에 대한 미 정책방향과 관련하여 그 의미가 클 것이며, 현재 논의가 시작되고 있는 동북아 내지 아.태 안보협의체 형성에 대한 미국의 입장과 관련하여, 동건 진전 동향을 예의 주시할 필요가 있음

<끝>

0133

1. Position of European and Northeast Asian nations

   A. Position of European nations

      o Britain, France, Italy and other EC nations strongly denounced Iraqi invasion of Kuwait, and in close cooperation with the US, have been actively participating in all international action against Iraq, including the adoption of nine UN Secuity Council resolutions and imposition of economic embargo.

      o Among the major measures EC nations have taken so far are :

      In economic field,

      - freeze all Iraqi assets and those of Kuwait controlled by Iraq
      - suspend crude oil import from Iraq and Kuwait
      - extend assistance to frontline states
        . At EC Foreign Ministers' meeting of 7 September, it was agreed to render $ 2 billion economic assistance to Turkey, Jordan and Egypt through 1991.
      - plan to hold EC-Arab ministerial meeting on 6-7 October to discuss ways to cooperate more closely with anti-Iraq Arab nations

      In military field,

      - send ground troops to the Gulf region including 6,000 British and 13,000 French soldiers
      - send combat planes (including 40 British and 40 French planes) and warships (including 7 British, 14 French, 5 Italian ships)
      - implement arms embargo against Iraq

0134

In political field,

- declare Iraqi annexation of Kuwait null and void
- reject Iraqi demand to withdraw foreign missions resident
  in Kuwait, and continue to maintain their embassies
- continue consultation among member states on possible military
  measures to ensure effective implementation of the economic
  sanction against Iraq

B. Position of Northeast Asian nations
   o Japan
   - respect UN Security Council resolutions and participate
     in economic sanction against Iraq
   - extend $ 4 billion assistance ; $ 2 billion in burden-sharing
     of militasy cost and $ 2 billion in economic assistance
   - send around 2,000 unarmed personnel to the Gulf area, perhaps
     as part of a newly proposed "UN peace-keeping cooperation corps"
   - suspend all economic cooperation with Iraq including "Yen loan"

   o PRC
   - support all UN Security Council resolutions
   - oppose military solution of the crisis
   - oppose large-scale US military presence in the Gulf region,
     saying it hightens tension in the area

2. Impact of Gulf crisis on Korea's economy
   o rising oil prices
   - Economic embargo against Iraq and occupied Kuwait took out more
     than 4 million b/d from the world crude oil market
   - Increase of oil production by 3.5 million b/d promised by Saudi
     Arabia and other countries is not enough to make up for the loss
     of Iraqi and Kuwaiti oil

0135

- Recent upsurge of world oil prices has more to do with speculation
  and mounting concern over possible outbreak of war, rather than
  with actual shortage in world oil supply
- Oil prices are expected to remain high, if the current stalemate
  in the Gulf continues
- For Korea, price increase of one dollar per barrel means
  $ 330 million in additional yearly burden

o loss in contruction field
- Korea is unable to collect around $ 1 billion of outstanding
  constuction payment, on account of its observance of UN economic
  sanction against Iraq
- Korea bans its companies from participating in new constution
  projects in Iraq and Kuwait

o loss in export earnings
- Korean export to Bahrain, Qatar and other Gulf countries have
  been considerably affected by the current crisis
- Korea suspends trade with Iraq and Kuwait, costing it around
  $ 200 million in export earnings

o some relevant statistics (projected)
- If oil prices are to stay $ 25 per barrel ;
  . Korea's GNP for 1991 will decrease by 2.5%
  . wholesale prices will increase by 3.7%
  . consumer prices will increase by 0.59%
  . overall economic loss for the first year will amount to
    $ 1.5-3 billion

0136

3. Position of ROK

   o   Respect all relevant UN Security Council resolutions, including
        resolution 662(1990) which denounced Iraqi invasion of Kuwait
        and pronounced the subsequent annexation null and void
        - Korea does not consider the closure of Korean Embassy in Kuwait

   o   Urge unconditional withdrawal of Iraqi forces from Kuwait

   o   Participate actively in international endeavour to achieve peaceful
        settlement in the interest of international peace and co-prosperity
        of mankind

   o   Adhere strictly to economic sanction against Iraq in observance of
        the relevant UN Security Council resolutions, thus joining in
        international efforts to penalize the aggressor
        - freeze Iraqi and Iraqi-controlled Kuwaiti assets, suspend oil
          import and ban all trade

   o   Pay its fair share of both military cost of multinational forces
        and economic assistance to frontline states. In this regard,
        $ 220 million package has already been announced.

   o   Express deep concern over the current crisis, particularly since it
        broke out amidst East-West rapprochement and at the time when all
        nations are cooperating to build a new international order

0137

페르시아만 사태

o 미국은 이라크의 쿠웨이트 철군과 쿠웨이트 합법정부 수립 그리고
  중동지역에서 이라크의 패권 및 주변국가에 대한 위협을 제거할 수
  있는 항구적 안보구조 확립이라는 전략 목표를 위해 이라크에 대한
  외교.경제 및 군사적 압력을 강화하고 있음. 그러나 이라크는
  쿠웨이트 철수 절대불가를 천명하고 反美 아랍민족주의 선동등을
  통한 反이라크 단합 저해 전략으로 맞섬으로서 양측간 긴장상태하에
  대치상황이 지속되고 있음

사태 전망

o 외교.정치적 해결가능성
  - 양측이 수용가능한 타협안 마련가능성 희박
    . 미국은 안보리결의 660호 완전실현을 주장하는 반면 이라크는
      쿠웨이트 포기 절대불가 입장
    . 이라크는 쿠웨이트 철군을 이스라엘의 점령지역(West Bank, Gaza
      지구) 반환 문제와 연계시킴으로서 아랍권의 호응을 얻으려 하고
      있으나 미국은 동 연계를 절대반대

0138

o 군사적 충돌 가능성
   - 미국은 이라크의 도발이 없는 상태에서 선제공격 감행은 어려움
     . 미국이 군사력을 사용할 경우 현재의 반 이라크 국제적 consensus에
        균열을 초래할 가능성
     . 아랍권 국가들의 대미 감정악화 및 군사력 사용후 미군의 페만지역
        주둔 명분 약화 가능성
   - 이라크의 선제 군사력 사용가능성 또한 낮음
     . 다국적 군에 비해 전투력 열세로 승산이 없으며 전쟁시 이라크
        초토화 가능성
     . 이스라엘 공격 대안도 공군력의 열세로 실행 가능성 희박
   - 그러나 이라크의 쿠웨이트 병합 영구화나 핵무기등 대량 파괴무기
     개발로 중동 안보에 중대한 위협을 초래할 경우, 이를 저지하기
     위한 미국의 군사력 사용가능성을 배제할 수 없음

o 대치상태 장기화 가능성
   - 현재 진행중인 경제 제재조치는 이라크 경제구조의 취약성을 감안
     할 때 효과가 있을 것으로 기대되나, 훗세인이 경제적 어려움 때문에
     쉽게 굴복할 것으로 보이지는 않음
   - 훗세인은 쿠웨이트 병합을 굳혀 일단 목표를 달성하고, 시간을
     끌면서 반 시오니즘, 아랍민족주의등을 조장, 보수 아랍 국가내의
     정치불안 유발등을 통해, 반 이라크 연합의 단합을 와해시키고 현
     대치 상태를 미국 대 아랍민족주의의 대결 구도로 변화시켜 자신의
     입지를 강화시키려 할 것으로 예상
   - 미국은 군사력 사용에 의한 사태 해결이 어려운 상황에서 정치.
     경제적 수단을 통한 대 이라크 압력을 강화하는 한편, 아랍권내
     반 이라크 단합을 공고히 하여 미군의 중동주둔 명분확보와 미국주도의
     중동 안보구도 확립 추구 예상

0139

가. 분쟁 관리의 국제화.다국화

 ○ 탈 냉전의 전환기적인 국제정세 하에서 미.소의 대립후퇴로 양극
    체제하에서 억제되었던 다양한 분쟁요인의 현재화로 지역분쟁 발생
    빈도 증대 가능성

 ○ 이라크 사태는 지역분쟁 해결에 미.소가 협조하고 다수의
    국가들이 이에 동참하므로서 탈 냉전시대의 위기관리의 국제화.
    다국화 경향 초래. 특히 UN 안보리가 강대국간 합의 도출에
    성공하므로서 향후 국제안보 문제에 UN의 역할증대 기대

나. 미국의 주도적 역할

 ○ 미국은 금번 사태를 탈.냉전시대 지역분쟁 관리의 시험대로 인식,
    사태의 원상회복을 통해 군사력 사용을 통한 국가이익 추구는
    용납될 수 없음을 국제관계의 기본 규범으로 확립코자 함

 ○ 상기 국제화.다국화 현상하에서 최근 소련이 국내사정으로 국제
    문제에 관여할 여력이 감퇴하므로서 향후 국제정치에 당분간
    미국의 주도권 행사 예상. 아울러 금번 사태에 대응하는데 국제적
    지지 뿐 아니라 실제 관련국간 비용분담을 실현하므로서 향후 여타
    지역분쟁 발생시 선례로 작용 가능성

다. 집단 안보체제 강화 경향

 ○ 지역분쟁에 대한 효과적인 대응을 위하여 냉전시대의 유물인 지역
    안보체제가 다시 강화될 것으로 전망

0140

UN을 利用한 對 이라크 군사행동 방안

90. 9. 27

N Y T

o 부시대통령은 UN의 경제제재 조치가 이라크군의 쿠웨이트 철수에
   성공하지 못할 경우, 멀지 않은 장래에 군사력을 사용할 것임을
   시사하고 있음. 그러나 이라크가 먼저 무력도발을 해오지 않는한
   미국의 선제 군사력 사용은 많은 문제점 수반 예상.

(국내적)

. 의회지지 문제

   의회는 지금까지 부시대통령의 대중동 군사정책을 지지해 왔으나
   이는 방어적 목적이라는 전제에 따른 것임. 공격으로 전환시
   의회지지는 미지수이며 공화당의원도 소수 포함된 영향력 있는
   일부 의원들은 미국의 전쟁돌입 결정에 의회가 주도적 발언권을
   갖을수 있는 formula 모색중.

. 국민지지문제

   국민들은 지금까지 부시대통령의 정책을 전폭 지지해 왔으나
   이는 사우디 및 기타 아랍국의 방어 목적이라는 전제에 따른
   것이며 공격으로 전환시 국민의 지지 역시 미지수. (수주일간의
   단기전은 지지할지도 모르나 그이상 시간이 지날 경우 지지급감
   예상)

0141

공람	안보과	90 9 27	담당	과 장	심의관	국 장	차관보	차 관	장 관
			김수권	정.					

(국제적)

. 세계 많은 나라들이 지금까지 미국의 정책을 지지, 군대 파견, 경제
  원조등으로 동참해 왔으나 미국 단독결정에 의한 개전에는 적극
  반대.(일부 유럽국가들간에 조속한 군사행동 보다는 현재 진행중인
  경제제재 조치를 계속 추진, 효과 추이를 보고 결정하자는 의견이
  있음)

o 지나치게 느리고 공개적이라는 단점이 있으나 UN을 통한 사태 해결이
   상기 문제들을 극복할 수 잇는 대안이 될 수 있음. Baker 국무장관도
   지금까지의 UN의 역할에 만족을 표명하고, 유엔에 군사행동 허가
   (authorize)를 요청하는 대안을 배제하지 않고 있음을 언급

o 그러나 UN을 통한 군사력 사용에 대한 미.소간 의견 불일치
   - 소 측 : UN 합동참모위원회 구성을 통한 UN 통제하의 군사력
                사용 제안
   - 미 측 : UN의 허가는 필요하나 UN 지휘하에 자국군을 맡기는
                것에는 반대
   - 타 협 안 : UN이 군사력 사용은 허가하되 실제작전에는 관여하지
                않는 방안
                * 현 해상봉쇄는 이런 형태를 띠고 있음

0142

Options for Bush

If There Is No Provocation by Iraq, The U.N. May Offer a Route to Unity

By R. W. APPLE Jr.
Special to The New York Times

AKRON, Ohio, Sept. 26 — If Iraq should sanction a major terrorist strike, harm American hostages or attack a United States warship or warplane, President Bush would certainly respond with military action, citing "provocation" by President Saddam Hussein to explain his decision.

"That much is clear," said a senior White House aide. "If we have a pretext, a casus belli, we go. But the much more difficult question is how we proceed if the weeks and months go by, and there is no provocation."

President Bush has suggested, without ever actually saying so, that at some point soon, if United Nations economic sanctions do not persuade Iraq to pull its troops out of Kuwait, he will use force to get them out. But it is not as simple as issuing an order to his commander in the Persian Gulf, Gen. H. Norman Schwarzkopf.

There is the matter of Congressional acquiescence. Key Democrats on Capitol Hill insist that their support for Mr. Bush's policies in no way constitutes a mandate for offensive operations against Saddam Hussein.

This time, there will be no hastily passed, open-ended measure like the Gulf of Tonkin resolution, which Lyndon B. Johnson and later Presidents used to justify their military actions in Vietnam. Indeed, some influential lawmakers, including a few Republicans, are searching for a formula that would give Congress a major say in deciding when or whether to go to war.

There is the matter of public support. All the evidence in the opinion polls suggests that the President has the backing of the overwhelming majority of the American people for what he has done so far. So does the warmth with which he has been received on his political forays out into the country, such as the one he began today in Akron, Ohio and Chicago.

But so far Mr. Bush has sought support only for defensive action: guarding Saudi Arabia and other Gulf nations. Neither the White House nor anyone else really knows how enthusiastic the public would be, and for how long, about a desert campaign against the Iraqi Army or an air offensive.

Interviews with Bush partisans who turned out for a fund-raising lunch here today suggested that their support is highly conditional. Stuart Giller, an Akron businessman, said: "People are solidly behind Operation Desert Shield, but they have their doubts about an Operation Desert Strike. They'd support a short war — a week or so — but beyond that, heavy losses, body bags, he loses support quickly, especially if we fire the first shots."

Playing in Paris

A dental assistant who declined to give her name said, "I'm afraid they've thought a lot in Washington about how to get into battle and not enough on how to get out."

Finally there is the matter of allied participation. "This administration has made a basic decision that it can't handle this alone," says one of its principal policymakers, and Mr. Bush is well aware that a justification for war that may sell on Capitol Hill and in Peoria may be much less effective in Paris, Damascus and Moscow. So the search is on for a predicate that would allow the preservation of allied unity, or most of it.

The route, it appears, may lie through the United Nations.

French diplomats are making it clear that despite President François Mitterrand's fury over Iraqi penetration of the French embassy in Kuwait, and the dispatch of crack French troops to the Gulf, Paris has little enthusiasm for a war policy. Other European countries that have backed Mr. Bush are firmly opposed to a unilateral United States decision to attack, even if it were dressed up with a round of "consultations" about the next step.

"Bush has three choices," said a minister from one European country who is visiting the United States. "He can do nothing, he can risk our opposition or he can use the U.N. None perfect, but that's the way it is."

The trouble with the United Nations in this context, from the Administration's point of view, is that it is too slow and it is too public. But Secretary of State James A. Baker 3d made it clear last Sunday that an appeal to the international organization to authorize military action has by no means been ruled out.

Describing himself as "extraordinarily pleased" by the role of the United Nations to date, Mr. Baker said on the NBC News program "Meet the Press." "If the President felt it was necessary to use force, I think he would want to move in a manner that would seek to preserve as much of the international consensus as we could, and hopefully all of it." The Administration has been thinking hard, he said, about "how to implement U.N. resolutions" calling for Iraqi withdrawal from Kuwait "in the absence of some specific act of provocation."

Tom King, the British Defense Minister, said in Washington last week that his country had placed no limitations on its support for Mr. Bush. But in New York on Tuesday, a senior British official, speaking on condition that he not be identified, said that when Mr. Bush and his allies "take stock of the situation" sometime before Christmas, war would not be the only option; the decision might be to give the sanctions more time.

Foreign Minister Eduard A. Shevardnadze of the Soviet Union indicated in a General Assembly speech that, however cumbersome the United Nations Military Staff Committee might be, giving it a major role might be Moscow's price for participation in any military operations against Saddam Hussein. If it had been working properly, he said, "there would be no need now for individual states to act unilaterally."

That could cause problems in Washington, which is reluctant to put United States forces under a United Nations flag, but a compromise might be reached under which the United Nations authorized but did not control military action. Such a deal was worked out to permit the imposition of a naval blockade.

A United Nations mandate might also make it easier for the Egyptians, Moroccans and Syrians to commit their troops to battle alongside the Americans, despite the opposition that might arouse from the Arab masses in their capitals and elsewhere.

Sept. 27, 1990
NYT

외 무 부

종 별 :

번 호 : USW-4459

일 시 : 90 1002 1100

수 신 : 장관(미북,미안,중근동,국연)

발 신 : 주미대사

제 목 : 미국의 대이락정책

연: USW(F)-0212

1. 연호 10.1 부쉬 대통령이 대유엔 연설에서 미국은 현 GULF 만 사태가 우선 외교적으로 해결되기를 희망한다는 점을 명백히 천명함에 따라 금 10.2. W.P.,NYT등 미언론들은 BUSH 대통령이 외교적 해결에 중점을 둔새로운 기회를제시하고 있다는 해설 및 사설을 계재하였음.

2. 특히 금번 BUSH 대통령의 제안은 기존의미국의 입장에서 이탈하는것은 아니나,이락의 쿠웨이트로부터의 철수후 이락-쿠웨이트간 제반 분쟁의영구적 해결모색,걸프지역의 안정을 위한 역내국가간의 협력체모색,아랍.이스라엘간 화해를포함한 중동평화 추진등 3개항으로 집약되는 정책방향은 군사적 대안으로부터 외교적 해결로 미국이 정책의 중점을 옮기고 있는것으로 당지 언론에서는 관찰하고 있음.

3. 또한 BUSH 대통령이 동연설에서 사태의 해결후(미군의 임무종료후),주 사우디 미군의 완전철수를 강력한 어조로 희망한 점도 주목됨.

.(THE AMERICANPEOPLE AND THIS PRESIDENT WANT EVERY SINGLE AMERICAN SOLDIERBROUGHT HOME AS SOON AS THIS MISSION IS COMPLETED.)

4. 여사한 BUSH 대통령의 정책 표명은 사태의 조속한 해결, HUSSEIN 의 제거를 포함한이락의 군사능력감소등 이락에 대한 강력한대응이 필요하다고 주장한 키신저 등의 제안(9.30 WP 지 계재 논설 참조)과 대조되고 있음.

(대사 박동진-국장)

미주국   미주국   중아국   국기국

90.10.03   01:10 CT

외신 1과 통제관

0144

외 무 부

종 별 :

번 호 : USW-4592 일 시 : 90 1011 1855

수 신 : 장 관 (미북, 동구1, 서구 1)

발 신 : 주 미 대사

제 목 : CHENEY 국방장관 구주순방

1. 금 10.11. 국방성 정례 브리핑시 CHENEY 국방장관의 구주순방 계획이 발표된바, 10.13-16간 영국, 10.16-19간 소련, 그리고 10.19-22간 불란서를 방문한다 함.

2. CHENEY 장관은 영국, 불란서에서는 국방장관등 고위관리들과의 면담을 통해 양자관계 지역문제, 전략문제등을 협의할 예정이라고 함.

3. 소련방문은 작년 DMITRI YAZOV 소련국방장관의 미국방문에 대한 답방형식으로이루어지는 것으로, CHENEY 장관은 YAZOV 장관외에 SHEVARDNADZE 외상, 경제학자, 일반시민등과도 만나게 된다고 발표됨.

첨부: 브리핑내용(USW(F)-2565)

(대사 박동진-국장)

미주국   1차보   구주국   구주국   정문국   안기부   국방부

PAGE 1   90.10.12   08:42 FC

외신 1과 통제관

0145

As many of you know, I think as we announced earlier this morning, the Secretary will leave Washington on Saturday -- Secretary Cheney -- for a trip to the Soviet Union, stopping off in London on the way and in France on the way back. He will leave here, as I said, Saturday the 13th. He'll be in London October 13th through 16th; Moscow October 16th through the 19th; and Paris October 19th through the 22nd -- returning to Washington -- arriving Andrews -- on the evening of the 22nd.

While he's in London, the Secretary will meet with the Secretary of State for Defense, Tom King, and other senior British government officials. In Paris, he'll meet with Minister of Defense Jean-Pierre Chevenement and other senior French government officials. And then in Moscow, that's a reciprocal visit for the visit to the United States by the Soviet Defense Minister Dmitri Yazov, here just about a year ago. He will also meet with the Foreign Minister, Shevardnadze; also with Minister of Defense Yazov and other senior Soviet government officials and some Soviet economists and Soviet citizens and so forth.

And in each place, he will be discussing bilateral, regional, and strategic matters of interest to both governments. There'll be a background session here at 2:00 this afternoon on the Secretary's trip, right here in our Pentagon Public Affairs Studio, conducted by a senior Defense official. So we invite you to come to that as well.

And those are my only announcements.

Charlie?

Q   Pete, is he going to meet with Thatcher, Gorbachev, and Mitterrand?

MR. WILLIAMS: He certainly hopes to. I think the general rule is -- the general protocol around here is that we never announce those meetings with heads of state in advance because their schedules are obviously subject to sudden changes. But that is

certainly our hope.

Q   Does he plan to try and talk the Soviets into sending anything more into the Gulf in the way of forces than they have now?

MR. WILLIAMS: That's not something that he's going over there to do. That's not a mission of the trip.

0146

Force in Gulf Reflects Colin Powell's Vision; It's Big and It's Mobile

Top General Learned a Lesson In Vietnam: If You Go In, Go With Enough to Win

Will He Replace Dan Quayle?

By ANDY PASZTOR and GERALD F. SEIB
Staff Reporters of THE WALL STREET JOURNAL

WASHINGTON — Months before Iraqi tanks rumbled into Kuwait, Gen. Colin Powell, the chairman of the Joint Chiefs of Staff, made a crucial decision that paved the way for the fast U.S. military buildup in the Persian Gulf.

Despite grumbling by some Pentagon brass, who thought their existing plans were just fine, he quietly ordered strategists to overhaul contingency plans for a crisis in the Mideast. Out went the old plan to halt a Soviet drive through Iran toward the Gulf. In came a new plan to defend Saudi Arabia's giant oil fields against threats from its neighbors.

In July, Gen. H. Norman Schwarzkopf, one of Gen. Powell's favorite commanders, used those concepts to have his staff run elaborate, computerized war games pitting about 100,000 U.S. troops against Iraqi armored divisions.

In August, just after Kuwait fell, President Bush summoned Gen. Powell to Camp David. The chairman was able to plop down a plan for the fastest large-

Colin Powell

scale deployment of U.S. forces since World War II—a plan that administration aides say has been changed remarkably little.

The giant military machine now in the Persian Gulf bears the unmistakable imprint of the nation's top general: 53-year-old Gen. Powell, a Vietnam veteran who is the youngest man—and the first black—ever to head the Joint Chiefs. He also may be the most talked-about chairman of the panel, which includes the top officer of each armed service, since it was set up in its current form in 1947.

The size of the U.S. operation in the Gulf—slipping in and sustaining nearly a quarter of a million men and women in one of the world's harshest environments—embodies Gen. Powell's belief in fast, massive military operations. "Light and lethal is good," he said recently. "But you also need heavy and lethal."

A master bureaucratic operator by virtue of years in Pentagon and White House jobs, Gen. Powell personally intervened to boost U.S. firepower at the last minute, squelching the skepticism of some lower-ranking generals who wanted to move more cautiously. Since then, his calm presentation of the policies and his affable approach to life have started some Republicans thinking of him as a 1992 vice presidential candidate. Perhaps in reaction, the general has taken a low profile; he declined to be interviewed for this article.

'Refreshing Change'

Moreover, Gen. Powell's approach is dispelling the doubts lingering over the U.S. military ever since Vietnam. Former Defense Secretary Caspar Weinberger, who once employed Gen. Powell as his personal military assistant, says the general believes that "you go in with overwhelming force, you go in very quickly, and once it's over you get out. That is a refreshing change from the Vietnam era."

Adds National Security Adviser Brent Scowcroft, "The military side is marked by quiet, cool efficiency, no histrionics, no visible handwringing. It has just been an extremely professional operation, which is the hallmark of Colin Powell."

But the cheering could stop quickly if body bags begin carrying Americans home from the Gulf. The very size of the American force he has assembled is designed to increase the odds of American success—but it also guarantees that any war with Iraq will be a bloody brawl between large armies, not a limited skirmish.

The chances of war remain high. President Bush's anger over Iraq's pillaging of Kuwait has shortened the time he is likely to allow economic sanctions alone to work against Saddam Hussein, administration officials say. U.S. troops are stepping up their activities, ranging from night training to amphibious-landing exercises. Meanwhile, Baghdad keeps saying its takeover of Kuwait is irreversible.

Military Outlook

If war comes, Gen. Powell's plan envisions air superiority and attacks from multiple routes breaking Iraq and minimizing American casualties. The U.S. forces eventually will include at least 210,000 troops on the ground, more than 1,000 helicopters, more than 500 front-line combat planes and more than 60 ships.

Gen. Powell's military outlook, like that of many officers of his generation, was shaped by Vietnam. His Gulf strategy emphasizes being versatile as well as big, using technology to fight at night and at great distances from the enemy.

The U.S. would first seek control of the skies, using advanced radar-jamming gear to disrupt communications and long-range missiles to knock out anti-aircraft batteries and command centers. Next, it would disrupt supply lines and cut off tank columns from ground support. Then it would rely on coordinated attacks from air, land and sea to wipe them out.

Gen. Powell well knows that air power can't do it all, however. Administration aides say he warned President Bush from the start that an all-out military drive to push Iraq out of Kuwait could produce thousands of U.S. casualties.

Some fault Gen. Powell for failing to explain to U.S. troops why such an enormous sacrifice might be necessary. Sen. Bob Kerrey, a Nebraska Democrat, recently criticized President Bush but also declared that he was "angry at Colin Powell for not recognizing that his troops—professional, loyal, capable—do not possess the clear and essential understanding of why they have been called to battle." The troops are ostensibly there to defend Saudi Arabia, the senator worried, but their very presence could provoke the fight with Iraq the administration says it wants to prevent.

That broadside from a fellow Vietnam veteran was an exception. Gen. Powell gets raves on Capitol Hill, where he sometimes employs a cautious, low-key style that evokes an ambassador more than a soldier. "A powerful nation has to wield its power with care," he recently told the Senate Armed Services Committee. Back in the privacy of his Pentagon conference room, officers say, he is more forceful, persistently advocating giving the president clear-cut military options.

Political Speculation

Such abilities have stirred talk about his entering politics, even replacing Dan Quayle as the 1992 GOP vice presidential candidate. "He brings two marvelous elements to a Republican ticket," says Democratic pollster Peter Hart. "Obviously, he is black, which would give them an entree they have never had on the Republican side, and he brings them solid credentials on national defense."

Jesse Jackson, who periodically talks privately with Gen. Powell, thinks his emergence is "having a profound impact on Republican and Democratic party politics," and increasing pressure on Democrats to put a black on their own ticket. But most Republicans say the politically untested Gen. Powell looks better in theory than he would in practice. "He doesn't have a base, he doesn't have a state," says GOP theorist Kevin Phillips. And his background in national security overlaps the president's expertise, Mr. Phillips adds.

Still, the very idea that Gen. Powell's career might resemble Dwight Eisenhower's represents a remarkable success

Oct. 15, 1990
WSJ

2602-1

story. The son of hard-working Jamaican immigrants who settled in New York's South Bronx, he didn't attend West Point but got his lieutenant's bars through the Reserve Officers' Training Corps at City College of New York.

A Knowledge of Yiddish

His upbringing in New York's ethnic melting pot has given him, among other things, a working knowledge of Yiddish that sometimes stuns Jewish acquaintances. He picked it up as a teen-ager clerking in an infants' furniture store and listening to Jewish shoppers.

The trim, seemingly unflappable general doesn't often talk about his black heritage in public, but he has noted it quietly. His first in-depth interview after becoming chairman was with Ebony, a magazine aimed at blacks. The Rev. Jackson says they agree on the importance of education and family but disagree on some issues because "generals are for military solutions to problems."

In his first tour in Vietnam, starting in 1962, Mr. Powell served as a field adviser to Vietnamese infantry and was wounded when he stepped on a punji stick near the Laotian border. In his second tour, he joined the Americal 23rd Infantry Division three months after a division platoon commanded by Lt. William Calley massacred more than 100 Vietnamese at My Lai.

Today, veiled references to the U.S. public's distaste for a long war pepper his comments. They are echoed by many field commanders now in Saudi Arabia.

But although some older, more senior military leaders came away from Vietnam leery of combat, Gen. Powell's current generation of Pentagon leaders is more willing to use military force—provided politicians explicitly agree to pour in enough strength to win quickly.

Politically Sensitive Jobs

After Vietnam and service in Korea, Mr. Powell became a Nixon-era White House fellow, serving under Mr. Weinberger at the Office of Management and Budget. During the Carter administration, he worked for the deputy defense secretary. When Mr. Reagan became president, Mr. Weinberger summoned Mr. Powell to the Pentagon as his top military aide.

He showed a deft political touch. During planning for the invasion of Grenada, he sensed that the Pentagon's press office would welcome advance warning and persuaded Defense Secretary Weinberger to give it a day's notice. The press office kept the secret but was prepared for questions. At the White House, by contrast, John Poindexter, then deputy national security adviser, froze out presidential spokesmen, creating a furor by prompting them to mislead the press about the operation just before it began.

Three years later, Gen. Powell had Mr. Poindexter's job. President Reagan promoted him to national security adviser, and last year President Bush made him chairman of the Joint Chiefs. Gen. Powell has developed a reputation as a smooth but coy bureaucratic operator, skilled at working the government system while steering clear of politically nasty fights.

"Colin Powell is a good friend," says Prince Bandar bin Sultan, Saudi Arabia's ambassador to Washington. "But in my talks with him, I feel very happy about what he tells me, but when I leave I'm not sure what he's told me." The prince, once a squash partner of Gen. Powell, says that when he tries to pin the general down, "he says, 'You're talking to the wrong guy. Talk to my civilian superiors.'" In the Reagan years, Gen. Powell strongly backed the Contra rebels in Nicaragua yet avoided the political damage suffered by others on both sides of the issue.

During his years in high-tension jobs, Gen. Powell has developed a stress-management "therapy": He repairs and rebuilds Volvos in his spare time. Car parts are often scattered about his driveway and basement, irking his wife, Alma, "a little bit," Mr. Weinberger says.

Barely hours after becoming head of the Joint Chiefs, Gen. Powell was thrust into planning last fall's invasion of Panama. The action bore his stamp: U.S. forces went in with overwhelming size and speed. Gen. Powell is the first chairman to take office with the expanded powers that Congress gave the post in 1986. They explicitly make him the president's personal military adviser, not just the representative of the various service heads.

During their marathon weekend of planning to launch the Saudi operation, Gen. Powell and Gen. Schwarzkopf, now his top Mideast commander, decided to increase the number of tank-killing Apache helicopters, A-10 ground attack jets and heavy M-1 tanks from earlier projections. Only four days after the Iraqi invasion, Defense Secretary Richard Cheney flew to Saudi Arabia and presented details to King Fahd. Gen. Powell waited back at the Pentagon for the phone call authorizing him to order the first wave of fighters and cargo planes into the air. What unfolded was "certainly not one of our static plans, which we write and keep on the shelf for 10 years," says Air Force Gen. Donald Kaufman.

In contrast to Vietnam, the White House and top civilians at the Pentagon approved the overall plans and then essentially stood aside. "The three-stars and the four-stars have been left alone to do their jobs," a State Department official says.

Oct. 15, 1990
WSJ

2602-2

Domestic crisis builds while Bush focuses on Gulf

<table>
<tr><td>**Analysis**</td></tr>
</table>

By Jack Nelson

Los Angeles Times

WASHINGTON — President Bush's near-total absorption with the Persian Gulf crisis has led to such dramatic missteps and equivocation on how to cut the federal deficit that the budget is mushrooming into a second domestic crisis — sowing confusion within Bush's own party and eroding his authority in Washington.

By shaking public confidence in his leadership, it could even cut down his political freedom to deal militarily with the Iraqi invasion of Kuwait.

Dismayed political leaders and analysts in both parties say that Bush, preoccupied with the Gulf crisis, has not only failed to provide effective leadership in resolving the budget impasse but has stumbled badly in failing to spell out for Congress or the American public how he ultimately hopes to resolve either issue.

"Clearly, this is the most challenging moment of his presidency, with a major foreign policy crisis and a major domestic crisis happening

See BUSH, Page 8

0149

Bush ———

● From Page 1

simultaneously," said a senior administration official who is involved in Gulf strategy.

The twin crises could not come at a worse time. Congressional elections are less than a month away, financial markets are already shaky and the country is teetering on the brink of a recession. Unless the budget crisis is resolved soon, some analysts say, Bush could suffer lasting political damage and his long-term ability to sustain the deployment of 200,000 troops in the Gulf could be seriously eroded.

The potential impact on Bush's freedom to maneuver in the Gulf is indirect but potentially significant.

Before the budget crisis burst upon him, Bush enjoyed extraordinarily high public opinion ratings and projected the image of a commanding, sure-footed leader. From a position of such political strength, he could exercise his military and foreign policy authority with confidence that voters would support him. Now, with his approval ratings tumbling and his footwork in question, he might command far less public confidence if he abruptly led the nation into war.

BUSH "HAS GOT this budget thing so screwed up he can't go to war now," said House Armed Services Committee Chairman Les Aspin. "With so much uncertainty about the budget," he said, the president cannot now plunge into the even greater uncertainties of a war because the public might "back off and not support it."

Confidence in Bush's leadership has been shaken even among GOP loyalists. Said a former top Republican official who declined to be identified:

"What's happening is unbelievable. I've just come from a meeting of Republicans and we can't understand what's happened to the president. Our boys are over there in the sand, the economy is going to hell and we've got a budget crisis that he's just turned over to the Congress. Nobody seems to know what's going on."

Bush's sudden difficulties over the budget spring primarily from two factors, GOP sources say:

● The president's decision to turn over management of the politically explosive deficit negotiations to White House Chief of Staff John H. Sununu, budget director Richard G. Darman and Secretary of the Treasury Nicholas F. Brady so that he himself could concentrate on foreign policy.

● The deep divisions within his own administration and the Republican Party over how to deal with the deficit and what strategy to pursue against the Democrats on the question of higher taxes vs. lower spending.

Said a senior administration official Thursday:

Bush points to his hips and says 'read my hips' after being asked if he had thrown in the towel on capital gains while jogging at Al Lang Stadium in St. Petersburg, Fla., Wednesday. (AP)

"There is confusion about strategy on the budget — are we truly committed to the bipartisan approach . . . or is there a reasonable alternative of trying to unify the Republicans, come up with our own package, paint the Democrats as the party of tax-and-spend and go to the voters with that?"

"There is a genuine tug-of-war among the president's advisers" on that, the official said, with Vice President Dan Quayle, Secretary of Housing and Urban Development Jack Kemp and others advocating fighting the Democrats while Sununu and Darman advocate sticking with the bipartisan route. The way the president is handling the budget problem, says Senate Armed Services Committee Chairman Sam Nunn, D-Ga., "goes beyond Bush and to the heart of the Republican Party and their entire political strategy and I believe that's what is haunting the president right now.

"He has a very divided party and he's obviously trying to hold the party together. He's got to choose between being a responsible president and an effective leader of his political party and it's a hard choice for him," Nunn said. As for leaving the budget negotiations to senior aides, some administration officials now say that Sununu, Darman and Brady got so committed to the negotiations between White House and congressional leaders that they failed to prepare fall-back positions to be used if the process failed — as it did last weekend.

SOME WASHINGTON insiders go so far as to question whether Sununu, Darman and Brady can survive as leaders of the administration.

"It's baffling, stunning," said John Deardourff, a Republican political consultant. "It's worse than a Chinese fire drill at the White House. Nobody knows who's calling the shots and they keep backing and filling. The average American must wonder what the hell is going on in Washington."

Whether deliberately or not, the president is still keeping members of Congress of both parties off balance on both the budget and the Gulf.

He has more-or-less taken a hands-off attitude on the budget since the House of Representative rejected the compromise package that he supported and when he has spoken out he has repeatedly sent conflicting signals. And he has not briefed members of Congress on the Gulf crisis in several weeks.

For his part, Bush insists that he has not been damaged by the budget impasse.

"NOBODY THINKS you can be popular by standing up and having to take, in a compromise, ingredients that you wouldn't necessarily want," he said earlier this week. "And so I'll do what I think is best and take the slings and the arrows that go with it. And I haven't felt too much pressure or anything."

House Majority Leader Richard A. Gephardt, D-Mo., on the other hand, charges that Bush "has failed to use the bully pulpit to communicate clearly with the American people what his policies are on the budget or on the Persian Gulf crisis. Only a president can mold public opinion in such crucial situations."

Senate Budget Chairman James R. Sasser, D-Tenn., said that he has "come to the glum conclusion" that there will be a war and "with all our domestic problems and no domestic priorities, it's frightening to me that one way to distract people from these problems is to get into some kind of military adventure abroad. That has been done in times past."

0150

관리번호 90-2099

원 본

외 무 부

종 별 :

번 호 : USW-4697 　　　　　　　　　일 시 : 90 1018 1825

수 신 : 장관(미불, 미안, 중근동)

발 신 : 주 미 대사

제 목 : 페르샤만 사태에 대한 국무장관 인책론

　　1., 최근 미 정계, 언론계 일각에서는 GLASPIE 주이락 미국대사가 HUSSEIN 대통령 면담시 이락-쿠웨이트 분쟁과 관련 유화적 입장을 표시한 점등 미 국무부가 이락의 대 쿠웨이트 침공 가능성에 대해 효과적으로 사전 경고를 하지 못한점을 들어 <u>BAKER 국무장관의 책임론</u>을 비롯 미 행정부에 대한 비판이 대두되어 왔음.

　　2. 이와 관련 금 10.18. W.P 지는 BAKER 장관이 이에 대한 마땅한 책임을 지고 사임할것을 촉구하는 MICHAEL KINSLEY 의 기고문 을 게재 하였음(별전 팩스참조)

　　3. 동 논설은 BAKER 장관이 평소 문제가 있을 경우, 이에 정면 대치하지 않고 거리를 두는 작전을 쓰고 있으며, 자신의 입장을 변명할수 있는 STORY 를 의도적으로 언론에 유출 시켰다고 지적하고 있는바, <u>페만 사태와 관련한 SCOWCROFT안보 보좌관의 적극적 역할을 보도</u>하최근 NYT, WSJ 의 기사와 대조 되고 있음.

　　(대사 박동진- 국장)

　　예고:90.12.31. 일반

미주국 안기부	장관	차관	1차보	2차보	미주국	중아국	정문국	청와대

외 무 부

종 별 :

번 호 : USW-4724

일 시 : 90 1019 1757

수 신 : 장 관(중근동,미북)

발 신 : 주 미 대사

제 목 : PRIMAKOV 미국 방문

1. 고르바쵸프의 중동 특사 자격으로 미국을 방문중인 PRIMKOV 는 작 10.18.
BAKER 장관과 요담한데 이어 금 10.19. BUSH 대통령을 백악관으로 예방함.

2. PRIMAKOV 방미전 미 언론에서는 동인이 '' 페''만 사태 해결을 위한 고르바쵸프
대통령, 또는 후세인 대통령의 멧세지를 전달할것 이라는 추측이무성 하였고, BAKER
장관 및 BUSH 대통령면담후 기자들은 동건에 대해 집중 질문 하였으나, PRIMAKOV 는
이러한 멧세지 전달을 부인함.

3. 대신 PRIMAKOV 는 (1) 쿠웨이트 철수 조건으로 이라크에 반대 급부를 주어서는
안되며, (2) UN 결의안의 평화적 시행을 기초로 '' 페'' 만사태가 해결 되어야한다는
입장을 강조하고, (3) 이라크에 체재중인 소련 군관계 인사들을 군사고문 (MILITARY
ADVISOR) 이 아니고, 소련이 과거에 이라크에 제공해온 무기 보수를 위한 기술자
(MILITARY SPECIALIST) 라고 주장함.

4. BUSH 대통령 예방후 PRIMAKOV 가 기자들과 가진 인터뷰 내용을 팩스편 송부함.

첨부: USW(F)- 2687

(대사 박동진- 국장)

중아국   1차보   미주국   정문국   안기부

90.10.20   09:04 WG

외신 1과   통제관

0152

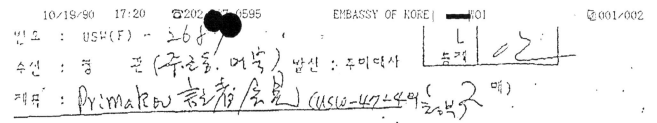
REMARKS BY YEVGENY PRIMAKOV, MEMBER, USSR PRESIDENTIAL COUNCIL
AT A PRESS STAKEOUT FOLLOWING HIS MEETING WITH PRESIDENT BUSH
THE WHITE HOUSE DRIVEWAY, WASHINGTON, DC/ FRIDAY, OCTOBER 19, 1990

          Q   (Interpreted from Russian.) After the meeting with the
President can you say that we are nearer the settlement of the
crisis?

          MR. PRIMAKOV: (Through interpreter.) The crisis is so comlex
and difficult, and the situation in the Persian Gulf area is
developing in such a complicated way that belief that, even with a
help of a discussion with the President, it would be possible to get
closer to the solution of the crisis would be assuming too much on
my part.

          But I would like to emphasize that the US President is indeed
thinking about the new world order, with that one cannot allow a
situation where actions which are incompatible with the civilized
society would be applauded. And he also believes and thinks that
all the objectives that have been set must be accomplished for
complying and implementing the United Nations resolutions. In this
our positions are there same.

          Q   Did you have any new ideas about how to resolve the
crisis in the Persian Gulf? Did you bring anything from President
Gorbachev or maybe some ideas from President Saddam Hussein?

          MR. PRIMAKOV: I cannot say that I have brought some specific
or convoluted ideas or detailed ideas. But at the same time, we,
the Soviet Union -- Soviet leadership -- are trying to do their
utmost in order to obtain the objectives that were set in the United
Nations resolutions through peaceful means.

          Q   Are you --

          Q   Well, do you think there can be a peaceful --

          Q   Did you talk about the continued role of Soviet military
advisors in Iraq?

          MR. PRIMAKOV: You are asking the question in a wrong manner.
We do not have military advisors in Iraq. What we have is a few
dozen -- about 60, I believe -- specialists, military specialists,
who are there in connection with the equipment supplies which took
place in the past. At this point, all supplies have been cut.

          Q   Are you -- do you think there is still a chance for a
peaceful settlement, or are you more optimistic or more pessimistic
as a result of your meeting with the President?

          MR. PRIMAKOV: You see, I cannot say that I have become less
moderately optimistic than I used to be before.

                         2687 -1

                                        0153

Q   ' Do you think a peaceful settlement is possible, sir?

MR. PRIMAKOV: I believe we should not rule out the
possibilities of a peaceful solution until we have exhausted all
options.

END

2687-2

외 무 부

종 별 :

번 호 : USW-4790   일 시 : 90 1024 1858

수 신 : 장관(미북, 미안, 중근동)

발 신 : 주 미 대사

제 목 : 걸프 사태 전망

1. 금 10.24. 당지 HERITAGE 재단은 미국의 무력사용 가능성 문제를 중점으로 걸프사태 전망에 관한 세미나를 개최하였는바, 동 요지 하기 보고함

    (당관 임성남 2 등서기관 참석)

    동세미나에서는 JENNETH ADELMAN 전 군축처장, AMERICAN ENTERPRISE INSTITUTE 소속 JOSHUA MURAVCHIK 연구원, HERITAGE 재단 국방정책 연구실 JAY KOSMINSKY 부실장 의 3 인이 주제 발표를 하였으나, ADELMAN 전 군축처장외의 발표는 별다른 주목을 받지 못하였음(아래 요지는 주로 ADELMAN 전 군축 처장의 발표 내용임)

    가. 사우디 주둔 미군 전력의 실전 배치 완료, 11 월 이후 걸프지역 기온 하강등을 이유로 당지 일부 언론 및 학계 일가등에서 미국의 대이락 공격 임박 가능성을 언급하고 있음. 특히 무력사용을 통해 이락의 화학무기, 핵 시설등을 제거하지 않고, 외교적 타협에 의해 금번 사태가 해결되는 경우는 이락측에 의한또다른 쿠웨이트 침공 사태가 재현될수도 있다는 점을 지적, 여사한 대 이락 공격 주장을 전략적 차원에서 정당화 하기도 함.

    나, 그러나 대 이락 전재응로 인한 인명의 손실과 현 단계에서는 예상키 어려운 전쟁의 파급효과 등을 감안할때, 부쉬 행정부가 세간의 소문처럼 대이락 공격 결정을 쉽게 내리기는 어려울것으로 봄.

    다. 오히려, 미측으로서는 당분간 대 이락 경제봉쇄 정책을 계속 실시해 나갈 가능성이 클것으로 추측되는바, 2-4 개월 내에 그 효과가 보다 더 가시화될것으로 봄. 이러한 전제하에 향후의 사태 진전 씨나리오를 다음과 같이 예상해 볼수 있음.

    -(2-4 개월 이내) 이라측의 경제난 심화

    -아랍 제국간 합의를 통해 이라크군을 쿠웨이트로 부터 철수시키고 쿠웨이트 왕정을 복구

미주국 안기부	장관	차관	1차보	2차보	미주국	중아국	정문국	정와대

0155

-아랍권의 형제애를 바탕으로 쿠웨이트측은 이락에 부비얀도등 할양

-유엔은 대이락 경제 봉쇄를 해제하는대신 대이락 무기 금수 조치 실시

라. 다만, 전기 예상과 달리 미국이 대 이락 공격을 개시한다면 키신저가 걸프사태 초기에 주장했던 국부공격(SURGICAL STRIKE) 과 같은 방식으로는 승산이 없다고 보며, 일종의 전면전이 불가필 할것으로 봄.

2. 최근 당지에서는 미 행정부가 중간선거가 끝나는 11 월 중순이후 대이락군사행동을 취할것이라는 추측이 나돌고 있는바, 이러한 추측에 동조하는 견해도 꾸준히 제시되고 있음.GEORGE WASHINGTON 대의 BERNARD REICH 교수(중동학과장)는 10.22. GE 대의 비공개 COLLOQUIUM 시 (김영목 서기관 참석), 미국이 무력 사요외에 여타 대안이 없음을 강조하고, 다음과 같은 분석을 제시함.

-POST COLD WAR 질서에 있어 미구의 4 대 목표 철회, 타협의 어려움

-경제 봉쇄의 완전한 효과 기대 곤란 (특히 적절한 시간내 효과 거양 불가)

-사태의 외교적 수습시, 계속되는 이락의 엄청난 군사적 위협 및야심의 제거 필요성등

-사막전에서의 기후조건(11-12 월이 작전에 바람직)

-년말전 사태의 수습이 필요한 미국내 사정(걸프만 군사개입에 대한 지지 감소, X-MAS 전후 반전 주장 강화 전망)

-걸프만 사태 장기화시 미국경제에 미치는 영향 및 동 경제사정 이 92 년 대봉령 선거에 결정적 작용예상

-가급적 명년 라마단 개시 이전에 외국군 철수를 희망하는 사우디의 입장

3. 한편, GORDON GRAY 국무부 소련과 중동 담당관은 당관 김영목서기관 접촉시 걸프만 사태와 관련한 미소 협력관계에 관해 다음과 같은 견해를표시함.

-소련은 POST -COLD WAR 시기에 있어 새롭게 형성된 미소 협력관계를 발전시켜나가려는 의지가 있으며, 이락에 대한 미국의 정책을 지지하여 왔음.

-미국과 련의 대 이락 정책은 기본적으로 동일하나, 소련은 평화적 해결 부분을 미국보다 강조하고 있는것이 차임임.

-평화적 해결이 불가하여, 무력이 사용될수 밖에 없는 상황이 되면, 소련은미국의 군사 행도에 반대치 않을것으로 전망함.

-PRIMAKOV 의 방미시(10.17. BAKER 장관 면담, 10.18. BUSH 대봉령 면담) 미측은 4 대입장에 따른 기본 목표를 재강조하고, 이락의 부분적 철군이나, 원치에 위배되는

PAGE 2

타협은 있을수 없음을 재강조했음. PRIMAKOV 는 동인과 HUSSEIN 간 면담시 인상을 전달했으나 (그간 보도와 대부분 동일), HUSSEIN 의 특별한 제안또는 미소간 비밀 협의 제안등은 일체 없었음.

4. 현재 , 미국내 일각의 11 월 대이락 공격설에 불구, 동 군사작전에는 많은 정치적, 군사적, 경제적 위험 및 대가가 수반되어야 하는 사정과 아랍구간의 복잡한 이해관계에 비추어, 미측 주도에 의한 신속한 군사행동이 반드시 용이할것으로는 예상되지 않음.

한편 대 이락 무력 공격 방안과 외교적 해결 방안의 상대적 COST 를 비교해볼때, 일견 후자의 해결 방안이 보다 더 손쉬운 선택 방안으로 보이는것은 사실이나, 지금까지 미국이 금번 페르시아 사태를 탈 냉전 시대 최초의 국제적 위기로 규정하면서, 무력에 의한 타국 침략행위는 결코 용납될수 없다는 점을 대내외적으로 강조해온 원칙론적 차원에서 볼때 미국이 타협택을 수용할 기미는 상금관찰되지 않고 있음(행정부 실무자들은 최선의 해결 방식이 후세인의 자발적 철수라고 지적)

다만 미측으로서는 현재 미군사력이현지에 완전히 증원되어 있는 만큼, 군사대안을 포기하지 않고 , 제반 정세의 진행을 예의 주시하고 있는 형편인 것으로 관찰됨.

(대사 박동진- 국장)

예고:90.12.31. 까지

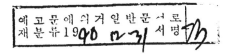

원 본

외 무 부

종 별 : 지급

번 호 : USW-4805

일 시 : 90 1025 1834

수 신 : 장관(미북,미안,중근동)

발 신 : 주 미 대사

제 목 : 걸프 사태 관련 미군 증파 추진

별반문서로 재분류(1990.12.31.)

연: USW-4790

1. 금 10.25 자 WP 지의 -US. CONSIDERS SENDING MORE FORCES TO GULF- 제하의 기사(USW(F)-2774)가 쿠웨이트내 이락군의 방위 태세 강화(주둔 병력 증원,사우디 국경 지역에의 지뢰 매설, 대전차 장애물 설치, 참호선 설치등을 통한 요새화 작업등)에 따른 미군 증파 가능성을 보도하고, 또한 금일 오전 체니 국방장관이 NBC, ABC, CBS 등 당지 주요 방송의 TALK SHOW 에 출연, 미군 병력 약 10만명의 증파 가능성을 시사함으로서 (NBC 방송 대담 내용은 USW(F)-2785 로 송부)당지 일각에서는 이러한 미군 증파 가능성을 연호 2 항의 대이락 공격 추진 임박설과 연계 해석하는 시각이 대두하고 있음.

2. 이러한 시각은 금일 실시된 국방부 정례 브리핑시 기자들의 질문과정에서도 여실히 들어 났는바(정례 브리핑 내용은 USW(F)-2784 로 발췌송부)CHENEY 국방장관의 방송 출연시 발언 내용및 국방부 대변인 답변 내용에서 나타난 미측 입장은 다음과같음.

가. 미군의 걸프만 파견 관련 당초, 상한선이 정해진바 없었음.

나. 기본적으로 파병 미군의 규모는 쿠웨이트등에서의 이락군 동향, 규모등걸프 지역의 상황과 연계되어 검토될것임.그러나 미군의 병력 수준과 특정 군사적 대응 방안을 직접 연계시키는것은 곤란함.

다. 현재 쿠웨이트 배치 이락군의 병력 수준은 약 43 만에 달하고 있는바, 병력 수준및 방어 태세등에 있어서 걸프 사태 초기와는 다른 양상을 보이고 있으며, 이러한 요소를 미군 병력 규모 검토시 고려하지 않을수 없음(국방부 브리핑시 인용된 WEBSTER CIA 국방 발언 내용 참조)

라. 미측으로서는 현재의 대이락 봉쇄 전략이 효과적으로 실시되고 있는것으로

미주국   차관   1차보   미주국   중아국   정와대   안기부   대책반

봄.즉 현재 상황에서 미국의 대이락 전략은 봉쇄 전략을 계속 강화해 나가는것임.

　마. 그러나, 대이락 무력 공격을 포함한 모든 OPTION 이 계속 선택 가능함.

　3. 연호 4 항으로 보고한바와같이 미측은 현재 군사적 대안을 포기하지 않고 제반 정세의 진행을 예의 주시하고 있는것으로 보이는바, 미군 병력 증파 계획을 대이락 공격 임박설로 직접 연계 해석하는것은 다소 성급한 분석으로 보임.오히려 이러한 증원 계획은 이락측의 방어 태세 강화에 대한 대응 조치로서의 성격이 보다 더 강한것으로 보임.

　다만, 미군의 페만 증파는 유사시 긴급 작전을 용이하게할수 있는 태세의 보완측면이 있으며, 이러한 조치를 통해 이락에 심리적 압박을 가해 자진 철군등굴복을 얻어 내려는 의도도 있다고 보임.

　(대사 박동진-국장)

　90.12.31 일반

관리 번호	90-2167

외 무 부

종 별 : 지 급

번 호 : USW-4859   일 시 : 90 1029 1933

수 신 : 장관(미북,미안,중근동)

발 신 : 주 미대사

제 목 : 걸프 사태 관련 베이커 장관 연설

    1. 금 10.29 베이커 장관은 라성 소재 WORLD AFFAIRS COUNCIL 에서 걸프 사태 관련하여 하기 요지 연설을 행한바, 연설문 전문 별첨 FAX(USW(F)-2839)송부함.

    가. 이락의 쿠웨이트 침공은 탈 냉전 시대의 세계 평화를 위협하고 있는바 미국은 결코 대이락 유화 정책을 택하지 않을것임.

    나. 중동 지역의 지정학적 특수성과 금번 사태가 세계 경제에 대해 갖는 영향에 대해서도 유념하여야함.

    다. 대 사우디 파병을 통한 미국의 군사적 목표는 다음과같음.

    -이락의 대 사우디 공격 억제

    -미국인의 인명 보호

    -유엔 안보리 결의에 따른 경제 제재 조치의 효율적 이행

    -(이락의 선제 도발등)상황 변동에 따른 군사적 대응 조치 강구

    라. 유엔 안보리 결의에 따른 금번 사태의 평화적 해결을 강력히 희망하나,대이락 무력 사용을 포함하는 모든 방안이 고려되고 있음.

    마. 현재 시간이 지날수록 대 이락 봉쇄 조치의 효과가 나타나고 있는바 미국으로서는(영토할양등의 방식을 통한)금번 사태의 부분적 해결을 반대함.

    2. 금일 연설의 촛점은 전기 라 항(FAX 상의 4 페이지 후반부)에 담겨져 있는바 현재 미국으로서는 이락을 계속 심리적, 군사적으로 압박해 나가는 한편, 대이락 경제 봉쇄 조치를 강화해 나감으로서 이락의 굴복을 받아내려는 의도가 강한것으로 보임.

    첨부 USW(F)-2839

    (대사 박동진-국장)

    90.12.31 까지

미주국	차관	1차보	미주국	중아국	청와대	안기부	대책반

10/29/90
｜２ : USW(F) - 2839
선 : 장   관 (미북, 기안, 북동)발신 : 주미대사
제 : Baker 국 장관 연설 (걸프 사태 관련) (7 매)

REMARKS BY SECRETARY OF STATE JAMES A. BAKER III TO
THE WORLD AFFAIRS COUNCIL/LOS ANGELES, CALIFORNIA, *Monday Oct. 29, 1990*

SEC. BAKER: (Applause.) Thank you, ladies and gentlemen.
Thank you very much. Thank you. Thank you very much.

Thank you, Dick. Thank you, ladies and gentlemen. I'm very
glad to be here in Los Angeles today. And, as you've probably
heard, I want to talk to you about why America is in the Persian
Gulf. In so doing, I'm going to try and be brief enough that I save
some time for questions when we're finished.

Being brief, though, does remind me of the story about the
little girl that went to church on Sunday morning with her
grandmother, and the grandmother had a preacher who was a
long-winded fellow who never gave a sermon that lasted less than an
hour and a half. And, as they sat there in church on that Sunday
morning and the sermon droned on and on, the little girl looked
about her, and there extending along both walls of the church all
the way down to the altar were these American flags. And underneath
each flag was a little gold plaque. The sermon drones on and on.
Finally, the little girl can't stand it any longer. She turns to
her grandmother, and she says, "Grandma," she says, "what are those
flags up there for?" And her grandmother says, "Why, Sarah," she
said, "those flags commemorate those who died in service." The
little girl said, "Oh, really?" she said. "The 9:00 service or the
11:00 service?" (Laughter, scattered applause.) So, I'm going to
try and be brief enough in my formal remarks that I don't lose you
in that part of the service. (Laughter.)

But before I begin, I've got to let you know that I accepted
this invitation with some trepidation. Last October I was
scheduled to give a speech in San Francisco, and an earthquake
struck. (Laughter.) And then last week we announced that I was
coming to California to give another speech, and another earthquake
struck. So now I'm here in Los Angeles, and if another earthquake
strikes, I know there will be scientists at the Berkeley seismic
station who will probably say that they don't have any direct
scientific proof -- (laughter) -- that these speeches are causing
these earthquakes; but maybe next time I might be asked to speak
someplace where they really need an earthquake, someplace like
Washington, DC. (Laughter and applause.)

These are days, though, ladies and gentlemen, as all of us
know, of great upheaval, and today, as I said, I'd like to speak to
you about one of the most important of those upheavals, and that is
the situation in the Persian Gulf. As members of this World Affairs
Council, you, I know, have long understood how distant international
events can affect all of us here at home. But I will say here today
that rarely has such an event as Iraq's invasion of Kuwait been more
challenging to America's future and to the future of many other
nations as well.

2839 -1

0161

Of course, as we all know, at this very moment there are thousands of Americans who are standing guard in the sands of Arabia. Maybe your son or daughter, a marine or a soldier or sailor or an airman who was stationed, perhaps, at Fort Ord or Camp Pendleton or the Alameda Naval Air Station or trained at Twenty-nine Palms is among them. Or maybe you know a neighbor whose job has been affected by the economic dislocation of this conflict. And certainly it goes without saying that we are all paying higher prices at the gas pump.

Of course, this conflict was not something that we sought, but it's not going to simply go away all by itself. We think it is a vital struggle in which we and the rest of the international community have got to prevail. So let me start, if I might, by telling you what's at stake as we see it.

And the first thing that's at stake is that Iraq's aggression challenges world peace. We happen to be living in one of those rare transforming moments in history. The Cold War is indeed over, and an era which is full of promise has begun. Just this month -- I was just -- we were just having a conversation here during lunch. Just this month, we have welcomed a new Germany, united in peace and freedom -- something that we've been waiting for a long, long time for. The peoples of Central and Eastern Europe have freed themselves through democratic and very peaceful revolutions. After decades of conflict, the United States and the Soviet Union are writing new rules of cooperation between those nations. And after a very long period of stagnation, the United Nations is becoming a more effective organization. The ideals of the United Nations charter are becoming realities.

But this happens also to be an era full of challenges and full of dangers. Ethnic and sectarian conflicts are intensifying. Nuclear, chemical, and biological weapons, and the advanced means for delivering these weapons are proliferating. Terrorism and narcotics continue to be scourges without boundaries or limits. Saddam Hussein's aggression shatters the vision of a better world in the aftermath of the Cold War. As President Bush and President Gorbachev stated in their joint statement in Helsinki, no peaceful international order is possible if larger states can simply devour their smaller neighbors.

The rest of the world, I think, is trying to forward with the 1990s, but Saddam Hussein is trying to drag us all back into the 1930s. And I think we really know what that means: the tempting path of appeasing dictators in the hope that they will not commit further aggression; the self-defeating path, if you will, of pretending not to see what really is happening as small nations are conquered and larger nations are endangered; and then finally, at the end, war with its terrible costs. In the 1930s as we all know, the aggressors were appeased. In 1990 our President has made our position very plain. We are not going to

2839-2

0162

appease this aggression.   (Applause.)

While the international community is trying to build on the successful ending of the Cold War, Saddam Hussein seems hellbent on a revival of hot war. He marries and old-style contempt for civilized rules with modern destructive methods, chemical and **biological** weapons, ballistic missiles, and if he could get them, nuclear weapons.

What can be the long-term meaning of Iraq's extensive chemical and biological weapons programs? Why is the Iraqi dictator spending billions of dollars to build weapons of mass destruction including a nuclear bomb? And why has he turned Baghdad into a safe haven for international terrorists? Surely not because he expects this aggression, first against Iran and now against Kuwait to be his last.

So Iraq's invasion of Kuwait is a clear, indeed historic challenge to the rest of the international community. If we reverse this aggression we will help define a world that lies beyond the Cold War as a place where civilized rules of conduct do apply. If we do not, the bright promise of the post Cold War era could be eclipsed by new dangers, new disorders, and a far less peaceful future.

Secondly, Iraq's aggression is a regional challenge. While might makes right is bad policy anywhere, it's especially dangerous in the Middle East, just as when an event occurs can give it greater significance, where it happens gives it meaning also. As we know, the Middle East is already disturbed by unresolved conflicts, sectarian and social strife, and by vast economic disparities. When you add weapons of mass destruction and much of the world's energy supply, it becomes a truly explosive mix.

Today the Middle East is at a crossroads. One of these roads leads to peace and frankly, the other leads to war. If there is one lesson that we have learned, it is that no one is immune from the effects of conflict in the Middle East. There can be no hope of resolving other problems in the region unless peaceful change becomes the wave of the future in the Middle East and in the Gulf. But Saddam Hussein's way is not the way of peace. His is a prescription for war. And ladies and gentlemen, let me say this very bluntly: If his way of doing business prevails, there will be no hope for peace in this area.

Third, Iraq's aggression challenges the global economy. Obviously, we've got to do more to reduce our energy dependence. But for better or worse, the health of the global economy will depend for the foreseeable future on secure access to the energy resources of the Persian Gulf. Neither we nor the rest of the international community can afford to let just one dictator control that access. Just consider the consequences.

If the entire world were to be thrust into a deep recession by an Iraqi stranglehold on Gulf energy resources, American industry, farmers, and small businesses would be hit especially hard. But so

2839 -3

would the Democratic reformers of Eastern and Central Europe. So
would the other emerging democracies -- those in Latin America, in
Africa and in Asia. All of them would suffer profound setbacks in
their ability to deliver the economic growth needed to sustain
confidence in the democratic process. And all of us, therefore,
would lose from this economic tyranny. And all of us know how
Saddam Hussein would seek to exploit his economic leverage in
pursuit of larger ambitions.

Led by the United States, the international community, I
think, has recognized these vital stakes. President Bush has
outlined four goals of our policy: first, the immediate, complete,
and unconditional withdrawal of all Iraqi forces from Kuwait as
mandated by United Nations Security Council Resolution 660;
secondly, the restoration of Kuwait's legitimate government; third,
the protection of the lives of American citizens held hostage

complying with ten Security Council resolutions.

On the military track, we and some 27 other countries have sent
troops or material to the Gulf in support of the Security Council
resolutions. Many thousands of Arab and Moslem soldiers in Saudi
Arabia now stand guard together with Americans and Europeans. And
this multinational force on land has been joined by powerful
multinational forces at sea and in the air. In contrast, if you
think about it, only 14 other countries contributed military forces
during the Korean War.

We must be clear, though, I think about our military mission.
Our military objectives are to deter an Iraqi attack on Saudi
Arabia, to protect American lives, and to ensure the effective
implementation of the United Nations Security Council resolutions.
Without such forces, Iraq's neighbors would be subject to attack if
they tried to enforce economic sanctions.

Our military forces are also there to provide an effective and
decisive military response should the situation warrant it. Saddam
Hussein must realize that there is a limit to the international
community's patience. He must also realize, and I'd like to stress
this point, that should he use chemical or biological weapons, there
will be the most severe consequences. (Applause.)

The President has made our position clear. We strongly prefer
a peaceful solution which is consistent with the mandate of the
Security Council resolutions. And as I think you can see from what
I've just related to you in terms of what we have done in the United
Nations and elsewhere, we are exhausting every diplomatic avenue to
achieve such a solution without further bloodshed. But again, we
have to say that all options are being considered. And let no one
doubt, we will not rule out a possible use of force if Iraq
continues to occupy Kuwait.

2839-4

0164

Since the invasion, I've spent a lot of time traveling, visiting our allies and friends both in the region and outside the region, and bringing the message that all of us share responsibilities for seeing this matter through. And ladies and gentlemen, they have all responded. Our friends in the Gulf and Asia and Europe have committed an additional $20 billion in resources to support both frontline states which are hardest hit economically by the crisis -- namely, Egypt, Turkey, and Jordan -- and to support our own military buildup. We are confident that additional support will be forthcoming should this conflict carry over into 1991. All told, there are 54 -- 54 nations contributing either militarily or economically or both to the effort against Iraq's aggression.

So I think we are on course. Ever day as the sun sets, Iraq gets weaker. Every day as the sun rises, the international community remains firmly committed to implementation of the Security Council resolutions. Sooner or later, and of course we all hope sooner, even the Iraqi dictator is going to notice that he's in trouble and the trouble is getting deeper. Sooner or later, ladies and gentlemen, and one way or another Iraq is going to have to comply with the Security Council resolutions. When it does, the prospects for peace in the Gulf and the Middle East as a whole will undoubtedly brighten. When it does, the prospects for a peaceful new international order will brighten too.

Meanwhile, the United States opposes any attempt whatsoever to reward Iraq for its aggression, even if it plays the siren's song of a partial solution. And should there be any doubt about the awful consequences of a partial solution, I would urge a close look at what Saddam Hussein has been doing to the people of Kuwait. Because he controls access to the true story of Kuwait, this is a story that is not told frequently enough, but it's a story of barbarism in its most crude and evil form: the rape of Kuwait.

Many of the reports seem altogether unbelievable. There's the report of a couple taking two sick children to a hospital, and on their way, they were stopped at an Iraqi checkpoint. When they asked for mercy to be allowed to continue on their way, the Iraqi soldier summarily shot their children, "curing them" in his words.

And consider the Kuwait City Zoo. Iraqi soldiers released the lions and tigers, and then used them for target practice. That might not be so bad, but their efforts were not completely successful, and a young Kuwaiti girl was mauled by one of the lions which had escaped.

He's also making political and economic war on our citizens, American citizens, still in Iraq and Kuwait. At strategic installations in Iraq, more than 100 American citizens are being held hostage as human shields. These Americans are being forced to sleep on vermin-ridden concrete floors. They are kept in the dark during the day, and moved only at night. They've had their meals cut to two a day, and many are becoming sick as they endure what is indeed a terrible ordeal. The very idea of Americans being used as human shields is simply unconscionable.

2839-5

Life for those who have escaped Saddam's soldiers is really not much less odious. Their days are lived with terror. Obtaining food and water, the most basic of human necessities, carries with it the risk of death.

So we all agonize for these people, innocent Americans, as well as the innocent nationals of other countries that are trapped by this man's deadly ambitions. In most cases, we cannot concern our concern and sympathy directly to these Americans, but that doesn't lessen the pain we feel at their plight, nor does it diminish our desire to banish all specters of Iraq's aggression.

We understand the concerns of their families here at home. The courage that they have shown in the face of these manipulations is great. We salute their will and spirit, and we salute as well their unity in the face of adversity. We shall not forget them.

This aggression extends beyond our citizens to that small band of American diplomats, men and women, who still fly the American flag high over Kuwait City. For weeks now, months, they have been denied supplies of food, water, or electricity, but they are not without courage.

Since the second of August, I have spoken often to Ambassador Nat Howell in Kuwait City, most recently just last Wednesday or Thursday. He and our other diplomats in Kuwait continue to serve this nation in an absolutely superb fashion. They continue to fight back. They are not giving in, and of course neither will we.

At the beginning of this conflict, the President and I and all of those concerned with this problem had to ask ourselves the same question that you have either asked yourselves or must be asking yourselves. And that is, why is it that America has to take the lead? Why is it that our kids have to be out there in the desert? Now that the Cold War is over, isn't this one that we can pass up?

Ladies and gentlemen, this struggle is about the kind of world that we want to live in. It's about the kind of nation that we are. And it's about the kind of legacy that we want to leave for our children.

The Cold War is over. We fought, and we sacrificied, and we persisted for over 40 years because we would not accept a world that was safe for the likes of Joseph Stalin. The American people have not come this long, hard way to make the world safe for the likes of Saddam Hussein.

So, let no nation think it can devour another nation and that the United States will somehow turn a blind eye. Let no dictator believe that we are deaf to the tolling of the bell as our fundamental principles are attacked. And let no one believe that because the Cold War is over, the United States is somehow going to abdicate its international leadership.

2839-6

May I remind you that America's involvement in world politics
came about from conviction based on hard and terrible experience.
We're not in the game just to play one inning and then go home. And
we certainly cannot be short of breath for the long haul. And
whatever the noise of naysayers, our moral principles, as well as
our material interests, make us a leader. That's why we're in the
Gulf, and that's why we have to prevail.

Will we have the courage and the fortitude to stand up for what
we know in our heart is right? Is Saddam Hussein's kind of world a
legacy that we want to leave for our children? Are the nations of
the world, all of them, practically without exception, gathered in
vain to defend the principles of the United Nations charter?

I think you know the answer to these questions. There is a
morality among nations. Aggression cannot be permitted to succeed.
And America, as it always does, will do what's right.

Thank you all very, very much. (Applause.)

2839-7

외 무 부

원 본

종 별 :

번 호 : LAW-1364
일 시 : 90 1030 1240

수 신 : 장 관(미북)

발 신 : 주 라성 총영사

제 목 : 베이커 국무장관의 오찬연설

1. BAKER 미국무장관은 10.29. LOS ANGELES WORLDAFFAIRS COUNCIL 주최 오찬에서중 동사태에 대한 미국정부 입장에 관한 연설을 행하였으며, 약1,700명의 청중이 참석하 였음.

2. 동 연설은 강경한 내용이었으며, 이락군의 KUWAIT 로 부터의 무조건 철수없이는 어떤 타협도있을수 없으며, 무력사용을 배제할수 없음을 되풀이 강조하는 동시에이락군이 쿠웨이트에서 행한 잔악행위 사례도 몇가지 열거하였음.

3. 동 장관은 또한 중동사태에 대한 미군출동을 지원해준 국가가 약 50개국에 달한 다고 말하고 년말까지 해결되지 않으면 금년을 넘길 준비를 진행하고 있다고 말함. 일본정부에서 중동에 군대를 파견하기 위한 관계법 개정문제에 관한 질문에 대하여 이는일본의 국내문제이므로 COMMENT 할수 없다고 말함.(질문자는 일본의 군비강화는 또 다른문제를 야기시킬 가능성이 있다는 의미에서 질문하였음.). 끝.

(총영사 박종상-국장)

미주국   1차보   아주국   정문국

PAGE 1
90.10.31   06:47 CG
외신 1과 통제관

0168

외 무 부

종 별 :

번 호 : USW-4875   일 시 : 90 1030 1747

수 신 : 장 관(미북,중근동, 동구1)

발 신 : 주 미 대사

제 목 : BAKER 장관 중동 및 구주방문

1. 국무부 TUTWEILER 대변인은 금 10.30 정례브리핑을 통해 BAKER 국무장관의 중동 및 구주방문계획을 발표한바, 동내용을 하기 보고함.

11.3 10:00 워싱턴 출발

11.4. 바레인

11.5. 사우디 TAIF 거주하는 쿠웨이트왕 면담, 제다 방문

11.6. 이집트, 터키

11.7 프랑스

11.8 영국

11.9 세바르나제 외상 면담, CFE, START 등 군축문제 및 폐만 사태 논의 (장소는 쏘련이 아닌 유럽에서 이루어질 예정이나 상금 미정)

2. 동건 상세 일정 확인시 추보 위게임.

(대사 박동진-국장)

미주국   1차보   구주국   중아국   정문국   안기부

정 리 보 존 문 서 목 록					
기록물종류	일반공문서철	등록번호	2012090522	등록일자	2012-09-17
분류번호	772	국가코드	US/XF	보존기간	영구
명　칭	걸프사태 : 미국의 대응, 1990-91. 전6권				
생 산 과	북미과/안보과	생산년도	1990~1991	담당그룹	
권 차 명	V.3 1990.11-12월				
내용목차	* 1990.11.8 Bush대통령, 걸프지역 미군 증파 시행 공식 발표				

0001

외 무 부

<table>
<tr><td>관리
번호</td><td>70-2186</td></tr>
</table>

종   별 : 지 급

번   호 : USW-4931   일   시 : 90 1101 1932

수   신 : 장관(중근동,미북,미안)

발   신 : 주 미 대사

제   목 : 걸프 사태 전망

대: WUS-3547

연: USW(1) 3731, (2)4037, (3)4790, (4)4859

대호 관련, 걸프 사태 귀추및 금후 전망등을 하기 보고함.

1. 정세 개요

가. 당관이 연호(1)로 기보고한 바와 같이 지금까지의 걸프 정세는 미국이 대이락 봉쇄 전략을 계속 추구해 나가는 가운데 지구전 성격의 군사적 교착 상태가 지속되어 왔음.

나. 여사한 대이락 봉쇄 전략을 통해 미국은 이라군의 쿠웨이트로 부터의 자진 철수등 소위 걸프 사태 해결을 위한 4 대 원칙을 일관되게 추구해 왔으나, 연호 (3)으로 기보고한바와같이 주로 아래 고려를 바탕으로한 대 이락 공격 임박설이 미국내 중간 선거를 앞둔 현 시점에서 당지 언론등 일각에 의해 강력하게대두하고 있음.

-무력 사용을 통해 이락의 화학 무기 , 핵 시설을 제게하지 않고, 외교적 타협에 의해 금번 사태가 해결되는 경우 이락측에 의한 또다른 쿠웨이트 침공 사태가 재현될 수도 있다는점.

- 미국이 금번 사태를 탈 냉전시대 최초의 국제적 위기로 규정하면서, 무력에 의한 타국 침략 행위는 결코 용납될수 없다는 점을 대내외적으로 강조, 쿠웨이트 영토 일부 할양등에 의한 외교적 타협책을 일관되게 거부해온점.

- 사우디 주둔 미군의 실전 배치 완료 및 병력 10 만 증파 추진

-11 월 이후 기온 하강으로 인한 사막전 수행 환경 양호

-대이락 경제 봉쇄 전략이 상금 이락에 대해 심각한 타격을 가하지 못하고 있는점.

다. 그러나 이락으로서도 사우디-쿠웨이트 국경 지대의 지뢰 매설 및 참호선

중아국   1차보   미주국   미주국   청와대   안기부   대책반

외신 2과 통제관 BT

0002

구축등을 봉해 강력한 방어 태세를 구축하고 있고, 미군의 공습에 대비한 방공망 강화 조치를 취하고 있을뿐만 아니라, 미국이 이락을 공격하는 경우 이락은이스라엘 공격등의 조치를 취함으로서 현재의 걸프 사태를 PLO 문제등과 연계할 가능성이 클것으로 예상되므로, 부쉬 행정부가 세간의 소문처럼 대이락 공격 결정을 쉽게 내리기는 어려울것으로 봄.

라. 이러한 상황하에서 미측은 연호(4)로 보고한 베이커 장관의 10.29 라성WORLD AFFAIRS COUNCIL 연설을 봉해 대이락 무력 사용 가능성을 강력하게 암시한 이래, 중간 선거 관련 지방 유세 연설등을 봉해 부쉬 대통령도 과거보다 훨씬강력한 어조로 이락의 만행을 규탄하면서 미측으로서는 금번 사태의 평화적 해결을 강력히 희망하나 대이락 무력 사용을 포함하는 모든 방안이 검토되고 있다는점을 반복, 지적하고 있음.

마. 여사한 미측의 RHETORIC 상의 태도 변화를 미측이 보다 더 진지하게 대이락 무력 사용 문제를 검토하고 있는 징후로도 해석할수 있는바, 작 10.31 U.S RAISES THE PRESSURE AND THE RISKS 제하의 W.P 지 기사도 이러한 관점에서 11 월이나 12 월중으로 부쉬 대통령이 대이락 공격 여부를 결정해야만 할것이라고 보도한바 있음.

2. 현재 상황에 관한 미측 평가

전기 W.P 지 보도와 같이 미국이 걸프 사태 관련 무력 사용 문제등에 관해 결정을 내리는 경우는, 우선 무엇보다도 이락의 자진 철수를 봉한 금번 사태의 외교적, 평화적 해결 가능성 및 대이락 경제 봉쇄의 효과에 관한 나름의 평가를 바탕으로 사안을 검토할것으로 보임 (이하는 주로 당관 임성남 서기관의 국무부 이락. 이락과 JOSEPH MCGHEE 부과장및 국무부 정책 기획실 STEPHEN GRUMMON 중동담당관 접촉 결과임)

가. 금번 사태의 외교적, 평화적 해결 가능성에 관한 평가

-두차례(10.5 및 28)에 걸친 프리마코프 특사의 후세인 대통령 면담및 붙소정상회담(10.29)등 외교적 노력을 봉한 금번 사태의 평화적 해결 가능성에 관해 언론 등에서 많은 추측 보도를 하고 있으나 미측으로서는 여사한 외교적 노력이 별다른 성과를 거두지 못한것으로 평가하고 있음 (금 11.1 자 WP 지의 ARAB ALLIES SEE SAUDIS AFFER SOVIET'S VISIT 제한의 기사도 프리마코프의 이락 방문이 별다른 성과를 거두지 못하였다고 보도함)

-프리마코프 특사의 이락 방문 기간중 이락측은 동 특사의 동정을 상세 보도하는등 언론 플레이를 봉해 이락이 국제적 고립에 빠져 있지 않다는 사실을 국민들에게 주지

PAGE 2

0003

시키고자 하였으나, 사실상 소련측은 이락군의 쿠웨이트로부터의 자진 철수 필요성을 강력하게 언급하는등 미국의 대이락 요구와 보조를 일치하였는바, 후세인 대봉려은 이에 대해 크게 실망하였다함.

- 또한 프리마코프 특사 자신도 이락측으로부터 사태 해결을 위한 어떠한 언질도 받지 못하였는바, 여사한 외교적 노력에 관한 미측 평가는 회의적인것이 사실임.

나. 대 이락 경제 봉쇄 의 효과에 관한 평가

-대이락 경제 봉쇄로 인해 이락내 각종 산업 가동률이 저하되고 있는것은 사실이나, 일부 생필품의 경우는 쿠웨이트로부터 약탈한 각종 물자가 이락 국내 시장에 반입됨으로 인해 오히려 가격이 하락하고 있기도함 (이락측은 쿠웨이트로부터 심지어 공중전화 박스까지 뜯어가는등 문자 그대로 쿠웨이트의 공동화를 추구하고 있다함)

-결론적으로 경제 봉쇄 조치로 인해 이락측이 심각한 정도의 추역을 받고 있는것으로는 보지 않으나, 또한 기본적으로 경제 봉쇄 전략은 당기간내의 승부를 목표로 하는것이 아니며 비교적 장기간에 걸친 대이락 고사 효과를 추구하고 있다는점을 유념해야함.

-이러한 관점에서 본다면 경제 봉쇄의 효과가 이제야 서서히 나타나고 있는것으로 보인바, 비록 시행후 곧 폐지하기는 하였으나 개솔린 배급제의 실시도 그지우로 볼수 있으며, 또 원유 수출을 약 3 개월간 실시치 못함으로 인해서 재정적 어려움도 겪고 있을것으로 봄(MCGHEE 부과장은 사견임을 전제로 금년 연말까지는 경제 봉쇄의 효과가 보다더 가시화 될것으로 본다고 언급함)

- 일단 경제 봉쇄 조치가 보다 더 심각한 영향을 초래케되면, 우선 군부의 사기가 저하될것으로 보며, 여사한 상황하에서 실용주의자인 후세인은 자신의 정치적 생명을 유지키 위해 걸프 사태 직후 대이락 관계 개선을 위해 전쟁 포로 석방등의 유화적 조치를 취했던 것처럼 보다 더 현실적인 태도를 취할것으로 봄. 즉 경제적인 어려움으로 인해 수니파와 시아파간의 갈등이 심화되는등 국내 정치의 안정 기반이 흔들리는 상황보다는 차라리 쿠웨이트로 부터 철수하는것이 후세인 대통령으로서는 보다 나은 선택이 될것임.

이하 USW-4932 로 계속됨.

검 토 필 (1986. (23)hh)

액고문에 의거 일반문서로 재분류 19

0004

외 무 부

종 별 : 지급

번 호 : USW-4932   일 시 : 90 1101 1941

수 신 : 장관(중근동, 미북, 미안)

발 신 : 주 미 대사

제 목 : USW-4931 의 계속

3. 미국의 전략

가. 전술한 바와 같이 외교적 해결의 가능성이 높지않고, 경제 봉쇄 전략이이락에 대해 심각한 충격을 가하지 못하고 있는 현 상황하에서 미국으로서는당연히 무력 사용 문제를 검토 할 것으로는 추측되나, 다음과같은 요인등을 고려시 부쉬 행정부가 금명간 대이락 공격 결정을 내릴 가능성 보다는 당분간 경제봉쇄 전략을 계속 추구해 나가는 동시에 사우디 주둔 미군의 임전 태세를 강화함으로서 이락에 대한 심리적 압박을 가중시키는 한편, 대이락 무력 사용 결정시에는 군사력 부입이 신속히 이루어질수 있도록 만반의 준비를 갖추어 나갈 가능성이 큰것으로 보임.

　-사태 발생직후 부터 미국의 기본 전략은 경제 봉쇄를 통한 이락의 자진철수 유도에 있었는바, 미측이 지금까지 여사한 기본 전략의 변경 가능성을 제시하지 않고 있는점

　-걸프 지역의 항구적 안정을 위해 이락의 화학 무기 체제 및 핵 무기 개발 시설등을 제거해야한다는 주장도 설득력이 있으나, 궁극적으로 이락의 국내 정치적 관점에서 볼때는 이락 사회 전체에 뿌리 깊이 박혀 있는 바쓰당 중심의 독재 체제의 제거가 필요 하다는점 (즉 이락의 비재래식 공격 능력 제거는 역내 안정을위해 하나의 필수 조건일뿐임)

　-대 이락 경제 봉쇄의 지속적 강화 시행및 대규모 미군 병력의 사우디 파견에도 붙구, 이락측이 여하한 태도의 변화도 보이지 않고 있는바, 이는 이락측이 미국의 군사력 배치를 진정한 위협이라기 보다는 일종의 시위(BLUFF)로 받아 들이고 있기 때문인것으로 봄.

　- 기후 조건으로 볼때 4 월이 되어야 기온이 급상승하기 시작 하므로 3 월까지는 작전 수행 환경이 비교적 양호한점 (전쟁 수행 부적합 기간이라할수 있는라마단도

중아국　　1차보　　　미주국　　미주국　　정와대　　안기부　　대책반

3.17 부터 시작함)

나. 이상과같은 고려에서, 미국은 경제 봉쇄 전략이 효과를 거두지 않는 경우 무력을 사용 한다는 점을 이락측에게 확실히 알려 주고, 미국의 위협이 단순한 시위가 아니라는점을 인식시키기 위해 일종의 극한 정책(BRINKMANSHIP)을 택하고 있는것으로 보임. 즉, 전술한바와같이 미국으로서는 경제 봉쇄 조치를 강화함과 동시에 대이락 임전 태세를 공고화 함으로서 이락측이 미국의 의도와 주변상황을 재검토케 하려는 목적인것으로 보임.

다. 따라서 향후 어느 정도는 미국으로서도 이제 막 채택한 극한 정책의 효과를 주시할것으로 보이며, 대이락 무력 사용 문제에 대해서는 여사한 극한 정책이 실패한 것으로 판단될때에 보다 더 심각하게 고려할것 보임.그러나 극한 정책의 적용 기간을 얼마나 길게할지는 부쉬 대통려등 최고위층외에는 아무도 알수 없는 상황이므로 대이락 무력 사용 시기를 예측 하기는 곤란할것임.

4. 결론

가. 따라서 걸프 사태의 향후 해결 방향은 다음 세가지 경우중 하나일것으로 보이며, 당분간 미국으로서는 현재의 극한 정책을 계속 추구할것으로 보임.

-미국의 극한 정책으로 인한 압력에 이락측이 굴복, 쿠웨이트로 부터 철수하는 경우

- 미국의 대이락 전면 공격

-아랍제국간 협의를 거쳐, 이락이 쿠웨이트로부터 철수 하는 대신 쿠웨이트는 아랍권내의 형제애를 바탕으로 영토 일부를 이락측에 할양하는 아랍식 해결

나. 특히 전기 아랍식 해결 방안에 따라 일단 사태가 수습된후, 아랍권 국가 군대로 구성된 평화 유지군이 동 지역에 주둔하고 대이락 무기 금수등의 보완조치가 취해진다면, 이러한 방안이 아랍권 내부의 합의 사항인 이상 미국으로서도 별다른 이견을 제시할수 없을것이라는것이 국무부 실무선의 반응임(이락에 의한 쿠웨이트 침공 직후 채택된 유엔 안보리 결의 660 호 3 항에서도 이락-쿠웨이트간 직접 교섭 및 아랍 제국간 협의를 통한 금번 사태의 해결을 촉구하고 있음이 주목됨.

다. 한편 부쉬 대통령은 금일 메사추세츠주 지방 유세 연설시 -WE ARE GIVING THE SARCTIONS THE TIME TO WORK. BUT THERE WILL BE NO COMPROMISE ON THE STATED OBJECTIVES OF THE UN SECURITY COUNCIL RESOLUTIONS.- 라고 언급함으로서 대이락 무력 공격 가능성을 강력한 어조로 언급한 10.29 상항 연설 등과는 대조를 이루었음.

PAGE 2

0006

(금일 연설문은 USW(F)-2880 으로 발췌 송부)

(대사 박동진-국장)

91.6.30 일반

검 도 필 (19 80.12.31 제공)

대고문에 의거 일반문서로 서명
재분류 19

FRESIDENT GEORGE BUSH SPEAKS TO GOP FUNDRAISDER, BURLINGTON,
MASSACHUSETTS, THURSDAY, NOVEMBER 1, 1990

On August 2nd **Iraq** invaded **Kuwait**. They literally raped,
pillaged and plundered this once peaceful land. This nation that is
a member of the **Arab League**, a member of the **United Nations**, and
Iraq began then to brutally and systematically dismantle Kuwait.
There is a historical analogy here between what's happened to Kuwait
and what happened to Poland when the world stood still, sat on
the sidelines, including our country in the late '30s.

They began to systematically dismantle it by shipping its
medical equipment, its machines, its record, its assets back to
Baghdad. Brutal, systematic dismantling. And they've tried to
silence Kuwaiti dissent
encouraged with an old way of doing that. I'm talking about the
firing squads. In one incident a 15 year-old boy gunned down. His
family forced to watch. His crime? Passing out leaflets.

The United States and the rest of the world united in anger and
outrage, determined to force Saddam Hussein out of Kuwait. On
August 5th, he announced that he was pulling his forces out of
Kuwait. And at that very moment he sent his armor and his troops
South to mass along the Saudi Arabian border, threatening yet
another member of the United Nations, another member of the Arab
League. And subsequently the United Nations Security Council passed
10 resolutions of condemnation and disapproval.

On August 5th, I said that Saddam Hussein's aggression will not
stand. And today I am more determined than ever; this aggression
will not stand!

(Applause.)

This morning, right now, over 300 innocent Americans,
civilians, are held against their will in Iraq, denied the freedoms
granted all under international law. Many of them are reportedly
staked out as human shields near possible military targets,
something that even Adolf Hitler didn't do. Many more Americans are
in hiding in Kuwait, hidden by courageous Kuwaitis, their lives at
stake, a number imprisoned.

And an embassy of the United States right there in Kuwait City.
And they are cut off from food and other supplies. And they are
surrounded by Iraqi troops. And our flag does still fly. But the
rights of these American citizens are at this very moment being
denied by Iraq's brutal dictator.

0008

So let me be clear. We have no argument
with the Iraqi people, none at all. We bear no hostility to the
Iraqi people, nor to any of the other 25 countries represented on
land and sea standing with us shoulder to shoulder in the Gulf. Our
problem is with Saddam Hussein alone.

And I want desperately to have a peaceful resolution to this
crisis. Indeed, we've worked closely with the United Nations in
putting sanctions into effect, in passing resolutions, in speaking
with one voice against the invader's aggression. We are giving the
sanctions the time to work, and I hope that there will never be a
shot fired in anger, but let me be very, very clear: There will be
no compromise on the stated objectives of the United Nations
Security Council resolutions -- none at all. (Applause.)

The brutality -- the brutality against innocent civilians --
will not be tolerated and will not stand. Saddam's clear violations
of international law will not stand. And that means, yes, his
brutal aggression will not stand. No one wants a peaceful crisis --
peaceful end to this crisis more than I do, but no one is more
determined to see this aggression turned back than I am, and I will
not change on that fundamental point of morality. (Applause.)

Now, as to our own kids, our own forces in the Gulf, they are
the best. They're the best young men and women ever to serve in our
armed forces. (Applause.) They're all volunteers. They're all
volunteers. They're all well-trained. They are all highly
motivated. They are your sons and daughters. They're your neighbors ki
They're the finest, and we owe them an enormous vote of thanks.

You know, these men and women don't take democracy for granted.
Thousands upon thousands of them are going to be sending in absentee
ballots from the Saudi desert, or opon the seas of the Gulf of Oman

and near the Straits of Hormuz. And if they can find the time to
vote under such challenging conditions, so can every single American
here at home. We have an obligation to show these extraordinary GIs
that we don't take democracy for granted, either. So let's make
them as proud of us as we are of them.

- 끝 -

2880-2-

0009

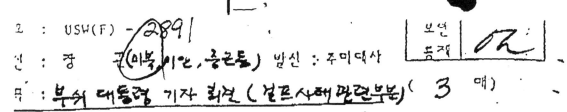
PRESS CONFERENCE WITH PRESIDENT BUSH/ ORLANDO, FLORIDA
ZC-4-1   page# 1   THURSDAY, NOVEMBER 1, 1990

PRESIDENT BUSH: Let me just make a brief statement and then I'll be glad to respond to questions.

I want to begin today by simply restating for the American people some of the key points about our efforts to turn back aggression in the Persian Gulf. I believe that it is essential that the American people fully understand the objectives of the United States and the United Nations, as well as the magnitude of the outrage perpetrated by the government of Iraq.

The United States and the rest of the world are united in the condemnation of Iraq's invasion of Kuwait. We have no quarrel with the Iraqi people. Our problem is with Iraqi's dictator Saddam Hussein.

I want a peaceful resolution to this crisis. We're giving the United Nations sanctions imposed on Iraq time to work. But let me be very clear, there will be no compromise on the stated objectives of the United Nations Security Council resolutions. Iraq's brutality against innocent civilians will not be permitted to stand, and Saddam Hussein's violations of international law will not stand; his aggression against Kuwait will not stand.

And now I'd be glad to take questions. I think, Tom, you have the first one.

Q   Yes, Mr. President, -- (inaudible) -- say that your comments in recent days have been aimed at least in part in preparing the American people for the possibility of war. Is that true? (And do you think the American people are ready, that they have no problems with it?)?

PRESIDENT BUSH: Tom, I want to have a peaceful resolution to this question. And our dealing through the
United Nations and working with them for common objectives I think is evidence of that. I've indicated we're prepared to give sanctions time to work, and I'll repeat that here again today. But I am not ruling out further options, and I'm not trying to prepare our country for war.

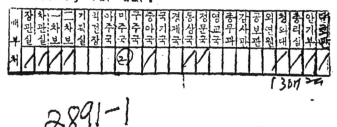

2891-1

0010

We have a little bit of a hiatus, because of the attention on the budget and other matters, from keeping in focus our objectives in Iraq. There's been a little less attention to it in some quarters, and I want to -- it's -- in a sense, Tom, it's a little bit awkward because here we are just a few days before an election, and I want to continue to work for Republican candidates, but I must continue to keep our objectives regarding Iraq in focus. And so what I try to do is separate out the foreign affairs, the Iraq question, from domestic politics. But it is essential that I do the latter, but it is not -- in doing that, I am not trying to sound the tocsin of war, but I am trying to point out the concerns that I feel, for example, on the hostage question. And I'll continue to do that.

Q   Mr. President, I know you say that you're not trying to prepare the American people for war, but could not your message of today and this week be summed up as that you are seeking a peaceful resolution if possible -- if possible, but a military one if not?

PRESIDENT BUSH: Well, I think that I've made those statements before. I think I've been rather consistent in pointing out that I would not rule anything out. If you go back and look at the things I've said, I -- I believe I've been on the record before with that -- that kind of comment, Brit.

Q   Mr. President, in the beginning of this crisis you held out little hope for a diplomatic solution. Today --

PRESIDENT BUSH: Did you say "a little hope" or "little hope"?

Q   Little hope for a diplomatic solution. Today you talk about hoping that there's a peaceful resolution. I'm just wondering, are we any closer to possibly having a diplomatic solution?

PRESIDENT BUSH: I don't see that. I don't see that we are. I've said from the very beginning I hoped that the sanctions would have an effect that would cause him to comply with the resolutions. I think they're having an effect. But our problem is, and the problem of our allies around the world is we can't certify for the world how disastrous or strong an effect these sanctions are having. But from the very beginning I've been saying I would hope that the sanctions would be effective. And we'll give them time. Again, my problem is, and the problem with those with whom I consult very closely, is we can't say how much is enough in terms of the sanctions or how much time it would take.

Q   Well, sir, if you do not expect a diplomatic solution, but you're hoping for a peaceful resolution, does that mean you expect Saddam will just give up?

PRESIDENT BUSH: That's what I would like to see, yeah. That's what the United Nations calls for -- calls for him to withdraw; calls for the restoration of the rulers. And so that's exactly what he ought to do. And I think if we hold firm -- and we are holding firm in this coalition with some 25 countries in the Gulf or on the sea there, plus the solidarity that the United Nations has demonstrated -- I think he'll eventually -- you know, the hope is

2891-2

eventually he might do that. But we can't guarantee to the American people how long will it take.

Q   Mr. President, -- (inaudible) -- Mr. Quayle said yesterday that the United States must -- (inaudible) -- Iraq's chemical, psychological, and nuclear -- (inaudible).

PRESIDENT BUSH: Well, I think from the very beginning an objective -- we spelled out some objective, but one that I think has been clearly spelled out has been ensuring the security and the stability of the Gulf. And that obviously is affected by the possession of these chemical and biological weapons and things of that nature. So I don't think that the goalposts are being moved. I think it's just simply a statement of reality.
If you're going to have a stable and you're going to have a secure Gulf after Kuwait is freed and the Iraqis have withdrawn their invasion, you're going to have to have some arrangements, I'm sure -- I think others would agree with this around the world -- that guarantee the peace there.

And I would hope that, as I've said early, I want all United Nations -- United States forces out of there as soon as possible, every single soldier. And it's important I keep repeating that, because there's this -- the allegations by some over in that part of the world that we want to keep forces there. That's not what we want to do. We want to come out. But there has got to be some security arrangments worked out, absolutely.

Q   Mr. President, you said earlier in the press conference the sand is running through the glass now. It sounds like suddenly time is no longer on your side, or you seem to be hinting that it may be shifting. Is that the reason why you've begun to emphasize the military option more, or what exactly -- (inaudible)?

PRESIDENT BUSH: I'm not sure I've emphasized military option more. I don't recall discussing military option per se, except to say I'm not ruling things out. But I do think that, in a sense, time might be on our side, because if these sanctions are to have any effect, they should be having more effect now than they did when they started, and hopefully more tomorrow than they do today. But I just -- I don't think that status quo can go on forever and ever. And I don't know how long, as I've tried to be very frank with you all -- I don't know how long is long enough. But
I've just got to keep putting the focus there and keeping everybody on notice that we are going to be successful. But it's, you know -- I'd leave it right there.

2891-3

0012

외 무 부

종 별 :

번 호 : USW-4948   일 시 : 90 1102 1744

수 신 : 장 관 (미북,중근동,동구1,아이)

발 신 : 주 미 대사

제 목 : BAKER 장관 중동 및 구주 방문

연: USW-4875

1. 연호로 보고한 BAKER 장관 일정중 변동및 추가사항을 하기 보고함.

11.3 09:00 워싱턴 출발

11.6 이집트 방문기회를 이용 QIAN 중국 외상면담

11.7 쏘련

11.8 세바르나제 외상 면담

11.9 영국

11.10 프랑스 방문, 워싱턴 향발

2. QIAN 외상 면담의 주요 목적은 페만 사태 논의라고 함

첨부: 미국무부 브리핑(USW(F)-2907)

(대사 박동진-국장)

미주국   1차보   아주국   구주국   중아국   정문국   안기부

PAGE 1   90.11.03   09:20 FC

외신 1과 통제관

0013

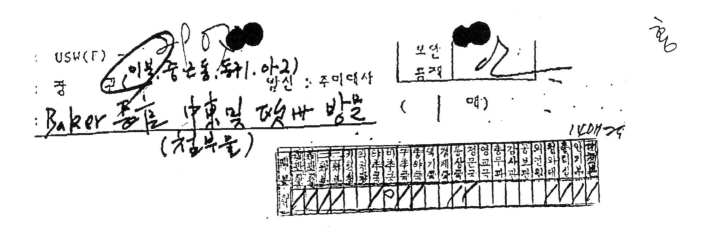

STATE DEPARTMENT REGULAR BRIEFING, BRIEFER: MARGARET TUTWILER
12:10 PM (EST), FRIDAY, NOVEMBER 2, 1990
S-5-1 page# 1
    dest=dsd,dos,forpolus,ussr,egypt,prc,iraq,kuwait,mme,mideast,pergulf
data

    MS. TUTWILER: I have several things I'd like to talk
about, the first being Secretary Baker's trip. I would like to
tell those of you who are traveling with us that we are now
leaving one hour earlier tomorrow. Instead of 10:00 AM, which
we told you, we're now leaving at 9:00 AM. I would like to tell
you that Secretary Baker will go to Moscow on Wednesday,
November 7, arriving there sometime that evening. He will meet
on Thursday, November 8th, with Foreign Minister Shevardnadze.
We will depart then, for those of you who are going with us.   On
Friday, we will end up in London. And on Saturday, we will be in
Paris and will return home.

    Another addition that I would like to announce is the
Chinese Foreign Minister has a previous planned trip in the region,
while we're there in the region, and we will see him in Cairo on
Tuesday, November 6th.

    Q   Margaret, can you explain exactly why the Secretary is
going to meet with the Chinese Foreign Minister? Is this to discuss
the Gulf only or are there other issues that --

    MS. TUTWILER: Well, the Chinese Foreign Minister, he hasn't
seen since September when we were in New York at the Security
Council meeting. And as you know, he is a permanent -- his country
is a member of the Permanent Five, and there, we have to assume,
are -- continue to be United Nations resolutions for one reason, and
they obviously have other things they can discuss. But since they
are both there in the region, both Foreign Ministers, both readily
thought that it made a lot of sense to get together.

    Q   Can you say what besides the Gulf they would discuss?

    MS. TUTWILER: Something besides? Off the top of my head,
Carol, I don't know, but I am sure there will be other issues. But
that is obviously the main issue.

외   무   부

종   별 :

번   호 : USW-4956   일   시 : 90 1105 1609

수   신 : 장 관(미북,미안,동구2,서구1,중근동,연기)

발   신 : 주 미 대사

제   목 : BUSH 대통령 구주및 중동순방

연: USW(F)-2911

백악관은 11.2. BUSH 대통령의 구주및 중동순방계획을 발표한바, 하기보고함.

11.16. 워싱턴 출발

11.17 첵코 방문, VELVET REVOLUTION 1 주년 계기 HAVEL 대통령등 면담

11.18. 독일 방문, KOHL 수상 면담

11.19-20 파리 방문, CSCE 외상회담 참석

이집트 방문 MUBARAK 면담

11.22. 사우디 방문, FAHD 왕, 쿠웨이트왕 MSFB마 및 추수 감사절을 계기로 한

주사우디 미군 위문

(대사 박동진-국장)

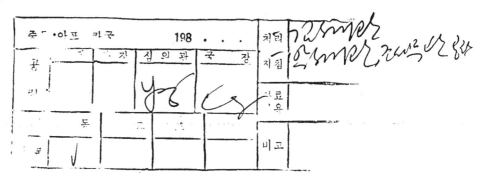

미주국	1차보	미주국	구주국	구주국	중아국	정문국	외연원	안기부

PAGE 1

THE WHITE HOUSE

Office of the Press Secretary
(Rochester, Minnesota)

For Immediate Release   November 2, 1990

STATEMENT BY THE PRESS SECRETARY

The President will depart November 16 for a trip that will begin
in Europe and conclude November 23 in the Middle East. He will
arrive in Prague on November 17, the first anniversary of
Czechoslovakia's "velvet revolution," for meetings with President
Havel and leaders of the Czech and Slovak Republics. On November
18, he will visit Germany to meet with Chancellor Kohl at the
Chancellor's residence in Ludwigshafen, continuing on that
afternoon to Paris, where he will participate in the summit
meeting of the 34 nation Conference on Security and Cooperation
in Europe, November 19-20.

The President will then travel on to Egypt and Saudi Arabia for
consultations on the situation in the Gulf with King Fahd,
President Mubarak and the Amir of Kuwait. He also will spend
Thanksgiving Day with U.S. forces deployed in the area.

\# \# \#

0016

미-사우디간 지휘체계 합의

(90.11.6. New York Times 및 Washington Post지 기사요약)

90. 11. 7

미주국 북미과

1. 합의 내용(11.5. Baker 미 국무장관과 Fahd 사우디 국왕간)

ο 사우디 영토로부터 개시되는 이라크에 대한 무력 공격 결정권 : 부쉬 미 대통령 및 Fahd 사우디 국왕이 공동으로 행사

 - 무력공격 개시를 위해서는 양지도자의 사전 승인이 필수.

ο 무력공격 방침 결정후 지휘 및 통제권 행사 : 미측이 독자적으로 행사

ο 이라크에 의한 사우디 공격시 방어작전의 지휘 및 통제권 : 현재 사우디 주둔 미군과 사우디군간 설치 운영되고 있는 합동 지휘 체제에서 행사

 - 단, 사우디측이 우월적 지휘 및 통제권 행사

2. 의의 및 효과

ο 사우디 영토로부터 이라크에 대한 무력공격은 미국이 독자적으로 결정 하지 않는다는 보장을 사우디에 제공

ο 대이라크 무력공격 준비와 관련, 커다란 장애 제거

 - 종래 사우디측은 사우디 영토를 대이라크 공격작전에 사용할 수 없다는 입장 견지

0017

o 부쉬 대통령의 <u>대이라크 무력사용 위협이 수사(rhetoric)에 그치는 것이</u>
   <u>아니라는 점을</u> 부각시키므로써 이라크에 대한 압력 증가

o 금번 미-사우디간 지휘체계 합의는 타 다국적군에게는 부적용
   - 미국과 다국적군 참여 국가와의 <u>별도의 개별 합의 필요</u>

0018

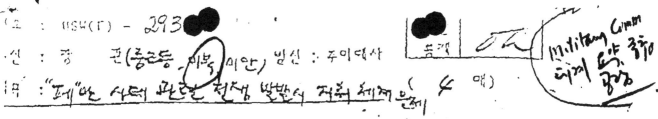

Saudis to Give Free Hand to U.S. If Attack on the Iraqis Is Approved

By THOMAS L. FRIEDMAN
Special to The New York Times

JIDDA, Saudi Arabia, Nov. 5 — The United States and Saudi Arabia tightened their pressure on Iraq today by agreeing on new command arrangements they would follow if they mounted an offensive strike, senior American and Saudi officials said.

In a step clearly intended to demonstrate the credibility of American military options, the two sides agreed that any offensive against Iraqi troops in Kuwait, or against Iraq, begun from Saudi territory would be undertaken only after President Bush and King Fahd both gave their approval.

But it was agreed that once an attack was authorized by the two political leaders, American forces would be free to plan and execute the attack entirely under their own commanders, without interference from the Saudi military leadership, officials said.

If Iraq should attack Saudi Arabia and a defensive military operation is required, the two sides agreed that the joint command structure set up since American troops began arriving on Saudi soil in the week after the Iraqi invasion on Aug. 2 would remain in force.

The Saudi-American understanding on command and control was reached during lengthy talks this evening between Secretary of State James A. Baker 3d and the Saudi Foreign Minister, Prince Saud al-Faisal, and King Fahd. The accord is significant for several reasons.

First, it clears away an important obstacle to any military operation against Iraq by reassuring the Saudi leadership that American troops on their soil will not undertake any unilateral offensive, while assuring the American military commander in Saudi Arabia, Gen. H. Norman Schwarzkopf, that if his forces have to take the field against Iraq he will be free to carry out the operation as he deems fit.

Second, the fact that the Saudis would agree to such an arrangement marks a clear development in their internal deliberations. Two months ago, the Saudi Defense Minister, Prince Sultan, declared flatly that Saudi territory could not be used for "offensive" operations against Iraqi forces. And

for the first three months of the crisis, the two countries had no firm understanding on how to coordinate any offensive strike.

Third, the decision should enhance the credibility of the mounting threats of force that President Bush has been making to persuade President Saddam Hussein of Iraq to withdraw from Kuwait unconditionally. The understanding is intended to make clear to Iraq that Washington now has a degree of flexibility in using Saudi territory for such an operation.

Baker Sees 'a New Phase'

"This crisis is entering a new phase," Mr. Baker told reporters before today's talks, "and while we are still seeking a peaceful, political and diplomatic solution, we have to, I think, put ourselves in a position where we would be able to exercise any options that might be available. I don't think that we can, nor should we, rule out resort to force, if that should be necessary."

Nevertheless, senior American and Saudi officials insisted that the command-and-control understanding did not foreshadow any imminent offensive military operation.

Both nations said they still wanted to try to work through the United Nations. They apparently agreed in principle to work together in the near future to try to persuade the Security Council to adopt a resolution authorizing the use of force if it is deemed to be the only way to evict Iraq from Kuwait.

Saudi officials said the fact that American troops based in Saudi Arabia would be allowed to operate independently in an offensive should not be read as a signal that no Saudi forces would take part in such an operation.

"We are trying to enhance the United Nations measures that will give us a peaceful solution," a senior Saudi official said. "If that doesn't happen, we will cross that bridge when we come to it. You would be very wrong to leave this place thinking that we have closed the door on diplomacy."

Coordination With Americans

If Saudi Arabia or other nations decide that they want their forces to take part in an offensive against Iraqi troops, they will have to coordinate the operation with the American military. Officials said Mr. Baker, who goes on

Tuesday to Egypt and Turkey, and then on to Moscow, London and Paris, would confer with other key members of the international force confronting Iraq about how they would like to coordinate any offensive. At the moment, each military contingent in Saudi Arabia has its own arrangement with the Saudi Army command.

Explaining today's understanding, a senior American official said of the procedures: "They are different when talking about matters of the defense of the Kingdom of Saudi Arabia as opposed to elsewhere. If it goes beyond Saudi borders, American commanders will command American troops."

If the operation is offensive, and aimed outside Saudi Arabia, the senior official added, "the authority for planning and approving those types of operations with respect to United States forces will rest with The United States command. There will be an agreement at the highest political level between the two Governments if those kinds of activities are undertaken."

Meeting With Kuwaiti Emir

Before his meeting this evening with Saudi officials, Mr. Baker flew to the Saudi mountain resort of Taif, where

Nov. 6, 1990

NYT

2936-1

0019

he met with the exiled Emir of Kuwait, Sheik Jaber al-Ahmed al-Sabah. Speaking to reporters before his talks with Mr. Baker, the Emir said his Government would like to see the Iraqis evicted in any way necessary and as soon as possible.

"As far as I am concerned," Sheik Jaber said, "I would like my country to be liberated today and before tomorrow. I would like to see the liberation of Kuwait as soon as possible, whether through the Security Council or not."

Mr. Baker spent Sunday visiting with American troops of the First Cavalry Division, which is stationed in eastern Saudi Arabia near the border with Iraq.

On the financial front, Mr. Baker told the Emir that the funds that the Kuwaiti leader had committed two months ago to support the military operation in the gulf would be used up by the end of the year. Sheik Jaber promised Mr. Baker that he would make an unspecified commitment of fresh funds for 1991, a senior Administration official said.

The Secretary also asked Sheik Jaber if he would consider providing financial assistance to the fledgling new democracies of Eastern Europe, where fragile economies have been badly hurt by the steep rise in oil prices. Sheik Jaber said he had dispatched a mission to Poland, Czechoslovakia and Hungary to assess their needs.

Yahya al-Sumait, Kuwait's exiled Minister of Housing, told reporters in Taif that the Kuwaitis were eager to bring the Iraqi invasion to a close before the Iraqis managed to forcibly expel all of Kuwait's citizens.

"We believe that with every day that passes in Kuwait, our people are being humiliated, tortured and killed by the hour," Mr. Sumait said. "This kind of atrocity cannot be tolerated anymore. To us, to our people, inside and outside Kuwait, we need a resolution, a solution, an immediate one."

Already, the Kuwaiti Minister said, 60 to 70 percent of the one million Kuwaitis are outside the country. Most are in Saudi Arabia, Egypt, Bahrain or Western Europe.

Gulf Special Aid: $13 Billion

ROME, Nov. 5 (Reuters) — Twenty-four of the world's wealthy nations said today that they would give $13 billion in special aid to the countries suffering most from the Persian Gulf crisis to harden their resolve on trade sanctions against Iraq.

Most of the money is to go to Egypt, Jordan and Turkey, hardest hit by the United Nations sanctions imposed after Iraq's invasion of Kuwait in August.

The pledge was made by the Gulf Crisis Financial Coordination Group, which includes the United States, the European Community, Japan and Persian Gulf oil-producing states as well as Kuwait's government in exile.

Several members of the group, set up by President Bush in September, had already made individual pledges of aid. Now, a figure has been put on the total commitment, spokesmen told a news conference.

"We are very satisfied with these commitments, which are very sizable," said David C. Mulford of the United States, Under Secretary of the Treasury for International Affairs, who presided at the meeting.

Egypt, Jordan and Turkey are to receive $10.5 billion by the end of 1991, and $2.5 billion is to go to other countries backing the sanctions campaign, an Italian Treasury Under Secretary, Mario Sarcinelli, said.

Officials declined to name the other recipients. However, Morocco, Pakistan and the Philippines have been mentioned in the past.

2936-2

Nov. 6, 1990
NYT
0020

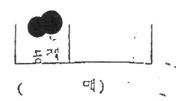
Baker, Fahd Set Command Plan

Accord Helps Prepare for Possible Attack

By David Hoffman
Washington Post Staff Writer

JIDDAH, Saudi Arabia, Nov. 5— Secretary of State James A. Baker III and King Fahd of Saudi Arabia agreed tonight on a framework for command and control over American and Saudi military forces here if the confrontation against Iraq turns to war, according to U.S. and Saudi officials. But Baker also indicated he wants to give diplomatic sanctions against Iraq more time to work.

The command agreement appeared to remove one persistent obstacle to preparation for a possible military strike against Iraqi President Saddam Hussein, and the announcement that both sides are now satisfied with the arrangement seemed to be yet another effort to increase the pressure on him.

Baker said earlier today that a "new phase" had begun in the Persian Gulf crisis in which the global community is prepared to "resort to force" if a peaceful solution is not found.

But senior U.S. officials emphasized today that Baker, while turning up the pressure on Saddam, would also like more time before using the military option, to give political and diplomatic efforts a better chance to resolve the crisis.

Recalling Baker's visit with the 1st Cavalry Division in the desert this week, a senior U.S. official told reporters tonight, "Before we commit young Americans" to war, "I think we owe it to them and to others to have done everything we possibly can to try to pursue the diplomatic, political and peaceful means of solving this crisis."

A senior Saudi diplomat said of the political and diplomatic pressure campaign against Saddam, "It beats the heck out of shooting."

With its simultaneous talk of war and diplomacy, the Bush administration appeared today to be trying to send different signals to different global audiences. For the U.S. public, the message appeared to be that conflict is not imminent despite the strident rhetoric recently from Baker and President Bush.

According to a senior U.S. official familiar with the talks, Baker and Fahd agreed to leave in place the current military command structure, which includes a separate U.S. command over American forces and an Arab command under Saudi leadership. The commander of U.S. forces in the region, Gen. H. Norman Schwarzkopf, works in tandem with Saudi Lt. Gen. Khalid bin Sultan, who commands all Saudi, Arab and some other multinational forces.

But the question of lines of command and who could decide to go to war involves extremely sensitive issues of national sovereignty, and both American and Saudi officials have been reluctant to talk publicly in recent weeks about their disagreement over who ultimately would be in charge if war came. Even tonight, the senior Saudi diplomat denied that there had been any disagreement.

But the high-ranking American official said Baker and Fahd had given their blessing to an arrangement that would give Saudi Arabia preeminence in decisions about defending the kingdom, while giving American commanders full control over U.S. forces for any operations beyond Saudi borders.

"There will be certain ways of handling matters if the issue is one of the defense of the kingdom, and other ways of handling things if the issue should become one of actions, let's say, outside the kingdom," said the U.S. official, who spoke to reporters after the Baker meeting with Fahd on condition he not be named.

At the same time, the official said, any large decision to go to war would still have to be approved by "the highest political levels" of the two governments. The official said the resolution of command-and-control questions between the United States and Saudi Arabia does not bind the other nations that have contributed to the multinational force and that further talks would have to be held with those countries.

Baker's meeting with Fahd tonight came at a critical juncture in the allied effort to drive Saddam from Kuwait. Officials said Baker wanted to get a first-hand account of how the Saudis would view armed conflict to liberate Kuwait, and Baker was joined in meetings earlier today with Saudi officials by Schwarzkopf.

Other senior State Department, Pentagon and White House officials involved with the crisis gathered here as well for meetings that also focused on other tactics to tighten the screws on Saddam, including new U.N. Security Council resolutions.

A Saudi official noted that so far, the formal mission of the 300,000-member multinational force remains to defend Saudi Arabia and that Bush and Fahd have not yet decided whether to declare it formally an offensive fighting force.

Officials did not explain how the new agreements would translate into specific guidelines for such problems as joint training excercises or military operations. But the American official said that "the authority for planning and approving" operations outside Saudi borders "will rest in a U.S. command."

The official said Baker and Fahd had discussed sending additional U.S. troops to the kingdom. The official said the Saudis have set no limit on the size of the American deployment, now at 200,000 troops. Secretary of Defense Richard B. Cheney recently suggested the Bush administration might send another 100,000 to join Operation Desert Shield.

In meetings today, Saudi officials vowed anew not to accept "partial solutions" to Iraq's invasion of Kuwait, such as a deal giving Saddam rights or ownership of some piece of

2936-3

nov. 6,
1990'
Wf

0021

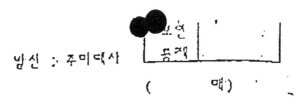
Kuwait, according to the U.S. official. The pledge follows a suggestion made recently by the Saudi defense minister that such a land swap might be a satisfactory way out of the crisis—a remark that infuriated some U.S. policy-makers in Washington.

Baker was expected to talk with Fahd about how long the anti-Iraq coalition could wait for the economic and political isolation of Saddam to have some effect. Bush has recently expressed impatience, saying he was fed up with mistreatment of American hostages in Iraq. But tonight the official said, "I think there is a general agreement that sanctions should be given time to work." The official said Baker is sounding out the alliance partners on how long they will wait.

Baker also held talks today with Saudis and the exiled ruler of Kuwait about possibly extending economic aid to front-line states—Turkey and Egypt—into next year if necessary. This was seen as another indication that some U.S. policy-makers believe the crisis may not be resolved by the end of this year.

Nov. 6, 1990
WP

2936-4

0022

관리 번호	ㅏ0-2376

원 본

외 무 부

종 별 : 지 급

번 호 : USW-5022

일 시 : 90 1108 1909

수 신 : 장관(미북,미안,중근동)

발 신 : 주 미 대사

제 목 : 걸프사태관련 미군증파 공식 발표

연:USW-4805,4931

1. 금 11.8. 부쉬 대통령은 백악관에서 행한 특별기자회견을 통해, 사우디 주둔 다국적군의 공격 능력을 충분히 확보키위해(TO ENSURE THAT THE COALITION HAS AN ADEQUATE OFFENSIVE OPTION) 금일부로 걸프 지역에 대한 미군증파를 시행한다고 공식발표하였는바, 부쉬 대통령발표 내용 및 질의응답 요지하기 보고함.(부쉬 대통령기자회견 내용 전문은 USW(F)-2973 FAX 편 송부)

가. 미국은 쿠웨이트로부터의 이락군의 무족건 전면철수, 쿠웨이트 합법정부의 북구등 지금까지 제시해온 걸프사태 관련 4 대 목표를 계속 견지해 왔음.

나. 현재 걸프지역 주둔 미군병력은 <u>23</u> 만에 달하는바, 미군과 사우디 주둔다국적군은 이락이 또다시 침략행위를 감행하는 경우 이를 방어하기에 충분한 능력을 보유하고 있음.

다. 사우디등 동맹국과의 협의를 거쳐, 전기 목표 달성을 위해 필요하게되는 경우 사우디 주둔 다국적군의 공격능력을 충분히 확보키 위해, 금일부로 걸프지역에 대한 미군 증파를 시행함.

라. 미국으로서는 물론 유엔 안보리 결의안에 따라 이락측이 쿠웨이트로부터 자진 철수함으로써 금번 사태가 평화적으로 해결되기를 희망함. 그러나 대이락 봉쇄 전략이 여의치못할 경우의 무력 사용 가능성은 상존함.(대이락 봉쇄 전략의 시행종료 시점에 대해서는 구체적 언급 회피)

마. 금번 미군 종파를 통해 미국이 얼마나 진지하게 전기 4 대 목표를 추구하고 있는지를 훗세인이 인식함으로써 정신을 차리게되기를 희망함.

바. 베이커 장관의 중동 지역 순방을 통해서도 금번 사태 해결에 관한 관련국간 결의를 재확인하였는바, 소련과도 현재 보조를 일치하고 있음.

미주국	장관	차관	1차보	2차보	미주국	중아국	정문국	청와대

2. 상기 부쉬 대통령기자회견에 이어 체니 국방장관도 백악관에서 기자들과질의응답을 가졌는바, 주요 언급 요지 하기 보고함.

(질의 응답 전문은 연호 USW(F)-2973 의 P.10-12 참조)

가. 당초 부터 걸프 지역 파견 미군 병력의 상한선은 정해진바 없었음.

나. 금번 증파병력의 구체적 규모는 밝힐수 없으나, 서독 및 미본토로부터 상당 규모의 육해공군 병력이 추가 부입될것이며, 이에 따라 예비군도 추가 동원될것임.

다. 금번 병력 추가 부입 작전은 금일 오전부터 기 시작되었음.

3. 한편 체니 국방장관 및 파웰 합참의장은 상기 백악관 기자 회견에 이어 국방부에서 공동 기자회견을 갖고 주로 금번 병력 추가 부입 작전의 세부 시행사항(부입 부대명등)에 관해 질의 응답을 가졌는바, USW(F)-2974 로 FAX 편송부한기자회견 전문 참고 바람.

4. 관찰 사항

가. 당지 언론등의 보도에 의하면 금번 추가 파병 규모는 최소 약 10 만명에 달할것으로 보인다하며, 여사한 병력의 이동에만도 최소 6-8 주가 소요될 것으로 예상되므로 미국이 대이락 공격 결정을 내리는 시점은 내년 1,2 월이될 가능성이 클것으로 본다 함.

나. 금일 부쉬 대통령의 기자 회견은 연호(USW-4805)로 기보고한 미군 증파설을 공식 확인한셈인바, 부쉬 대통령은 동 추가 파병 공식발표 시점을 중간 선거 직후로 잡음으로서 여사한 증파 추진이 선거 결과에 미칠 영향을 최소화 하려는 의도였던 것으로 보임.

다. 금번 증파되는 부대중에는 최신에 M1A1 탱크를 기본장비로 갖추고 있는제 1 기계화 보병 사단 및 각급 기갑부대가 포함되어 있는바, 미국으로서는 여사한 증파 작전을 통해 이락에 대한 압력을 점증시켜 나가는 한편, 대이락 경제봉쇄 전략의 대이락 전면 공격 전략으로의 전환 시점이 임박해 있다는 점을 이락측에 대해 강력히 암시함으로써 이락군의 자진 철수라는 평화적 해결책을 실현 시키려는 의도로 보임.

라. 특히, 금일 연설을 통해 증파 사실을 공식 발표했다는점은 물론 미군의걸프 지역파병목적이 대이락 공격에도 있다는 사실을 분명히 밝힌점이 주목되는바, 이로써 미국의 대이락 공격 가능성이 보다 더 가시화된것으로 평가됨(일부언론등에서는 훗세인 대통령이 자신의 정치적 사활에 민감한 현실주의자 이므로, 전쟁발발 일보직전에 이락측이 쿠웨이트로부터 철수함으로써 미국의 여사한 BRINKMANSHIP 이

PAGE 2

0024

소기의 성과를 거둘것이라는 낙관적 견해를 제시하고 있기도함.)

   (대사 박동진-차관)

   예고:90.12.31 일반

2. 주요 국제군사동향

   미, 중동파견 군사력 증원결정

   > 체니 미 국방장관은 11.8(현지시간)기자회견에서 부시
   > 대통령의 지시에 따라 현재 중동에 투입된 미군을 증원
   > 하기 위하여 지상군과 해군력을 대규모로 증파할것이며,
   > 이는 현파병 규모가 방어에는 충분하나 공세작전을
   > 수행하기에는 부족하기 때문에 내려진 결정이라고 밝혀
   > 군사작전에 의한 사태해결 가능성과함께 군사력에 의한
   > 미국의 대이락 압력이 더욱 강화될것임을 시사하였음.
   > (주미무관 보고)

   〈분석 및 평가〉

   ○ 체니 장관이 밝힌 증원부대 목록

      - 육 군
        · 독일주둔 제7군단 본부
        · 독일주둔 제1기갑사단
        · 독일주둔 제3기갑사단
        · 독일주둔 제2기갑사단예하 1개여단(제2기갑사단
          (-1)은 본토주둔)
        · 독일주둔 제2기갑사단 수색연대(독립연대)
        · 독일주둔 제2 전투지원단
        · 미 본토(캔사스 Fort Riely) 주둔 제1기계화
          보병사단

26 - 16   0026

352 걸프 사태 미국 동향 1

- 해병대
  . 제2해병 원정군(노스캐롤라이나,Camp Lejene)
  . 제5해병 원정여단(캘리포니아, Camp Pendleton)
  . 해군 사전배치선단(MPS,노포크)

- 해 군
  . 아메리카 항모 전투단
  . 레인저 항모전투단
  . 루즈벨트 항모전투단
  . 1개 전함 기동단
  . 제3상륙전단(캘리포니아, 샌디에고)

* 공군은 현재까지 특정부대를 선정하지 않았으나 필요시
  증원예정

o 이상의 전투력 증파외에도 체니장관은 미 육군과
  해병대의 전투예비군 동원령을 내릴것이라고 발표
  (11.6)한바 있으며

- 대상부대로는
  . 제48기계화 보병여단(조지아)
  . 제155 기갑여단(미시시피)
  . 제256 기계화 보병여단(루지애나)
  . 해병대 약 3,000명 등이며,

26 - 17

0027

- 이중 육군부대는 캘리포니아 사막지역에서중동적응
  훈련을 받은후 상황에 따라 중동투입 여부가 결정될
  것이나,

- 해병대 병력은 제5해병원정 여단에 편입되어 중동에
  파견될 것으로 알려졌음.

ㅇ 체니 장관은 이러한 부대증파 조치로 증가되는 병력의
  숫자와 구체적인 시기는 밝히기를 거부하였으나

- 지상군 7만여명, 해군 및 해병 3만여병등 증파규모는
  10만명을 상회할것으로 판단되며

- 중동도착 까지는 수주로 부터 수개월간이 걸릴것으로
  보임.

* 항공모함 2척은 성탄절 이전에 중동해역 도착예정.

ㅇ 독일 주둔 미군의 대규모 이동과 관련, 체니 장관은

- 소련과의 유럽재래전력 감축협상(CFE)진전에 따라
  독일 주둔 미군 5만여명의 감축이 이미 예정되어
  있었으며,

- 따라서 금번 조치는 단순히 철수예정부대의 이동
  배치로써,

- 이들 부대들은 현재의 편제장비를 그대로 보유하고
  중동에 투입될것이라고 밝혔음.

26 - 18

0028

o 이와같은 미측의 중동투입 군사력 증강조치는

- 현 중동사태를 조기 해결키 위한 미국의 대이락
  무력시위 효과와 함게

- 현재까지 중동에 투입된 경무장 지상군의 기갑전력
  부족을 보충함으로써 공격작전 감행시 예상되는
  막대한 미군사상자 발생을 방지하며,

- 항모전투단의 항공세력 보강으로 개전초 공중우세를
  달성하고 이락군의 준비된 진지 방어작전을 일시에
  무력화 시키기 위한 전술적 조치로 평가되고있음.

o 사실 사우디 현지의 미군지휘부는 최근,

- 시간이 경과함에 따라 이락군이 지뢰와 철조망으로
  보강된 강력한 방어진지를 구축하였으며, 방어진지
  에 다량의 네이팜 및 유류를 확보하여 공격부대에
  대하여 화공전을 기도하고 있을뿐 아니라,

- 미공군기에 의한 1-2일간의 폭격으로는 이락군의
  전방 방어진지 무력화가 곤란하므로써 지상작전의
  조기병행시 대량의 미군인명 손실이 우려된다고
  판단하고 있음.

- 따라서 미군지휘부는 지금까지 공중폭격에 중점을
  두고 지상작전 을 동시 병행하는 속전속결 작전
  방안을 구상하여 왔으나

26 - 19

0029

- 수일간의 대규모 공중폭격으로 이락군의 전방방어
  진지를 무력화 한후 강력한 기갑부대에 의한 지상
  공격으로 방어진지를 완전 극복하는 방안이 강구
  되고 있음.("호너" 현지 공군사령관 기자회견)

o 한편, 사우디 주둔 다국적 군사력의 지휘권 문제와
  관련한 질문에 대해 체니장관은,

- 과거보다 많이 향상되었으며 장차 더 발전할것이라고
  답변하므로써

- 최근 베이커 국무장관의 사우디 방문시 군사지휘권에
  대한 사우디측과의 합의로 상당한 진전이 있었음에도
  불구하고 아직도 많은 부분에서 세부합의가 필요함을
  시사 하였음.

o 베이커 국무장관은 11,5 사우디 젯다에서 "파드"사우디
  국왕을 예방하고 군사지휘권에 대한 기본적 합의를
  이룩하였는바, 주요내용은 다음과 같음.

- 중동에서의 군사력 사용은 미국과 사우디 정부의 최고
  책임자로 부터 승인을 받아야함.

- 사우디군과 아랍 및 다국적 군사력은 사우디군 총사
  령관(KHALID BIN SULTAN 중장)이, 미 군사력은 미
  중앙사령관이 지휘,

26 - 20

0030

- 사우디 국경밖(이락,쿠웨이트)에서의 작전시 미군은
  미군사령관의 지휘.

- 다국적 군사력 지휘시는 당사국과 직접 대화와 협상을
  가져야 하며 미국과 사우디간 합의가 군사력에 영향을
  미치지 못함.

ㅇ 위와같은 양국 군사지휘권에 대한 합의로 대이락 군사
  행동시의 주요 장애요인이 해소된것으로 보이나,원활한
  군사작전을 위해서는 보다 구체적인 합의가 필요할것으로
  평가되고 있음.

26 - 21

0031

90. 11. 13

아랍圈 페灣평화해결 外交활발

美해병 사우디서 수일내 上陸훈련

美共和의원들 武力사용승인 특별의회 소집촉구

【위싱턴·니코시아·모스크바 AP·로이터連合】 美國의 페르시아灣 군이 질질 승인했으며 국방부 또 한 쿠웨이트접경부근의 사우디해안에서 수일내에 수천명의 美해병이 상륙공격훈련을 은 이날 페灣사태가 폭발점에 가까워지고 있다고 경고하면서 이라크의 쿠웨이트철수를 거듭 촉구했으며 아랍-페灣위기사태를 평화적으로 해결하기 위해 의회의 절차가 필요하다고 말했다.

공화당소속 상원 의원들과 중진의원들이 13일 조지부 시대통령에게 특별의 회를 소집해 해군예비역의 추가소집 과 美해병이 상륙공격훈련을 실시한다고 발표함으로써 페灣에서의 군사행동과 관련, 美정부와 의회의 의견이 엇 갈리고 있다.

로버트 돌 공화당 상원 원내총무와 상원 공화당 제2 인자인 외교위원 리처드 루가 의원은 美國이 의회에 정식 선전포고를 요청해야 한다는 것을 세계에 과시하기 위해 의회의 절차가 필요하다고 말했다.

한편 피트 윌리엄스 美국 방부 대변인은 도널드 애트 우드 美국방부 부장관이 지난 9일 해군예비역의 소집 상한선을 기존의 6천3백명에서 1만명으로 늘릴 수 있도록 조치했다고 전했으며 陸軍 공군 등의 다른 예비役들에도 이와 유사한 추가 소집이 승인이 있어야 할 것 이라고 말했다.

윌리엄스 대변인은 또 페灣에 정박중인 군함에서 최소 한 2천명의 해병대원들이 이라크가 급파되는 무기의 사정거리내에서 실시된 다고 발표했다.

윌리엄스 대변인은 또 상륙훈련의 구체적인 시기 및 장소는 이번주중 추후에 발표될 것이라고 말했으나 익 명을 요구한 국방부의 한 관계자는 쿠웨이트와의 국경으로부터 불과 16km 떨어진 사우디해안에서 대부분의 훈련이 실시된다고 밝혔다.

美國의 이같은 움직임과는 달리 이라크는 페르시아灣 위기를 담보기 위한 아랍 정 상회담 개최문제를 논의하기 위해 13일 모로코 튀니지 및 리비아에 특사를 파견하는 편 후스니 무바라크 이집트 대통령이 리비아 국가원수 무아마르 카다피와 회담을 갖기 위해 리비아를 방문하는 등 아 랍진도자들의 페灣사태를 평화적 해결을 위해 활발한 외 교활동을 전개하고 있다.

이같은 아랍권의 움직임에 맞추어 소련외무부의 알렉산 데르 벨로노고프차관과 블라 디미르 페트로브스키 차관이 13일 페르시아灣 위기사태를 논의하기 위해 中東과 北아 프리카를 1주일 일정으로 모스 크바를 떠났다고 정부기관지 이즈베스티야紙가 보도했다.

한편 이라크의 쿠웨이트철 수를 촉구하면서 아랍國 장이 명확히 밝혀지지 않 고 있기 때문에 정부정책에 대한 국민의 지지가 감소되 고 있다면서 이라크를 응징하려는 政策에 한마음으로 뭉쳐 있어야 한다고 부시대통령이 말했다.

투거 의원은 TV프로에서 페灣사태에 대한 美의회의 입 장이 명확하게 밝혀지지 않 고 있는데 있어 의회의 지지선 언을 부시대통령이 얻어야 한다고 말했다.

페灣開戰 아직 때가 아니다

제임스 레스턴 칼럼

〈뉴욕타임스=本社特約〉

歷史는 「참을성없는 戰士」 편든적 한번도 없어

이라크封鎖로 후세인 목죄기 충분

0033

페르시아만 사태 무력 사용 문제

(11.13자 NYT지 기사 요약)

90.11.14.

북 미 과

1. 군사적 대치 상황 장기화에 따른 정책 변화 가능성 점증

   o 최근 미 행정부의 폐만사태 무력 해결 가능성 시사에 대한 비판 여론이
     대두되고 있음.
     - 대이라크 경제 제재조치 계속 효과를 기다리지 않는 조급한 태도라 비판
       * 부쉬 대통령은 15만명의 추가 파견을 통해 91년초까지 폐만 주둔
         병력 수준을 40만까지 증강하고 부대 순환 배치 계획도 취소

   o 사우디내 대규모 미군의 장기 주둔은 아랍 민족주의 운동의 표적이 되어
     보수적인 사우디 사회의 불안 요소로 작용할 가능성에 대한 우려도 점증
     되고 있음.

   o 사태 장기화시 미군의 무력 사용 가능 시점 상실 가능성도 지적되고 있음.
     - 뜨거운 하절기보다는 동절기 작전 수행이 용이

2. 정책 변화에 대한 비판 대두

   o 넌 상원 군사위원장(민, GA), 다니엘 모이니헌 상원의원(민, NY)등은
     대이라크 경제제재 조치의 효과를 꾸준히 기다리지 못하는 행정부의
     조급한 태도를 비난하기 시작했음
     - 무력 사용시 미군측 피해는 예상보다 클 것임을 지적

0034

o 루가 상원의원(공, Ind.)은 11.13(화) 부쉬 대통령에게 미의회를 소집
  대이라크 전쟁 선포 문제를 토의토록 권고 예정이라 함.
  - 공화당 지도부 및 동료 공화의원 지지 획득 실패

3. 백악관 양대 정책 계속 추진 강조

o 피츠워터 백악관 대변인을 기존 경제 제재조치 계속, U.N. 결의 존중,
  대의회 협의 계속등 기존 정책 무변화를 강조함.
  - 대규모 미군 증파등 사태해결 가속화 노력 해명에는 언급 회피

4. 대규모 미군의 대 사우디 증파 의미

o 91년초까지 15만을 증파, 사우디 주둔 미군 병력이 40만에 달한다고 하는
  사실은 페만사태 처리에 관한 미 행정부 정책 변화의 이정표가 될 것이며
  아래 사항을 전제로함.
  - 대이라크 경제제재 조치로만은 이라크의 쿠웨이트 철수 실현은 기대난
  - 미측은 이러한 이라크 태도를 수수방관할 수 없다는 입장

0035

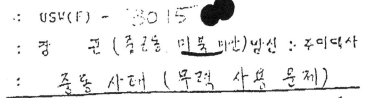

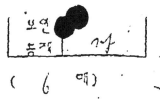

When to Threaten Iraq?

Only Prospect of Early War Might Induce Hussein to Leave Kuwait, Officials Believe

By MICHAEL R. GORDON

Special to The New York Times

WASHINGTON, Nov. 12 — To critics who ask why the United States should not wait a year or more to see if economic sanctions force Iraq to withdraw from Kuwait, Administration officials say they have valid reasons for threatening a war this winter.

News Analysis

President Bush's decision last week to nearly double the American military force in the Persian Gulf and to cancel troop-rotation plans, they say, was based on the assumption that only the threat of early war can persuade President Saddam Hussein of Iraq to withdraw his forces from Kuwait.

In addition, said a senior Administration official who asked not to be identified, the White House was worried that keeping a large number of American soldiers in the Persian Gulf region for a prolonged period might provide a political target for Arab nationalists and contribute to the destabilization of Saudi society.

Dulling the Fighting Spirit

American soldiers might also lose their fighting edge if the crisis went on too long and some specialists note that the coming winter months are better fighting weather than the broiling summer.

In the end, the President can turn away from a military confrontation and look for other ways to end the crisis. His aides say Mr. Bush has not yet made a decision whether to go to war. But they acknowledge that it will be difficult to sustain the large deployment of American forces in the Persian Gulf for a prolonged period and would be politically embarrassing to withdraw them without having achieved the Administration's objectives.

Mr. Bush's troop decision has led to the first serious challenge to his policy from some leaders in the political mainstream, like Senator Sam Nunn, Democrat of Georgia and chairman of the Armed Services Committee. They say that the White House is moving too quickly to bring the crisis to a turning point and to move toward the use of force.

Senator Daniel Patrick Moynihan, Democrat of New York, asserted today that the Bush Administration was poised to go to war without either a genuine effort to see if the economic sanctions would be effective or to provide a thorough explanation to the American public.

"Why not stay the course we started?" Senator Moynihan asked. "If ever a blockade might work, it's here."

Mr. Bush is "not preparing Americans for what's happening," Senator Moynihan declared.

Lugar Moving on His Own

Senator Richard G. Lugar of Indiana, senior Republican on the Foreign Relations Committee, is expected to recommend on Tuesday that President Bush call Congress back into session to debate a declaration of war, according to an official familiar with the Senator's thinking. Mr. Lugar has scheduled a news conference for Tuesday morning, but is not among the bipartisan Congressional leadership group that will be meeting with President Bush to discuss the Persian Gulf.

The official said that Mr. Lugar was acting on his own and had not sought a consensus of Republican leaders.

Senator Nunn, reflecting the wariness of some American military commanders, says that war in the Persian Gulf would be bloodier than Bush Ad-

Continued on Page A14, Column 3

ministration policy makers seem to anticipate and that economic sanctions may yet work, dispensing with the need to put American servicemen and women at risk.

Seeking to contain the growing debate, the White House spokesman, Marlin Fitzwater, said today: "We don't want to go to war. President Bush will say the same things these Congressmen are saying — be cautious, follow the policy, support the U.N. resolutions, consult with Congress."

But Mr. Fitzwater's statements, while apparently aimed at quieting the critics, did not provide a public explanation for the Administration's speeded-up timetable for resolving the gulf crisis.

A senior Administration official in private did not hesitate to explain that the White House has put its political and military campaign to evict Iraqi troops from Kuwait on a fast track.

How Vulnerable?

"There is some doubt as to how long we keep our forces there. This is not Germany," the official said, suggesting that the longer American forces remain in Saudi Arabia, the greater the possibility that the foreign presence might undermine the conservative traditions of Saudi society and even lead to instability.

He said the presence of large numbers of American troops in Saudi Arabia "is a point of vulnerability" for the Saudi leadership that Iraq has tried to exploit. "How much of a vulnerability we do not know," he added.

The senior Administration official also said that "American troops are out there in the most forbidding terrain and may lose their edge," a concern that must be balanced by the apparent desire of some senior military commanders to avoid a rush to war.

The senior official argued further that Eastern Europe nations and other countries were being seriously hurt by the oil-price rises, adding to the need to resolve the gulf crisis soon.

Finally, the official explained, the White House was concerned that Mr. Hussein was simply not taking the United States seriously because Iraq had continued to build up its forces in Kuwait and was continuing to plunder

Nov. 13, 1990
NYT

0036

3015-1

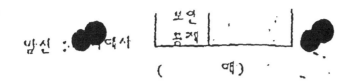
the country. Mr. Hussein, this official said, was still trying to drive a wedge through the alliance and appeared to believe that time is on his side.

Achieving the New Order

Critics have raised other important questions:

Is the "new world order" that Mr. Bush seeks best established by a decisive defeat of the invading Iraqi forces at the hands of the American military, or by waiting to see if economic sanctions take their toll?

Is the threat of war this winter a shrewd application of shock therapy against a recalcitrant Saddam Hussein, or does it reflect a lack of confidence in the multinational coalition to hang together in its opposition to Iraq's taking of Kuwait?

The developing debate is a far cry from August, when the Bush Administration decided to dispatch American forces to Saudi Arabia to defend the West's oil supply against an Iraqi attack. The stated mission of the American military at that time was to "deter and defend," a mission that has since been accomplished, and the Administration received broad backing from members of both parties.

And Now, a Milestone

President Bush also stated at the time that Iraq's invasion of Kuwait would not stand, and pointedly noted that no military options had been excluded. But the Administration emphasized that it was relying primarily on worldwide economic sanctions to persuade Mr. Hussein to withdraw from Kuwait. Echoing this line, Administration officials repeatedly argued that time was on Washington's side.

President Bush's decision to send an additional 150,000 troops to the gulf area bringing the total to nearly 400,000 by early next year, marked a milestone in the Administration's handling of the gulf crisis because it appeared to be based on the calculation that either economic sanctions would not force Mr. Hussein to withdraw or that Washington could not afford to wait to see if they did.

Making a comprehensive public case for its decision to accelerate the timetable for resolution of the crisis may not be easy for the White House, which clearly does not want to highlight concerns it may have over the endurance of the multinational coalition or Saudi sensitivities to a long-term American troop presence there.

Nov. 13, 1990
NYT

3015-2

0037

Milton Viorst

War and Consequences

It would be ironic if, by the law of unintended consequences, the Gulf crisis ends where it began—with revolutionary Iran, the most powerful state in the Middle East, threatening Arabs and Israelis alike with its militant pietism.

Indeed, once the genies of war are let loose, it is possible to imagine a range of unintended consequences: the overthrow of moderate regimes in Egypt and Jordan by Islamic radicals, multiplying the vulnerability of Israel; the collapse of the fragile sheikdoms of the Gulf, sending the price of oil soaring for the next decade; a quixotic uprising of Kurds, shaking the regimes not just in Iraq but in Syria, Turkey and Iran.

Out of the mix of possible consequences, however, the greatest likelihood is an abrupt end to the equilibrium on the Iraq-Iran border, which was Saddam Hussein's gift—Gen. H. Norman Schwartzkopf, U.S. commander in the Gulf, said as much in a recent interview in The New York Times—to international stability.

A decade ago, the Middle East was in serious jeopardy from the legions of the Ayatollah Khomeini, bent on spreading their Shiite fundamentalist faith into the Arab world. Iraq's Shiites, a majority of the population, were tipping to their side. So were strong Shiite minorities in Saudi Arabia and Kuwait.

Historians may debate whether Saddam committed gratuitous aggression or was provoked into initiating war, but the fact is that he took on Khomeini, fused his own deeply heterogeneous people into a nation with a single purpose and fought the fundamentalist revolution to a dead halt.

The Iraqis did not wage a pretty war. Outnumbered three to one in population, they enjoyed greater firepower and used poison gas to win battles when they had to, though military experts generally agree that gas was not the key to their ultimate victory. Mostly, they won by digging in and inflicting heavier losses than they took, going on the offensive only when the Iranians were badly weakened by the attrition of their manpower.

It seemed obvious as the war approached an end that Iraq's battle-hardened army of a million men was likely to be a loose cannon in the region once it had no enemy. Rather wisely, the United States made serious efforts at that juncture to overcome the animosity that had long marked its relations and to reach a rapprochement that might contain a restless Iraq.

But dealing with a brutal, dictatorial regime that is insensitive to international public opinion was not easy. Critics glibly assert that the State Department did too much to accommodate Saddam Hussein. The real question, I believe, was whether we did enough to bring him into a system of international order.

We know Saddam is an unsophisticated, insular man who yearns for respect from other world leaders. He believed he had earned it by his triumph over Iran, and perhaps he had. Would it have made a difference if he had been invited to Washington or Paris to take a few bows? I suspect it would, but after he gassed his own Kurds insurgents, but Iraqi citizens—no Western head of state could have received him on an official visit.

And so the scenario of the loose cannon came to pass.

It alighted on Kuwait, for reasons that also came out of the war. Throughout eight years of bloody fighting, the Kuwaitis, like the Saudis, looked on—as they are looking on now while others prepare to fight for them. They supported Iraq with money, which seemed only reasonable; but unlike the Saudis, they demanded full repayment, with interest. Expecting the debt to be forgiven, the Iraqis were stunned, and the dispute became increasingly acerbic until it exploded on Aug. 2 with the invasion.

It is no defense of that invasion to say that President Bush must now decide whether it is in America's interest to settle up with Iraq or make war—and that is where the law of unintended consequences comes in. Do the president's advisers really believe, even if we win quickly and with minimal losses, that our Army would be able to pack up and come home?

It would take a monumental effort to put the Humpty-Dumpty of the Middle East back together, and the United States—with its money and its men—would be stuck with doing it.

Iran would be at the top of the agenda. It is naive to think that the revolution, though currently demoralized, has outgrown expansionism. Khomeini, before he died, made clear his belief that the cease-fire was temporary. If we now destroy Iraq, we would still have to re-create it as a military power—unless we are prepared ourselves to remain for years on the Euphrates.

What makes far greater sense is for us to figure out what kind of order we can live with in the Middle East—taking into account not just Kuwait but arms and oil prices, and maybe even the Israeli-Palestinian dispute. Then we ought to get on with negotiations, because even a victorious war would bring no end of surprises, unpredictable in nature but surely unpleasant.

Milton Viorst, a Washington writer, covers the Middle East for The New Yorker.

Nov. 13, 1990
NYT

3015-4

0038

결전 시기의 임박

(11.13.자 CSM 지 기사 요약)

90. 11. 14.
북 미 과

o 부쉬 부통령의 대규모 미군 증파 지시로 페만 주둔 미군의 공세 개시를 위한
  카운트 다운이 시작됨.

  - 대규모 미군의 전비 태세를 장기간 유지시키기는 곤란

o 무력이 사용될 경우 신속히 사용되어야 함.

  - Baker 장관의 중동 및 유럽 우방국 순방은 이를 위한 협의 목적

  - 무력 사용에 제일 미온적이었던 중국측도 대이라크 설득 작업에 협조

    · 11.12. 전기침 외상 이라크 방문시 동 메세지 전달

o 부쉬 대통령의 페만 주둔 미군 증파 지시는 놀라운 사실은 아님.

  - 15만에서 20만 정도의 병력 증파

    · 3½ 중무장 육군 사단, 해병 원정대, 3대의 항공 모함 전단 및 전투기
      대대등

o 병력 증파에 따라 대규모 병력이 장기간 전비 태세만을 유지할 수 없게되는
  결과를 초래함.

  - 기존 파병 병력의 순환 배치 계획도 보류되어 사기 유지에 문제점 대두

  - 사막 배치 대규모 병력에 대한 보급도 큰 문제

  - 해군의 경우, 6대의 항공 모함 전단 배치

o 이러한 병력 증파는 후세인에게 쿠웨이트로부터 철수케 하기 위해 무력
  사용을 심각히 고려중이라는 것을 인식케 해야 함.

  - 한편 병력 증파가 완료되는 향후 6주간은 무력 사용이 없을 것이라는
    안도감을 후세인에 줄 우려

  - 이라크측이 동 조치에 위협을 받고 있다는 증후 무

0035

o 후세인은 자신의 정치적 생존을 최대 목표로 삼고 있어 전쟁을 원치 않고
  있다는 분석도 가능함.

  - 주쿠웨이트 미국 대사관 방치 사실등 사태 발발 이후 대미 도발 자제
    태도를 지적

o 11.13자 NYT지는 '전쟁과 그 결과' 제하 칼럼을 통해 미국이 무력 사용을 통해
  이라크를 궤멸시킬 경우 이란을 중동 지역내 최강국가로 남게해 더욱 복잡한
  고민을 안게될 것이라는 우려를 표시함.

  - 이라크와의 전쟁 결과 혁명이란 정부와의 대결이라는 원치 않는 결과로 원점
    회귀할 가능성 지적

Clock Ticks Away on Standoff

Increased military buildup signals troops will have to be used quickly, analysts say

By Peter Grier
Staff writer of The Christian Science Monitor

═══ WASHINGTON ═══

THE countdown toward a United States military offensive in the Persian Gulf appears to have begun.

By ordering a massive deployment of yet more American troops to the Gulf, President Bush has pushed the button on a timer, say military analysts. When the buildup is completed in several months, US forces in the region will be so large that it will be difficult to sustain them at full readiness for long.

If they are to be used, they will then have to be used quickly. Secretary of State James Baker III's blitz tour of the Middle East and Europe last week appears to have been designed to convey the message that the clock is now running – both to US allies, and to Iraq's Saddam Hussein.

"We must heighten the pressure further ... by laying the foundations for the use of force," Secretary Baker said before leaving his last stop, Paris.

Despite reports that France, for one, is hesitant about its troops joining the US in an anti-Saddam offensive, Baker said his tour found no serious difference of opinion on implementing UN resolutions calling for Iraq to leave Kuwait.

"There is no question with respect to the unity of the coalition," he said.

Even China, the member of the UN Security Council thought most reluctant to resort to force, seems to be telling Saddam that unless he backs off there is no hope of peace. Chinese Prime Minister Qian Qichen delivered that message to the Iraqi leader personally during a Monday visit to Baghdad.

Mr. Qichen and Saddam supporter

Palestine Liberation Organization leader Yasser Arafat said they backed King Hassan of Morocco's call for an emergency Arab summit to avert war in the Gulf. But Iraq rejected the proposed summit Sunday.

The members of the anti-Saddam coalition don't all agree, however, about the effect so far of economic sanctions. "There are some differences of opinion with respect to which sanctions are already working and are having a bite," Baker said.

President Bush's announcement last week that more US forces will be sent to the Gulf came as no surprise. Pentagon officials had been hinting for days that such an action would be forthcoming, with the only questions being how many troops would be sent, and if units now in the Gulf would be replaced and rotated back home.

The new deployment will result in the addition of from 150,000 to 200,000 US personnel to those already in the Gulf region, approximately doubling US military strength. Major units to be sent include three and a half heavy Army divisions, an additional Marine expeditionary force, three more aircraft carriers, and an undisclosed number of Air Force fighter and attack jets.

The resulting concentration of force will be too large to sit and wait for a lengthy period, according to military analysts. Two main facts point to this conclusion. One is Secretary of Defense Richard Cheney's admission that units that were the first to arrive in Saudi Arabia will, in fact, not be sent home when the reinforcements arrive.

Military officials have said such a rotational policy is important to maintaining morale – if US troops are to be sitting and waiting for a long time.

Secondly, the sheer logistics of supporting such a force will be difficult in the Saudi desert. Analysts point in particular to the Navy's situation. When the newly deployed ships arrive, there will be six US carrier task forces in the

region, an almost unprecedented concentration of naval power in the post-Vietnam era.

Operations at sea, however, are very demanding of Navy pilots and crew, and drink up massive amounts of jet fuel.

"You can't maintain six aircraft carriers there for long," says Greg Weaver, a senior military analyst at the SAIC Corporation.

US officials maintain that the new deployments should show Saddam that the United States is serious when it says it will use force to oust him from Kuwait. In announcing the deployment, the word "offensive" passed Mr. Bush's lips for the first time.

The flip side of the deployment announcement, however, is that Saddam Hussein probably believes that no military action will occur until the new forces are in place, which will take six weeks at least. He has a breathing space in which to continue hunkering down and contemplating his next move.

"This indicates to Saddam he has considerable time," says Raymond Tanter, a political science professor at the University of Michigan who served on the National Security Council under President Reagan.

To this point the Iraqi leader has shown little indication that the US-led military buildup in the Gulf is changing his mind about his occupation of Kuwait, and Professor Tanter believes that he won't be coerced into giving up his gains.

"I think he thinks the US is not willing to stay the course," he says.

Other analysts believe he may be biding his time before concessions. "I don't think this man wants war," says a Pentagon Middle East expert who is part of a US government task force analyzing the Gulf situation.

"He has not challenged us anywhere," says the expert, pointing to such potential flashpoints as the embattled US Embassy in

Nov. 13, 1990 CSM

0041

미국의 군사행동 지연 사유

(11.13.자 WSJ 지 기사 요약)

90. 11. 14
북 미 과

o 부쉬 대통령이 대이라크 전쟁을 연기하는 데는 여러 이유가 있음.

　- 추가적인 군비 증강을 위한 기간 필요

　- 우방국의 전쟁 수행을 위한 국민들의 지지 확보

　- 이라크측 보급 악화로 인한 사태의 평화적 해결 가능성 기대

o 또한 행동지연에 따른 부작용도 증대되고 있음.

　- 무력 사용을 통한 사태 해결에 대한 국민 열기 분산 조짐 대두

　　· 넌, 모이니헌 상원의원은 무력사용 가능성에 우려 표시

o 부쉬 대통령은 대규모 추가 파병 방침 발표와 동시에 무력 사용 시점의
　몇달 연기를 시사함.

　- 연기의 직접적 사유는 추가 병력 배치에 소요되는 기간이나 또다른 이유는
　　우방국들과의 공동 보조를 맞추는데 있음.

o 미 고위관리들도 이라크측이 무력 사용 가능성에 위협을 받지 않고 있음을
　인정하나 경제 제재 조치의 효과는 일부 군수 및 산업 분야에서 나타나고
　있음.

　- 헬기용 건전지등 부족 상황 시현

　- 이라크 군부내 불만 고조에 대한 정보 보고도 산건

o 이라크, 쿠웨이트산 원유 공급 중단에 따른 원유 수급 불균형 상태는 여타
　산유국 증산으로 해소되어 가고 있어 원유 시장 질서 회복을 위한 사태의
　조기 해결 필요성을 감소케 함.

0042

o 91.3.의 라마단 및 91.6. 성지 방문 시기등도 미 전략 수립의 참고 사항임.
  - 명년초까지는 선택을 위한 충분한 시간 보유

o 무력 사용을 위한 최적기 선택은 매우 어려운 작업이기도 함.
  - 사태 계속에 따른 국내 불만 점증, 이라크 억류 미국인 인질 및 외교관
    들의 고생 기간 장기화등이 부정적으로 작용 예상
  - 이라크측의 화학무기 및 핵무기 증강 기간 부여 가능성에 대한 우려
  - 동 기간중 이라크측은 서방측 결속 와해를 위해서도 계속 노력 경주할
    것으로 예상됨.

o 영국, 사우디등이 무력 사용에 적극적이며 이집트, 시리아등은 즉각적인
  무력 사용에는 미온적 태도를 보이고 있음.
  - 프랑스는 무력 사용을 위한 별도의 UN 결의를 전제 조건으로 주장
  - 소련도 UN 결의 필요 주장과 함께 외교적 해결 노력 추가 경주 필요성
    강조

0043

Bush Has Reasons to Put Off Action in the Gulf But the Delay May Further Weaken His Position

By Gerald F. Seib
Staff Reporter of The Wall Street Journal.

WASHINGTON — President Bush has compelling reasons to delay before unleashing a war with Iraq—reasons ranging from the need for a further military buildup to allies' need to build public support for war in their own countries to Iraq's worsening logistical problems.

But waiting also carries a huge risk for Mr. Bush. At home in the U.S., all the momentum in public sentiment is moving away from a desire for war, a trend that will accelerate unless Mr. Bush somehow moves to reverse it. Yesterday, Sen. Daniel Moynihan (D., N.Y.) expressed misgivings about a move toward war, warning that if Mr. Bush isn't careful, his presidency could "die in the Arabian desert."

Sen. Moynihan joins other prominent Democrats such as Sen. Sam Nunn of Georgia who have expressed misgivings about war, and some Republicans are growing more uneasy as well.

Mr. Bush signaled two things last week: He is building up a military force explicitly designed to blast Iraqi troops out of Kuwait, but he also is inclined to wait weeks or perhaps months before pulling the trigger.

The immediate reason for the delay, of course, is that weeks will be needed for some 120,000 additional U.S. ground troops and thousands more sailors Mr. Bush is dispatching to reach the Persian Gulf. But that is only one factor in answering the agonizing question of whose side time is on in the showdown with Iraq.

A quick turn to war now could easily splinter the international coalition opposing Iraq, which is going to be buffeted by political and diplomatic strains in coming weeks even if there isn't any fighting. Some allies are telling the U.S. they need time to convince their people there isn't any alternative to war, some insist that a United Nations resolution authorizing force be passed first, and none is sure exactly who would control troops from the various countries in hostilities. "You've got slow erosion [of the coalition] sitting tight," says former defense secretary, James Schlesinger. "You've got rapid disintegration if you turn to unilateral war."

Just yesterday, Egypt's President Hosni Mubarak underscored the delicate task the U.S. faces in meeting all the desires of its coalition partners in planning any military strike. Mr. Mubarak was quoted in an Egyptian newspaper as saying that Egyptian troops would be willing to enter Kuwait as "peacekeeping" forces but wouldn't drive into Iraq itself.

In addition, senior U.S. officials now

On Duty
Additional U.S. active duty forces being sent to Persian Gulf

ARMY
1st Armored Division, Ansbach, Germany

2nd Armored Division, Garlstedt, Germany

2nd Armored Cavalry Regiment, Nuremberg, Germany

3rd Armored Division, Frankfurt, Germany

2nd Corps Support Command, Stuttgart, Germany

1st Infantry Division, Fort Riley, Kansas

VII Corps Headquarters, Stuttgart, Germany

NAVY
Aircraft carriers USS Theodore Roosevelt, USS America and USS Ranger, with escorts

Battleship USS Missouri, with escorts

Amphibious Group Three, San Diego

MARINES
2nd Marine Expeditionary Force, Camp Lejeune, North Carolina

5th Marine Expeditionary Brigade, Camp Pendelton, California

Maritime Prepositioning Ship Squadron 1, Norfolk, Virginia

Source: Defense Department

candidly admit that Iraq's Saddam Hussein so far hasn't taken seriously the threat of war. Now, some time will have to pass to judge whether the addition of tens of thousands of fresh U.S. troops will be sufficient to sober the Iraqi leader into backing out of Kuwait.

Beyond that, while the delay so far has given Iraqi troops more time to dig into Kuwait, there are new indications that time is working against the Iraqi forces in some ways.

Economic sanctions, while they clearly aren't starving Iraq or grinding it to a halt, appear to be pinching in sensitive military and industrial areas. The Pentagon assumes that Iraq's supply of military spare parts, lubricants and other essential materials is getting more precarious. One senior U.S. official notes, for instance, that some Iraqi helicopters need special batteries available only from U.S. manufacturers—batteries that aren't reaching Iraq because of the U.N. trade embargo.

U.S. intelligence officials also say that new signs of dissent within the Iraqi military are emerging in interviews with Iraqi officers and soldiers. Pentagon officials

point to evidence of recent high-level military demotions and shake-ups.

In addition, intercepted Iraqi communications "show there is lots of uncertainty and even some disputes inside the military about how to proceed," says one senior Pentagon planner.

Equally important, U.S. officials are relieved that increased oil production in other countries appears to have more than made up for the oil exports lost to the world by the embargo on Iraqi and Kuwaiti oil. That relieves pressure the Bush administration once felt to resolve the showdown with Iraq simply to restore order to the oil market.

The Islamic calendar also is increasingly going to play a role in American planning. The U.S. and its Arab allies clearly would like to resolve the confrontation with Iraq before the Islamic holy month of Ramadan, which begins in March, and the time of the annual Islamic pilgrimage to the holy sites in Saudi Arabia in June.

That suggests the U.S. might have good reasons to wait until early next year to start a military operation, but not much longer than that. All told, "we have arguably five months or so to play with to get this resolved," says Barry Rubin, an analyst at the Washington Institute for Near East Policy. "So we have some time."

Of course, the question of whose side time is on in the showdown with Iraq has been agonizingly difficult to resolve throughout the three-month Iraqi crisis, and the answer remains far from clear. There are also some powerful forces creating pressure for a quick military strike, including the prospect of increasing uneasiness in Mr. Bush's own back yard the

Nov. 13, 1990

WSJ

3015-5

0044

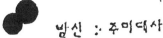
longer the delay continues.

Iraq's systematic dismantling of Kuwait, the growing fear of mistreatment of U.S. hostages and the plight of U.S. diplomats holed up in the embassy in Kuwait City all are factors that suggest time isn't on Mr. Bush's side.

In addition, there are continuing fears that a delay only gives Saddam Hussein's regime more time to build up its chemical and nuclear-weapons programs. Certainly, Iraq will use any delay in military action to probe for fissures in the international coalition by hinting at willingness to compromise, perhaps by explicitly offering to withdraw from just part of Kuwait.

Most important, a delay creates increased opportunity for criticism and second-guessing inside the U.S., fraying the initial bipartisan support for Mr. Bush. In just the week since the Nov. 6 election, Democrats have grown more vocal in questioning the wisdom of turning to war on behalf of Kuwait and in insisting that Congress be asked to approve any offensive action in advance.

Mr. Bush, who isn't good at swaying U.S. public opinion with personal appeals, risks seeing political and public backing for the military option evaporate. The administration then may have to hope that domestic skeptics will be swayed when more time has passed and it's clear that economic and diplomatic pressure won't budge Iraq.

It's also possible that time also could push America's international partners toward war rather than away from it. Among these partners, Britain is the most willing to turn to war quickly, with Saudi Arabia, Egypt and Syria somewhat less eager for immediate action. France insists that a new U.N. resolution authorizing action be passed first. And the Soviet Union, which the U.S. would like to bless any military move, also has favored a U.N. resolution and more time for diplomacy.

The unease with the war option may change, though, if more time passes without progress. "Internationally, there's still a lot of doubt and questioning about the use of military force," says Mr. Rubin. But, he adds, "as time goes by and the sanctions neither produce an Iraqi retreat nor Iraqi flexibility, we have seen a tendency of these countries to be more willing to support military action."

—*Andy Pasztor contributed to this article.*

Nov. 13, 1990
WSJ

3015-6

"부쉬 대통령의 실책"

(90.11.13.자 N.Y.T. 게재 A.M.Rosenthal 기고문 요약)

o 부쉬 대통령은 페만 사태 초기, 이라크 제재 조치 필요성에 대한 <u>명확한</u>
<u>이유를 제시하지 못하므로써 중대한 실책을 범함.</u>

   - 미군 파견 및 전세계적 차원의 대이라크 금수 조치의 가장 <u>중요한 이유</u>는
     수백만의 인명 살상과 파괴를 자행할 <u>사담 후세인을 저지하기 위한 것임.</u>

   - 그러나 부쉬 대통령이 상기 이유를 제시하지 못하므로써 사우디 사막에서
     미군이 전투를 직면하고 있는 현시점에서 미군 <u>파병 이유에 대한 논란</u>이
     야기되고 있음.

o 부쉬 대통령이 제시한 목표는 미국민들에게 <u>만족스러운 것이 아니었던 바</u>
  이유는 다음과 같음.

   - 이라크의 침략 격퇴 : 과거 중국의 티벳트 침략, 소련의 동구 침략,
                        아랍 국가간 침략등의 경우 미국은 침략 국가에
                        대해 금번과 같은 전쟁 태세를 취하지 않았던바
                        금번 사태는 왜 그토록 중요한지 납득하기 어려움.

   - 쿠웨이트 정부 복귀 : 쿠웨이트 왕정을 복귀시키기 위해 목숨을 버리거나
                        생명의 위험을 무릅쓸 미국민은 단 한사람도 없음.

   - 독재자에 의한 세계 원유 공급 장악 방지 : 이 목표는 경제적, 정치적으로
                        현실적인 것이기는 함. 그러나 미국은 원유의 원활한
                        확보를 위해 강력한 에너지 절약 추진, 휘발유세 인상,
                        서구제국과 연합하에 OPEC 카르텔 와해 노력 등의
                        방법을 강구해 볼 수도 있는 것임.

0046

o 부쉬 대통령은 미국이 사담 후세인과 대치하고 있는 이유는 <u>그를 권좌에서
제거하기 위한 것이라는 것을 하루속히 미국민에게 솔직히 천명해야</u> 함.

- 페만 사태와 관련 부쉬 대통령은 매일 많은 이야기를 하고 있으나 오로지
사담 후세인이나 U.N.을 향하여 발언하고 있는 듯한 인상을 주고 있음은
문제임.

0047

ON MY MIND
A. M. Rosenthal

The President's Mistake

President Bush made one profound mistake immediately after Iraq conquered Kuwait. Every day it becomes more important that he correct it before United States ground forces go into action against Saddam Hussein.

Mr. Bush failed to state the single most important reason for going to war against Iraq — or even for organizing the worldwide embargo. That is to eliminate Saddam Hussein's power to cause more death and destruction. Other reasons do not justify the deaths of Americans — or placing them in deadly jeopardy.

Perhaps Mr. Bush himself was reluctant to face it in the beginning. Certainly Presidential candor was not a happy prospect for Administration officials who designed and pushed the failed, disgraced policy of strengthening Saddam Hussein and appeasing him almost up to the hour of invasion.

If they really wanted to convince Saddam Hussein of American determination to oppose him at last, the resignation of Secretary of State James Baker and some of his top Middle East hands would have been one inexpensive, bloodless way of showing it.

Whatever the reason, Mr. Bush came up with war goals that simply do not satisfy a large part of the American public. The public support needed by the President and every soldier depends not so much on the length of a war but whether it sits well in the American stomach.

Mr. Bush told the country that one goal was to turn back aggression. Every American intelligent enough to fight is intelligent enough to know that the United States did not feel compelled to go into battle against other aggressions — China against Tibet, the Soviet Union against the world of Eastern Europe, and Arab against Arab time and again. Why was was this one so important?

Americans were told that another objective was to restore the royal family of Kuwait. Name one American you know who thinks that is worth dying for, or even facing the possibility of death. Just one.

And Americans were told that the country could not allow a dictator with a proven taste for power and blood to stand astride much of the world's oil supply. That is an economic and political reality. But it is not convincing enough to Americans who know that there are steps the U.S. has not yet taken to preserve its oil independence. Among them: tougher conservation, higher gas taxes, real attempts to break the OPEC cartel with a Western Hemisphere consortium benefiting us and our neighbors.

So, with American men and women facing combat in the desert, the U.S. debates why they are there. Mr. Bush has done well preparing the country militarily for the possibility of war, but has failed to prepare it politically and spiritually.

He has not said the bone truth: Left in power, Saddam Hussein will use his missiles and chemical arsenal in the future as he has in the past. And if Israeli destruction of his nuclear plant in 1981 had not set him back a decade or so, Iraq would be a nuclear power today.

Does anybody truly believe that when he acquires them, Saddam Hussein will not use nuclear weapons as blackmail? Or never slip a few to some of his terrorist gangs and allies like Libya? Does anybody truly believe that he would not use nuclear power as a first resort or certainly a last if he ever again faces a strong coalition that threatens his rule?

Stop this man before he can kill millions. That is the only war goal worth putting before American soldiers as a reason for risking their lives. And it is the reason that U.S. and allied air power should have been used to destroy his arsenals before American armies were shipped abroad. It is the reason that air power should still be tried before they are sent into combat. The country and the President need matters of heart from each other — trust, confidence and respect. But on the edge of war, he wasted his dignity and dwindling time by running around fighting local political battles.

When he decides he must send more hundreds of thousands of Americans into danger, he breaks the news to reporters at the White House, instead of telling the parents himself, in their living rooms.

He talks almost every day, but always gives the impression that he talks to be heard only by Saddam Hussein or the U.N. In the timetable of the Mideast crisis, the date that counts most is when the American President decides to address the American people in full openness — rectifying the error he made, telling them that the reason to confront the power of Saddam Hussein is to end the power of Saddam Hussein. □

Nov. 13, 1990

NYT

0048

Pentagon Paying High Prices For Shipping Supplies to Gulf

By KEITH BRADSHER

To support the rapid American military buildup in the Persian Gulf, the Defense Department has been paying high prices to charter vessels and book space aboard regularly scheduled freighters — sometimes twice the standard commercial rate.

Some shipping experts suggest that the Government has greatly overpaid for charters, particularly in the first two months of the gulf crisis. Robert W. Kesteloot, a shipping consultant in Reston, Va., who retired in 1986 after six years as the Navy's director of strategic sealift, termed the rates that shipowners are charging the Government for chartering some of the larger vessels "mind boggling." He added, "They'd never get that in peacetime."

Ship brokers, freight agents and shipping executives agree that higher prices have meant more profits for shipowners. But they defend the surge in rates as inevitable because the military deployment has sharply increased the worldwide demand for shipping and because the Pentagon makes some special demands that commercial shippers do not.

The Government's costly transportation contracts are likely to receive greater scrutiny in the coming months if the United States' military commitment in Saudi Arabia continues. The Government is currently operating 173 vessels for the sealift to Saudi Arabia, a larger fleet than was ever used at one time during the Vietnam War, in which the American buildup of ground troops was spread over three years.

The most expensive shipping agreements were struck in the weeks immediately after Iraq invaded Kuwait on Aug. 2. The military was forced to pay a premium to persuade shipping companies to take some of their vessels out of commercial service and to cut back commercial space aboard freighters.

For example, the Military Sealift Command, which manages ocean transportation for the Navy, has been paying nearly $8,000 for each standard 40-by-8-by-8½-foot steel container that it uses to send supplies to the Persian Gulf from the East Coast of the United States. This price is double what some commercial shippers now pay.

In response to a question, the sealift command said in a statement issued on Dec. 15 that in October it had begun negotiating a new contract but was interrupted by President Bush's announcement on Nov. 8 that up to 200,000 more troops would be sent to Saudi Arabia. "It is the Government's intention to reprice the contract as soon as we are able to accurately define our requirements," the agency statement said.

The sealift command is also paying $7,000 to $8,500 a day to charter the medium-size multi-deck freighters needed to carry small trucks, jeeps and other supplies. The same class of freighters fetched $6,000 to $8,500 a day last summer, ship brokers said. Commercial interests are also paying the higher rates now, unless they

An estimate of $1.56 billion could double, Pentagon officials say.

booked vessels long in advance.

And the military has been paying up to $35,000 a day for long-term charters of so-called ro-ro's, which are built like automobile ferries to allow vehicles to roll on and off, and which are the only vessels that can efficiently transport large numbers of heavy tanks.

'Paying in Excess of Top Dollar'

"They were paying in excess of top dollar," said James L. Winchester, a shipping analyst at Mabon, Nugent & Company, a New York brokerage. "It was ludicrous."

Yet, ship brokers describe the surge in ship charter prices as a simple matter of supply and demand. The demand for charters rose sharply, and so did the price, they explain. "It's like other markets — like stocks and bonds," said John Weale, the vice president of Fednav Ltd., a Montreal shipping company that has supplied a ro-ro to the sealift.

The military, to be sure, would have paid less if it had arranged for charters over a six-month period. But it needed to move troops and equipment quickly to the gulf in August. The Government thus had to pay a higher price, just as an airline passenger who needs to book a ticket the day before a flight departs pays more than the bargain hunter who buys a ticket months in advance.

Original Estimate Doubles

Vice Adm. Francis R. Donovan, the commander of the Military Sealift Command, responded with a statement to questions about the agency's chartering expenses. His statement said the rates paid "were not particularly high in light of the short-term requirement, diversion of ships from commercial employment and uncertain condition in the Middle East."

Most of the military equipment and supplies sent to Saudi Arabia has gone by sea, although tanks, guns and many troops have been sent by air. The Defense Department said in September that the sealift would cost it $336 million for August and September and another $1.56 billion from October 1990 through September 1991.

Pentagon officials estimate that the $1.56 billion figure could double as a result of President Bush's order on Nov. 8 to send another 200,000 troops to Saudi Arabia.

The Defense Department estimated in September that the airlift to Saudi Arabia would cost $2.24 billion in the 1991 fiscal year, but much of this cost has been for the military's own large fleet of transport planes.

Disadvantage in Public Bidding

The military's urgent need for many vessels prevented it from playing shipowners against one another, which is standard Government practice with private companies.

Government rules requiring that large contracts be awarded through public bidding have put the sealift command at a disadvantage, said Dimitris Kastriotis, the chartering manager at Alltrans International Group Inc., a ship brokerage in Wayne, N.J.

If an oil company, for example, wanted to charter five tankers, it might quietly and separately approach 10 shipowners and ask each for a single vessel. The oil company would take the five cheapest deals available and announce them all the same morning.

"Had you known they wanted five, not one, you would have charged them 20 or 30 percent extra," another broker explained.

Shipping companies have also benefited during previous crises. For example, charter rates briefly doubled when the Arab-Israeli war in June 1967 closed the Suez Canal.

NYT
12/24/90

0043

외 무 부

관리번호 90-2405

종 별 :

번 호 : USW-5099

일 시 : 90 1115 1630

수 신 : 장관(미북, 미안, 중근동)

발 신 : 주 미 대사

제 목 : 걸프 사태 관련 최근 미국내 동향 종합 보고

연:USW-5072 (1), 5022 (2), 4931 (3)

당지 언론 분석 및 주재국 각계인사 접촉을 통해 파악한 연호 (2) 부쉬 대통령의 미군 증파 공식발표 이후 관련 동향 및 사태진전 내용을 아래 종합 요약 보고함.

1. 미 행정부의 극한 정책(BRINKMANSHIP) 추진

가. 미 행정부는 10.29. 라성 WORLD AFFAIRS COUNCIL 에서의 베이커 국무장관 연설을 시발로, 부쉬 대통령의 중간 선거 지원을 위한 각종 유세 연설등을 통해 매우 강경한 용어를 사용, 이락의 쿠웨이트 침공을 규탄하고 대이락 무력 사용 가능성을 강력하게 암시함으로써 소위 RHETORIC 상의 변화를 보이기 시작하였음.

나. 특히 중간선거 직후인 11.8. 부쉬 대통령이 OFFENSIVE OPTION 의 확보를 위한 미군 증파를 공식 발표하고, 곧이어 11.9. 채니 국방장관이 사우디 주둔미군의 로테이션 계획을 부인함으로써 여사한 미측의 움직임은 상기 RHETORIC 상의 변화와 함께 미국의 대이락 공격 가능성을 보다 더 분명하게 가시화시켜 주었는바, 11.14. 자 NYT 사설은 이러한 미 행정부의 입장 변화와 관련, DESERT SHIELD 작전이 DESERT SWORD 작저으로 변형 되었다고 표현 함.

다. 한편, 다음과 같은 요인들은 이락측이 쿠웨이트로 부터 자진해서 무조건 철수하지 않는경우, 대규모 증파를 통해 공격 위주로 전환된 사우디 주둔 미군은 실제 전부작전은 내년봄 이전 개시할 가능성을 시사하고 있음.

-사우디 주둔 미군의 로테이션 취소를 기 파견 부대의 작전부입 시점이 임박한 것으로 해석할수있는 점.

-군수 및 보급 차원 뿐만 아니라 40 만에 달하는 대군을 특정지역(특히 외국 군대의 주둔에 민감한 반응을 보여온 사우디)에 장기 주둔 시키는 것은 정치적, 외교적 측면에서도 곤란하다는 점.

미주국	장관	차관	1차보	미주국	중아국	청와대	안기부	대책반

90.11.16   07:34

외신 2과 통제관 BT

0050

-또한 미 국내 정치적 관점에서 볼때, 미국이 이미 천명한 목표를 달성하지못한채 여사한 대규모 병력을 철수하게 되면 이는 부쉬 대통령의 정책적 실수로 인식될 것이라는 점.

-3 월이 되면 "성지 순례"가 시작되고 기온이 상승하기 시작함으로써 군사적으로 작전환경이 불리해지는 점.

-대 이락 경제 봉쇄 전략이 실시된지 3 개월이 경과 했는대도 이락측 이 쿠웨이트로 부터의 철수 움직임을 전혀 보이지 않고 있는점.

라. 그러나 기 보고한바와 같이 현시점에서 미국은 무력사용을 결정한것은 아니며 이러한 극한 정책을 통해 미군사력 배치가 단순한 시위가 아니라 진정한 위협이며, 대 이락 경제 봉쇄 전략으로 부터 대 이락 전면 공격 전략으로의 전환시점이 임박해 있다는점을 이락측에 대해 강력히 암시함으로써, 후세인에 대한압력을 가중, 이락군의 자진 철수를 유도하려는 의도로 보임.

2. 미 의회 반응

가. 행정부의 전기 극한 정책에 대한 미 의회의 반응은 연호 (1) 로 보고한바와 같이, 사우디 주둔 미군 병력 증강 사유에 대한 보다더 상세한 대국민설득이 필요하다는 입장이며, 이러한 토론과정을 통해 행정부의 대 이락 정책이 의회와 국민의 강력한 지지를 받게 되면 이락측이 미군등 다국적군 의 자국 공격 가능성을 보다 더 심각하고, 진지하게 받아들일것이라는 점을 지적하고 있음.

나. 의회의 이러한 움직임은 청문회등 토론 과정을 통해 대 이락 공격에 의해 이룩 하려는 정치적 목적과 전쟁으로인한 인적, 물적 손실과의 보다 구체적인비교 분석을 행하려는 의도로 보이며, 특히 NUNN 의원과 같은 경우는 미국이 보다 더 인내심을 갖고 대 이락 경제 봉쇄 전략의 효과를 주시하여야 할것이라는점을 지적하고 있기도 함.

다. 한편, 연호 (1) 보고와 같이, 11.13. 공화당의 외교봉 중진 의원인 LUGAR 상원의원은 사우디 주둔 미군의 대규모 증강으로 인해 미국이 사실상 이락과의 COLLISION COURSE 에 놓이게 되었으므로, 의회 소집을 통해 미국의 군사력 증강 문제등과 관련한 걸프 사태 대응 방안을 공개 논의할것을 제의한바 있으나, 작일 백악관에서 있었던 행정부 및 의회 수뇌부간 회동에서는 의회 특별회기 소집대신 청문회를 포함 현재와 같은 비공식협의를 계속해 나가기로 일단 합의함.

(민주당 지도부는 여사한 특별회기 소집이 결과적으로 민주당도 BUSH 대통령의

PAGE 2

입장을 지원하는 결과가 될지도 모른다는 점에서 반대하고 있음).

3. 미 언론 및 여론 반응

가. 전기 의회 반응으로 마찬가지로 , 미 언론 및 언론에 나타난 미국내 여론은 대부분 공개 토론을 통한 미국내 여론 수렴의 필요성을 강조하고 있음.

특히 "TOO FAR TOO FAST IN THE GULF" 제하의 11.11. 자 NYT 사설은 부쉬 대통령이 의회와 국민에 대해 거의 아무런 사전협의도 없이 새로운 대이락 공격 노선을 택하고 있다고(WHEN MR. BUSH DICTATES A NEW OFFENSIVE POLICY WITH BARELY A NOD TO CONGRESS OR THE BUPLIC. THE SHOWS MORE IMPERIAL IMPATIENCE THAN UNIFIED STRENGTH.) 지적함으로써 상당히 강도 높게 부쉬 대통령의 대 이락 정책을 비판하고, 사우디 내의 미군 공세 전력 강화가 일종의 관성적 반응으로 인해 전쟁으로 치달을 수도 있다는 점을 지적하였음.

나. 또한 11.12 자 NYT 에 실린 ANTHONY LEWIS 의 " THE LOGIC OF WAR " 제하의 논설도 공개 토론을 통한 미국의 대이락 공격 지지 여론 형성이 후세인의 굴복 유도에 필수적임(PRESIDENT BUSH MUST CONVINCE CONGRESS AND THE PUBLIC THAT THE STAKES ARE WORTH THE RISK OF WAR. ONLY BY DOING SO CAN HE CONVINCESADDAM HUSSEIN THAT HE MUST FEAR MILITARY ACTION.)

을 지적하고 있음.

이하 USW-5100 으로 계속

PAGE 3

외 무 부

종   별 :

번   호 : USW-5100   일   시 : 90 1115 1634

수   신 : 장관(미북)

발   신 : 주 미 대사

제   목 : USW-5099 계속분

한편 , 이락의 군사적 완전 무력화를 주장하는 강경론자인 A.M. ROSENTHAL 및 걸프 사태 발발 초기부터 대이락 무력 공격을 주장해온 HENRY KISSINGER 조차도 의회등을 통한 공개 토론의 필요성에는 모두 공감하고 있는 형편임.

다. 또한 금 11.14. 자 NYT 에 게재된 TOM WICKER 의 " THE WRONG STRATEGY" 제하의 논설은 미국민이 보다 더 인내심을 갖고 대이락 경제 봉쇄 전략의 추이를 지켜볼것("UNTIL IT IS CRYSTAL CLEAR THAT THE EMBARGO AND BLOCKADE ARE FUTILE, MANY AMERICANS WILL BE HESITANT TO ACCEPT HEAVY CASUALTIES FOR ANYOF THESE GOALS)을 주장하였음.

4. 관련 국제 동향

가. 한편 베이커 국무장관의 최근 중동 및 구주 순방시 걸프 사태 관련국들은 자국의 이해 득실에 따라 다음과 같이 상이한 반응을 보인것으로 알려짐.

(순방 결과 관련 기자회견 내용은 작일 팩스편 송부한 USW(F)- 3046 참조)

1) 걸프 사태 해결을 위한 관련국간 공동 보조 필요성 및 쿠웨이트 영토 일부 할양등을 통한 동 사태의 부분적 해결 반대등 기본 원칙에 있어서는 견해 일치를 보였으나 다만 대 이락 경제 봉쇄 전략의 효과에 대한 평가 및 동 전략의 적용기간에 관한 견해는 각각 상이함.

2) 사우디, 이집트, 시리아등 소위 전선국가들은 대 이락 무력 공격을 통한이락의 군사적 무력화를 선호하는 반면, 소련, 중공, 프랑스, 터키등은 대이락경제 봉쇄 및 무력 시위를 통한 이락의 쿠웨이트로 부터의 자진 철수 유도 방안을 선호 하고 있음.

3) 쿠웨이트 망명 정부를 제외한 대부분의 관련국들이 향후 2-3 개월은 대 이락 무력공격을 자제함으로써 대 이락 경제 봉쇄의 효과를 좀더 기다려 보자는 입장임.

(다만 이집트, 사우디등 아랍국들은 대이락 공격 결정 이전 이락측에 대해 충분한

미주국   장관   차관   1차보   미주국   중아국   청와대   안기부   대책반

시간적 여유를 주었다는 명분론적 입장에서 여사한 입장을 취하고 있는 반면, 소련, 중공, 프랑스, 터키등은 동 기간중 이락측이 쿠웨이트로 부터의 철수 결정을 내리거나 이락내 반 후세인 세력에 의한 쿠데타 발생등을 기대하고 있음.)

4) 아랍권 각국들은 이락측이 상금 사우디 주둔 다국적군을 진정한 군사적 위협으로 받아들이지 않고 있는것으로 봄.

즉, 후세인 대통령은 전쟁이 임박하지 않는 한 쿠웨이트로 부터의 철수를 진지하게 고려할 인물이 아니므로, 미측의 금번 병력 증파 결정에 대해서는 대부분 지지를 표함.

나. 또한 11.11. 모로코의 하싼 왕은 아랍 형제국간의 전쟁을 피하기 위한 긴급 아랍 정상회담 개최를 제의하였는바, 주요 이해 당사국인 사우디가 이락군의 쿠웨이트로 부터의 철수를 회의 참석의 전제조건으로 내세우는 등 상금 회의 자체의 개최 전망이 불투명한 실정임.

5. 결론

가. 걸프 사태와 관련, 현재 부쉬 행정부가 직면하고 있는 가장 큰 어려움은 대이락 압력 가중과 더불어 다국적군 참여국간 결속유지 및 적절한 수준의 대의회, 국민 설명을 통한 범국민적 지지 확보라는 3 가지 서로 다른 차원의 목표를 동시에 추구하여야 하는데에 있음.

즉, 미측이 대이락 위협을 보다더 CREDIBLE 하게 머어 가는 과정이 관련국은 물론 의회와 미 국민들의 눈에는 전쟁임박의 조짐으로 비치고 있으며, 이에 따라 특히 전쟁개시 가부에 관한 미국내의 여론이 비등함으로써 미국의 군사적 위협의 신뢰도를 오히려 저하시키고 있는 역설적 상황이 현재 BUSH 행정부가 처해 있는 딜레마임.

나. 요약컨데, 부쉬 행정부로서는 국내적으로 민주적 방식에 따라, 또 동시에 국제적으로는 관련국간의 CONSENSUS 를 통해 대 이락 공격 여부를 결정해야 하는 어려운 상황인바, 이러한 절차를 통해 미측이 국내 여론을 결집함으로써 소위 애국심을 통한 단결(RALLY-AROUND-THE-FLAG) 의 효과를 거양하는 경우는 이락측에 보다 더 심각한 심리적 압박을 가할수도 있겠으나 , 의회 논의등을 통해서도 행정부 조치에 대한 명백한 지지를 유도치 못하는 경우 이락측은 미국의 군사력을 계속 진정한 위협이 아닌 단순한 무력시위의 차원에서만 인식하게될것임.

즉 엄청난 파괴력을 보유하고있는 초강대국임에도 불구, 미국은 자국의 국내정치 체제에 내재하고 있는 특수성으로 인해 걸프지역에 배치중인 약 40 만의 대군을

군사적 위협수단으로 충분히 활용치 못하고 있는 형편임(이와 관련, 작일기자회견시
베이커 국무장관은 현재와 같은 긴급 상황하에서는 민주주의가 아닌 독재체제
방식으로 정부를 운영하는것이 더 쉬울것이라는 요지의 언급을 함으로써 미 행정부가
현재 체해 있는 어려운 상황을 솔직하게 토로한바 있음.

    (대사 박동진-차관)
    91.6.30. 일반

검 토 필 (1990.12기

예고문에의거 일반문서로
재분류 1901 630 서병

외 무 부

관리번호 90-2423

종 별 :

번 호 : USW-5149

일 시 : 90 1116 1826

수 신 : 장관(미북,미안,중근동)

발 신 : 주 미 대 사

제 목 : 걸프 사태관련 미 종교계 동향

연:USW-5099

연호 사우디 주둔 미군 부대의 공세 전력 강화 결정 이후 미국내 반응 관련, 금 11.16 자 NYT 보도에 따르면, 미 전국 교회 협의회(NATIONAL COUNCIL OF CHURCH)가 걸프 지역으로 부터의 미군 철수 및 금번 걸프 사태와 팔레스타인 문제의 연계 해결을 주장하는 요지의 결의안을 작일 채택 하였다 하는바 (동 기사 전문은 USW(F)-3101 로 팩스편 송부) , 미종교계 내의 여사한 비판적 움직임도 부쉬 행정부로서는 부담 요인이 될것으로 보이기에 참고로 보고함.

(대사 박동진- 국장)

91.6.30. 일반

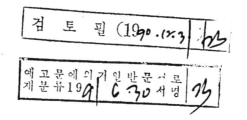

검 토 필 (1990.12.3

예고문에 의기 일반문서로 재 분류 19   6 30 서명

미주국   1차보   2차보   미주국   중아국   안기부

90.11.17   08:44

외신 2과 룡제관 BW

0056

외 무 부

종 별 :

번 호 : USW-5201   일 시 : 90 1120 1836

수 신 : 장 관(미북,동구1,중근동,미중)

발 신 : 주 미 대사

제 목 : BUSH 대통령 해외 방문계획

연: USW-4593

금 11.20. 파리에서 있은 백악관 정례 브리핑시 발표된 부쉬대통령 해외 방문계획을 하기 보고함.

가. 11.26-27 MEXICO,MONTEREY 방문, SALINAS대통령과 회담 (연호 참조)

나. START 협정 서명을 위해 내년도중 소련방문, 1월이라는 언론보도와 관련, 구체적인시기는 결정되지 않았다고 함.

다. 내년 상반기중 터키 공식 방문

(대사 박동진-국장)

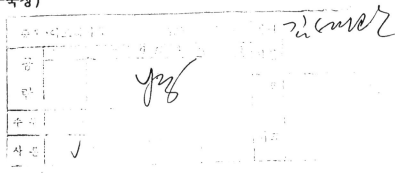

미주국   1차보   미주국   구주국   중아국   정문국   안기부

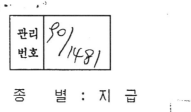

외 무 부

관리
번호 801/1481

종 별 : 지 급

번 호 : USW-5209

수 신 : 장관(미북,동구일,미안,구이,중근동)

발 신 : 주 미 대사

제 목 : 미.쏘 관계

연 USW-5155

1. 당관 김영복 서기관이 11.20 JOHN ORDWAY 국무부 소련과 부과장과 접촉시 현재
주요 미소 관계 진전 동향에 대한 동 부과장 설명요지를 다음 보고함. 기에 예고군에
의거 일반문서로 지 분류됨.

가. 소련 국내 정세에 대한 평가

-GORBACHEV 가 지난주말 소연방 회의에서 첫번째 행한 연설(11.16)은 심각한
실패작이었으나, 연방 정부 구조 개편을 제의함으로서 위기가 극복된것으로 보임. YELTSIN 이 동 안에 대해 부정적 입장을 표시 하였으나, GORBACHEV 는 엘친과 최소한
동반의 수단을 제공했다고 평가됨.

- 미 행정부로서는 현 단계에서 GORBACHEV 의 지위 변화 여부를 판단할수 없으나,
GORBACHEV 의 국내적 지지가 급속히 하락한것은 분명한 사실이며, 만일 연방
최고회의나 인민 대표회의가 현 상태에서 선거를 실시한다면, 고르바쵸프의 지지 기반
확보는 불가능할것으로 보임.다만 고르바쵸프는 최소한 현 시점에서 연방 최고회의를
그런대로 리드(CONTROL) 하고 있는것으로 관찰됨.

-미 행정부는 소연방 체제의 변화과정, 고르바쵸프와의 여타 공화국 지도자간의
권력 분배 조정 과정을 예의 주시하고 있으며, 새로운 현상이 있을경우 이를 현실로
수용해야한다는 인식을 갖고 있으나, 현 단계에서 특별한 대책을 강구하고 있지는
않음.

나. GULF 만 사태 대처에 대한 미소 협조

-금번 CSCE 정상회담중 BUSH-GORBACHEV, BAKER-SHEVARDNAZE 간 GULF 만 사태
대처와 관련 집중적 협의가 있었음(상세 내용 상금 미접)

-그간 BAKER 장관-SHE 외상간 접촉(BAKER 장관의 11.8 모스크바 방문등)을
종합해볼때, 소련은 여하한 경우에도 미.소간 협조 체제에서 이탈하지 않을것임을

미주국	차관	1차보	2차보	미주국	구주국	구주국	중아국	정와대
안기부								

분명히 했으며, -고- 대통령과 -쉐- 외상은 HUSSEIN 에 대해 매우 강경한 입장을 표시했음.

-양측은 향후 유엔 이 할수 있는 추가 조치(무력 사용 허가 결의안 추진등 의미)에 대해 상세히 협의했음.

구체적 조치와 관련 양측이 즉각적인 합의를 보지 못서것은 사실이나, 양측은 이견이 공개적으로 표시되지 안도록 상호 녀력해 오고 있음. 쏘련도 궁극적으로 무력 사용의 대안을 배제하지는 않는다는 기본 입장을 보였음.

다. 향후 미소 관계

-미.소 양측은 당초 계획대로 11 월중 정례 외무장관 회담을 개최치는 못했으나 12 월중 이를 개최토록 추진중임. 쏘련측은 금번 파리에서 양국 정상간 회담시, 1 월중 모스크바에서 미소 정상회담을 갖을것을 제의하고, 이를 발표 하였으나, 미측으로서는 우선 START 협상이 순조롭게 종료되어야 한다는 입장임.이와관련 양측은 제네바 협상팀의 노력을 평가하고, 동팀에 대해 보다 큰 재량권을 부여키로 합의했음.

-BAKER 장관은 11.8 미소 외상 회담시 소련에 대한 MFN 지위 부여, 미소 통상 협정 비준을 위해 이민법의 통과를 다시한번 강조한바, 소측은 12 월중 처리가 가능할것이라고 답변함(최근 SAM NUNN 의원도 미 행정부가 소련의 이민법 통과에 구애받지 않고 , MFN 지위를 부여하고 소련에 대한 경협등 호혜적인 경제 관계 활성화를 추진한것을 제의)

2. 당관 관찰

-미측은 금번 CSCE 정상회담 기간중 GULF 만 사태와 관련 무력 사용 결의안에 대한 소련의 협조 확보를 위해 집중적 노력을 기울일것으로 보임.이와 관련 소련측은 TIMING 과 관련 유보적 입장을 갖고 있으나, 헬싱키 합의 정신을 바탕으로 미측 입장과 절충코저 하고 있는것으로 보이며, 미소 양국 대통령의 대변인간 공동 기자 회견(11.19 파리)을 통해 미소간 협력 관계를 재강조토록 배려한것으로 관찰됨.

-한편 미측은 그간 CSCE 정상 회담은 CFE 협정이 마무리 되어야 가능한다는 일관된 입장을 견지하여 왔었는바, 차후 미소 정상회담 개최를 위해서도 START6 가 마무리 되어야한다는 입장을 견지할것으로 보이나, 동 정상회담 개최에는 -페-만 사태 대처 전략 추진, 소련 국내 사정 변화등 요인도 감안될것으로 예상됨(소련측은 1 월 초순 정상회담 개최를 강력히 희망)

(대사 박동진-국장)

90.12.31 일반

0060

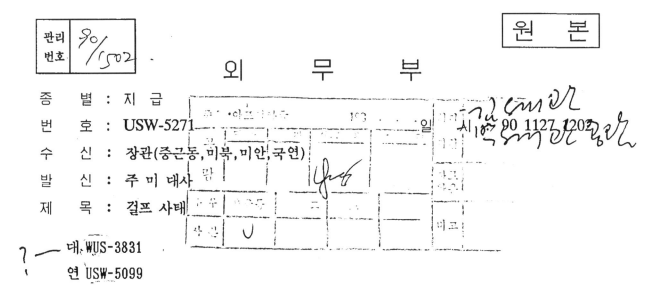

관리 번호 90/1502

외 무 부

종 별 : 지급

번 호 : USW-5271

수 신 : 장관(중근동,미북,미안,국연)

발 신 : 주 미 대사

제 목 : 걸프 사태

대. WUS-3831

연 USW-5099

1. 대호 관련 금 11.26 자 NYT 지등 당지 언론보도에 따르면 미국등 유엔 안보리의 5 개 상임 이사국은 이락에 대해 쿠웨이트로부터 철수할수 있는 마지막기회를 부여하되, 일정 시한까지 철수치 않는 경우는 이락에 대해 모든 필요한수단(ALL NECESSARY MEANS)을 사용할수 있다는 요지의 결의안 초안에 합의하고이에 따라 BAKER 국무장관등 안보리 이사국 외무장관 참석하에 11.29(목) 동 결의안에 대해 표결 예정이라함(결의안 초안 전문은 USW(F)-3210 로 FAX 편 송부)

또한 전기 대이락 철수 요구 시한에 관해서는 상임 이사국간에 상금 합의가이루어지지 않은것으로 알려지고 있으며(미측은 91.1.1 을 소련측은 1.15 을 주장), 중국측의 태도에 다소 불분명한점이 있기는 하나 동 결의안의 통과는 비교적 낙관시 되고 있다함.

2. 당관 관찰

가. 여사한 유엔 안보리 결의안 통과는 대이락 무력 사용 가능성을 보다 더 가시화 시킴으로서 훗세인 대통령에 대한 압력을 가중시킬것으로 보이며,또한 미 국내 정치적으로는 부쉬 행정부가 대 사우디 병력 증파등을 통해 추진해온 극한 정책(BRINKMANSHIP)에 대한 보다 더 광범위한 국민적 지지를 유도해 나가는데에 도움이 될것으로 봄.

나. 다만 미군 증파 병력의 대 사우디 수송 작전에 상당 시일이 소요되므로내년 1 월 까지도 미군 병력의 실전 배치가 완료되지 못할 가능성이 크고, 또한 미측으로서는 대이락 공격 효과의 극대화를 위해 기습 작전을 전개할 가능성이 크므로 이락에 대한 철수 요구 시한(내년 1.1 이나 1.15)을 대 이락 작전 개시일과 동일시 하는것은

중아국   차관   1차보   2차보   미주국   미주국   국기국

90.11.28   08:40

외신 2과 통제관 FE

0061

곤란할것임.

　다.　한편　이처럼　군사적　위협과　국제적　압력이　증대되는　상황하에서
이락측으로서는　인질문제를　흥정　대상으로　삼아　시간을　벌면서　대이락　경제　봉쇄
참여국간의　분열을　유도할것으로　보이며,　또　동시에　쿠웨이트　사태와　팔레스타인
문제의　연계　해결을　계속　주장함으로서　국제　여론의　분산을　모색해　나갈것으로　보임.

　(대사 박동진-국장)

　91.6.30 일반

19 9I. 6 . 30. 에 여고문에
의거 일반문서로 재 분류됨.

PAGE 2

외 무 부

종 별 :

번 호 : USW-5294

일 시 : 90 1127 1822

수 신 : 장 관(아이,미북)

발 신 : 주 미 대사

제 목 : QIAN 외상 방미

1. BOUCHER 국무부 부대변인은 금 11.27 국무부정례 브리핑을 통하여 유엔 안보리 참석차 방미예정인 중국외상이 11.30 워싱턴을 방문, 일련의 공식회담을 갖게된다고 발표함.

2. QIAN 외상 워싱턴 방문시의 주요 의제로는 폐만사태, 캄프챠 문제, 중국내 인권 문제등 이거론될 것으로 보임.

3. 이에 대해 기자들은 동외상의 워싱턴 방문이 미국이 천안문 사태이후 중국에 대해 적용하고 있는 고위 방문금지에 위배되는것이 아닌지에 대해 집중질문한바, 이에 대해 BOUCHER 부대변인은 1)의례적인 교환 방문 (EXCHANGES) 과 실질적 문제 해결을 위한 접촉 (CONTACT) 은 차이가 있으며, 2) 기왕에도 BAKER-QIAN 외상간에 4차례에 걸친 접촉등 실질문제해결을 위한 접촉은 계속되어 왔음을 거론하면서 미국의 대중국 제제정책에 변화가 없음을 강조하였음.

4. 정례 브리핑 내용 FAX USW(F)-3216 송부함

(대사 박동진-국장)

아주국   1차보   미주국   정문국   안기부

PAGE 1

: USW(F) - 3216

: 경   권 (아미, 미부)   발신 : 주미대사   보안
                                              좀겨

: Qian 外相 訪美 (첨부물) USW-5294의 중간부

STATE DEPARTMENT REGULAR BRIEFING, BRIEFER: RICHARD BOUCHER
12:57 P.M. (EST), TUESDAY, NOVEMBER 27, 1990

    Q   Can you provide us with some information on the plans the
US government has to meet with the Foreign Minister of China,
please?

    MR. BOUCHER: The Secretary has invited all the foreign
ministers of the UN Security Council member states to meet in New
York to discuss the continuing crisis in the Gulf, as well as the
next steps the UN Security Council might take in response to Iraq's
continued illegal occupation of Kuwait.

    Given China's role as a permanent member of the United Nations
Security Council and our common interest in advancing a range of
global and regional issues, including Cambodia, we believed it
useful to invite Foreign Minister Qian to Washington for a
comprehensive review of those matters as well as an in-depth
discussion of bilateral issues.

    Foreign Minister Qian will be in New York, November 28th and
29th, and he will hold official meetings in Washington on Friday,
November 30th.

    Q   Does this put an end, then, to the ban on high-level
contacts?

    MR. BOUCHER: No, Jim. We've consistently said that we would
hold meetings with Chinese officials in pursuit of vital US
interests. This will be the fifth meeting between Secretary Baker
and Foreign Minister Qian since mid-1989. I have a list of the
meetings here.

    They met in Paris on July 31, 1989; at the United Nations in
New York on September 28, 1989; at the United Nations in New York on
September 28, 1990; and in Cairo most recently on November 6th.

    While Minister Qian is in Washington we intend to explore ways
to strengthen cooperation on global and regional issues and seek
understandings on ways to achieve improvement in bilateral
relations, including further progress in the area of human rights
that would permit a gradual return to normal high-level exchanges.

    Our approach in this matter is consistent with the policies of
the European Community, Japan, and other friends and allies which
they have adopted with respect to China.

    Q   Would you agree that inviting him to Washington sends a
different kind of signal? A signal that you are prepared to improve
relations?

-1

0064

'2 : USW(F) -

:신 : 정 관   발신 : 주미대사   보연
                                                      동정

'무 :   (예)

MR. BOUCHER: Bill, I think the President and the Secretary
have always made clear the basis on which relations could be
improved. We have many vital issues with a country such a China.
We have vital issues with China right now, in the Persian Gulf and
with the progress on Cambodia. We have always said that we would
maintain official contacts. We have always made the distinction
between contacts and exchanges.

Q   Richard, if this visit

doesn't violate the ban on exchanges, can you give us some
indication of something that might violate the ban on exchanges?
What is -- what is prohibited?

MR. BOUCHER: Well, I can run down the specifics that we talked
about at the time and the specifics that are still suspended. The
suspension of normal high level exchanges, particularly those of a
formal and ceremonial nature remains in effect. These include
cabinet-level exchanges under the Joint Commission on Commerce and
Trade -- that's a Commerce chaired group; the Joint Economic
Commission -- that was the Treasury chaired group; and the Joint
Commission on Science and Technology.

Q   Richard, there was also a report that a high-level
Chinese trade official was due here -- speaking of trade.

MR. BOUCHER: There was a lot of focus on that. I can give you
the rundown on that visit, but it's nothing unusual.

Q   Why would that not violate this ban on high level --

MR. BOUCHER: Well, let me give you the rundown on it and I
think you'll understand. Commerce Undersecretary Michael Farren has
invited Chinese Trade Minister Gu Yongjiang to come to Washington
December 10 and 11 to hold discussions on bilateral trade matters.
The decision to invite Vice Minister Gu was made several weeks ago
in response to an expression of interest on the part of the Chinese
government to have trade talks following Gu's planned trip to Canada
beginning in late November.

The visit is consistent with US policy of continuing our
commercial relationship with China and maintaining official contacts
that serve important US interests. US-China bilateral trade is
expected to reach $20 billion this year. We think we clearly have
an interest in keeping open channels of communication on trade
issues. Vice Minister Gu is the senior official responsible for
trade with the United States in the Chinese Ministry of Foreign
Economic Relations and Trade.

Let me also note that this visit is not unusual. Oh, for the
past year, we've had other contacts with China at the senior level

-2

0065

to discuss trade matters. For example, the Aerospace Vice Minister
has visited several times on matters related to the export of
satellites; a member of the Chinese National People's Congress
Standing Committee had meetings with senior US officials in October
in connection with the visit of a Chinese buying mission to the
United States.

        Q   Absent from your remarks is any characterization of what
is apparently a tightening grip on the part of the Chinese
government on the expression of freedom of the press, freedom of
speech, freedom of religion, freedom of travel. All of those
things are getting worse in China rather than better.
You did mention that one of the things you would like to talk about
is the general category of human rights. But there is no expression
of the direction China appears to be going in response to the
opening up of contacts with the United States.

        MR. BOUCHER: We have spoken, I think, in some detail before
about specific cases, and about our dialogue on human rights.
We have discussed bilateral issues in all our previous meetings with
the Chinese, including human rights, and we would expect to do that
in this one.

        I'd just say that the recent news that China is planning to try
dissident journalist Wang Juntao and Chen Zeming on sedition charges
highlights the need to speak directly to senior Chinese officials
about our human rights concerns. These will be among the principal
issues to be discussed when the Foreign Minister visits Washington.

        Q   Richard, will Foreign Minister Qian see anyone higher
than Secretary Baker?

        MR. BOUCHER: I don't have any specific schedule of his
meetings at this point.

                    ―――――――

                              -3 (END)

                                              0066

종 별 :

번 호 : USW-5333　　　　　　　일 시 : 90 1129 1722

수 신 : 장관(미북 미안, 중근동,구이)

발 신 : 주 미 대사

제 목 : 부쉬 대통령 유럽, 중동 순방 결과 브리핑

1. 최근 BUSH 대통령의 유럽 및 중동 방문관련, 금 11.29. 당지에서는 국무성이 주선하여 BLAIR HOUSE 에서 대사들을 대상으로 백악관 NSC 의 구주 및 중동담당관(DAIVD C. GOMPERT, RICHARD N. HAASS) 에 의한 브리핑이 있었음.

2. 내용에 있어서는 이미 알려진 바에 특별히 추가할 만한것이 없으나 금번방문 에서 우방들이 미국의 GULF CRISIS 에 대한 POLITICAL OBJECTIVE 를 전폭적으로 지지하며 IRAQ 의 침략을 반대하기 위한 제반조치에 적극 참여하는 자세를 확인하였을 뿐 아니라 문제 해결에 대한 SENSE OF URGENCY(시급성)를 미국과 같이 공감하는 입장을 감지하였다는 점등을 강조 하였음.

3. 문제 해결을 위한 SENSE OF URGENCY 와 관련, 현 미국의회 일각에서의 신중론 의 대두로 일반 사람들의 오해의 소지가 있으나 사실은 정부와 의회사이에는 지금까지 취해온 백악관의 제반 조치의 충분한 이해와 협조관계가 이루어져있으며, 11 월 29 일 UNSC 에서 채택될 추가 결의가 통과되면 미 의회의 입장은 더욱 이해적인 방향으로 발전될것이라고 전망하고, 11 월 30 일에는 BUSH 대통령과 의회 지도자들과의 간담회가 다시 개최될 예정으로 있다고 설명함.

4. 미국은 IRAQ 에 대하여 최대의 압력을 가하여 평화적으로 사태를 수습하는 정책을 현재 추진중이나, 끝까지 목적을 달성하지 못할때는 최후의 조치도 불가피하게 된다는 점을 밝히고, 최대의 압력을 동원하기 위해서 SYRIA 같은 나라와의 정상 접촉을 가지게 된것은 외교의 현실성에 비추어 충분히 있을수 있는 일이라고 설명하였고, ISRAEL-PALESTINE 문제 해결의 시도는 IRAQ 침략문제가 잘 해결된후 논의될수 있는 안건이라 설명함(질문에 대한 답변 부분)

5. 유럽과 관련하여 동서 냉전 종식의 공식적 선언과 민주적 정치질서의 확대 발전이 금번 CSCE 의 의제라고 설명하고, 장래는 경제협력과 국제무역, 특히 자유무역

미주국	차관	1차보	2차보	미주국	구주국	중아국	정와대	안기부

PAGE 1

체제의 신장이 중요한 세계 문제로 등장하게 된다는 사실을 강조 하였음.

　　(대사 박동진- 국장)

　　90.12.31. 일반

0068

외 무 부

관리번호 90-2494

종 별 : 지급

번 호 : USW-5367

일 시 : 90 1130 1824

수 신 : 장관(미북, 미안, 중근동, 국연)

발 신 : 주 미 대사

제 목 : 걸프 사태관련 부쉬 대통령 기자회견

연:USW-5271

작일 유엔안보리에서의 대이락 무력 사용 허용 결의안 봉과등과 관련, 금 11.30. 부쉬 대통령은 백악관에서 특별 기자회견을 가졌는바, 동 회견 요지 및 당관 평가등 하기 보고함(부쉬 대통령의회견 모두 발언 내용 전문은 USW(F)-3300 로 질의 응답내용은 USW(F)-3301 로 각각 팩스편 송부함)

1. 부쉬 대통령 언급 요지

가. 금번 걸프 사태 해결을 위한 미국의 4 대 원칙에는 전혀 변함이 없는바, 작일의 유엔 안보리 결의안 봉과를 계기로 이락 군대가 쿠웨이트로 부터 철수해야만 한다는 점을 후세인 대통령이 보다 더 분명하게 인식하게 되기를 희망함.

나. 구체적으로 , 금번 사태관련 본인은 현재 다음과 같은 점들에 대해서 우려를 갖고 있음.

-기본적으로 무력에 의한 주변국가 점령이 용납되어서는 안된다는점.

-주 쿠웨이트 미국 대사관원의 안위 문제

-이락측의 쿠웨이트에서 자행하고 있는 각종 약탈 행위

-이락의 핵무기 개발 가능성

다. 이락측에 대해 군사 행동을 취하는 경우, 여사한 군사작전은 결코 월남전식의 장기전(PROTRACTED, DRAWN- OUT WAR)이 되지 않을것임.

라. 금번 사태의 평화적 해결을 위한 추가 조치의 일환으로, AZIZ 이락 외상이 12 월 둘째주 후반부에 워싱톤을 방문, 본인과 회담을 갖고, 또 BAKER 국무장관은 12.15-1.15. 사이이 바그다드를 방문, 후세인 대통령과 회담을 가질것을 제의함.

동 회담을 통해, 미측은 기 통과된 각종 유엔 결의안의 범주내에서 금번 사태의 제반 측면을 토의코자 함.

미주국 안기부	장관 대책반	차관	1차보	2차보	미주국	중아국	국기국	청와대

PAGE 1

2. 당관 평가

가. 금일 부쉬 대통령 언급 내용중 가장 주목되는 점은 상기"라"항의 <u>미-이락</u>
<u>양국간 외무장관 교환 방문 제의인바</u>, 미측은 동 교환 방문을 통해,
이락측이쿠웨이트로 부터 철수하지 않는 경우 무력 사용도 불사할것이라는 미국의
확고한 결의를 후세인 대통령으로 하여금 분명히 인식케 하고자 하는 의도로 보임.
즉, 연호 유엔 안보리결의안 통과에 이은 훗세인 대통령과의 직접 대면을 통해,
미측은 이락측의 주변상황 재평가를 유도함으로써 금번 사태의 평화적 해결(
즉, 이락군의 쿠웨이트로 부터의 자진 철수)을 도모하고자 하는것으로 보임(부쉬
대통령은 질의 응답시, 훗쎄인 대통령의 측근 인사들이 동 대통령에게 나쁜 소식은
보고하지 않기 때문에 훗쎄인 대통령이 현재 정보 판단의 차원에서 다소 고립된 상황에
처해 있으며, 따라서 미국이 무력사용도 불사코자 하는 확고한 결의를갖고 있다는
사실을 제대로 인식하지 못하고 있다고 설명)

나. 따라서, 금일 회담시 부쉬 대통령이 수차 강조한바 와 같이, 미측이 상기
접촉을 통해 금번 사태의 <u>부분적 해결 방안을 수용할 의사가 전무하다는 점을분명히</u>
<u>밝힌 이상</u>, 이락측이 외무장관 교환 방문 제의를 수락하는 경우, 동 접촉은 사실상
미국의 대이락 멧쎄지 전달을 위한 일방 통행로로만 활용될 가능성이 큼

다. 또한, 설사 이락측이 이러한 측면을 고려 동교환 방문 제의를 거부하거나 혹은
여사한 접촉이 대이락 설득의 차원에서 아무성과없이 끝난다 할지라도, 부쉬
대통령으로서는 <u>대외적으로나 국내적으로 걸프 사태의 평화적 해결을 위해 끝까지</u>
<u>노력했다는 인상을 줄수 있으므로 미국 주도의 대 이락 군사 행동에 대한국내외의</u>
<u>지지를 확보하는데에 도움이 될것으로 봄.</u>

라. 비록 금번 걸프 사태와 팔레스타인 문제의 연계 해결등 전제 조건을
내세우기는 했으나, 이락측이 지금까지 대화를 통한 금번 사태의 해결을 주장해온
이상 전기 미측 제의를 거부하는데에는 다소의 어려움이 있을것으로 보임. 그러나
이락측이 동 제의를 적극 수용, 미국과의 대화 유지를 통해 일종의 지연 전술방안을
강구할수도 있을것임.

마. 한편, 부쉬 대통령은 금일 회견시 대 이락 공격 작전이 월남전과
같은장기전의 성격을 띄지는 않을것이라고 언급하였는바, 이는 미측이 단계적
확전이나 국부 공격이 아닌 <u>일종의 전면 공격 방식을 통해 이락군을 작전 초기</u>
<u>단계부터 압도하려는 의도임을 시사한것으로 보임(</u> 이러한 미측 작전 계획의

PAGE 2

0070

밑바탕에는 월남전이나 한국전과 같은 장기전에 비해 최근의 파나마, 그레나다 침공과 같은 전격전이 비교적 국민들의 지지를 더많이 확보했었다는 국내정치적 차원의 고려가 깔려 있는것으로 보임.)

　　(대사 박동진-차관)

　　91.6.30. 일반

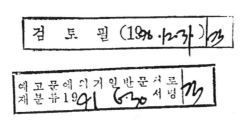

PAGE 3

0071

걸프사태 : 미국의 대응, 1990-91. 전6권 (V.3 1990.11-12월) 397

*EPF512   11/30/90
BUSH DOUBTS SANCTIONS ALONE WILL FORCE IRAQI PULLOUT
(Transcript: Bush statement, news conference) (6060)

Washington -- Although President Bush believes the United Nations
sanctions imposed on Iraq following its invasion of Kuwait
"clearly...are having some effect," he expressed doubt November 30
that those measures alone will compel Iraq to withdraw from Kuwait and
restore its legitimate government.

"I can't tell you that the sanctions alone will get the job done," he
said at a White House news conference, "and thus, I welcome
yesterday's United Nations action" authorizing the use of all
necessary means to liberate Kuwait from Iraqi occupation if the troops
are not withdrawn by January 15.

Bush pointed out that the new democracies of Eastern Europe and the
developing countries of Africa and the Western hemisphere "are being
severely damaged by the economic effects" of Iraqi President Saddam
Hussein's aggression.

The president said those who feel that there is no penalty for
"waiting months and months" for the sanctions to force Iraqi
compliance with the U.N. resolutions "must consider the devastating
damage being done every day to the fragile economies of those
countries that can afford it the least."

Following is the transcript of the president's statement and the news
conference which followed:

(begin transcript)

BUSH: I have a statement, an opening statement, that is a little
longer than normal and I'd ask your indulgence, and then I will be
glad to respond to questions.

We're in the Gulf because the world must not and cannot reward
aggression. And we're there because our vital interests are at
stake. And we're in the Gulf because of the brutality of Saddam
Hussein. We're dealing with a dangerous dictator all too willing to
use force, who has weapons of mass destruction and is seeking new
ones, and who desires to control one of the world's key resources --
all at a time in history when the rules of the post-Cold War world are
being written.

Our objectives remain what they were since the outset. We seek Iraq's
immediate and unconditional withdrawal from Kuwait. We seek the
restoration of Kuwait's legitimate government. We seek the release of
all hostages and the free functioning of all embassies. And we seek
the stability and security of this critical region of the world.

0072

We are not alone in these goals and objectives. The United Nations,
invigorated with a new sense of purpose, is in full agreement. The
U.N. Security Council has endorsed 12 resolutions to condemn Iraq's
unprovoked invasion and occupation of Kuwait, implement tough economic
sanctions to stop all trade in and out of Iraq, and authorize the use
of force to compel Saddam to comply.

Saddam Hussein has tried every way he knows how to make this a fight
between Iraq and the United States and, clearly, he has failed.
Forces of 26 other nations are standing shoulder-to-shoulder with our
troops in the Gulf. The fact is that it is not the United States
against Iraq, it is Iraq against the world, and there's never been a
clearer demonstration of a world united against appeasement and
aggression.

Yesterday's U.N. Security Council resolution was historic. Once
again, the Security Council has enhanced the legitimate peacekeeping
function of the United Nations. Until yesterday, Saddam may not have
understood what he's up against in terms of world opinion, and I am
hopeful that now he will realize that he must leave Kuwait immediately.

I'm continually asked how effective are the U.N. sanctions -- those
put into effect on August 6 -- and I don't know the answer to that
question. Clearly, the sanctions are having some effect but I can't
tell you that the sanctions alone will get the job done. And thus I
welcome yesterday's U.N. action.

The fledgling democracies in Eastern Europe are being severely damaged
by the economic effects of Saddam's actions. The developing countries
of Africa and in our hemisphere are being victimized by this
dictator's rape of his neighbor, Kuwait. Those who feel that there is
no down side to waiting months and months must consider the
devastating damage being done every day to the fragile economies of
those countries that can afford it the least.

And, as Chairman Alan Greenspan testified just the other day, the
increase in oil prices resulting directly from Saddam's invasion is
hurting our country, too. And our economy, as I said the other day,
is at best in a serious slowdown. And if uncertainty remains in the
energy markets, the slowdown will get worse.

I've spelled out once again our reasons for sending troops to the
Gulf. Let me ell you the things that concern me most.

First, I put the immorality of the invasion of Kuwait itself. No
nation should rape, pillage and brutalize its neighbor. No nation
should be able to wipe a member state of the United Nations and the
Arab League off the face of the earth. And I'm deeply concerned about
all the hostages, innocent people held against their will in direct
contravention of international law. And then there's this cynical and
brutal policy, forcing people to beg for their release, parceling out
human lives to families and traveling emissaries like so much chattel.

0073

I'm deeply concerned about our own embassy in Kuwait. The flag is still flying there; a handful of beleaguered Americans remain inside the embassy, unable to come and go. This treatment of our embassy violates every civilized principle of diplomacy. And it demeans our people, it demeans our country. And I am determined that this embassy, as called for under Security Council Resolution 674, be fully replenished and our people free to come home.

What kind of precedent will these actions set for the future if Saddam's violation of international law goes unchallenged?

I'm also deeply concerned about the future of Kuwait itself. The tales of rape and assassination, of coldblooded murder and rampant looting, are almost beyond belief. The whole civilized world must unite and say this kind of treatment of people must end and those who violated the Kuwaiti people must be brought to justice.

I'm deeply concerned about Saddam's efforts to acquire nuclear weapons. Imagine his ability to blackmail his neighbors, should he possess a nuclear device. We've seen him use chemical weapons on his own people. We've seen him take his own country, one that should be wealthy and prosperous, and turn it into a poor country, all because of insatiable appetite for military equipment and conquest.

I've been asked why I ordered more troops to the Gulf. I remain hopeful that we can achieve a peaceful solution to this crisis. But if force is required, we, and the other 26 countries who have troops in the area, will have enough power to get the job done.

In our country, I know that there are fears about another Vietnam. Let me assure you, should military action be required, this will not be another Vietnam. This will not be a protracted drawn-out war. The forces arrayed are different; the opposition is different; the resupply of Saddam's military would be very different; the countries united against him in the United Nations are different, the topography of Kuwait is different, and the motivation of our all-volunteer force is superb.

I want peace. I want peace, not war, but if there must be war, we will not permit our troops to have their hands tied behind their backs, and I pledge to you there will not be any murky ending. If one American soldier has to go into battle, that soldier will have enough force behind him to win and then get out as soon as possible, as soon as the U.N. objectives have been achieved. I will never, ever agree to a halfway effort.

Let me repeat. We have no argument with the people of Iraq. Indeed, we have only friendship for the people there. And, further, I repeat that we have no desire to keep one single American soldier in the Gulf a single day longer than is necessary to achieve the objectives set out above.

0074

No one wants to see a peaceful solution to this crisis more than I do, and, at the same time, no one is more determined than I am to see Saddam's aggression reversed.

And lastly, people now caution patience. The United States and the entire world have been patient. I will continue to be patient, but yesterday's U.N. resolution, the 13th by the Security Council, properly says to Saddam Hussein, "Time is running out. You must leave Kuwait, and we've given you time to do just exactly that."

Many people have talked directly to Saddam Hussein and to his foreign minister, Tariq Aziz. All have been frustrated by Iraq's ironclad insistence that it will not leave Kuwait.

However, to go the extra mile for peace, I will issue an invitation to Foreign Minister Tariq Aziz to come to Washington at a mutually convenient time during the latter part of the week of December 10th to meet with me. And I'll invite ambassadors of several of our coalition partners in the Gulf to join me at that meeting.

In addition, I am asking Secretary Jim Baker to go to Baghdad to see Saddam Hussein, and I will suggest to Iraq's president that he receive the secretary of state at a mutually convenient time between December 15 and January 15 of next year.

Within the mandate -- within the mandate of the U.N. resolutions, I will be prepared, and so will Secretary Baker, to discuss all aspects of the Gulf crisis. However, to be very clear about these efforts to exhaust all means for achieving a political and diplomatic solution, I am not suggesting discussions that will result in anything less than Iraq's complete withdrawal from Kuwait, restoration of Kuwait's legitimate government, and freedom for all hostages.

QUESTION: Now that you have a clearcut U.N. resolution on use of force, doesn't that force you into a position -- if these talks between the secretary of state break down -- doesn't this force you into the position of having to use force on January 15 if Saddam Hussein hasn't left? And if not, won't we be seen as the one that blinked first?

ANSWER: No, the date was not a date at which point force had to be used.

Q: If I could just follow up with another question. Are you going to ask Congress for approval of this -- this resolution? Would you like to see Congress pass the same kind of resolution as the United Nations?

A: I'd love to see Congress pass a resolution enthusiastically endorsing what the United Nations has done, yes. But we're in consultation on that, and I have no plans to call a special session. I'm not opposed to it. But we are involved in consultations right now. I have talked to several members of Congress. I've talked to leaders in the House. I've talked to several on the Republican side

0075

and Democratic side in the Senate.   And I want to be sure that these consultations are complete.

Some feel a lame duck session is not good, that the new members should have a right to have a say.   Others feel that we ought to move right now.   The Congress, as you know, in their adjournment resolution had a provision in there that they could come back and take this up.   They are a coequal branch of government.   They can do that if they want to.

But we will continue our consultations.   They'll follow, incidentally, today, this meeting with the leadership.   So I'll get a little better feel for that as we go along.

Q: You say you're confident that American troops will prevail against Saddam if called upon.

A: Oh, absolutely.

Q: But at what price?   How many Americans?

A: Well, I can't give you that, any figures, of course.   But I can say that the movement of this additional force safeguards the lives of every American and every one of our allies in the Gulf.

Q: In recent days, senior members of the administration have emphatically rejected the idea of any special emissaries or diplomatic envoys to or from Iraq to discuss this on your part.   What changed your mind, sir?

A: The U.N. resolution, I think, has a good chance of making Saddam Hussein understand what it is he's up against.   I have not felt that he got the message.   I hope this will do it.   But I am convinced that these two direct meetings that I've discussed here will guarantee to all the people of the world, certainly to the American people, that Saddam Hussein not misunderstand, not misinterpret -- I keep hearing, "Well, people won't give him the news."   Unlike the president of the United States, who gets good news and bad news very faithfully, I am told that Saddam Hussein's troops don't bring him the bad news.   And I'm told that he is somewhat isolated.   And I think this U.N. resolution will help in a sense to de-isolate him.   And I think the two proposals that I've made here will help.   And so, it's just going the extra step, that's what it is.   And it's a decision that I personally made.

Q: You indicate that this date is not actually a deadline for the use of force, merely a date after which force would be permissible.   How do you avoid the impression, should that date come and go without military action, that the U.S.-led coalition has, in fact, blinked?

A: Well, we've got to look at events at the time.   But I don't think there will ever be a perception that the United States is going to blink in this situation.   That's why I had some of the words in this statement that I had.

0076

Q: You've just spoken about the weapons of mass destruction and nuclear weapons, and also that one of your goals is to try to reach stability in the region. Can you reach stability in the region with Saddam Hussein in power?

A: I think most countries -- members of the United Nations -- feel that there have to be some safeguards put into effect in terms of guaranteeing the security and stability of the Gulf. And so, I would think that the status quo ante will not be enough, and I think there will be -- there are sanctions in place now, and I think it would be very.proper to discuss what those safeguards should be after there has been a -- a total compliance with the United Nations resolutions.

Q: I just noticed that when you were originally -- when you outlined your goals you included stability in the region. You seemed to summarize them when you talk about these talks with Saddam Hussein, but you didn't -- you only mentioned the first three; you didn't mention stability in the region.

A: Well was I talking about the U.N. resolution -- which security and stability I don't think was a part of the U.N. resolution. It is certainly part of the world's objective, however. I think that may be the technical difference.

But look, it is critical, and it is very, very important.

Q: I want to ask if your comments about the Kuwaiti embassy -- whether it's fair to conclude, based on those, that you will neither close the embassy nor permit those Americans to be starved out.

A: I will not say exactly what I will do or exactly what I won't do.

There is a very interesting report that we got in this morning saying that some Iraqis showed up at the Kuwaiti embassy, our embassy in Kuwait, and had delivered fruit, vegetables, and a case of Iraqi cigarettes to Embassy Kuwait. And apparently there's going to be another delivery tomorrow, including soda pop. And they asked what medical supplies were required. And --

Q: (Military ?) --

A: It doesn't say that. And the embassy will apparently provide a list tomorrow. And the electricity is still cut off.

So this is kind of an interesting little development. But I -- somebody said to me, "Well, hey, what about if there's some provocation?" They asked me in the leadership meeting. I said, "Consider me provoked when it comes to the U.S. embassy. Consider me provoked when I see Americans without proper food and medical equipment."

Q: Do you take it from that communique that you've received there that the Iraqis have the message and want to eliminate that as a potential tripwire?

0077

A: I don't know. It's too -- it's the best question, right on
target, one that we were discussing inside. And I -- let's try to be
optimistic and say this is -- this could be a positive sign. But it's
so far short of compliance with international law that I can't be
rejoicing. But it is a very interesting development.

Q: You've been getting some pretty negative comments up on the Hill
in these hearings, as you know, this week. Now this morning you said
this would not be a long, protracted Vietnam-type war. However,
General Odom of the -- former head of the NSA, testified just this
morning before the Senate Armed Services that in fact we'd have to be
there for decades. Now presumably he means even after military combat
we'd have to have people in place there as part of a peacekeeping
force. Do you see our commitment there to extend that far?

A: No, I don't.

Q: Let me ask you something else. Al Gore yesterday takes issue with
your comments and the comments of some of your aides, such as Brent
Scowcroft, about Saddam being able to churn out a nuclear weapon
within a matter of months. Gore, who's had some private briefings
apparently from some of these people, indicates that your
administration's statements are misleading --

A: I disagree with the senator, and if he wants to gamble on the
future about the construction of atomic weapons by Saddam Hussein, I
don't. And I know what the intelligence says, every bit of it. And I
can't share it, obviously, because we don't comment on intelligence
matters. But I am concerned, and the very first time I spoke on this
subject, I think· in August, I mentioned weapons of mass destruction, I
believe, but certainly early on. And I am concerned about it. And if
Senator Gore has a difference of opinion and is not concerned about
it, we just have an honest difference there.

I am concerned about Saddam Hussein's attempt to accelerate the
possession of a -- construction or possession of a nuclear weapon, and
I might as well share that as honestly as I can.

Q: Are you saying you think he could develop a warhead next year?

A: I'm not giving you a time frame, but there -- you've seen the
estimates, some of which, I guess, are accurate, in the papers. And
there's a lot of scientists that come down on different sides. And
Senator Gore, I'm sure, is an intelligent fellow, and he -- but I
don't think he has access to absolutely all -- maybe he does -- but I
am not going to err on the side of under estimation when it comes to
this question.

Q: Your announcement about Tariq Aziz and Secretary Baker -- have you
had any signals, any indications from the Iraqis, that they would
welcome this, that they are indeed looking for this kind of
communication?

0078

A: No. The only thing I've heard is that they want to talk. There's an opportunity, but no, I have not had any -- even diplomatic signals or signals of other kinds.

Q: And of those 26 nations that you list in the area, how many of those are equally committed to offensive action, rather than just defensive action?

A: I can't give you the answer to that because I don't really know. But I expect that there is enthusiasm in all quarters of those countries for the U.N. action that was taken yesterday.

Q: With all respect, shouldn't you know how many would follow your troops into battle?

A: I know that what I said is true about the -- if we have to go into battle, and I am satisfied I know enough about that. I went over in detail, as one will imagine a president should because I have the responsibility as Commander-in-Chief, what might happen if we have to use force. I repeat, I hope we'll never have to have one single shot fired in anger.

Q: Iraq has been constantly calling for dialogue. Aren't you concerned that those two missions, Tariq Aziz and James Baker, will lead Saddam Hussein to claim that the United States is showing a sign of weakness?

A: That what?

Q: That the United States is weakening?

A: Because Baker goes to Baghdad?

Q: Aren't you concerned that that would be the position of Saddam Hussein?

A: No, I'm not. I'm concerned some might say this is an ultimatum in which it is an effort to be sure that he understands the commitment of the United States, that he understands that anything that is done must be done inside the confines of the U.N. resolutions that have been passed, that there will be no contingency. There can be no face saving. That's not what this is about. This is to be sure that he understands how strongly the president of the United States feels about implementing to a tee, without concession -- the U.N. position.

And some have told me that he's not getting the message of how determined we are. And I can't think of any better way to do it at this juncture, in the wake of the U.N. resolution, than this face-to-face meeting. I'm not sure he'll agree to it.

Q: Today's press conference seems to amount to, again, more talk of preparation for war. Can you describe what you think your responsibilities are, in terms of Congress, as we head into this

0073

period, since they seem to think that and agree that you're consulting
-- talking, but not -- you seem reluctant to go and get a resolution
that mimics the U.N. resolution. What do you think your
responsibilities are to Congress and to the people that elected them?

A: Full consultation.

Q: Any more than telling them before you do something?

A: I'm leveling with them on where I think -- think matters are right
now, and you've put your interpretation on my remarks. There was
plenty of comments in there about hoping that we will have a peaceful
resolution; that the best answer to get a peaceful resolution is to
have Saddam Hussein know how determined everybody is.

You see, I think yesterday's U.N. resolution was a step towards peace,
not a step towards war, because I believe that when Saddam Hussein
finally gets the message and understands what he's up against in terms
of world opinion and other things, that he will do that in Kuwait
which he did in Iran.

Q: The Soviet Union did indeed vote on our side as far as the
resolution, allowing force if it's necessary. Are we going to offer
the Soviet Union any compromise on export credits? As you know, that
there's some concern that they think there's a de facto grain embargo
going on because we won't offer export credits in their very needy
time.

A: The matters are totally separate and unrelated, but I am concerned
about this, and I've talked with Mr. Gorbachev of a willingness to
entertain proposals for food, particularly if the reports prove to be
accurate in terms of the severe winter and the hardship that this will
inflict on the Soviet people.

I have asked our own top people here to come up with recommendations
for me next week as what to do about Jackson-Vanik. It has been my
position that the Soviets should pass the necessary emigration
legislation. That has not taken place. But some are saying that I
now have a clearer waiver authority than I thought. And I do not want
to work hardship on any sector of the American economy. I'm one of
those strongest proponents against a grain embargo, and yet I'm told
that some in middle America think that our position is really almost
resulting in a grain embargo. And I want to dispel any notion that I
am for the grain embargo.

The Soviets are concerned about many aspects of this legislation. So
I am facing a decision as to what to do. Should we try to waive
Vanik, and should we then extend credits under the CCC? There are
other agricultural programs that I think we can go forward with
immediately without a waiver of Jackson-Vanik. But it's a very
evolving issue, question here, and I don't know exactly what I am
going to do, because we're caught between some strong and
understandable economic interests at home, and, on the other hand, a
position of wanting to stand for free and fair emigration. 0080

One thing that is important to note, however, is that the amount -- the exodus of Soviet Jews from the Soviet Union is high, and I'd like to take some credit for our administration in this because we've been steadfast in encouraging the exodus of Soviet Jews. And so that will weigh on my consideration when I get down to have to make this final decision about the waiver of Jackson-Vanik.

Q: On that, would you consider another increase of, you know, the quota that -- the number of people that could immigrate to the United States? Would we increase the amount that we'd accept?

A: We're reviewing the whole policy at this juncture.

Q: Arab experts suggest that Saddam Hussein has hinted in his remarks that he would like to have some sort of deal, but he wouldn't necessarily hold to his demands. Now you're saying you're willing to meet with him. Are you willing to offer him anything in these meetings in return for a pullout, such as a conference on the Middle East?

A: No. Those two items are totally separate. We've made that very, very clear. And what I have said is that this will be -- this -- these discussions will be done within the U.N. mandate. I'm not all that hopeful that what -- that we'll get big results out of all of this. It's going the extra mile; it's taking the extra step. But I can't tell you that I think we're going to have great success on all of this because our partnership in the world is together on the fact that we cannot stop short of total fulfillment without condition of the U.N. resolutions.

Q: Well, what then is the point of the meeting? Are you just delivering ultimatums?

A: No, this isn't an ultimatum, at all. And I hope what it does is demonstrate that we are prepared to go face to face and tell him how committed we are to the U.N. resolutions. I've told you, I don't think he has felt this commitment. As I said earlier, he may feel it a little more strongly now that we did what many skeptics thought couldn't happen -- that the U.N. Security Council did -- and that is come together and pass this very important resolution.

So one thing is, we got to -- he's got to understand what the alternatives are to complying with the U.N. resolution. And the best way to get that across is one on one -- Baker looking him right in the eye. I've been told that he doesn't necessarily believe that I am totally committed to what I've been saying, and here's a good opportunity to have him understand that, face to face.

So we want to make the case to him, directly, for complying with the U.N. resolutions; make the case to him, from a secretary of state who's incessantly worked to get this resolution through, of the strength of the commitment of the international community. And then try to persuade him that -- to reconsider his position and to take the steps necessary for a peaceful resolution of the crisis. 0081

But it isn't, you know, a trip of concession. When you've done what he's done, I don't -- I don't see that there's -- there's room for concession, there's room for giving something to save face. That's not the way you treat with aggression and we're not going to treat it any differently than I've outlined here.

Q: With high oil prices hurting the world --

A: You're whipsawed today, it's terrible. The statement was so long at the beginning; I apologize for that.

Q: You mentioned the damage that high oil prices are doing to the world economy. Should Saudi Arabia and other producers share more of their windfall?

A: I think they're doing a pretty good job in underwriting the costs to various countries and helping third -- third party countries that have been hurt by all of this. But I think everybody should go the extra mile to help others.

And I was pleased when I was talking in Mexico, for example with President Salinas, that he is selling oil at -- trying to help the burden by selling oil at bargain prices off of this inflated world price. So I think everybody should try to help. And I think the Saudis have made a lot of commitments to countries in trying to help out, and I hope they'll continue to do that, and I'm confident they will.

Q: If I could follow, sir, should Saudi Arabia have a military draft?

A: That's for the Saudi Arabians to decide. I don't think the United States needs one, incidentally.

Q: If you ultimately feel that you have to ask Americans to support the use of force, what that, of course, means is that you have to ask some parents to give up the lives of their children.

A: I know it.

Q: And what I was wondering was, we all know how important your children are to you. Do you feel that this issue is important enough to you that you could conceive of giving up one of their lives for it?

A: You know, you've put your finger on a very difficult question. People say to me, "How many lives, how many lives can you expend?" Each one is precious. And I don't want to reminisce, but I've been there. I know what it's like to have fallen comrades and see young kids die in battle.

And it's only the president that should be asked to make the decision: Is it worth it? How many lives is it worth? Is it worth it to commit one life, put one life in harm's way to achieve these objectives? And that's why I want to get a peaceful resolution to this question.

0082

You ought to read my mail. It is so heart moving. Supportive, and yet, "please bring my kid home. Please bring my husband home." And it's a tough question, but the president has to make the right decision, and these are worldwide principles of moral importance. And I will do my level best to bring those kids home without one single shot fired in anger. And if a shot is fired in anger, I want to guarantee each person that their kid whose life is in harm's way will have the maximum support, will have the best chance to come home alive, and will be backed up to the hilt.

And that's why -- because of that question that weighs on my mind, I added that language this morning about how this will not be a Vietnam. They can criticize me for moving force, and if we've got one kid that's apt to be in harm's way, I want him backed up to the hilt by American firepower and others as well. And that's why I'm working as hard as I am, not only to hold this coalition together, but to strengthen it. And the best way to safeguard the lives of Americans is for Saddam Hussein to do that which he should have done long ago. And if force has to be used, the best way to safeguard lives is to see that you've got the best and you're willing to use it. And that's my posture.

Q: Why do you seem to be avoiding the people's representatives having an opportunity to talk on this and to express their opinion? You know Congress, and yet you're avoiding it. And you know that the Constitution gives them power not only to declare war, to provide the money and to say other things about what shall be done with troops. That's the Constitution. Yet you seem to be avoiding that. The experts on Capitol Hill say that what you have done by pre-notification, calling two or three members and saying to them, "We're on the way," you've already made the decision, you're just notifying them, that's pre-notification; that's not consulting with Congress. They say you should sit down and have a back-and-forth with them -- and I will remind you that when Foley speaks as Speaker of the House, he may be Speaker of the House, but he sure as hell doesn't represent Florida or Texas.

A: Well, now, therein you brought up the -- properly brought up the dilemma I face. There are 435 members of the U.S. Congress. There are 100 members of fine. They have the power under the resolution of adjournment to come back 20 seconds from now, and to take a voice, to stand, to take a common position. If they want to come back here and endorse what the president of the United States has done and what the U.N. Security Council has done -- come on, we're ready. I'd like to see it happen.

But what I don't want to do is have it come back and end up where you have 435 voices in one House and 100 on the other saying what not to do, and saying -- kind of a hand-wringing operation that would send bad signals.

I welcome these hearings. We are having hearings. We are consulting. I've told you I'm consulting. I'll be honest with you. I

0083

cannot consult with 535 strong-willed individuals. I can't do it, nor
does my responsibility under the Constitution compel me to do that.
And I think everyone would agree that we have had more consultations
than -- than previous administrations.

Q: Sir, we have a majority rule in this country, and you seem to be
afraid of it.

A: No, I am not afraid of it at all. We have a tripartite form of
government, and I know my strengths and I know the limitations on the
presidency.

This is an interesting debate. And I know my limitations. And I know
what I can do, and I know what previous presidents have done. And I
am still determined to consult the extra mile.

Do you want to continue to debate? You've --

Q: Well, sir, you seem to give -- you and Jim Baker give the other
countries a chance to talk, and you give the United Nations a chance
to talk, but you won't give the United States people a chance to
debate with you.

Q: Is there a question in there somewhere?

A: Well, now, that's an absurd comment, from a bright person like
you. That is absolutely absurd. They're holding hearings. They're
talking. They have the power under the adjournment resolution to
reconvene this minute. Some in the House want to come back now. Some
want to talk about it later on. Some in the Senate want to come right
back now and immediately endorse what the president has done and what
the Security Council resolution is, and I'm for that. But some
don't. And so consultation is going on. Please do not assign to me
improper motives. We're -- they're talking right now. They're having
endless hearings by endless experts up there, each one with a slightly
different view. And that's the American way. And that's fine. And I
know what the responsibilities of the president are, and I am
fulfilling those responsibilities.

(end transcript)
NNNN

0084

외 무 부

관리번호 90-2611

종   별 :

번   호 : USW-5410   일   시 : 90 1204 1836

수   신 : 장관(미북,미안,중근동,국연)

발   신 : 주 미 대사

제   목 : 걸프 사태관련 국무부 브리핑

연:USW-5367

1. 금 12.4. 당관 유명환 참사관은 국무부 근동국 DAVID MACK 부차관보가, 현재 다국적 오퍼레이션에 참여하고 있거나, 이에 기여하고 있는 국가를 중심으로 당지 외교단을 위해 실시한 걸프 사태관련 브리핑에 참석하였는바, 동요지 하기 보고함

(당관 임성남 2 등서기관 배석)

가. 걸프 사태 관련, 미국은 손실을 극속화 하면서 금번 사태를 평화적으로해결하기 위해 노력하고 있으나, 11.30. 발표된 부쉬 대통령의 미-이락 양국간외무장관 교환 방문 제의도 여사한 노력의 일환으로 보아야함.

즉, 미국으로서는 금번 사태의 평화적 해결이 불가능하다고 판단될때에야 비로소 무력사용에 의존할것인바, 그 이전에 모든 외교적 해결 가능성을 모색할것임(WILL EXHAUST EVERY DIPLOMATIC POSSIBILITY)

나. 현재 실시중인 대 이락 경제 봉쇄 조치는 원유수출에 의한 이락의 외화수입을 원천 봉쇄 함으로써 이락 경제에 심각한 타격을 가하고 있음. 그러나 후세인 대통령이 유엔 안보리의 각종 결의에 아무런 긍정적 반응을 보이지 않고 있는 점을 감안할때, 대이락 경제 봉쇄 조치가 동 대통령의 상황판단(CALCULATIONS) 에 까지 영향을 미치고 있다고는 보기 어려움.

오히려 이락측은 쿠웨이트를 자국의 행정구역으로 편입하고, 각종 약탈, 테러 행위를 자행하고 있는 형편임.

다.11.29. 통과된 유엔 안보리의 대이락 무력사용 허용 결의안은 이락측으로 하여금 주변상황을 정확하게 인식하도록 하기 위해 마지막으로 기회를 주고 있는것이며, 전기 미-이락 양국간 외무장관 교환방문 제의도 후세인 대통령에게 미국의 결의를 분명하게 전달하기 위해서임.

미주국	차관	1차보	2차보	미주국	중아국	국기국	청와대	안기부

즉, 동 교환 방문의 기본 목적은 사태 해결을 위한 "교섭"에 있는 것이 아니라, 이락 지도층에 대해 이락이 현재 처해 있는 국제적 상황을 분명히 인식시켜 주는데에 있는바, 동 교환방문을 통한 여하한 양보(이락의 체면을 살려주기 위한 부분적 해결 방안이나 팔레스타인 문제등 여타 국제문제와의 연계 방안등)도 생각할수 없음.

요약컨데, 이락 지도층은 유엔 안보리의 결의를 수락하든가 아니면 정권 몰락의 위험을 무릅쓰든가, 현재 양자 택일의 상황에 처해 있다는점을 분명히 인식하여야 함.

라. 한편, 이락측이 AZIZ 외무장관의 방미 초청을 수락함에 따라 현재 바그다드 에서 방미 일자를 양측간에 협의 중이며(베이커 장관의 이락방문 문제는 상금 미협의), 금번 사태와 여타 국제문제와의 연계 방안을 이락측이 거론할 가능성을 사전 배제키 위해 미국외에 여타 관련국도 대이락 협의에 참여케 하려던 당초의 방침을 변경, 미-이락 양국간 협의로만 진행 예정임.

마. 또한 미측으로서는 대 이락 경제 봉쇄 조치의 유지, 강화를 위해 계속 노력 할것이며, 금번 사태로 인한 국제적 부담의 공평한 분담을 지속적으로 추진할것임.

바. 현재 미측으로서는 대이락 공격 개시에 관한 여하한 결정도 내리지 않은 상태인바, 대규모 미군 병력이 걸프 지역에 파견되고 유엔안보리의 무력 사용허용 결의안이 통과되었다고 해서 전쟁이 불가피 하다고 보는것은 속단임. 금번 사태의 평화적 해결은 아직도 가능한바, 여사한 평화적 해결은 이락군의 쿠웨이트로 부터의 무조건 철수에의해서만 이룩될수 있음.

　2. 특기 사항

가. 상기 브리핑 내용은 기본적으로 연호 부쉬 대통령 기자회견 내용과 유사한바, 금번 외무장관 교환 방문 목적이 "교섭"에 있지 않다는 점을 거듭강조한점이 주목됨(동 브리핑 직후 질의 응답시, 이락측이 체면을 살리지 못한다면 평화적 해결의 가능성은 사실상 희박하지 않느냐는 지적이 다수 있었는바, MACK 부차관보는 이락측은 정권의 성격상 FACE-SAVING 을 필요로 하지 않는다고 언급하고, 기존의 정책을 180 도 전환하면서도 국민들에 대해서는 이를 이락측의 승리로 설명한 전례가 다수 있다고 부연함)

나. 또한 질의 응답시, MACK 부차관보가 금번 미-이락간 협의의 대상 의제가 사전 결정되어 있지 않은 상태 이므로 걸프사태 관련 제반 측면(예컨데, 이락측이 쿠웨이트로 부터 선 철수하는 경우의 사후 관련 문제등)을 논의할수 있을것이라고 언급한 점 및 설사 금번 미-이락간의 협의가 소기의 성과를 거두지 못하더라도

관련국간 협의에 다소의 시일이 소요될것이므로 1.16. 부로 대이락 공격을 개시키는 어려울것이라고 언급한점등이 주목됨.

  (대사 박동진-국장)

  91.6.30. 일반

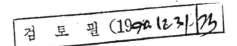

검 토 필 (1990. 12.31. 73

예 고 문 에 의 거 일 반 문 서 로
재 분 류 19 91 6.31 서 명 73

관리
번호 90-2518

원 본

외 무 부

종 별 : 지 급

번 호 : USW-5427

일 시 : 90 1205 1816

수 신 : 장관(미북, 미안, 중근동)

발 신 : 주 미 대사

제 목 : 미-이락 외무장관 교환 방문

연:USW-5410

1. 금 12.5. 국무부는 대변인을 통해 이락측이 11.30. 발표된 미측의 미-이락 양국간 외무장관 교환 방문 제의를 공식 수락했으며, 이에 따라 방문 일자등 구체 사항에 관한 협의를 현재 진행중이라고 발표 했음.

2. 동관련 진전 동향 추보 예정임.

(대사 박동진-차관)

91.6.30. 일반

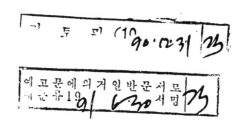

미주국   차관   1차보   미주국   중아국

PAGE 1

90.12.06   08:45

외신 2과 통제관 BT

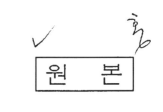

외 무 부

종   별 : 지급

번   호 : USW-5540   일   시 : 90 1213 1838

수   신 : 장관(미봉,중근동,미안,마그레브)

발   신 : 주 미 대사

제   목 : 미-이락 외무장관 교환 방문 추진동향

연:USW(F)-3464

1. 금 12.13. NYT 지는 표제 교환 방문관련, AZIZ 이락 외무장관의 방미 일자는 12.17 로 미-이락 양국간에 의견이 접근한 반면, BAKER 국무장관의 이락 방문일자는 이락측이 1.12. 을 고집하는데에 반해, 미측은 1.3. 이전을 주장함으로써 현재 양국간 교섭이 난관에 봉착해 있다고연호 보도함.

2. 이와관련, 금일 당관 임성남 2 등 서기관이 국무부 이란-이락과 JOSEPH MCGHEE 부과장으로부터 탐문한바에 따르면, 미측은 BAKER 국무장관의 이락방문 일자가 결정되지 않는한 AZIZ 이락 외무장관의 방미를 수락하지 않는다는것이 현재 입장이므로, 12.17 로 보도된 AZIZ 장관의 방미일자도 확정된것으로 보기는 어렵다는 반응을 보임.그밖에 회담 진전방향등에 관한 동부과장 언급 요지는 다음과같음.

가. 금번 걸프 사태에 관한 이락측 결정권은 훗세인 대통령이 독점하고 있으므로, AZIZ 외무장관은 부쉬 대통령 면담기회등을 이락의 기존 입장을 선전하는데에 주로 이용할것으로 보임. 즉 미측으로서는 BAKER 국무장관의 훗세인 대통령 면담에 보다 큰 비중을 두고 있음.

나. 금번 외무장관 교환 방문의 목적이 걸프사태 해결을 위한 교섭에 있지 않다는 점은 미측도 누차 강조한바 있으며, 팔레스타인 문제등 여타 국제분쟁과 금번 사태와의 연계를 수용할수 없다는 미측 입장에도 전혀 변함이 없음. 그러나금번 교환 방문시 미국으로서는 이락이 갖고 있는 제반 우려사항(CONCERNS)에 대해 토의를 할 용의는 있음.

다. 팔레스타인 문제등을 논의키 위한 국제회의 개최 구상관련, 여사한 문제가 이스라엘로서는 국가 자체의 존립에 직결되는 문제이므로 쉽사리 응할수 없는 입장이며, 여사한 이스라엘의 입장은 최근 샤미르 수상 방미시에도 확인한바 있음.

미주국   차관   1차보   미주국   중아국   중아국

사견이기는 하나, 여타 아랍제국들이 이스라엘을 국가로서 승인하는등 전향적 조치를 취한다면 이스라엘도 보다 유리한 반응을 보일수 있을 것으로 봄. 주지하다싶이, 미국으로서는 여사한 국제회의 개최가 시기적으로 이락의 요구와 연계되어 있다는 인상을 줄수 있으므로, 유보적인 태도를 취하고 있음.

　　라. 개인적 전망이기는 하나, 이락측이 3 월말 이전 부비얀도나 루말리아 유전지대를 제외한 대부분의 쿠웨이트 영토에서 철수함으로서, 일단 평화적해결의 실마리를 찾게될 것으로 봄.여사한 상황이 도래하는 경우 미국으로서는 무력사용이 곤란해질것이며, 다만 경제 봉쇄 조치는 일단 계속 이행하게될 것으로 봄.(대사 박동진-국장)

　　예고:91.12.31 일반

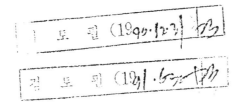

외 무 부

종 별 : 지 급

번 호 : USW-5561   일 시 : 90 1214 1845

수 신 : 장관(미북,중근동,미안)

발 신 : 주 미 대사

제 목 : 미-이락 외무장관 교환 방문 추진 동향(BUSH 대통령 기자 회견)

연 USW-5540

1. 금 12.14 백악관 기자회견을봉해 부쉬 대통령은 미-이락 외무장관 교환 방문 추진 관련, 이락측이 베이커 장관의 이락 방문일자를 1.12 로 고집하는것은유엔 안보리 결의안을 준수하지 않기 위해 일종의 지역 작전을 쓰려는 의도로 밖에 볼수 없다고 언급하고, 현재 AZIZ 이락 외무장관의 방미 문제도 보류상태(ON HOLD)에 있는것으로 본다고 언급함(기자 회견전문은 USW(F)3491 로 FAX 송부)

2. 그러나 부쉬 대통령은 이락측이 1.12 을 계속 고집하는 경우 미측의 대응 방안에 관해서는 구체적 언급을 회피하였는바, 현재 미 행정부는 이문제로 인해 다소 곤경에 처해 있는것으로 보임(부쉬 대통령은 11.30 외무장관 교환 방문 제의시 방문 일자를 보다 구체적으로 제시 하지 않은것이 실책 이었다고 언급)

3. 한편 금일 부쉬 대통령이 이락측을 공개적으로 비난한것은 후세인 대통령으로 하여금 유엔 안보리 결의안 주수의 당위성을 보다 심각하게 받아들이게 함으로서 베이커 국무장관의 이락 방문을 보다 조기에 실현 시키려는 의도로 보이는바, 동건 진전 사항 계속 추보 예정임.

(대사 박동진-국장)

91.12.31 일반

미주국   1차보   미주국   중아국   정와대   안기부

PAGE 1   90.12.15   09:41

외신 2과 롱제관 BT

0091

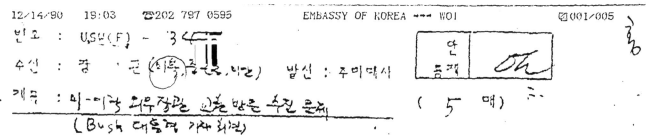

PRESS CONFERENCE WITH PRESIDENT BUSH PRIOR TO DEPARTURE FOR CAMP DAVID
THE SOUTH LAWN, THE WHITE HOUSE, FRIDAY, DECEMBER 14, 1990

And now I'd like to take up another subject, a second one. On
November 30th, in offering direct meetings between the United States
and Iraq, I offered to go the extra mile for a peaceful solution to
the Gulf question. And I wanted to make clear to Saddam Hussein the
absolute determination of the coalition that he comply fully with
the Security Council resolutions. Iraqi aggression cannot be
rewarded.

And so I have asked the Secretary of State to be available to
go to Baghdad any time up to and including January 3rd, which is
over five months after the invasion of Kuwait and only 12 days
before the United Nations deadline for withdrawal. That deadline is
real.

To show flexibility, I have offered any one of 15 dates for
Secretary Baker to go to Baghdad, and the Iraqis have offered only
one date. In offering to go the extra mile for peace, however, I
did not offer to be a party to Saddam Hussein's manipulation.
Saddam Hussein is not too busy to see, on short notice, Kurt
Waldheim, Willy Brandt, Muhammad Ali, Ted Heath, John Connally,
Ramsey Clark, and many, many others on very short notice. And it
simply is not credible that he cannot, over a two-week period, make
a couple of hours available for the Secretary of State on an issue
of this importance, unless, of course, he is seeking to circumvent
the United Nations deadline.

Look, I want a peaceful solution to this crisis. But I will
not be a party to circumventing or diluting the United Nations
deadline, which I think offers the very best chance for a peaceful
solution. And so I wanted to get out
my feeling about these -- these proposed meetings.

Yes, Jim?

Q   Mr. President, what's wrong with the January 12th date
that he set? Why would that dilute it, unless you're afraid that he
might come up with some offer?

PRESIDENT BUSH: Well, in the first place, the United Nations
resolutions that pertain say that he has to be out of Kuwait. I
wish now that I had been a little more explicit in my first
announcement on what I meant by "mutually convenient dates." But I
was not then, but now -- and am not -- not now prepared to have this
man manipulate the purpose of the Secretary of State's visit. So we
will -- we have made an offer of many, many dates, but remember, the
United Nations resolution calls for total withdrawal by this date.

3491 -/

Q   And does your statement today indicate that you would not
accept January 5th or 6th?

PRESIDENT BUSH: We've offered 15 days, and he ought to get
moving and do something reasonable, if he really wants to move for
peace. Yes?

Q   Mr. President, is there a date at which you would
withdraw the offer to meet -- the senators this morning say you're
willing to forgo talks now?

PRESIDENT BUSH: Well, we're not going to do them on terms that
-- that are -- would appear to the world to be an effort to
circumvent the United Nations resolution. I mean, he's got a
massive force there, and that force has to be out on the 15th of
January under the United Nations resolutions. So we'll see -- we'll
see how it goes. I -- I'm -- I would say that we've given so many
alternatives here that he ought to stay with -- accept one of these.
If he's serious.

Q   Are you --

PRESIDENT BUSH: Now, if it's simply that he is trying to
manipulate, that is what I will have no part of.

Q   Are you offering --

Q   Mr. President?

Q   -- are you telling him that --

PRESIDENT BUSH: Helen, we've just got to take what they call a
follow-on here.

Yes?

Q   Is there a deadline for him to accept your offer?

Q   No, we're not putting down deadlines on it. The Aziz
meeting is on hold, I guess. I mean, I say "I guess" because
we've made clear to them that it's kind of a home-and-home
arrangement here.

Yes, Helen?

Q   You've said the deadline is real, so that means you think
you have carte blanche to start a war after January 15th, or on
January 15th?

PRESIDENT BUSH: I'm saying that the United Nations resolution
is very clear as it regards January 15th, and I will continue now to
work for a peaceful solution.

3491 -2

0093

Q   Mr. President, when Congress --

Q   Well, you do think you can go to war after that, is that
right?

PRESIDENT BUSH: What do you mean, "can go to war"?

Q   You can start a war.

PRESIDENT BUSH: I -- I think that the United Nations
resolutions should be fully implemented.

Q   Mr. President, when Congress comes back in January, will
you ask Congress for specific authority to take offensive action?

PRESIDENT BUSH: I -- we're talking about that, and I'm very
pleased with the support we've had in Congress, and I'm very pleased
with the level of support from the American people. You see, as
these hostages have come home, I think the people have understood --
the American people -- much more clearly what's at stake. As
they've seen the testimony about the brutality to the Kuwaiti people
that was so compelling at the United Nations, I think people have
said, "Wait a minute, this policy deserves support."

So I am pleased with the support I think that's being
manifested in more support by the Congress. But I will be talking
to the leaders, continuing to consult. And what I -- I told the
leaders in the Cabinet Room a few weeks ago, if you want to come in
here and strongly endorse what I am doing or endorse the United
Nations resolution, I welcome that because I think it would send a
very strong, clear signal to the world.

Q   Well, sir, why are you afraid to go before Congress and
consult with them and get their advice and get their approval?

PRESIDENT BUSH: Hey, listen, Sarah, I was consulting with them
as recently as this morning -- five members of Congress. And we
will continue to consult with them.

Yeah?

Q   That's not 535 [members of the House and Senate].

Q   Mr. President, we're hearing if Saddam Hussein --

PRESIDENT BUSH: We're doing it all the time. I'm on the phone
almost every day to them. We've had leadership meeting after

leadership meeting. Oh listen! I explained this to you in the
press room awhile back -- (laughter) -- this same question! Come
on!

Q   (Off mike) -- but you should see my mail!

PRESIDENT BUSH: (Chuckles) You ought to see mine.

Q   Are you saying if Saddam Hussein won't meet by January
3rd, there simply will be no meeting?

3491 -3

0094

PRESIDENT BUSH: =m saying that he -- we've given him 15 dates
and he ought to take one of them. I don't like to draw deadlines in
the sand here. But I -- there'd have to be some compelling reason
for me to change it, because I don't want to move this up against
the United Nations deadline. If you'll read the UN resolutions,
you'll see that he should be totally out, totally out of Kuwait by
January 15th. That's a massive undertaking.

Yeah?

Q   Mr. President, if I may follow up?

PRESIDENT BUSH: Yeah?

Q ·   Are you saying that you may meet January 4th or 5th --

PRESIDENT BUSH: I'm not saying that, you're saying that. I've
put it as clearly as I can. I hope there's no obfuscation.

Yeah?

Q   Mr. President, what is your thinking today about Saddam
Hussein's nuclear and chemical capabilities? Will international
safeguards -- (inaudible) --?

PRESIDENT BUSH: I am very much concerned about it. I think
that Congress and the American people are getting increasingly
concerned about his -- not his -- it's not just nuclear which
concerns me,
but it's other unconventional war capabilities. I'm talking
about, for example in this context, chemical -- weapons that he has
used on his own people already.

So yes, I am very concerned about it, and any arrangement that
is going to keep the rest of the world happy will have to have --
address itself to these -- this unconventional war capability of
Saddam Hussein. Anybody that will take the reckless action he has
taken militarily against a neighbor must be contained in this --
in this era when we're all concerned about nuclear proliferation.

So I'm glad you brought it up, because this morning I met with
a group of people who are supportive of our policy and they are
emphasizing to me, as they go across the country, the concern by the

American people -- on the part of the American people -- about his
possession of these unconventional weapons and his desire to acquire
nuclear weapons.

And I told -- I believe that it was a press conference with
most of you present -- I said if I've got to err on the side of how
long -- I addressed myself to the question, how long does he ---
will it take for him to get weapons, I will err on the cautious
side, on the conservative side. And I am concerned that he could
acquire weapons in a very short period of time -- a weapon in a very
short period of time. And that is a factor that is serious as I
contemplate how he is compelled to live up to the United Nations
resolution.

8491 -4

0095

I've got time for one more, and then I really do have to go.

Q   Mr. President, right now the issue of chemical --
possession of weapons and nuclear weapons is not part of the United
Nations resolutions. Will you go back to the UN and get that made
part of one of the requirements for Saddam Hussein or will you move
on that unilaterally?

PRESIDENT BUSH: Well, I don't think it's unilateral because I
think all our coalition partners
share my concerns about his possession of unconventional weapons and
his attempt to get more. But I don't have plans at this moment to
take this to the United Nations, but believe me, it is very much in
my thinking as I contemplate what action to take to enforce the
United Nations resolutions.

Thank you all and have a great weekend.

                              END

3491 -5

0096

페만 사태 지원에 따른 미국내 의료요원 부족 현상

(12.19자 The New York Times 기사 요약)

1990.12.21

북 미 과

o 국무부가 전쟁 발발시 예상되는 부상자 치료를 위해 페르시아만에 파견할
   대규모 의료지원 체제의 구축을 서두름에 따라, 미국내 의료 혜택 제공에
   많은 지장을 초래함.
   - 이는 20,000명이 넘는 군의관, 간호원 그리고 기타 요원들을 병원선 및
     걸프만 지역에 있는 병원에 배치함으로써 야기된 현상임.

o 이런 현상은 농촌 지역에서 특히 심하며, 도시 지역에서도 몇몇 중요한 전문의
   들이 부족한 실정임.

o 페만에 파견되고 있는 많은 수의 의료요원이 예비역이나 주방위군에서 충원
   되므로, 예비역이 아닌 민간인 의사 및 간호원은 동원령에 영향을 받지 않음.

o 예비역, 현역을 막론하고 전장에 투입될 의료 요원의 수와 의료시설의 규모
   등은 기밀 사항임. 왜냐하면, 이런 정보는 이라크에 미 전략을 노출시킬 수
   있기 때문임.

o 현역 의료 요원의 페만 파견으로 발생한 결손을 보충하기 위해 예비역 의료
   요원이 미국과 유럽지역 미군 주둔지에 파견됨.
   - 그러나, 많은 미군 기지에서도 몇몇 중요한 전문의 부족 현상이 나타남.
   - 예비역 의료요원이 근무하던 민간 병원과 재향 군인회 등의 의료진 부족
     현상은 심각한 상태임.

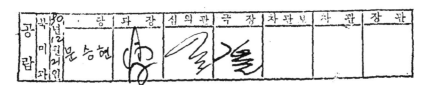

0097

- 전쟁 발발시는 인력 구조상 어느정도 여유가 있는 도시지역 민간 병원들도 의료요원 부족 현상을 일으키게 될 것임.

o 많은 예비역 내과의들은 현역으로 편성되게 되면, 50% 이상의 봉급 감소를 감당해야 됨.

o 전쟁 발발시, 미군은 부상자들을 병원선이나 사우디의 병원으로, 부상이 심한 경우는 본토로 송환해야 함.
- 전쟁이 심해지는 경우, 군 혹은 민간 병원을 막론하고 매일 수백명의 전쟁 부상자들을 치료해야 할 것임.

0098

USV(F) - 3521 II

: 경   관 (미부, 미안, 중근동) 빈신 : 주미대사

: 페만 사태 지원에 아른 미국내 의료요원부족현상 (2 맥)

Persian Gulf Buildup Disrupts Medical Care Back in the U.S.

By ERIC SCHMITT
Special to The New York Times

WASHINGTON, Dec. 18 — Medical care in parts of the United States is being disrupted as the Pentagon rushes a vast medical support system from home to the Persian Gulf to deal with possible wartime casualties.

Civilian hospitals and clinics and Department of Veterans Affairs medical centers across the country are juggling shifts, hiring temporary workers, paying overtime and postponing elective surgery. The steps are being taken to bridge the gaps created by the deployment of more than 20,000 military doctors, nurses and other personnel to hospital ships and medical centers in the gulf and to support hospitals in Europe and the United States.

Rural areas, which were suffering acute shortages of nurses and doctors even before the gulf crisis, are bearing the brunt of the medical drain. But the loss of a key specialist can hamper large urban medical centers, too.

"The abruptness of this has had a tremendous impact on rural communities and, to a lesser extent, on some urban areas that are chronically underserved," said Dr. Raymond Scalettar, an internist here who is a member of the American Medical Association's executive committee.

Classified Data on Doctors

Many of the medical personnel being deployed are from the military reserves and National Guard, which the Army relies on for 75 percent of its medical units. The Pentagon, responding to criticism that medical care in the gulf remains inadequate for a major war, expects to mobilize several thousand additional reservists in the next few weeks to bolster an elaborate triage and hospital network built from scratch in the Saudi Arabian desert.

Civilian doctors and nurses who are not in the reserves are not affected by the call-up.

Reservists make up only a small percentage of the approximately 600,000 physicians in the United States, but they are a larger percentage in rural areas, where military traditions are strong. For example, two of the five ear, nose and throat specialists in a broad swath of eastern Montana are reservists.

Measuring the precise impact of the call-up on medical communities is difficult. The number of American doctors, nurses and technicians — reservists and active military personnel — as well as the number of hospital beds and quantities of medical supplies available in the gulf is classified information. Pentagon officials say making it public would give Iraq a glimpse into projected American casualties and possible battle plans.

Many reservists have been sent to military bases in the United States and Europe to ease shortages created by the transfer of active-duty doctors to the gulf. But several Army base hospitals, including those at Fort Bragg, N.C., and Fort Campbell, Ky., remain critically short in important specialties like diagnostic radiologists, obstetrician/gynecologists, general surgeons and nurse anesthesists.

Only 450 reservists were sent to fill in for the 1,000 active-duty doctors, nurses and other personnel at the National Naval Medical Center in Bethesda, Md., who are manning the Comfort, one of the Navy's two hospital ships in the gulf. As a result, the center is handling only 275 in-patients, down from 350 before the deployment.

Plugging gaps at military hospitals, in turn, has drained the civilian hospitals and veterans centers where reservist doctors, nurses and technicians work full time.

Call and 'Hope for the Best'

In dozens of telephone interviews with health-care workers and their patients across the country, a picture emerges of urban areas adequately coping with the call-up while rural communities scramble to replace their doctors.

Dr. Wain Allen, a reservist, was the lone full-time physician serving two small northern Utah towns, Coalville and Kamas, before he was mobilized Dec. 6 to serve military dependents at an American military hospital in Germany. Active-duty doctors and nurses at the hospital were sent to the gulf.

Back in Utah, Charles Dahlin and his wife, Betty, were among those who relied on Dr. Allen for medical care. They now say that in the event of a medical emergency they will call 911 and "hope for the best."

"Here's a doctor that many people in this community need and depend on, and they're sending him to Germany to handle the runny noses of servicemen's kids," said Mr. Dahlin, 80 years old.

In the past month two large Army medical reserve units in Salt Lake City were called to active duty, depleting hospitals within a 60-mile radius.

Ted Baxter, director of planning and development at the Department of Veterans Affairs Medical Center in Salt Lake City, said the center had to close 10 percent of its 370 beds after losing nearly 30 doctors and nurses. Elective surgeries are being delayed by weeks, he said, and some patients will be referred to other hospitals.

'Just a Matter of Time'

The Department of Veterans Affairs Medical Center in Charleston, S.C., lost 10 percent of its doctors to a call-up of reserves. "Doctors are working extra shifts," said Charles Steinert, a hospital spokesman, "and we've backfilled with agency nurses to maintain our standards of care."

In urban areas, civilian hospitals are generally coping with the call-up without major problems, because they have larger medical communities to draw from. But administrators warn that if war breaks out many of those hospitals would lose crucial personnel who are on reserve alert.

"There hasn't been a significant impact on Long Island hospitals yet," said Robert S. Lord, executive vice-president of the Nassau-Suffolk Hospital Council, "but it's just a matter of time."

Carolyn Yordan, a spokeswoman for the Greater New York Hospital Association, which represents 124 nonprofit hospitals and nursing homes in New York City, said: "We have not experienced a tremendous amount of dislocation. Reservists make up a relatively small number of our staff doctors and nurses."

But rural communities have already been seriously affected, because the loss of one or two doctors, particularly specialists, takes a steep toll.

In eastern Montana, for instance, five ear, nose and throat doctors serve about 350,000 people scattered across hundreds of square miles. One of those physicians, Dr. Sheri Rolf, an Army reservist from Billings, was summoned last week, and another, Dr. Steve Butler, is waiting to be called up.

"It's like a doctor draft," said Dr. Stephen A. Kramer, one of the three non-reservist ear, nose and throat physicians in the area.

Indeed, the Army has exempted from call-up or has shortened active-duty service for only five medical re-

3521-1

Dec. 19, 1990 NY.

0099

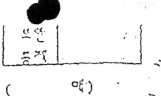

: USH( ) -
: 경 관   발신 : 주미대사

(액)

servists deemed hardship cases. Two were forensic pathologists in Harris County, Tex., which includes Houston. The county, which has a population of more than 2.5 million, has only five such specialists, and only when bodies in the morgue began backing up did the Army yield to pleas from county officials and send the doctors home, three months early.

In northeastern South Dakota, Day County stands to lose 25 percent of its family health care if Dr. Alan Bloom, 40, a major in the South Dakota Air National Guard, is called to active duty, as he expects will happen soon.

Dr. Bloom and three other family practitioners each serve about 30 patients daily, including many low-income patients from the Sisseton Sioux Indian Reservation and three nursing homes in the town of Webster.

His colleagues will cover for him while he is away, but Dr. Bloom worries that if the gulf crisis drags on and he is forced to stay longer than six months — as the Pentagon is considering for reserves — he might not be able to return to his practice.

"The trust factor with my patients will be blown," he said. "They'll all wonder, 'What if he's activated again and I'm left without my doctor?' "

Many physician reservists are taking pay cuts of more than 50 percent when called to active duty, and the fear of losing patients is aggravated by worries about personal bills.

Dr. Henry Russell, an Army reservist and the only chest surgeon in Williamson County, Tenn., shared these concerns shortly after he was activated last week. But four of his colleagues in Franklin, the county seat, banded together to hire his office staff and pay his $1,500 monthly home mortgage to tide over his practice and his family.

If war breaks out, the United States military plans to move casualties through several echelons of care, from battlefield medics to MASH units to one of the Navy's two 1,000-bed hospital ships in the gulf or a Saudi hospital staffed by American doctors and nurses. The most seriously wounded soldiers would be flown to American military hospitals in Europe and, if casualties were particularly heavy, to the United States.

If fighting was intense, domestic American hospitals — military and civilian — could be called on to treat several hundred war casualties a day.

The University of Utah Health Sciences Center, which operates a 372-bed acute-care hospital in Salt Lake City, was short 150 nurses, out of a staff of 1,600 nurses, even before the gulf crisis. Since then, 40 of its nurses have been called up.

Dec.19, 1990

NYT

3521-2 (END)

0100

외   무   부

종   별 : 지급

번   호 : USW-5566   일   시 : 90 1214 2017

수   신 : 장관(미북,미안,동구일,중근동,연기)사본주 쏘 대사-본부 중계요

발   신 : 주 미 대사

제   목 : 쉐바르나제 외상 방미

연 USW-5502,5520

1. 금 12.14 당관 이승곤 공사는 미국무부측 요청에 따라 금번 미소 외무장관 회담(12.10-11 휴스턴), 쉐 외상의 백악관 방문(11.12) 결과에 대한 대 동맹국 브리핑에 NATO, 일본, 호주 대사관측 대표들과 함께 참석 미측 설명을 청취한바, 미측에서는 BUTHOLMEW 안보과학 기술 지원 차관과 SEITZ 구주 차관보가 브리핑을 실시함(당관 김영목서기관 수행)

2. 개요

금번 회담에서는 START, CFE 등 군축 문제, GULF 사태, 아프가니스탄, 앙골라등 지역 문제및 기타 양자 문제가 협의되었으며, 고위 면담시에는 소련 국내 정세, 미국의 대소 경협 문제가 논의되었음(한반도등 아시아 지역 정세는 논의되지 않음)

3. 군축 문제

-BATHOLEMEW 차관은, 미측은 군축 문제 협의에 있어 많은 시간을 CFE 협정 문제에 할애 했다고 하며, START 협정 마무리와 관련해서는 매우 기술적인 문제에 협의가 있었다고 하고 오는 2.13 정상회담전 START 의 마무리를 낙관하였음.

-다만, CFE 협정의 이행과 관련, 미국측은 소련측이 협정 의무 우회및 일탈의 소지가 있는 징후를 보이고 있어 동 문제에 대한 명확한 답변과 향후 조치 내용을 강력히 요구하였다고함(감축 장비의 우랄 이동의로의 배치, 육군 군장비의 해군 상륙, 연안 사단으로의 전환등)

- 동 차관은 이와관련, 소 군의 구테타등 본격적 정치 개입을 할것으로는 보이지 않으나, 발언권을 강화하고 문민 정부의 결정에 일방적으로 순종치 않으려는 경향(상기 우회적 노력)을 보이고 있다고 평가함.

-한편, 소측은 향후 군축 분야의 진행과 관련, 단거리 핵무기 감축 협상의 조속한

미주국	차관	1차보	2차보	미주국	구주국	중아국	외연원	정와대
안기부								

개시를 주장하면서, 동 협상에는 탄두와 운반 수단의 생산, 보유국 뿐 아니라 자국 영토에 타국의 탄두와 운반수단을 배치하고 있는 국가도 포함되어야한다고 주장하였다고함.

4) 걸프만 사태

- SEITZ 차관보는 쉐 외상은 현재 미 행정부의 정책에 대해 매우 긍정적인 반응과 지지를 보였으나, 사태의 평화적 해결을 계속 강조하였다고 설명함.

- 쉐 외상은 현재 미국이 후세인으로 하여금 실제 위협을 느끼도록 하는 전술에 동의하면서, 일방 소측의 중동 평화 프로세스의 본격적 활성화를 재강조하였는바, 베이커 장관은 미국은 중동 평화 프로세스를 긍정적으로 보고 있으나 현사태와 팔레스타인 문제의 연계에는 극히 신중한 자세를 가져야한다는 입장을 보였음.

- SEITZ 차관보는 소련측이 1.15 이전 안보리 상임 이사국간 외상회의 또는정상회의를 제의하였으나, 미측으로서는 외상회의는 일단 검토 가능한 대안이나정상회의는 반대하였다고 하고 여사한 쏘측 제안은 5 개국간 공동 결의를 과시하는데 목적이 있는것으로 본다고 부언함.

- SEITZ 차관보는 쉐 외상은 중동의 비핵지대화안을 실제로 외상 회담시 제의치는 않았다고 하고, 중동에서의 핵.화학, 미사일 확산 방지 문제가 일반적으로 실무 협의시 토의되었으나, 동 외상의 기자 회견에서 핵지대화를 제기한것같이 발표하였다고 설명함.

5. 소련 국내 문제

- 쉐 외상은 소련 국내 사정에 대해 매우 어두운 상황으로 묘사하고, 규율의 붕괴, 부정과 조직 범죄의 성행, 지방 수준에서의 폭력및 무장충돌 발생등 상황을 감안할때, 법질서의 회복이 불가피하다고 설명하였음.

- 이에 대해 베이커 장관은 질서의 회복 노력은 이해하나, 탄압(CRACKDOWN)이 되어서는 안되며, 여사한 탄압이 있을경우 이는 미소 관계에 매우 부정적(DISRUPTIVE)인 영향을 미칠것이라고 경고 하였음.

- SEITZ 차관보는 이와 관련, 쉐 외상의 죠지아, 발틱등의 혼란한 상황을 예를 들며, 소 연방 체제및 사회 전체에 발생하고 있는 어려움을 설명하고, 소련의개혁 정치는 후퇴하지 않을것이라고 다짐하였다고 부언함.

6. 경제 문제

- 쉐 외상의 경제 문제의 어려움에 대한 설명이 있었으며, 부쉬 대통령과 베이커

PAGE 2

0102

장관은 소련이 장기적 안목의 근본적 개혁을 포기해서는 안된다는 위칙을 강조함(동 면담과 이에 따른 미측의 대소 경제 원조 결정 내용은 기보고 참조)

7. 기타 문제

-금번 회담시에는 아프가니스탄에 대한 공동 선언의 채택을 서하였으나, 소측이 -하향성 군사력 균형- 즉, 소 측이 대 나지블라 무기 공급 중단에동의치 않음으로서 일단 공동 선언의 채택은 보류되었으나, -과도 체제- 에 있어서는 진전이 있었음.

- 앙골라 문제에 있어 미 소 양측은 상호 교차 접촉에 합의한바, VAN DUNEM앙골라 외무 장관은 12.13 국무부로 베이커 장관을 방문, 면담하였으며, 쉐 외상은 이미 SAVIMBI 를 면담한바 있음.

- 양측은 KIEV 와 NEW YORK 에 총영사관을 추가 개설키로 한데 이어, 각국내에 소규모 영사관을 확대 설치키로 합의했음.

7. 당관 평가

-금번 회담은 START 를 마무리 함으로서 양국 정상회담을 기합의대로 명년초 실시한다는 목표에 따라 개최되었으나, 회담의 초점은 걸프만 사태의 타결과 소련 경제에 대한 지원에 주어진것으로 보임.

-연호 보고와같이, 쉐 외상이 정치적 차원에서 소련의 어려움에 대한 미국측의 이해와 협조를 요청하고 이에 대해 부쉬 대통령의 전격적 결정을 내린것은 미측이 소련의 곤경의 정도가 심각히 우려할 정도로 진행되고 있다고 판단하고 있는것으로 보이며, 베이커 장관의 기자 회견시 답변과 같이 소련의 안정은 미국뿐 아니라 많은 나라의 이익에 직결된다는 전략적 고려가 있었던것으로 관찰됨.

(대사 박동진-국장)

91.12.31 일반

90.12.31 검토필 조
90. 6. 30. 검토필 조

페만 사태 해결에 대한 미 외교정책의 합의 모색
- Kissinger와 Brzezinski의 견해차이

(12.17자 The Wall Street Journal지 기사 요약)

1990.12.18.

북 미 과

o 페만 사태 해결에 대한 양인의 견해차는 현재 미국의 외교정책 결정자들 및
  국민들간의 동 문제에 대한 양분된 견해를 반영함.

  - 이러한 견해차이는 장기적 관점에서 보면, 미국 외교정책의 Consensus였던
    소련의 팽창에 대한 봉쇄정책이 소련의 변화로 사라졌기 때문임.

  - 페만 사태 해결을 위한 미 외교정책에 있어서 Consensus의 결여는 90.1.15로
    된 최종 시한을 앞두고 있는 부쉬 행정부에게는 치명적임.

o Kissinger의 견해

  - 이라크를 쿠웨이트에서 축출하기 위한 군사적 선택을 지체해서는 안됨.

o Brzezinski의 견해

  - 전쟁은 피해야 하며, 협상을 통한 문제 해결을 모색해야 함.

0104

o 양인의 견해차이

구 분	Kissinger	Brzezinski
경제 제재의 효과	경제 제재가 효력을 발휘하고 있다는 아무런 증거도 없음.	경제 제재가 상당한 효력을 발휘하고 있으며, 1년 이상 지속되면 이라크에 치명타를 가하게 될 것임.
협상의 유용성	협상은 후세인에게 끌려다닐 것이며, 국제 협조의 붕괴를 가져올 것이고, 결국 미국은 이라크에게 어느 정도의 양보를 하지 않으면 안됨. 이런 관점에서 Baker 국무장관의 바그다드 방문을 반대함.	협상은 영토 문제 등에 관한 이라크.쿠웨이트간 분쟁에 수용할만한 결과를 산출할 수 있을 것이므로, Baker 국무장관의 바그다드 방문을 찬성함.
제한된 군사력 사용의 가능성	공군과 해군의 공격 등 제한된 군사력의 사용으로 미국은 이라크를 패퇴시킬 수 있을 것임.	광범위한 육상전이 불가피할 것임.
중동 지역의 장래	걸프만 지역에서의 이라크의 세력 확장 및 화학, 핵무기 개발을 억제하기 위해서는 필요한 조치가 취해져야 함.	군사적 충돌은 지속적인 반미 감정을 야기할 것이며, 이는 이 지역의 안정을 해치는 결과를 초래할 것임.

0105

외 무 부

관리
번호 90-2581

원 본

종 별 : 지 급
번 호 : USW-5665
일 시 : 90 1221 1832
수 신 : 장관(미북,중근동,미안,마그)
발 신 : 주 미 대 사
제 목 : 페만 사태 해결 전망

당지 언론 분석및 주재국 각계 인사 접촉등을 토대로 당관에서 작성한 표제전망을 하기 보고함.

1. 미국의 입장

가. 미 행정부는 금번 사태 관련, 이락군의 쿠웨이트로 부터의 완전 철수등미국의 기본 목표에는 여하한 변화도 없다는 점을 계속 강조하고 있으며, 걸프지역 주둔 미군 증파를 통해 이러한 목표가 달성되지 않는 경우의 무력 <u>사용 가능성을 강력하게</u> 암시하는등 소위 "극한 정책"도 계속 추구하고 있음.

나. 또한 11.29 유엔 안보리가 대 이락 무력 사용 허용 결의안을 통해 내년1.15 을 이락군 철수 시한으로 제시함으로서 미국의 여사한 극한 정책은 국제적 승인을 받게된 셈인바, 특히 미국의 이러한 강경 노선이 이락측이 인질 석방 결정을 내리게된데에도 주효한 것으로 보임.

다. 한편, 미측은 부쉬 대통령이 선 제의한 미-이락 양국 외무장관 교환 방문 관련, 베이커 국무장관의 이락 방문이 1.3 이전 이루어져야만 한다는점을 내세우면서 아지즈 이락 외상의 방미를 보류시키고 있는바, 이러한 미측의 태도에서도 금번 사태의 부분적 해결을 반대하는 부쉬 행정부의 입장이 분명하게 나타나고 있음.

2. 이락의 입장

가. 상기와같이, 미국의 병력 증파, 유엔 안보리 결의안 통과등으로 국제적압력이 가중되고 있는 상황임에도 불구, 이락측은 인질 석방 이외에 별다른 태도의 변화를 보이지 않고 있음.

나. 오히려 이락측은 베이커 국무장관의 바그다드 방문 일자를 유엔 안보리결의안상의 철수 시한 직전인 1.12 로 제시하는등 일종의 - 지연 작전-을 전개하는 한편, 금번 사태와 팔레스타인 문제의 동시 해결을 지속적으로 주장하는등

미주국   차관   1차보   2차보   미주국   중아국   중아국   청와대   안기부

90.12.22   10:23
외신 2과 통제관 FE

0106

일종의 -연계 작전-도 펴고 있음.

　다. 기본적으로 이락측은 여사한 시간끌기 작전으로 잃을것이 없다는 입장으로 보이며, 또 이러한 와중에서 미국내 여론이 보다 더 심각한 분열상을 보이거나 대이락 다국적 봉쇄 전선이 와해됨으로서 현재 상황에서 사태가 고착화되는것을 최대의 목표로 추구하고 있는것으로 보임.

　3. 전망

　가. 이락군의 부분적 철수 가능성

　-WEBSTER CIA 부장도 12.15 자 WP 지와의 인터뷰시 언급한것 처럼, 당지 일각에서는 이락측이 미군등 다국적군의 공격 임박 시점에 쿠웨이트 로부터 급작스럽게 부분 철수할것으로 기대하고 있음(또한 12.18 자 NYT 지 보도등 최근 당지 언론 보도에 의하면, 이락측이 루마일라 유전 지대및 페르시아만으로의 진출에 필수적인 부비얀도와 와르바도의 2 개 도서등 쿠웨이트 북부 지역만을 자국의 영토로 편입하기 위해 새로운 경계선을 확정하는등 부분적 철군의 움직임을 보이고있다함)

　- 현재 미국은 베이커 국무장관의 연례 NATO 외무장관 회담 참석 기회등을 활용, 여사한 부분 철군으로는 사태가 해결될수 없다는점을 대이락 봉쇄 전선 참여국등에게 설득시키기 위해 노력하고 있으나, 실제 이락측이 부분 철군을 행동으로 옮기는 경우 현재와같은 강도의 다국적 봉쇄 전선이 유지되기는 어려울것임(특히 쉐바르드나제 소 외상의 사임 으로 인해 소련측이 지금까지의 대미 공동 보조 노선에서 일탈하는 경우, 대이락 다국적 봉쇄 노선은 치명적 상처를 입게될것임)

　-한편, 걸프 사태의 당사자격에 해당하는 아랍권 일각에서 여사한 부분적 해결을 금번 사태의 궁극적 해결 방안으로 수락하는 움직임을 보이고, 이러한 움직임에 대한 국제적 지지가 확산되는 경우 미측으로서도 부분적 철수 이전과같은정도의 국제적 지지를 확보키는 어려울것임.

　- 또한 일단 이러한 여건이 조성되는 경우 미국내적으로도 반전 분위기가 보다 더 확산될것이며 의회 및 언론등의 대이락 공격 여부에 관한 논의가 보다 더 분분해 질것인바, 이러한 상황하에서 부쉬 행정부가 대이락 무력 사용 결정을내리기는 어려울것임.

　-즉 이락측이 전격적으로 부분 철군을 단행하는 경우, 미국으로서는 전면적무력 사용이 사실상 불가능해질것이며, 국제 여론과 국내 분위기도 이완 현상을 보일것인바, 이러한 상황하에서 페만 사태는 부분적 해결 상태의 고착화 방향으로

PAGE 2

0107

진전될것임.

　나. 미국의 대이락 공격 가능성

　-1.15 까지 이락측이 전면 철수를 하지 않는경우 대이락 공격을 개시한다는것이 지금까지 공표된 미국의 공식 입장이므로, 설사 전기와같이 이락군의 부분철수가 이루어 진다 할지라도 미국의 군사력 사용 가능성을 완전히 배제하기는어려운 측면이 있음.

　-다만, 이러한 경우 미측은 지상전을 통한 인명 손실을 최소화 하고, 이락의 반격 능력을 소멸시키기 위해 우선 집중적인 공중 폭격으로 이락의 세균 무기저장고등 군수 시설, 후방 보급선 및 미사일 기지등을 강타할 가능성인 클것으로 보임.즉 이락측의 부분 철군에 대한 대응 방안으로서, 미측은 공군력 사용이라는 제한적 작전을 전개함으로서 이락측 으로 하여금 미국의 전면 공격 가능성을 보다 더 심각하게 인식하도록 유도하고자 할 가능성이 있음.

　다. 참고 사항

　-쉐 소 외상의 사임등 예측하지 못했던 변수들이 등장하고 있고 금번 사태 향방의 관건을 쥐고 있는 훗쎄인 대통령의 내심을 아무도 정확히 해석하지 못하는 상황이므로 확정적 예측을 하기는 곤란하나, 현 상황하에서는 전기 -가-항의 부분 철수 가능성이 클것으로 보임.

　-훗쎄인 대통령은 이러한 부분적 해결을 얼마든지 자신의 외교적 승리로 설명할수 있을것이며, 부쉬 대통령으로서는 대이락 공격 여부에 관한 진퇴 양난에 빠질것임.

　- 특히 여사한 부분적 해결책이 아랍권의 공감을 얻는 경우, 미측으로서는 이러한 부분적 해결 방안을 거부하기 어려운 입장에 빠질것인바, 적어도 형식적으로는 미군 파병이 사우디측 요청에 의했던것이므로, 사우디측 요청으로 다시 철수 한다는 명분을 내세울수도 있을것임.

　-또한 부쉬 행정부는 지금까지의 논리를 발전시켜, 미국의 극한정책으로인해 그나마 부분적 철군이라도 유도할 수 있었다고 국내적으로 자신의 입장을 합리화 시킬수도 있을것이며, 국제적으로는 대이란 억지력으로서의 이락의 효용을 재평가 하는 한편 대이락 무기 금수등의 조치는 계속 유지하고자 할것임.

　-그러나 이락군의 쿠웨이틀부터의 전면 철수등 기존의 4 대 목표가 여한한 BLUFFIN 요소도 포함하지 않고 있는 미 행정부의 진전한 목표라면 전기 -나-항과같이 우선 공군력 사용이 부분적 철군에 대한 대응 방안 으로서 검토될것임.

PAGE 3

0108

(대사 박동진-차관)
91.12.31 일반

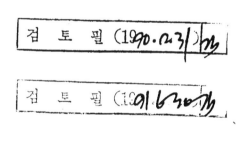

外 務 部

관리
번호 90-450

종 별 : 지 급

번 호 : USW-5662

일 시 : 90 1221 1806

수 신 : 대통령(사본 외무부 장관)

발 신 : 주 미 대사

제 목 : 중동 사태 관련 부쉬 대통령 면담

1. 금 12.21 당지 시간으로 1330 부터 약 30 분간 BUSH 대통령의 요청으로 백악관에서 중동 사태에 관한 우방 외교 사절들과의 회담이 있었는데, BUSH 대통령은 직접 몇가지 사항에 관해서 설명을 하고 또 참가국가들의 적극 협조를 요청하였읍니다.

2. 백악관 으로부터는 SUNUNU 비서실장, SCOWCROFT 안보 담당 보좌관, GATE차석 보좌관, 행정부에서는 BRADY 재무장관, EAGLEBURGER 국무부 부장관등이 배석 하였으며, 회의가 시작 되기 전에는 사진 기자들에게 공개 하였읍니다.

3. 초청된 우방은 한국, 일본등을 포함한 재정 지원 공여국 이외에 군대를 파견한 우방 일부와 SAUDI ARABIA, KUWAIT 도 포함되어 있었읍니다.

4. 부쉬 대통령이 오늘 참석한 외교 사절들에게 본국의 국가 원수들에게 충실히 전달할것을 부탁한 발언 요지는 다음과 같습니다.

가. 지금까지 IRAQ 침략 저지에 참여한 다수 국가들의 튼튼한 결속(TOGETHERNESS) 은 IRAQ 의 SADAM HUSSEIN 에게 강도 있게 표시된것으로 평가하며, 우방들의 적극적 자세를 미국은 감사하고 있음.

나. 미국은 참가 제국과의 긴밀한 협력관계와 상호 협의 태세를 앞으로도 계속 유지해 나가기를 희망하며, 중동 사태의 성공적 해결에 관해서 우방들로부터 유익한 의견이나 조언이 있을때는 이를 환영함.

다. IRAQ 에 대해서는 미국이 UN 안보리 결의를 관철하기 위해서 결단코 군사력을 사용할 용의가 있다는 사실과 군사작전에 착수할때는 막대한 타격을 가할것이고 비교적 속전 속결 주의로 나갈것이며 결코 월남전과같이 장기화 될수는 없다는 점이 명백히 인식되도록 다같이 노력할 필요가 있음.

라. 미국 의회측에서 여러가지 이견을 말하고 있으나 자신은 의회의 간섭을받지

정와대   장관

않고 필요한 시점에는 단연코 미국 병력을 사용할것인바, 제 3 자들이 착오 없기를 바람(병력 사용의 결의를 재삼 강조하였음)

마. IRAQ 의 KUWAIT 침략을 성공적으로 저지하는 여부는 냉전 체제 이후의 세계 신질서 수립을 위해서 매우 중요하며, 세계 평화와 법의 지배, 인간의 자유등을 확보 하려는 새로운 장래의 설계를 위해서도 IRAQ 의 침략은 방임할수 없으며 인명의 손상을 두려워 한다면 큰 목적을 달성하기 어려움.

바. IRAQ 의 침략을 성공적으로 저지하기 위해서는 참가 우방 사이의 책임 분담("RESPONSIBILITY SHARING") 이 필요하며 앞으로 참가 우방들이 재정적 지원을 적극 증대할것을 미국 대통령은 강력히 요청함.

6. 관측

UN 안보리 결의에서 지정한 평화적 해결의 시한이 임박하는데도 IRAQ 측과의 외교적 대화 노력이 무진전 상태임에 비추어, BUSH 대통령이 군사 작전 불사의 결연한 용의를 직접 표시하는 한편, 참가 우방국들의 책임 분담 확대를 강하게 호소하는것이 오늘 회동의 주 목적 이었다고 판단 됩니다. 끝

91.12.31 일반

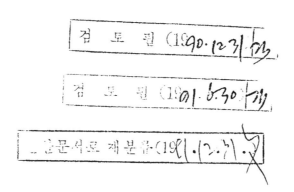

PAGE 2

0111

Iraqi Diplomats Fly Back Home For Quick Talks

By PATRICK E. TYLER
Special to The New York Times

BAGHDAD, Iraq, Dec. 24 — Iraq has recalled its ambassadors from leading European countries, the United States, Japan and elsewhere for urgent consultations this week over the diplomatic deadlock in the Persian Gulf crisis.

The recall of important members of Iraq's diplomatic corps appeared to some Western officials here to be a sign that President Saddam Hussein is preparing a diplomatic initiative before the Jan. 15 deadline set by the United Nations Security Council for an unconditional Iraqi withdrawal from Kuwait.

Among those recalled were Mohammed al-Mashat, the Ambassador to Washington, and Abdul Amir al-Enbari, the envoy to the United Nations, as well as the ambassadors to Moscow, London, Paris and Tokyo.

More Than Two Dozen Recalled

By this afternoon, Western officials said they had counted more than two dozen ambassadors who had been recalled, mostly from countries taking part in the military coalition against Iraq. Tonight, the ambassadors were meeting with senior Foreign Ministry officials, who were not available for comment.

Whatever the nature of the consultations, the summons injected drama into the stalemate that has settled heavily over this war-weary country.

A dreary mid-winter drizzle fell on Baghdad tonight as the nation's Christians, who make up more than 1 million of Iraq's population of 17 million, made last-minute Christmas tree purchases. Lines formed outside bread and pastry shops, where ovens worked overtime for the two-day Christian holiday in this predominantly Muslim country.

Shoppers Limit Spending

But by all accounts, the capital's merchants did not fare well with holiday shoppers, who limited their purchases to essential items. Many Christmas trees were left standing at the end of the day.

"People are not spending their money, and they're staying in their homes," said a woman from a prominent Baghdad family. "Last night we had a blackout. How do you think that makes you feel at Christmas?"

The blackout test, ordered Sunday night by the civil defense authorities, darkened about half the city for a short period just after 9 P.M. local time. The drill followed several days' instruction in the Arabic-language newspapers on

Continued on Page 6, Column 4

procedures for darkening homes and businesses in the event of air attacks.

The recall of diplomats follows the failure of Iraqi efforts to gain support in Arab and European capitals for an Arab mediation initiative to end the crisis, which would undermine or divide the international coalition that is using the threat of force to hold Iraq to the Jan. 15 deadline.

President Bush offered his own plan for a final round of diplomacy to avoid a military conflict, but Mr. Bush and Mr. Hussein have not been able to agree on the dates for such talks.

A United States official here said he did not see how an exchange of foreign ministers between Washington and Baghdad could occur unless the dispute over the timing of the visits is resolved by the end of this week.

Embargo Showing Effect

In the last several days, there have been new signs that the trade embargo against Iraq, now nearly five months old, has hit critical services.

Foreign technicians from the national water authority told an Asian embassy late last week that supplies of chlorine compounds to purify drinking water in Iraq were critically short and could run out by Jan. 5 or 6.

The technicians reported that a backup filtration system was available, but that it would not meet normal purification standards for drinkable water.

A breakdown in clean water supplies could worsen health conditions in Iraq, which are already deteriorating as people hoard goods in anticipation of possible war and medical supplies run short.

Dispute on Medical Supplies

Western diplomats here have criticized Iraq for not applying to the United Nations sanctions committee for humanitarian shipments of medical supplies. Medical supplies fall under the trade embargo unless specifically exempted for humanitarian reasons.

Iraq, which accuses the United States and its allies of being responsi-

ble for the deaths of more than 2,000 children since August, has declined to accept United Nations authority over medical shipments.

Western officials have challenged Iraq's count of infant deaths that could be attributed to the embargo. But as time passes, shortages of drugs and critical medical supplies are having a marginal effect on mortality rates, these officials acknowledged.

With the Jan. 15 deadline drawing nearer, Asian diplomats reported that Iraq was seeking new military aid from North Korea. The assistance was described as spare parts and technical expertise to maintain sophisticated Soviet warplanes and other weapons in the Iraqi arsenal.

The Iraqi Air Force is predominantly equipped with Soviet-made MIG-17, MIG-23, MIG-25 and MIG-29 warplanes, along with French-made combat aircraft.

North Korean Advisers Arrive

The first delegation of 20 North Korean military advisers has arrived in Iraq, Asian diplomatic officials said, and Iraq's senior arms purchaser, Hussein Kamil Hassan, a son-in-law of the President, is said to have led an Iraqi military cooperation mission to North Korea in recent weeks.

Iraq has been hostile toward North Korea for at least five years because North Korea supplied SCUD missiles and other weapons to Iran during the eight-year Iran-Iraq war. North Korea and Iraq have no diplomatic relations.

But Iraq, with its acute shortages of spare parts, may put the enmity aside in favor of pragmatic military considerations, diplomats here said.

As thousands of Soviet military advisers have left Iraq in recent months, Eastern European diplomats have reported a steady decline in the maintenance and combat readiness of Soviet-made aircraft and air defense radar and missile systems in Iraq.

Civil defense officials prepare the nation for a possible war.

0112

외교문서 비밀해제: 걸프 사태 34
걸프 사태 미국 동향 1

초판인쇄 2024년 03월 15일
초판발행 2024년 03월 15일

지은이 한국학술정보(주)
펴낸이 채종준
펴낸곳 한국학술정보(주)
주 소 경기도 파주시 회동길 230(문발동)
전 화 031-908-3181(대표)
팩 스 031-908-3189
홈페이지 http://ebook.kstudy.com
E-mail 출판사업부 publish@kstudy.com
등 록 제일산-115호(2000. 6. 19)

ISBN   979-11-6983-994-5 94340
       979-11-6983-960-0 94340 (set)